THE GENESIS
OF SHAKESPEARE IDOLATRY

The University of North Carolina Press, Chapel Hill, N. C.; The Baker and Taylor Company, New York; Oxford University Press, London; Maruzen-Kabushiki-Kaisha, Tokyo; Edward Evans & Sons, Ltd., Shanghai

THE GENESIS OF SHAKESPEARE IDOLATRY
1766-1799

A STUDY IN ENGLISH CRITICISM OF THE LATE EIGHTEENTH CENTURY

BY

ROBERT WITBECK BABCOCK, PH.D.

CHAPEL HILL
THE UNIVERSITY OF NORTH CAROLINA PRESS
1931

COPYRIGHT, 1931, BY
THE UNIVERSITY OF NORTH CAROLINA PRESS

PRINTED IN THE UNITED STATES OF AMERICA BY
EDWARDS & BROUGHTON COMPANY, RALEIGH, N. C.
BOUND BY L. H. JENKINS, INC., RICHMOND, VIRGINIA

THIS BOOK WAS DIGITALLY PRINTED.

To

MY MOTHER AND FATHER

PREFACE

This book is a regenerated doctoral thesis, which was written with the book more or less consistently in mind. Some changes have of course been made since its original presentation at the University of Chicago, and I take full responsibility for the revisions. They appear largely in the general reorganization, the Introduction, the chapter entitled "A Preliminary Survey" (which is wholly new), Part II, Part IV, Appendices A and B, and stylistically throughout.

Whatever success this book may have will be due almost entirely to the indefatigable efforts of Professor R. S. Crane of the University of Chicago. Mr. Crane carried it through several revisions to its final thesis form, and for his innumerable suggestions—always helpful and stimulating—I am most deeply grateful. I feel I speak for all his students when I remark that his insistence on accuracy, clearness, and force has been perhaps our greatest bane at the start, certainly our greatest blessing at the end. Though we shall never be Alexander Popes, he has always been our William Walsh.

To Professors G. W. Sherburn and C. R. Baskervill of the University of Chicago I also owe thanks for their kindness in reading and offering suggestions on the original thesis. Mr. Stanley B. Harkness of Chicago has given me literally pages of stylistic corrections which have been invaluable. The late Professor J. F. Royster of the University of North Carolina published Appendices A and B in *Studies in Philology* in May, 1929, and very kindly encouraged me to continue the study. I am happy now that it is his Press which is publishing the book. I am also under obligation to Professors R. D. Havens, H. S. V. Jones, and Baldwin Maxwell, editors of *Modern Language Notes*, *Journal of English and Germanic Philology*, and the *Philological Quarterly* respectively, for permission to reprint sections which appeared in articles of mine in their magazines.

Finally, with regard to the more mechanical processes of producing the book, I owe thanks to my sisters, Maritje and Heath; to Miss Ella M. Hymans, Miss Caroline G. Wilgus, and Miss Pauline G. Waite, for their persistently kind assistance in the McMillan Shakespeare Collection in the University of Michigan; to Dr. W. W. Bishop, Librarian of the University of Michigan; to my students in English 40 in Michigan for their coöperation in checking several important periodical references (many of their names appear in footnotes throughout the book); to Miss Margaret V. McIntyre for her amazingly accurate typing; to Dean W. L. Coffey of the College of the City of Detroit for his kindness in granting me residence privileges in Ann Arbor while finishing the book; to Mrs. Alice T. Paine, of the University of North Carolina Press, for her brilliant reorganization of the chapters, and to Dr. L. L. Hanawalt, of the College of the City of Detroit, for his able assistance in the very undelightful task of proofreading.

I present the book now with the sincere hope that it will be a worthy representative of Professor Crane's excellent training school. Ultimately I shall endeavor to make it merely one of a series extending from 1600 to 1800 (and perhaps further), embracing a history of Shakespeare criticism, in its various aspects, from "the beginnings" to the dawn of the nineteenth century. My original inspiration in this field, I should note, came from Professor Karl Young of Yale (then of Wisconsin) and was warmly fanned by Professor Hardin Craig of Stanford (then of

Iowa). "I feel sure," wrote Professor Craig over a year ago, with regard to my rather comprehensive plan, "that (if you don't kill yourself) you will carry it through." My main task, therefore, is to live on, in homage to Mr. Young, Mr. Craig, and Mr. Crane.

"In magnis voluisse sat est."

Ann Arbor, June, 1930 R. W. BABCOCK

CONTENTS

PREFACE.. vii
INTRODUCTION xvii

PART I

THE NEW INTEREST IN SHAKESPEARE

Chapter   *Page*
  I. A PRELIMINARY SURVEY, 1660-1765...... 3
      From 1660 to 1730—From 1730 to 1765—
      Knowledge of Shakespeare in this Period.

  II. THE SCHOLARLY INTEREST.............. 11
      Editions, Chronology, and Spurious Plays—
      Shakespeare Illustrated, Concordances,
      Glossaries, and Shakespeareana (Bibliographical)—Biography.

  III. THE POPULAR INTEREST................ 28
      Attacks on Commentators; Parodies—Sequels, Operas, and Imitations—Modern Characters from Shakespeare, Public Lectures, and Jubilees.

PART II

SHAKESPEARE DEFENDED AGAINST TRADITIONAL OBJECTIONS

  IV. THE UNITIES REJECTED.................. 45
      Shakespeare's Violation of the Unities—
      General Scepticism Concerning the Unities
      —Johnson's Rejection of the Unities—Other

Chapter		Page
	Arts and the Unities—Nature Greater than the Rules—The Historical Rejection of the Unities—Aristotle's Support of the Unities Denied.	
V.	SHAKESPEARE'S CLASSICAL LEARNING...... The Beginnings of the Controversy— Farmer's Denial of Shakespeare's Direct Knowledge of the Classics—The Reaction to Farmer's Work—Farmer's Point of View Corroborated by Other Critics—The Late Eighteenth-Century Point of View—Shakespeare Above the Ancients—Absolved from the Imitation of Models.	57
VI.	SHAKESPEARE AND DECORUM; OTHER POINTS OF ATTACK.................. Shakespeare's Violation of Decorum—The Historical Defense—Tragicomedy Attacked and Defended—The Appeal to Nature— Supernatural Characters Attacked and Defended—Puns and Blank Verse Accepted.	70
VII.	THE ATTACK UPON ALTERATION OF PLAYS The popularity of Alterations—The Growing Disapproval—The Turning of the Tide.	82
VIII.	THE REACTION AGAINST VOLTAIRE........ Voltaire's Mistranslation of Shakespeare— Voltaire's Strictures on Shakespeare—The Reaction of British Critics—British Reply to the Traditional Objections Made by Voltaire—British Attacks on Voltaire as a Writer—Attacks on Voltaire's Mistranslation of Shakespeare—Attacks on Voltaire's	90

Chapter	Page
	Ignorance of Elizabethan Drama—Attacks on Voltaire as a Man—Mrs. Montagu and the Reaction against Voltaire.

PART III

THE OLDER EULOGY DEVELOPS NEW EMPHASES

IX. THE PERSISTENCE OF THE OLDER EULOGY.. 113
Shakespeare as Poet—Shakespeare as Poet of Nature—Shakespeare, Original Genius.

X. NEW EMPHASES: SHAKESPEARE AS CONSCIOUS ARTIST AND AS MORAL PHILOSOPHER............................ 127
Shakespeare as Conscious Artist with Judgment Equal to His Genius—Shakespeare as Moral Philosopher.

XI. APPRECIATION OF CHARACTERS.......... 135
Historical Characters—Shakespeare's Women—Minor Characters—Iago and Shylock—King Lear—Macbeth—Falstaff—Hamlet—Conclusion.

XII. THE PSYCHOLOGIZING OF SHAKESPEARE.... 155
The Background of Psychological Criticism—Shakespeare's Depiction of the Passions—William Richardson as Psychological Critic of Shakespeare—The Reaction to Richardson—The Use of the Psychological Method—Minor Characters—Macbeth and Richard III—Falstaff—Hamlet—The Importance of the New Criticism—The Application of

Chapter *Page*

Theories of Association to Various Aspects of Shakespeare.

XIII. HISTORICAL CRITICISM IN THE LATE EIGHTEENTH CENTURY..................... 183
Shakespeare's Language—Shakespeare and British History—Shakespeare and His Audience—Sources of Shakespeare's Plays—Comparative Study—Stage History.

XIV. IDOLATRY AD ASTRA.................... 199

PART IV

THE EARLY NINETEENTH CENTURY AND SHAKESPEARE

XV. THE REFLECTION OF LATE EIGHTEENTH-CENTURY VIEWS IN COLERIDGE, LAMB, HAZLITT, AND THE MAGAZINES........ 211
Editions, Chronology, and Spurious Plays—Shakespeare Illustrated, Concordances, Glossaries, and Shakespeareana (Bibliographical)—Biography—Attacks on Commentators; Parodies—Sequels, Operas, and Imitations—Modern Characters from Shakespeare, Public Lectures, and Jubilees—The Unities—Shakespeare's Learning —Shakespeare, the Ancients, and Imitation of Models—Decorum: Tragicomedy and Supernatural Characters—Shakespeare's Puns and Blank Verse—On Alterations of Shakespeare's Plays — Voltaire — Shakespeare as Poet—Shakespeare as Poet of

Chapter		Page
	Nature—Shakespeare, Original Genius—Shakespeare's Judgment—Shakespeare as Moral Philosopher—Shakespeare's Characters—Psychologizing—Shakespeare's Language—Shakespeare and British History—Shakespeare and His Age—Shakespeare's Sources—Comparative Study—Shakespeare and Stage History—Idolatry ad Astra—Conclusion.	
XVI.	SOME CLUES TO THE DIRECT INDEBTEDNESS OF COLERIDGE, LAMB, AND HAZLITT TO EIGHTEENTH-CENTURY CRITICISM.......	228
	A Field Open for Investigation—Lamb and Hazlitt—Coleridge.	
XVII.	CONCLUSION	240

APPENDIX A..................................... 245
Primary Texts of Shakespeare Criticism in the Eighteenth Century.

APENDIX B..................................... 268
A Secondary Bibliography of Shakespeare Criticism in the Eighteenth Century.

INDEX.. 297

INTRODUCTION[1]

Thirty-eight years ago, Mr. George Hallam, writing for the New York Shakespeare Society, declared, "Plenty of records have been left us . . . from which to construct a history of the rise, ascendancy and permanence of Shakespearian criticism. We are only waiting for the Gibbon of literature to appear."[2] This book will attempt, with apologies, to answer Mr. Hallam's plea in part by tracing the rise of Shakespeare idolatry in England during the last thirty-four years of the eighteenth century—that is, from Johnson's famous *Preface* of 1765 to the close of the century.[3] It will show, therefore, the genesis of the early nineteenth-century super-idolatry.

So far no one apparently has concentrated on this field sufficiently to do it justice, and perhaps the typical attitude toward it is evinced by the earliest attempt to deal with it: Charles Knight's survey in 1847, of *The History of Opinion on the Writings of Shakspere*.[4] This work devoted about ten pages[5] to the discussion of the period in question, and within these ten pages Knight displayed distinct disgust for the texts he was forced to consider: " . . . the heap of these forgotten emanations of the critical mind."[6]

---

[1]Unless otherwise noted, the footnotes refer to the complete bibliographies listed in Appendices A and B, which are both arranged chronologically.
[2]"Contributions to a History of Shakespearean Criticism," *Shakespeariana*, IX (1892), 30.
[3]For a good brief survey of Shakespeare criticism before 1766, see J. Adler, *Zur Shakespeare-Kritik des 18. Jahrh.* (1906), pp. 8-16.
[4]In the introductory volume of *Studies of Shakspere*, London, 1847.
[5]Pp. 207, 208, 265-67, 271, 273, 275-76. Sir Sidney Lee apparently misdated this work as "first published in 1849."—Preface to C. H. Hughes, *The Praise of Shakespeare* (1904), p. vii.
[6]*Op. cit.*, p. 264.

Probably the next important general contribution to the history of this lost battalion of Shakespeare critics was an article published in the *Nineteenth Century* in 1882, by Mr. W. H. Pollock, entitled "Shakespearian Criticism."[7] Mr. Pollock, relying on Gervinus, surveyed the fluctuations of Shakespeare's reputation from early in the seventeenth century and remarked with regard to the eighteenth century, "Up to the time of Steevens and Malone all the criticisms and prefaces were written under the tyranny of French taste, which was ruled by Voltaire."[8] This was not quite fair to our critics from 1766 to 1799. And Mr. Pollock's concluding remarks were concerned with a study of the attitude toward one play, *Hamlet*—with particular reference to the adaptations. Actually, Steevens, Johnson, and Voltaire were the only eighteenth-century critics mentioned; yet there were many other "forgotten emanations" that might have been recalled by Mr. Pollock.

Mr. George Hallam's two papers, appearing in 1892 in the *Shakespeariana* of the New York Society, neglected English criticism of Shakespeare in the eighteenth century in favor of French and German. Thus Samuel Johnson received one paragraph,[9] Voltaire eight pages,[10] and the Germans ten.[11] And Mr. Hallam's conclusion was as infelicitous as Mr. Pollock's: "The criticism which reigned from Dryden to Coleridge was essentially French in its principles."[12]

In 1895 appeared Mr. E. Walder's *Shaksperian Criticism: Textual and Literary—From Dryden to the End of the Eighteenth Century*, which was divided into two sections, the first (pp. 5-71) presenting literary criticism, the second, textual. Now textual criticism can display idolatry at best only statistically, and hence there were here really but sixty-

---

[7] XI (1882), 915-33.   [8] *Ibid.*, p. 921.   [9] *Op. cit.*, p. 37.
[10] *Ibid.*, pp. 38-44, 80-81.   [11] *Ibid.*, pp. 82-92.   [12] *Ibid.*, p. 37.

seven pages devoted to the literary appreciation of Shakespeare during the whole eighteenth century. And even these pages showed Mr. Walder's preoccupation with the much exploited "French School"[13] as contrasted with "The Romantic School,"[14] the latter (pp. 45-71) being essentially the only section concerned with our neglected critics from 1766 to 1799. As a matter of fact, throughout his book Mr. Walder made errors that tend to destroy one's confidence in his general reliability. For example, he dated Rymer's *Plays of the Last Age Considered* as of 1664;[15] he gave Goldsmith's *Citizen of the World* a chapter XI, on the "Stage";[16] he attributed an edition of Shakespeare's *Sonnets* to Gildon in 1640;[17] he misdated Dibdin's *History* as of 1796,[18] whereas the dedication is actually dated "March 25, 1800."[19] More might be said in derogation of his discussion of Cumberland's *Observer*,[20] of the French school of Shakespeare critics,[21] and of "The Romantic School";[22] but one distinctly valuable contribution of his book appears in its recognition of "the beginning of the philosophical criticism of Shakspere"[23] by Maurice Morgann.

Paul Hamelius' formidable German dissertation, *Die Kritik in der Englischen Literatur des 17. und 18. Jahrhunderts* was published in 1897, but as a contribution to Shakespearean criticism in the eighteenth century it has little

[13] P. 6. [14] P. 45.
[15] P. 27 n. The title is *Tragedies*, not *Plays*, and the date is 1678.
[16] P. 13 n. This is Goldsmith's *Enquiry* (1759).
[17] P. 71 n. This 1640 Edition was printed by Thomas Cotes for John Benson.
[18] P. 20.
[19] See R. W. Lowe, *Bibliographical Account of English Theatrical Literature*.
[20] No. 69 is used on p. 21, but there is no reference to Numbers 68, 70, 71, 72, 73, and 74, also on Shakespeare.
[21] *Ibid.*, p. 42. Joseph Warton appears therein!
[22] *Ibid.*, p. 12. Johnson appears therein!   [23] *Ibid.*, pp. 18-19.

value. Our critics from 1766 to 1799 are lost beneath such sweeping generalizations as: "In der zweiten Hälfte des xviii. Jahrhunderts schimmert hinter jedem kritischen Streite der Name und der Einfluss Popes durch";[24] and "Das neoklassische Urteil über Shakespeare, welches sich bis ans Ende des xviii. Jahrhunderts behauptete. . . ."[25] Herr Hamelius was really much more interested in Spenser than in Shakespeare in the eighteenth century[26] and so misjudged slightly the attitude toward the greater Elizabethan. But some helpful aspects of his book will be indicated below.

By far the most promising, and yet perhaps most disappointing, modern scholar in this field is Professor David Nichol Smith, who produced in 1903 and 1916 a Preface and two Introductions on the subject of Shakespearean criticism in the eighteenth century. The first Preface and Introduction (both in 1903) very brilliantly gave the late eighteenth century its due in anticipating Coleridge in "the new criticism"[27] of Shakespeare: "The present volume will show how the eighteenth century could almost lose itself in panegyric of Shakespeare."[28] Professor Nichol Smith then quite logically pointed out the four successive phases of eighteenth-century criticism of Shakespeare: "The first deals with his neglect of the so-called rules of the drama; the second determines what was the extent of his learning; the third considers the treatment of his text; and the fourth, more purely aesthetic, shows his value as a delineator of character."[29] For these four stages he printed appropriate texts, but only two of these—those of Farmer and Morgann—represent our lost critics from 1766 to 1799.

---

[24]P. 159.   [25]P. 111.   [26]*Ibid.*
[27]*Eighteenth Century Essays on Shakespeare* (1903), Preface, p. vi.
[28]*Ibid.*, Introduction, p. xii.   [29]*Ibid.*, p. xiii.

As Mr. A. C. Bradley pointed out in his review of Professor Nichol Smith's first book in *The Scottish Historical Review*,[30] Theobald, Hanmer, and Warburton hardly deserved so much attention: "The gradual progress of the century in aesthetic appreciation would, perhaps, be clearer and Mr. Smith's book would also gain in interest for most readers, if some pages from Richardson, Warton, or even Mrs. Montagu, took the place of the Prefaces of Theobald, Hanmer and Warburton."[31] And even more pertinently Mr. Bradley continued: "But the change in the general level of taste is naturally better gauged by reference to less gifted writers. . . . There can be no doubt about this change, and it is coincident, of course, with the gradual dawn of the romantic movement, which becomes unmistakable in the last quarter of the century."[32] Mr. Bradley was at last directing some attention toward the "forgotten emanations."

Three years later, however, in 1906, Herr J. Adler's *Zur Shakespeare-Kritik des 18. Jahrh.* (*Die Shakespeare Kritik im Gentleman's Magazine*) devoted only one brief section (pp. 16-31) specifically to our critics from 1766 to 1799, giving W. Richardson and Mrs. Montagu, for example, only one paragraph each. Further, Herr Adler's dissertation, by virtue of its title, confined itself to merely one periodical.

C. F. Johnson's *Shakespeare and His Critics* appeared in 1909. Mr. Johnson was constrained by the scope of his study to devote only one chapter to our later eighteenth-century critics, and here he was a little disconcerting, at least, in some of his categorical statements. He announced, for example, that William Richardson was the first critic to note the beauty of Shakespeare's women[33] and that

---

[30] I (1904), 291-95.   [31] *Ibid.*, p. 294.   [32] *Ibid.*
[33] P. 149. Mr. Johnson may have been misled by something like W. Collins' *Epistle to Sir Thomas Hanmer*, 57-66.

Richardson also made the first attempt to analyze Shakespeare's characters.[34] An article on Richardson in the *Journal of English and Germanic Philology* for January, 1929, and the discussion of the same subject by Dr. T. M. Raysor, in *Modern Language Notes* for December, 1927, will indicate how startling that second assertion was. As for the first: Richardson's discussion of Shakespeare's women, which appeared originally in 1789, had often been anticipated before 1789, as will appear in Part III of this book. In the light of these two representative facts, one cannot help being somewhat disturbed by the unconditional statements of Mr. Johnson's chapter.

Professor Nichol Smith published his second book in 1916, another anthology of texts, this time proceeding from Condell to Carlyle, together with an Introduction of twenty-one pages. This book apparently attempted to follow Mr. Bradley's suggestion with regard to the earlier group of selections, for Whately, Richardson, Warton, and Kames were all represented; and even Mrs. Montagu appeared in a footnote.[35] But only three pages of the Introduction were concerned with our lost critics from 1766 to 1799—in the course of which discussion, however, one idea evolved was conspicuously impressive: "The older criticism had accepted Shakespeare as the 'mirror of life,' and the newer criticism now proceeded to supply the exposition."[36] This idea will be used below in this Introduction.

The next general work of importance in this forgotten field was published in 1925—Mr. C. M. Haines' *Shakespeare in France: Criticism—Voltaire to Victor Hugo*.[37] Inasmuch as

---

[34] P. 151: i.e., "as if they were real human beings." Note also his "Kendrick" for Kenrick (p. 125) and the misdating of W. Richardson's Essays as of "1794" for 1774 (p. 145). See my Appendix A for these texts.

[35] *Shakespeare Criticism*, p. 172.　　[36] *Ibid.*, p. xviii.

[37] I have discussed Mr. T. R. Lounsbury's *Shakespeare and Voltaire* (1902) in my chapter, "The Reaction Against Voltaire."

Mr. Haines' book touches only one (and that really a negative) aspect of the late eighteenth-century criticism of Shakespeare, it will be considered in detail in its proper place in Part II. At present, it is necessary only to remark that Mr. Haines has completed a very disagreeable task, the assemblage of all Voltaire's strictures on Shakespeare, and so ably has he done this that later students may proceed directly to the task of noting the English reaction to Voltaire.

The most recent, and without doubt the most respectful, consideration of our lost critics from 1766 to 1799 has been made by a Coleridge specialist, Dr. T. M. Raysor, with two articles in *Modern Language Notes* for January and December, 1927, the first on "The Downfall of the Unities in the Eighteenth Century," and the second on "The Study of Shakespeare's Characters in the Eighteenth Century." The first of these pointed out "that Nichol Smith errs . . . on the conservative side,"[38] and proposed "to discuss the very interesting periodical reviews of Dr. Johnson's Preface."[39] It then noted some twenty-one books which referred to the unities during the period from 1736 to 1799, together with about eleven periodical articles, four of the latter being reviews of Johnson's *Preface*, one of Lord Kames' *Elements*, and one of Dr. John Berkenhout's *Biographia Literaria*. Sixteen, that is, one-half, of the above references preceded 1766 and hence are really not our "forgotten emanations," though they provide a very interesting background study. The rest will be discussed below in the chapter on the unities.[40] Dr. Raysor's second article on "The Study of Shakespeare's Characters in the Eighteenth Century" was a briefer study and will be incorporated in the chapters on the subject in question.[41]

[38]XLII (Jan., 1927), 2.   [39]*Ibid.*   [40]Chap. IV.
[41]Chaps. XI and XII. Chap. II of Mr. S. A. Small's *Shaksperian Character*

The Oxford University Press has recently published Professor David Nichol Smith's latest book, *Shakespeare in the Eighteenth Century*. "These three lectures," writes Professor Nichol Smith (January, 1928), "were delivered in Birkbeck College, London, in November, 1927." The first lecture (pp. 1-27) treats of Jonson, Dryden, Rymer, and the early adaptations and stage productions of Shakespeare. The second (pp. 29-60) reviews the work of the eighteenth-century editors of Shakespeare. The third (pp. 61-91), and the only one that really deals with our lost critics, discusses "Shakespeare's critics in the eighteenth century," notably Pope, Johnson, Lloyd, Kames, Joseph Warton, Whately, Morgann, Mackenzie, and Richardson. Only eleven pages of this lecture (pp. 81-91), however, touch our critics from 1766 to 1799, and only the last three of these pages really add anything new to Professor Nichol Smith's previous publications.[42]

Interpretation: "The Merchant of Venice" (1927) briefly traces the history of eighteenth-century criticism, but Mr. Small is following only one play and even then misses F. Gentleman and the Exeter Society *Essays* on Shylock (see Chap. XI below). He also apparently overlooks W. Richardson's second (1784) and third (1789) series of essays.

[42]Professor Nichol Smith has a footnote on p. 84 referring to the *British Magazine* in order to show the development of interest in Shakespeare as a result of Johnson's edition in 1765. But as this *British Magazine* ran from only 1760 to 1767, should he emphasize that "Before 1765 the only articles on Shakespeare in this magazine are" those in June, 1760, and August, 1761? For the *British Magazine* did not run long enough to establish such a point. If he is to use any periodical at all, why not the *Critical Review*, which began in 1756, or, better, the *Gentleman's Magazine* (from 1731), *London Magazine* (from 1732), *Monthly Review* (from 1749) etc.? And as a matter of fact in the *British Magazine*, IV (1763), 333, was printed a "Parallel between Shakespeare and Milton"; and V (1764), 64, contained reference to Shakespeare. Professor Nichol Smith also apparently missed at least two other articles in this periodical from 1765-67. However, his footnotes are again excellent—see pp. 27, 46, 81, and even 84—and his emphasis on the historical development is important (pp. 49-51, 52, 53, 55, 57).

So, apparently, no one has given sufficient attention to our forgotten critics of the late eighteenth century; yet from the work of these predecessors of mine, as well as from independent study, have been derived the principles which have guided the writing of this book. For example, Mr. E. Walder wrote one very valuable paragraph in 1895: "This philosophic movement in Shaksperian criticism was undoubtedly brought about by the wider critical movement of which Locke, Berkeley and Hume were exponents."[43] This idea Mr. A. C. Bradley also touched upon: "Indeed if Morgann could be taken as a fair example of that generation, we should have to say that the century, some time before it closed, had reached *in principle* the whole position in which criticism has rested from the days of Schlegel and Coleridge."[44] Professor Nichol Smith in his Introduction in 1916 also suggested the same philosophic idea[45] as noted above, and Mr. Haines stated it emphatically from another point of view: "Taylor [1774] represents the last stage of the formalist school, who were now reduced to the attempt to rationalize those rules which in fact rested not upon reason but upon a tyrannical literary tradition."[46] Something therefore must be done with this psychologizing of Shakespeare in the late eighteenth century, and hence a large section of this book is devoted to the subject, "a task hitherto unattempted," as Morgann would put it.[47]

The second method by which this book has been largely guided—that is, the emphasis upon criticism in periodicals of the late eighteenth century—appeared first in Hame-

---

[43] *Op. cit.*, p. 19.
[44] *The Scottish Historical Review*, I (1904), 294. Morgann is essentially a psychological critic.
[45] *Shakespeare Criticism*, p. xviii.   [46] *Op. cit.*, p. 47.
[47] *An Essay on the Dramatic Character of Sir John Falstaff* (London: Davies, 1777), p. 16.

lius' dissertation in 1897: "Zunächst enthielt jede Lieferung einer Zeitschrift, wie im Spectator, einem einzelnen Essay, nach und nach änderte sich ihre Form, und sie wurden Magazines und Reviews genannt. Kritische Beiträge waren darin so häufig, dass im Jahre 1761 im British Magazine geklagt wird, dass die Leser nur politische und kritische Aufsätze kaufen wollen. (S. 199.) Viele der wertvollsten kritischen Arbeiten des XVIII. Jahrhunderts, u. a. die von Johnson und Warton, erscheinen zuerst in Zeitschriften."[48] And Mr. A. C. Bradley in 1904 remarked, as noted above, "But the change in the general level of taste is naturally better gauged by reference to less gifted writers."[49] Hence the chief substance of this book is the analysis of Shakespearean criticism as it appeared not merely in books of the period, but in "magazines," that is, general periodicals, from 1766 to 1799—once again "a task hitherto unattempted."[50]

These are probably the two main principles which have directed the production of this study of the lost critics. But other ideas have been picked up and applied. The general outline of the book, for example, is based, with some slight variation, upon Professor Nichol Smith's statement in 1903 (noted above) of the four successive phases of Shakespearean criticism in the eighteenth century. To these four phases has been added historical criticism, which Professor Nichol Smith until recently tended to neglect, though Mr. A. C. Bradley recognized its value: Farmer's *Essay* "shows that the century had come to realize how indispensable to a critic of Shakespeare is familiarity with the literature of his time";[51] and Herr Hamelius agrees: "Statt des einen,

[48]*Op. cit.*, p. 138.   [49]*Loc. cit.*
[50]J. Adler's dissertation, *Zur Shakespeare—Kritik des 18. Jahrh.* (1906) by virtue of its title confined itself to one "magazine" and even then never but once used more than two articles per play.
[51]*The Scottish Historical Review*, I (1904), 293. Professor Nichol Smith's

aus Aristoteles und seinem Nachfolgern entnommenen Massstabes, an welchem die Neoklassiker die ganze Literatur massen, gelangte nun eine historische Anschauungsweise zur Geltung."[52] Hence appears the section on historical criticism.

It was of course necessary to make some distinct limitations. Elimination of detailed study of textual criticism was the first check arbitrarily set,[53] because textual criticism can merely be used statistically to show rising idolatry. Newspaper items were also rejected since this material is not generally available in this country, and criticism of actors' versions of the plays—for example Bell's edition—was disregarded, for this book has no concern with such mutilated stage versions of Shakespeare. Modern criticism on all of the above omissions, however, has been supplied in Appendix B in a bibliography as complete as possible at the moment, and it should be noted that no such bibliography, I believe, has ever been hitherto proposed. The bibliography of primary texts in Appendix A is also, probably, the first attempt at such a study.[54] Hence this book is in reality merely an introductory study to the whole field and will provide inspiration, I hope, to other scholars to delve more deeply into the attitude toward Shakespeare in the eighteenth century as a whole.

In conclusion, it should be emphasized that this study is not concerned with criticism of Shakespeare before 1766. On the contrary, its purpose is to point out that the genesis of super-idolatry of Shakespeare lay *in the late eighteenth century*—that is, to propose this period as the

---

most recent book, *Shakespeare in the Eighteenth Century*, pressed the point: pp. 49, 50-51, 52, 53, 55, 57.

[52]*Op. cit.*, p. 162.

[53]References to the Sonnets and Poems in general have also been omitted.

[54]A preliminary draft of both of these bibliographies appeared in *Studies in Philology*, Extra Series I (May, 1929), 58-98.

background of the criticism of Coleridge, Hazlitt, and Lamb, and not to treat the background of this background. As it is generally true, however, that the ideas of 1766-99 often did appear sporadically before this precise period, there is suggested in footnotes at the beginning of each section material which will help an interested reader to trace the ideas of the late eighteenth century back into preceding criticism; and I have also introduced a chapter entitled "A Preliminary Survey, 1660-1765," which will indicate the general transition. This whole natural development should be particularly noted with regard to the second and third large divisions of the book.

Mr. J. O. Halliwell-Phillipps remarked superciliously in a letter October 12, 1888: "I do not care for anything of the *last* century unless it relates to Shakespearian *biography*, such as traditions, Stratford, etc."[55] But Professor Karl Young, whom I thank for starting me happily in this field several years ago by his vigorous teaching in Madison, continually stressed the importance of the eighteenth century, and Mr. A. C. Bradley noted with regard to Morgann:— "There is no better piece of Shakespearian criticism in the world."[56] This book will now support the contentions of Mr. Young and Mr. Bradley.

[55] Quoted by S. Lee in his *Shakespeareana*, I, 225.
[56] *The Scottish Historical Review*, I (1904), 291.

PART I

THE NEW INTEREST IN SHAKESPEARE

CHAPTER I

A PRELIMINARY SURVEY, 1660-1765

This brief and tentative chapter is presented simply to acquaint the reader with the main ideas to be discussed later in this book by surveying rapidly now the shifting attitude toward Shakespeare over two successive periods—from 1660 to 1730 and from 1730 to 1765—which lead, by direct transition, to the field of our lost critics, from 1766 to 1799.[1]

FROM 1660 TO 1730

During the earlier period, from 1660 to 1730, the traditional objections to Shakespeare generally held sway. That is, the critics castigated the poet for neglecting the unities, for ignoring the ancients, for violating decorum by resorting to tragicomedy and supernatural characters, and for using puns and blank verse.[2] But after 1730 there arose a definite emphasis upon a more defensive attitude toward Shakespeare with regard to the above points: critics appeared who rejected these traditional objections, and their defense was accompanied by an aggressive, apostrophizing mode of approach. Now, more than ever before, Shakespeare's characters were wholesomely applauded, the poet was promoted to the rank of conscious artist, and he was studied sympathetically with reference to his own age. Thus this important period from 1730 to 1765 really serves

---

[1] No attempt will be made to document this chapter thoroughly, for the accent throughout is on the ideas presented without particular reference to their absolutely precise source. *Periodical material on these ideas preceding 1766 will be found in the preliminary footnotes to chapters throughout the rest of the book.*

[2] Compare the chapter titles of Part II, in the Table of Contents. The late eighteenth century reacted against all these objections.

as a distinct introduction to that covered by this book,[3] and the whole development from 1660 to 1765 actually deserves a book by itself.[4] The present brief survey can do little more than sketch hastily this preliminary field, with the purpose of introducing to the reader these main ideas, to be referred to throughout the remainder of the book.

To begin directly: with regard to the unities, in the period from 1660 to 1730 critics generally favored them at the expense of Shakespeare.[5] Pope excused Shakespeare on an historico-comparative basis and a lack of knowledge of the ancients,[6] but Gildon argued in behalf of the poet's classical knowledge.[7] Dryden was not so sure.[8] Gildon, therefore, advanced the ancients above Shakespeare and preferred imitation of models,[9] but other critics lifted Shakespeare to at least a level with the ancients on the basis of his imitation of nature and natural genius.[10] In the matter of general decorum the critics generally attacked Shakespeare.[11] Similarly they rejected his tragicomedy,[12] but two, at least, applauded his supernatural characters.[13] The

---

[3]Compare the chapter titles of Parts II and III, in the Table of Contents.

[4]The present writer will attempt to write this book next, himself.

[5]Dryden, Preface to *Troilus and Cressida* (1679); the *Essay of Dramatic Poesie* wavers from 1668 to 1693 (3rd ed.); Rymer, *The Tragedies of the Last Age Considered* (London; R. Tonson, 1678), pp. 24, 106, and *A Short View of Tragedy* (London: Baldwin, 1693), pp. 2, 161; Gildon, *An Essay on the Art, Rise, and Progress of the Stage* (London: E. Curll, 1710), p. xxv.

[6]Preface to Edition (London: J. Tonson, 1725), pp. vi-vii.

[7]*Op. cit.*, p. vi.   [8]Preface to *All for Love* (1678).   [9]*Op. cit.*, pp. i-iii.

[10]Pope, *op. cit.*, pp. ii-vii; Dennis, *Essay on the Genius and Writings of Shakespear* (1712), reprinted in D. Nichol Smith's *Eighteenth Century Essays* (1903), pp. 41-42.

[11]Dryden, *An Essay of Dramatic Poesie* (1668); Steele, *Spectator*, No. 141, Rymer, *A Short View*, the second "Chap. V," pp. 124, 131, etc; Pope, *op. cit.*, p. v.

[12]Dryden, Preface to *Troilus and Cressida* (1679); *Of Poetry and Painting* (1695); Addison, *Spectator*, Nos. 39, 40, 42, 44; Gildon, *op. cit.*, p. ix.

[13]Addison, *Spectator*, No. 419; Rowe, *Some account of the Life* . . . *Shakespear* (London: J. Tonson, 1709), pp. xxiii, xxvi.

poet's puns were assailed by Addison,[14] and the use of blank verse by Dryden.[15] Yet one critic defended his blank verse,[16] and two others attacked alterations of his plays.[17] As a whole, however, the traditional objections were generally upheld throughout the period from 1660 to 1730.

On the other hand, within this same period, there was actually a slight movement toward the newer criticism suggested by the chapter titles of Part III. Six prominent critics praised Shakespeare's powers of characterization;[18] only Rymer[19] and Dennis[20] objected. And Rowe anticipated to some extent the late eighteenth-century argument over Falstaff by declaring him "cowardly."[21] Both Rowe[22] and Pope,[23] also, knew historical criticism.

FROM 1730 TO 1765

The next period, from 1730 to 1765—the transition period—shows a definite shift toward the attitude of the last decades of the eighteenth century. Hanmer in 1736[24] began to question the unities, and was followed by at least

---

[14]*Spectator*, No. 61. [15]*Essay of Dramatic Poesie* (by Neander).
[16]Dennis, *op. cit.*, p. 25.
[17]Addison, *Spectator*, No. 40; Gildon, *Remarks on the Plays of Shakespear* (London: E. Curll, 1710), pp. 265-66.
[18]Dryden, Preface to *Troilus and Cressida*; Hughes, *Guardian*, No. 37; Steele, *Spectator* No. 238; Rowe, *op. cit.*, pp. xvii-xx; Gildon, *Remarks*, p. 284; Pope, *op. cit.*, p. iii.
[19]*A Short View* (1693), pp. 86-147.
[20]In *Miscellanies* (1693) Dennis attacked Shakespeare's aristocrats.
[21]*Op. cit.*, p. xviii. [22]*Ibid.*, pp. xv, xxiii, xxvii, xxxi.
[23]*Op. cit.*, p. v. See also Professor Young's monograph, noted below, for other critics of this earlier period.
[24]*Some Remarks on the Tragedy of Hamlet*, pp. 1, 42. (This text is generally attributed to Hanmer.) Dr. T. M. Raysor in his article in MLN for Jan., 1927, has given a good background study of the breakdown of the unities before 1766. I shall therefore merely present a few illustrations, including John Brown's *Dissertation* (1763), which Dr. Raysor omitted. See also Chap. IV, below.

three critics.[25] Furthermore, Webb in 1762[26] and Johnson in 1765[27] definitely defended Shakespeare himself on this point. Both Hanmer[28] and the anonymous critic of *Hamlet* (1752)[29] denied Shakespeare's classical learning, but they were more than offset by several other critics.[30] The slowness of development on this point suggests at once the distinctly transitional aspect of the period.

E. Young in 1759 rescued Shakespeare from the accusation of the imitation of models,[31] and meanwhile Upton had defended the poet's general decorum in 1746.[32] But Upton stands alone on this, for four other critics all attacked Shakespeare.[33] Again, the transitional aspect of the period is to be noted. Tragicomedy, however, shows the rise of more well-balanced argument: three critics attacked it,[34] but two defended it.[35] It will take some time

[25] J. Upton, *Critical Observations on Shakespeare* (London: Hawkins, 1746), sec. 9; the anonymous author of *Miscellaneous Observations on the Tragedy of Hamlet* (London: Clark, 1752), p. v. (Jaggard assigns this to Johnson, but Courtney and Nichol Smith ignore it); John Brown, *A Dissertation on the Rise, Union, and Power . . . of Poetry and Music* (London: L. Davis and C. Reymers, 1763), pp. 114-15.

[26] *Remarks on the Beauty of Poetry* (London: Dodsley, 1762), pp. 103-7.

[27] *Preface* (1765), pp. xxv-xxxi. See Chap. IV, below.

[28] *Op. cit.*, pp. 40-41.   [29] *Miscellaneous Observations*, etc., p. iv.

[30] Upton, Warburton, Whalley, Grey, and Dodd. See my preliminary paragraphs in Chap. V, below.

[31] *Conjectures on Original Composition* (ed. E. J. Morley, 1918), pp. 34 ff; and see Hurd's *On Poetical Imitation* (1751), (London: Cadell and Davies, 1811), II, 125, 133, 142, etc.; and more especially his *On the Marks of Imitation* (To Mason, Aug. 15, 1757), (London: Cadell and Davies, 1811), II, 250, *240, *250, 311-12.   [32] *Op. cit.*, p. 107.

[33] Hanmer, *op. cit.*, pp. 28, 29, 33, 35, 36-37, 41; Anon., *Miscellaneous Observations* (1752), p. viii; G. Colman, *Critical Reflections on the Old English Dramatic Writers* (1761), in *Prose on Several Occasions* (London: T. Cadell, 1787), II, 113; Johnson, *Preface*, pp. xxi-xxii. See Chap. VI, below.

[34] Hanmer, *op. cit.*, pp. 19, 28, 31; Anon., *op. cit.*, pp. 46-48; Colman, *op. cit.*, II, 113.

[35] Upton, *op. cit.*, p. 106; Johnson, *Rambler*, No. 156 (Sept. 14, 1751), and *Preface*, pp. xiv-xv. See Chap. VI, below.

after 1765 for the later critics to exonerate Shakespeare on this point. Two commentators praised the poet's supernatural characters,[36] but two others also attacked his puns.[37] There was a definite rise of interest in blank verse in the criticism of Upton[38] and Webb,[39] and the attack on alterations set in, never to be relinquished till Shakespeare was finally redeemed: four prominent critics all rejected adaptations.[40] It is obvious, therefore, that, with reference to the traditional objections, the period from 1730 to 1765 was definitely turning toward a new, more defensive point of view—in short, the point of view of the commentators from 1766 to 1799.[41]

And this transitional period also developed an aggressive, apostrophizing mode of approach. Shakespeare's powers of characterization were approved by at least seven distinguished critics.[42] Hanmer had to some extent suggested the coming distrust of Hamlet by rejecting the speech over the King at prayer: " . . . very Bloody . . . so inhuman, so unworthy of a Hero"[43] and Upton had called Falstaff "a coward."[44] The psychologizing of Shakespeare had also begun with Upton,[45] Hume, Burke, and

---

[36]Hanmer, *op. cit.*, pp. 2, 25-26; Colman, *op. cit.*, II, 117. See Chap. VI, below.

[37]Hanmer, *op. cit.*, p. 41; Johnson, *Preface*, pp. xxiii-xxiv. See Chap. VI, below.

[38]*Op. cit.*, pp. 17-21, 28.   [39]*Op. cit.*, pp. 36 ff.

[40]Fielding, *Historical Register* (1736); Upton, *op. cit.*, pp. 14 n, 16, 147 (?). The last reference is to the dream, omitted in the second (1748) edition; Anon., *op. cit.*, pp. xi-xii; Goldsmith, *Enquiry* (1759), chap. XI.

[41]Compare the chapter titles of my Part II.

[42]Theobald, *Preface* (1733), reprinted in D. Nichol Smith, *Eighteenth Century Essays on Shakespeare*, pp. 64, 73; Hanmer, *op. cit.*, pp. 2, 18, 20, 41; Upton, *op. cit.*, p. 54 (on the women in *Macbeth*), 101; Anon., *op. cit.*, pp. v, 31; Joseph Warton, *Adventurer* (1753-54), No. 113, 116, 122, on Lear; Colman, *op. cit.*, II, 118-19; Johnson, *Preface*, pp. viii-xiii. For periodical material on this point see the introductory footnote to Chap. XI, below.

[43]*Op. cit.*, p. 33.   [44]*Op. cit.*, p. 85.   [45]*Ibid.*, pp. 42, 49, 51.

Kames.[46] Daniel Webb promoted Shakespeare to the rank of conscious artist[47] and the anonymous critic of *Hamlet* (1752) applauded Shakespeare as a moral philosopher.[48] Historical criticism had developed very rapidly:[49] seven prominent critics were applying it to the poet.[50] Even as early as 1736 Hanmer hesitated to find fault with Shakespeare because the poet was almost always right[51]—a distinct hint of the future idolatry. All in all, therefore, the period from 1730 to 1765 forms a definite transition in the direction of our lost critics of 1766 to 1799. It will perhaps be clearer now to the reader that this book will develop the revolt begun sporadically in the transition years before 1766.

Knowledge of Shakespeare in This Period

The late eighteenth century was at times disturbed over its predecessors' ignorance of Shakespeare. The Advertisement to the Reader in Johnson and Steevens' edition of 1773 points out with disgust that Steele in the *Tatler* quoted Betterton's alteration of *Macbeth*, not Shakespeare. The third edition, in 1785, of the same editors, chastises Dr. Hill for giving an extract in *The Actor* (1750) from

---

[46] For a discussion of Hume, Burke, and Kames on this point see the introductory paragraphs of Chap. XII, below.

[47] See Chap. X, below.   [48] *Op. cit.*, p. 15.

[49] In general for this point see Professor Karl Young's distinguished monograph, "Samuel Johnson on Shakespeare: One Aspect," in *Wisconsin Studies*, No. 18, 1923.

[50] Theobald, *op. cit.* (See Professor Young's monograph.); Hanmer, *op. cit.*, pp. 6, 27, 34, 38, 41, etc.; Upton, *op. cit.*, pp. 9-10 n, 37; Anon., *op. cit.*, p. 13; Mrs. Lennox, *Shakespear Illustrated* (1753-54). (See Professor Young's monograph.); Colman, *op. cit.*, II, 119. Johnson, *Preface*, pp. xxxii ff.

[51] *Op. cit.*, p. 25. Compare Hurd in *Notes on the Art of Poetry* (1749): "And now the genius of Shakespeare is idolized in its turn. Happily for the public taste, it can scarcely be too much so." Ed. of 1811 (Cadell and Davies), I, 277.

Romeo and Juliet as Shakespeare's when it was actually Otway's interpolation in *Caius Marius*.[52] This is Malone's note, and Malone goes on to quote Shirley's Prologues to *The Sisters* (1640) and *Love Tricks* (1667) to show, also, the seventeenth century's neglect of Shakespeare. Malone's *Preface* in 1790 to his own edition continues in this vein, but perhaps the best late eighteenth-century summary of criticism of Shakespeare preceding 1766 appears in the Exeter Society *Essays* in 1796.[53] This survey repeats the above items and adds emphasis on alterations of Shakespeare, noting Tate's assumption of the authorship of *Lear* in 1707:[54] "In the days of 'the hero William' . . . the plays of Shakespeare were seldom acted . . . Their fame is now established."[55] But all this derogatory judgment of the late eighteenth century on its predecessors is somewhat discounted by the development shown above in this chapter, for the periods from 1660 to 1730 and from 1730 to 1765. And as a matter of fact, the Exeter critic, Richard Hole, considerably weakens his case by proceeding to admit that Johnson and Steevens in their third edition (1785, Vol. I, p. 75) quoted as Otway's "some beautiful passages which he had stolen from Shakspeare"[56]—a remark which is rather curious in the light of Malone's note above. So perhaps the late eighteenth century itself should not be too supercilious toward its predecessors. Incidentally, one of its own newspaper critics, a man named Trinder, apparently reviewed a Shakespeare play as a brand new

---

[52]I, 77 n. When Garrick revived Shakespeare's *Macbeth* in 1744, Quin queried in astonishment: "What does he mean? don't I play *Macbeth* as written by Shakespeare?" (A. Murphy, *Life of David Garrick*, Dublin, 1801 p. 48.)
[53]*Essays by a Society of Gentlemen at Exeter* (Exeter: Trewman and Son, 1796), pp. 241 ff. The three essays on Shakespeare were by Richard Hole.
[54]*Ibid.*, pp. 244-45: "because Shakespeare was so little known."
[55]*Ibid.*, p. 241.   [56]*Ibid.*, p. 246.

play of the season. Both the *Gentleman's Magazine* in 1781[57] and *The Observer* (1785-90), No. 50, pounced on this luckless reviewer. If the late eighteenth century, which definitely idolized Shakespeare (as this book will attempt to show), could make such errors as this, it might have been more lenient toward its earlier brothers, who certainly prepared the way for its own criticism.

[57]LI (1781), 629.

CHAPTER II

THE SCHOLARLY INTEREST

The steady rise of idolatry of Shakespeare throughout the late eighteenth century may be suggested broadly in terms of tangible features lying outside the field of literary criticism. Though detailed study of such features has been deliberately excluded from this book,[1] nevertheless a general statistical survey[2] of such concrete development will serve as a valuable background for a subsequent analysis of the literary criticism of the period. This rising interest in Shakespeare's texts and Shakespeareana in general from 1766 to 1799 will therefore be suggested (using summaries whenever practicable); and, as such a study will represent an indirect aspect of the idolatry of the late eighteenth century, we may "By indirections find directions out" from two points of view, the scholarly and the popular "assays of bias": that is, editions, chronology, and spurious plays, Shakespeare illustrated, concordances and glossaries, Shakespeareana (bibliographical), and biography, for the scholarly "windlasses"; and attacks on commentators, parodies, sequels, operas, imitations, modern characters from Shakespeare, and jubilees, for the popular.

EDITIONS, CHRONOLOGY, AND SPURIOUS PLAYS

Editions of Shakespeare's Plays from 1766 to 1799 include: Steevens' *Twenty Plays* (1766), Johnson (1766, in Ireland), Theobald (1767), Capell (1768), Johnson (1768),

---

[1] See Introduction.
[2] The method used will follow roughly that of the article on "Shakespearian Statistics," in *N&Q*, March 19, 1864, pp. 232-33.

Pope (1768), Balfour (1769), Blair (1769, 1771), Ewing (1771), Hanmer (1771), Theobald (1772), Johnson and Steevens (1773), Theobald (1773), Bell's Theater Edition (1774), Jennens (5 plays, 1774), Theobald (1777), Johnson and Steevens (1778), Malone's *Supplement* (1780), Malone's Second Appendix (1783), "Stockdale's" (i.e., S. Ayscough, 1784), Johnson and Steevens (1785), Rann (1786), Nichols (1786), Bell (1787), Malone (1790),[3] Ayscough (1790, 1791, with Index), Bellamy and Harrison (1791), Johnson and Steevens (1793), Malone (1794), Blair (1795), Bellamy and Robarts (1797), Robinson (1797), Longman (1797), Ogilvie (1798), Baldwin (1798), Nichols (1798), Harding (1798-1800).

Connected with these many attempts to establish Shakespeare's text should be noted at least three important studies which were intended to influence editors.[4] The first was Joseph Ritson's *Remarks, Critical and Illustrative on the Text and Notes of the Last Edition of Shakspeare* (1783), in which Ritson attacked Steevens: "There have been no less than eight professed Editors of Shakspeare; and yet the old copies, of which we have heard so much, have never been collated by any one of them[5] . . . Mr. Steevens never collated any one of the folios . . . the text is no more finally settled at present than it was in the time of Theo-

---

[3]Malone in his Note preceding the second edition of the *Letter to the Rev. Richard Farmer* (1792) repudiated the seven-volume edition put out under his name. This *Letter* was published twice in 1792, both times by Robinson, and the two texts, except for this Note, are identical. In this book I happen to have used the second edition, consistently.

[4]In giving these representative texts, I have ventured to omit T. Tyrwhitt's *Observations and Conjectures upon Some Passages of Shakespeare* (1766), and E. Capell, *Notes and Various Readings* (1774-80). For similar works antedating 1766, see B. Heath, *Revisal of Shakespear's Text* (1765), and J. Upton's brilliant textual animadversions in Books II and III of his *Critical Observations on Shakespeare* (1746).

[5]London: Johnson, 1783, Preface, pp. ii-iii. Compare Chap. XIII, below.

bald,"[6] who was "the best of Shakspeares editors."[7] These *Remarks* were answered in the *St. James Chronicle*, June 5, 1783, by "Alciphron," presumably George Steevens, and Ritson replied with the *Quip Modest*, 1788, and *Cursory Criticisms*, 1792. Malone also took a hand in this battle with his *A Letter to the Rev. Richard Farmer* (1792), which replied to Ritson's *Cursory Criticisms*. In the course of his *Letter* Malone produced such decisive sallies as: "[Ritson's] *Remarks* are absolutely below a serious notice . . ."[8] "Such, I think, is the substance of this Quip, for so this writer chooses to denominate some of his shrewd and sagacious remarks, though he does not deal much either in *cranks* or *wanton wiles*."[9] The second book was J. M. Mason's *Comments on the Last Edition of Shakespeare's Plays* (1785), which pointed out that Steevens confined himself merely to "litigated passages" whereas "I have studied every line of these plays."[10] Mason's suggestions were given some recognition in Johnson and Steevens' fourth edition, 1793.[11] The third book was Whiter's *A Specimen of a Commentary on Shakspeare* (1794), which will be discussed in detail in Part III.[12]

Individual plays also appeared separately: e.g. *Henry VIII* (1786, 1787), *Othello* (1773), *King Lear* (1768, 1770, 1787, 1792), *Hamlet* (1773, 1789), *Julius Cæsar* (1774), *Macbeth* (1787), *As You Like It* (1787), *Merchant of Venice* (1787), *Twelfth Night* (1787), *Winter's Tale* (1782), *Richard III* (1787), etc. Rachael Randall's services in this field in 1787 may well be compared with those of J. Tonson in 1734.[13]

---

[6]*Ibid.*, pp. iv-v. [7]*Ibid.*, p. vii. [8]P. 38. [9]P. 37.
[10]London: Dilly, 1785, Preface, p. ix. [11]I, 342 ff.
[12]Chaps. XII and XIII.

[13]J. Tonson published *Julius Caesar* in 1729; *Merry Wives of Windsor* and *Henry IV*, Part 2, in 1733; *Richard III*, *Measure for Measure*, *Much Ado*, and *Midsummer Night's Dream* in 1734.

The attitude of critics toward the editors may be suggested briefly. The *Universal Magazine*, in 1777, following Morgann, declared that editors had not done Shakespeare justice: they have not eliminated "the disgraceful incumbrance of some wretched productions, which have long hung heavy on his fame."[14] The praise for Malone was always very fulsome: T. Davies speaks of "the accurate Mr. Malone";[15] and Samuel Ayscough says, "according to Mr. Malone's accurate investigations."[16] *The Bee* in 1791 rejected Pope and Warburton,[17] and the *Universal Magazine* at the close of the period expressed the general point of view, in summary: "Were Shakspeare to revisit this globe, the first thing that would surprise him would be, to learn that above one hundred and fifty thousand pounds have lately been devoted toward splendid editions of his works."[18]

---

[14] LXI (1777), 5. This appears in Morgann, *op. cit.*, p. 64.

[15] *Dramatic Miscellanies* (London: Davies, 1784), II, 259.

[16] Preface to *Index to the Remarkable Passages and Words . . . Shakspeare*, 1790. See also Johnson and Steevens', fourth edition (1793), *Advertisement*, p. xxi.

[17] IV (1791), 295.

[18] XCIII (1793), 184. But one will hardly get the full effect of the interest in these editions without resorting to a list of reviews of one editorial attempt, for example. The following contemporary survey of Johnson and Steevens' activity is merely suggestive of the popularity of the editing of Shakespeare during this period:

1773 Edition
  Monthly Review, XLIX (1773), 419.
  Critical Review, XXXVI (1773), 345, 401.
1778 Edition
  Monthly Review, LXII (1780), 12, 257.
  Critical Review, XLVII (1779), 129, 172.
1785 Edition
  Monthly Review, LXXV (1786), 81, 161.
  Critical Review, LXII (1786), 321.
  Gentleman's Magazine, LIX (1789), 587, 710, 810, 907, 1091, 1198.
  Ibid., LX (1790), 43, 125, 215, 306, 401, 506; LVI (1786), 235.

Supplementary to the editing of Shakespeare was the problem of the chronology of the plays, and this subject was the definite interest of Edmond Malone. His "An Attempt to ascertain the Order in which the Plays attributed to Shakspeare were written" appeared first in Johnson and Steevens' second edition, 1778,[19] and was reprinted in subsequent editions, with some modifications, such as were introduced especially in the second version of this list in Malone's own edition (1790).[20] J. Hurdis' *Cursory Remarks Upon the Arrangement of the Plays of Shakespear* (1792) commented on Malone and received considerable attention from the reviewers in the *Critical Review*,[21] the *Monthly Review*,[22] and the *Analytical Review*.[23] The Exeter Society *Essays* in 1796 also found some fault with Malone, with regard to *The Winter's Tale* and *All's Well That Ends Well*.[24]

1793 Edition
Analytical Review, XIX (1794), 350.
British Critic, I (1793), 54, 127.
Critical Review, LXXXII (1794), 390.
Gentleman's Magazine, LXVII (1797), 194.
Further interesting items connected with these editions in general include:
Scots Magazine, XLIX (1787), 8—on sums paid to editors of Shakespeare.
Gentleman's Magazine, LVII (1787), 76—on finances of editions.
Ibid., LXI (1791), 1098—on proposal for modernizing Shakespeare.
Ibid., LXIV (1794), 327—on a new edition proposed by the ladies.

[19] I, 269-346.
[20] I, 261 ff., with revisions, as noted in the Preface, p. lxi.
[21] LXXVI (1792), 228. [22] XII (1793), 110. [23] XIV (1792), 76.
[24] Pp. 260-61. The *Sonnets* received little attention during the period. Steevens reprinted them in 1766 from G. Eld's version of 1609 but omitted them in his later editions, referring to Malone as "their only intelligent editor" (Advertisement, Edition of 1793, p. vii). Malone had printed them in vol. I of his *Supplement* (1780). Further reference to them may be noted in the *Monthly Mirror*, VIII (1799), 361. For a modern point of view on the sonnets in the eighteenth century see G. Crosse's article in the *London Mercury*, IV (1921), 623-32.
 That the English were taking some notice of foreign translations of Shakespeare appears from the fact that the *Monthly Review* in 1776 discussed both

Another editorial problem was that of establishing the Shakespeare canon. Steevens printed *Pericles, Titus Andronicus,* and the three parts of *Henry VI* in 1766. The next year Farmer questioned sections of *Pericles* and threw out *A Yorkshire Tragedy* and Theobald's *Double Falsehood*;[25] and the same year Capell accepted the three parts of *Henry VI, Taming of the Shrew, Titus Andronicus,* and *Love's Labour's Lost.*[26] Richard Warner in 1768 also favored *Titus,*[27] as the *Macaroni and Theatrical Magazine* did *Henry VIII* in 1772;[28] but the *Lady's Magazine* flatly rejected *Titus.*[29] Meanwhile Mrs. Griffith included *Titus, Two Gentlemen of Verona, Henry VI* (3 parts), and *Henry VIII* in her work in 1775 on the general principle that anything that merely *hinted* of Shakespeare should be included.[30] Morgann, curiously enough, abruptly threw out *The Taming of the Shrew* in 1777,[31] together with the first part of *Henry VI.*[32] Colman in 1778 questioned *The Two Noble Kinsmen.*[33] Finally Malone in 1780 printed all the possible apocrypha and re-

German and French versions: LIV (1776), 399, 575 (the German was J. J. Eschenburg's *Shakespeares Schauspiele*); and in 1788 reviewed a complete German translation: LXXVIII (1788), 637. Meanwhile Steevens had attacked e Tourneur in his edition of 1788 (I, 210), and in 1793 the *Analytical Review* devoted a review to J. J. Eschenburg alone: XVII (1793), 120. But such German and French works fall generally outside the scope of this book.

[25]*Essay on the Learning of Shakespeare* (Cambridge: J. Archdeacon, 1767), pp. 16-17. He also eliminated spurious translations from Ovid (pp. 32-33) and assigned other pseudo-Shakespeare material to W. Stafford (p. 34) and George Peele (p. 38).

[26]Introduction to Edition (1768), pp. 36-37, 39, 40, 41.

[27]*A Letter to David Garrick* (London: Warner, 1768), p. 12.

[28]October, 1772, p. 77: ". . . it carries the sacred imprimatur of Shakespeare."

[29]IX (1778), 532.

[30]*The Morality of Shakespeare's Drama* (London: Cadell, 1775), pp. 403, 25, 303 325 respectively.

[31]*Op. cit.*, p. 50 n.

[32]*Ibid.*, p. 49. He wrote a long note on the other two parts, pp. 49-50 n.

[33]*Prose on Several Occasions* (London: Cadell, 1787), II, 160.

jected all but *Pericles* and *A Yorkshire Tragedy*.[34] Two years later the *Biographia Dramatica* eclipsed Malone by eliminating *Pericles* and *A Yorkshire Tragedy*, as well as *Locrine, Sir John Oldcastle, Titus Andronicus, The Puritan, The London Prodigal, The Life and Death of Cromwell*.[35] By this time the tide had fully set in against the apocrypha. T. Davies threw out *Henry VIII* in 1784,[36] though Mason was inclined to accept it in 1785.[37] Mason also seemed to favor *Pericles* slightly, though he rejected all the other plays which Malone had published in 1780.[38] In 1790 Malone again returned to *Pericles*,[39] and in 1792 declared he had discovered manuscripts to support his contention in 1780 that five of the plays he printed had not a line of Shakespeare.[40] Finally Mason in 1798 definitely assigned *The Two Noble Kinsmen* to Beaumont and Fletcher.[41] Further material to show how Shakespeare was redeemed, as Morgann had vigorously requested in his comment on Voltaire,[42] appeared in the *Monthly Review* in 1770,[43] the *British Critic* in 1793,[44] and the *Gentleman's Magazine* in 1797.[45] All of these developments should readily suggest the popularity of editing Shakespeare in the late eighteenth century.

---

[34]Advertisement, p. vii. The list included 7 plays: *Pericles, Locrine, Sir John Oldcastle, Life and Death of Lord Cromwell, The London Prodigal, The Puritan, A Yorkshire Tragedy*.

[35]I, 404-05. [36]*Op. cit.*, (1784), I, 339.
[37]*Op. cit.*, (1785), pp. 233-45. [38]*Ibid.*, Preface, p. xv.
[39]Preface to 1790 Edition, p. lix. He had thrown out *Titus* in 1780.—Advertisement, p. viii.
[40]*Letter to the Rev. Richard Farmer*, p. 5 n.
[41]*Comments on the Plays of Beaumont and Fletcher* (London: Harding, 1798), p. 343.
[42]*Op. cit.*, p. 64.
[43]XLIII (1770), 494—"*Arden of Feversham* not by S."
[44]I (1793), 128—"*Henry VI* not by S."
[45]LXVII (1797), 931—on "Pseudo-S."

Shakespeare Illustrated, Concordances, Glossaries, and Shakespeareana (Bibliographical)

S. Felton in his Advertisement to *Imperfect Hints toward a New Edition of Shakespeare . . . 1782* (1787) called for illustrations of Shakespeare's text—that is, pictures. This perhaps stimulated Boydell's activity from 1787 to 1802, though Malone himself expected to do the task, as he wrote to Farmer in 1792.[46] Meanwhile J. Hall had produced some *Illustrations of Shakspeare* in 1773 and J. H. Mortimer offered *Shakspeare's Characters, 12 Illustrations* in 1775. This type of text was supplemented by C. Taylor's *Picturesque Beauties of Shakespeare* in 1783-87, H. W. Bunbury's *Shakespeare* in 1792-96, and S. and E. Harding, *Shakspeare Illustrated*, in 1793.[47]

Boydell's activity just mentioned, in collecting (1787-1802) portraits for an edition of Shakespeare is well known. He published catalogs, in 1787, 1789, 1790, and 1791, for example, and the edition appeared in 1802. E. Jerningham in 1791 had dedicated a poem to him with the Advertisement: "The following poem does not pass any judgment upon the Pictures that are now exhibited in the Gallery; but attempts to point out new subjects for future exhibitions." And the interest in Boydell's work is obvious in the light of the many articles on it.[48]

In 1787 Andrew Becket published *A Concordance to Shakespeare . . . in which The Distinguished and Parallel passages*

---

[46] Pp. 9-10 n.

[47] See also *Gentleman's Magazine*, LIX (1789), 1184 n.—"Historical Dramas to be illustrated."

[48] *Universal Magazine*, LXXXIV (1789), 274; *Analytical Review*, IV (1789), 107; *European Magazine*, XV (1789), 412; *Gentleman's Magazine*, LIX (1789), 442; *Ibid.*, LX (1790), 1088; *Monthly Review*, I (1790), 427; *Hibernian Magazine*, 1791, Part I, p. 8; *Ibid.*, 1793, Part II, p. 2; *Anthologia Hibernica*, I (1793), 399; See also: C. Taylor, *Shakespeare Gallery*, 1792, and F. G. Waldron, *Shaksperian Museum*, 1794.

in the Plays of that justly admired Writer are methodically arranged. Becket remarked in his Advertisement: "The intention in the present selection is, to make the poet sometimes speak in maxims, or sentences"[49]—for example, on "Abstinence," "Acquaintance," etc. The reviewers did not wholly approve of this book: "Not unfrequently *words* or *terms* are introduced merely for the sake of a note to illustrate them." Nevertheless he is a "young but zealous critic."[50] And the *Monthly Review*: "The Author, in endeavoring to make it a *readable* book, has not paid sufficient attention to it as a *Concordance*, or a complete book of reference."[51]

S. Ayscough published his "Index to the remarkable passages and words . . . Shakespeare" in the third volume of his 1790 edition. To him the *Monthly Review* gave "encouragement which we are decisively of opinion he deserves."[52]

In 1768 R. Warner declared Hanmer's Glossary incomplete and added: "I propose to go farther," that is, beyond obsolete words to "technical terms, local words, and common words used in an uncommon sense. . . ."[53] Further, this glossary will have another advantage, and which has never yet been attempted . . . it will be made also to serve as an Index."[54] He appended a specimen of his proposed Glossary, covering the letter "A." That it was generally approved by contemporaries becomes evident when one considers the reviews, for example, in the *London Magazine* and the *Monthly Review*. The latter remarked: ". . . we have nothing more at heart than the promotion of this valuable work."[55] About twenty-two years later

---
[49]P. viii. [50]*Gentleman's Magazine*, LVII (1787), 1092.
[51]LXXVIII (1788), 220. Compare also *Scots Magazine*, L (1788), 136, and *Critical Review*, LXV (1788), 107.
[52]IV (1791), 422. [53]*Op. cit.*, p. 21. [54]*Ibid.*, p. 65.
[55]XXXVIII (1768), 346. For the *London Magazine* see XXXVII (1768), 334.

appeared George Mason's *Collection of English Words used by Shakespeare* (c. 1790).

Early bibliographical data were supplied by Garrick with his "Testimonies to the Genius and Merits of Shakespeare," appended to his Ode (1769), but most of these obviously preceded 1766. However, Johnson and Steevens' second, third, and fourth editions and Malone's Preface (1790) all listed "Detached Pieces of Criticism." For example, the second edition began with Rymer's *Short View* (1693) and continued with Gildon's *Remarks* (1710), Dennis' *Essay* (1712), Theobald's *Shakespeare Restored* (1726), Roberts' *Answer to Pope's Preface* (1729), etc. The last entry was Voltaire's *Letter to the French Academy* (1777).[56] The third edition concluded with Mason's *Comments* (1785),[57] and the fourth with Hurdis' *Cursory Remarks* (1792).[58] In 1780 the *Critical Review* noted E. Capell's *Shakesperiana*,[59] John Ireland produced *Shakespeariana* in 1786, and R. Farmer's *Bibliotheca Farmeriana* appeared in 1798.[60]

BIOGRAPHY

The interest in aspects of Shakespeare's life increased rapidly during the period, from Capell's *Hints* in 1767[61] to Malone's documents in 1796.[62]

---

[56]See I, 248-52.   [57]See I, 261-66.
[58]See I, 462-71. The last two editions of Johnson and Steevens and Malone's Preface all gave also a survey of the actors in Shakespeare's plays. F. Gentleman and Tom Davies had further developed the acting traditions in their books of 1770 and 1784, respectively.
[59]XLIX (1780), 79.
[60]*Shakespeare's Jests* was published in 1770 and 1795, and allusions to Shakespeare appear *passim* throughout the period. I shall not even attempt to estimate them.
[61]Introduction to Edition (1767), pp. 71-74.
[62]See text below. According to Maggs Brothers' *Shakespeareana* (1927, No. 493, pp. 99-100), as early as 1771 one Herbert Lawrence had broached the Baconian Heresy in his *The Life and Adventures of Common Sense: An Historical*

In 1778 Johnson and Steevens' second edition offered some biographical details,[63] and the third and fourth editions followed example, the latter appropriating Malone's remarks of 1790. Malone in his own edition had added many footnotes to Rowe's Life of Shakespeare and provided Additional Anecdotes of the poet;[64] his minute scholarship appears, for example, in his rejection of an anecdote of Shakespeare and Jonson.[65] Malone, in fact, is the final authority, for his *Historical Account of the English Stage* (to 1741) is an epitome of scholarship and shows his supreme value as an historical expert.[66]

However, a few other minor notations might be made, chiefly from periodicals. The *European Magazine* in 1793 announced: "It is highly gratifying to an Englishman to observe, that every new discovery tends to confirm the opinion that Shakespeare was as estimable for the goodness of his private life, as he was superior in genius to every one of his contemporaries."[67] W. Whiter in 1794 scouted the Shakspeare-père-Davenant theory,[68] and finally the Exeter Society *Essays* in 1796 had a few pages on Shakespeare's life.[69] Further general biographical material will be given in a note to show the rapidly rising interest in this aspect of Shakespeare.[70]

Allegory. But Prof. C. R. Baskervill of the University of Chicago remarks, "I see no hint in it of the heresy."

[63] I, 196-212.   [64] I, Parts I and II.   [65] I (Part I), 387 ff.

[66] I (Part II), 1-284. Compare the comments on Malone by his contemporaries, p. 14 above.

[67] XXIV (1793), 185. For this note I am indebted to Mr. D. L. King of the University of Michigan.

[68] *A Specimen of a Commentary on Shakspeare* (London: Cadell, 1794), pp. 98, 100 n.

[69] Pp. 248-49. Meanwhile M. Sherlock had noted in 1786 that Shakespeare "was also an actor,"—*A Fragment on Shakspeare* (London: Robinson, 1786), p. 14.

[70] *Biographia Dramatica*, I (1782), 401-03; J. Jordan, *Families of Shakspeare*

Johnson wrote to Mrs. Thrale, June 13, 1775: "Mr. Green has got a cast of Shakespeare, which he holds to be a very exact resemblance." Johnson and Steevens' second edition (1778) printed a list of the portraits of Shakespeare.[71] The principal ones include the Chandos (1719, 1743, 1783), the Soest or Zoust (1725), the Janssens (1770), and the Felton (1792).[72] W. Richardson[73] in 1794 wrote *Proposals for engraving the Felton Portrait of Shakespeare.*[74]

The spelling of Shakespeare's name greatly troubled the late eighteenth century. Colman in 1778 was worried about it;[75] so was Ritson in 1783;[76] and Johnson in 1785 apparently gave it up as a bad job.[77] It is interesting to note

---

and Hart, 1790; *Gentleman's Magazine*, XXXIX (1769), 344—House at Stratford; *Ibid.*, LIX (1789), 25—Biography; *Ibid.*, LXI (1791), 602—Shakespeare's Chair and Mulberry Tree; *Ibid.*, LXIV (1794), 1067—Shakespeare's Crabtree; *Hibernian Magazine*, 1782, pp. 65, 121—Biography; *Literary Magazine*, X (1793), 321—Memoirs of Shakespeare; *London Magazine* XLII (1773), 490—Records of Shakespeare's Family; *Macaroni and Theatrical Magazine*, I (1793), 21—Life of Shakespear; *Monthly Review*, XLIX (1773), 421—Shakespeare's Indifference to Fame; *Ibid.*, LXII (1780), 258—Sir T. Lucy and Shallow; *Scots Magazine*, XXXI (1769), 393—Life of Shakespeare; *Universal Magazine*, LXXVI (1785), 109—Anecdote of Shakespeare;

Items on Shakespeare's character appeared in the *Analytical Review*, VI (1790), 427, and the *Universal Magazine*, XCIII (1793), 171.

[71] I, 213-15.

[72] See Catalogues of the Manchester-Whitworth Institute (1916) and the Grafton Galleries (1917).

[73] This man was a "print-seller," not *the* William Richardson. (See Appendix A under 1774, 1784, 1789.)

[74] For reference in periodicals, to portraits of Shakespeare see: *Gentleman's Magazine*, LXII (1792), 613; *Ibid.*, LXIV (1794), 1068, 1183; *European Magazine*, XXVI (1794), 277, 388.

Busts and monuments include the Vertue Bust (1725) and the C. R. Grignion (1786), the Westminster Abbey Monument (1741, by A. Miller); the Garrick Statue (1765), and the Shakespeare Gallery Monument (1796).

[75] In *Prose on Several Occasions*, II, 164 n., 165 n.   [76] *Remarks*, pp. 1-2.

[77] Boswell's *Life* (ed. Hill), V (1785), 124. Further interest in this demor-

the significant advertising value of the poet's name as apparent in its application to a school in 1793: "Shakspeare's-Walk Charity School."[78]

One curious item of posthumous biography was the writing of messages from Shakespeare in Paradise. This began, for example, as early as 1752, with *A Poetical Epistle from Shakspeare in Elysium to Garrick*, followed by the *Critical Review*'s "Interview at the Shrine of Shakspeare" in 1757[79] and the *Universal Magazine*'s "Shakespear's Ghost" in 1765.[80] In 1777 appeared an *Epistle from Shakspeare to his Countrymen*,[81] and the *Monthly Mirror* in 1796 reviewed "Verses from the Ghost of Willey Shakspeare to Sammy Ireland," a satire primarily on the father of W. H. Ireland.[82]

This reference to Samuel and S. W. H. Ireland leads at once to one of the most spectacular biographical incidents in the eighteenth century, the Ireland forgeries.[83] It is not within the purpose of this book to go into this subject in detail, for the matter is not strictly an affair of literary criticism. But it indicates very concretely the extreme rise of interest in Shakespeare—especially in the poet's life—toward the close of the century and by virtue of this aspect deserves some attention here.

The background of these forgeries was really a seedbed of romantic idolatry: the "popular enthusiasm independent of the critics";[84] the craze for Shakespeare quartos with

---

alizing subject appears in the *Gentleman's Magazine*, LIV (1784), 253, 264, 505; LVII (1787), 25, 125, 204, 478, 480, 689; LVIII (1788), 33; and LIX (1789), 494. These volumes of this periodical are here numbered for the two parts together.

[78]*Monthly Review*, XII (1793), 468.   [79]*III* (1757), 176.
[80]XXXVII (1765), 268.   [81]See *London Magazine*, LXVI (1777), 217.
[82]II (1796), 160.
[83]For a list of these documents see S. Lee, *Shakespeareana*, II, 265, or Maggs Brothers' *Shakespeareana* (1927), pp. 237-38.
[84]*London Mercury*, IV (Oct., 1921), 623 ff. A more recent account appears

the resulting fancy prices noted by Steevens in 1778; the inability of Rowe and Malone to satisfy this "public enthusiasm," which rushed headlong into Ireland's trap, Ireland being merely the climax of minor forgeries and Elizabethan "discoveries," such as Walpole's *Winter's Tale* idea[85] and Plumptre's *Hamlet*-Mary-Queen-of-Scots theory,[86] Theobald's *Double Falsehood*, the *Compendious Examination* detected by Farmer in 1767,[87] and the pamphlet on the relations of Shakespeare and Jonson which fooled even the joker Steevens but which did not fool Malone. All these paved the way for the Irelands.

Of the two men, Samuel and his illegitimate son William H., the father was "an engraver and dealer in prints," the son a clerk to a conveyancer and a devotee of archaic chirography. In 1794, when William was seventeen, they visited Stratford together and were told by the owner of the Clopton House that he had just destroyed a sheaf of papers with Shakespeare's signature to make room for some young partridges. This gave William the idea of concocting the false documents, which he first announced in the autumn of 1794, one of them including a letter to the Queen with a lock of Shakespeare's hair. He then forged manuscripts of *Hamlet* and *King Lear*, omitting the ribaldry to prove the players put it in; and the public, wildly eager for such papers, swallowed them all whole. In February, 1795, twenty-one prominent men recognized them and Boswell fell on his knees to kiss the letters. William "invented an ancestor . . . who saved Shakespeare from drowning" as the source of these documents. So far so good.

---

in the *New York Times Magazine*, Feb. 21, 1926. As stated on p. 11 above, I shall use such summaries whenever possible.

[85]See pp. 33ff below.   [86]See Chap. XI below.

[87]Crosse dates this as "1765," strangely enough (*loc. cit.*, p. 626). See Farmer's First Edition (1767), p. 34. He also misdates Steevens' publication of the Sonnets as 1760 (p. 630) for 1766.

But William went one step, at least, too far. He "discovered" a new Shakespearean play, *Vortigern and Rowena*, and followed it up with another, *Henry II*. He had made special ink, but the paper bothered him, and clumsy spelling and style finally tripped him. Porson and Steevens began to question; Ritson scared Ireland badly; and then Malone rose to the attack, breaking up the *Vortigern* performance on April 2, 1796. Ireland confessed his forgeries, ran away from his father, who rose to his defense (and died still believing, in 1800), and expanded his confession in 1805.

This is merely a brief sketch of the situation, but the following texts should be noted to show the intense contemporary interest in the development: W. H. Ireland published his documents under the title, *Miscellaneous Papers and Legal Instruments under the Hand and Seal of William Shakespeare*, December, 1795. James Boaden immediately attacked Ireland in *A Letter to George Steevens . . . on S. Ireland . . . W. H. Ireland*, 1796. Ireland was defended by "Philalethes" (Colonel F. Webb), January, 1796; by M. Wyatt, February, 1796; and W. C. Oulton, February, 1796. He was attacked by F. G. Waldron, February, 1796, and by E. Malone in the famous so-called "Vindication," March, 1796. (Porson also indirectly attacked him.) *Vortigern and Rowena* was played April 2, 1976, and collapsed before ridicule. Ireland confessed his forgeries with the *Authentic Account of the Shakesperean MSS.*, December, 1796.

As it was Malone's famous document which did most to destroy Ireland's activity, its full title-page should be given:

An
Inquiry
into the Authenticity
of Certain
Miscellaneous Papers
and
Legal Instruments
Published Dec., 24, 1795
and attributed to
Shakespeare, Queen Elizabeth
and
Henry, Earl of Southampton
by E. Malone London: T. Cadell and W. Davies, 1796

Samuel Ireland, utterly unable to believe his son's confession even though that son had fled, came to his boy's defense with *Mr. Ireland's Vindication*, Jan., 1797, and *An Investigation of Mr. Malone's Claim to be the Character of a Scholar or Critic*, August, 1797. In 1800[88] the father died still believing in the authenticity of the documents, the son, now living from hand to mouth, having inadvertently got married and completely alienated his father.

Meanwhile George Chalmers had been lured by these documents into attacking Malone and declaring that the *Sonnets* were addressed to Queen Elizabeth. For this "new hare," see the following texts: George Chalmers, *An Apology for the Believers in the Shakspeare Papers*, 1797; *Supplemental Apology*, 1799; *Appendix to Supplemental Apology*, 1800. But this leads us into the nineteenth century.[89]

---

[88]Compare *N&Q*, CXLVIII (June 6, 1925), 408.

[89]The interest of periodicals in all this biographical controversy started by the Irelands is appalling. The following are merely a few articles, with special emphasis on the number of periodicals involved: *Analytical Review*, XXIII (1796), 317, 320, 380, 448; *Ibid.*, XXV (1797), 51, 53; *British Critic*,

There is no doubt, therefore, that there was tremendous scholarly interest in Shakespeare in the late eighteenth century—both editorially and biographically—and it will now be appropriate to turn to the more popular interest.

VII (1796), 522, 630; *Ibid.*, IX (1797), 572; *Critical Review*, LXXXVI (1796), 361; *Ibid.*, XCII (1798), 173, 177, 239; *European Magazine*, XXXI (1797), 34, 118; *Gentleman's Magazine*, LXV (1795), 209, 285, 457; *Ibid.*, LXVI (1796), 7, 92, 138, 267, 286, 297, 363, 463, 492, 562, 1101; *Ibid.*, LXVII (1797), 778; *Ibid.*, LXIX (1799), 601; *Hibernian Magazine*, 1796, Part I, pp. 343, 443; *Monthly Epitome*, I (1797), 29; *Monthly Magazine*, II (1796), 488; *Monthly Mirror*, I (1795-96), 34, 169, 230, 291, 359; *Ibid.*, II (1796), 160, 481, 490; *Ibid.*, III (1797), 38, 110; *Ibid.*, IV (1797), 98; *Monthly Review*, XX (1796), 342; *Ibid.*, XXII (1797), 111, 236; *Scots Magazine*, LVIII (1796), 100, 258, 885; *Universal Magazine*, XCVIII (1796), 274, 315.

On *Vortigern and Rowena*: *Hibernian Magazine*, 1795, Pt. II, p. 522; *Monthly Mirror*, I (1795-96), 371; *Monthly Review*, XVIII (1795), 233; *Universal Magazine*, XCVIII (1796), 280.

On Chalmers: *Anti-Jacobin Review*, III (1799), 383; *British Critic*, IX (1797), 512; *Gentleman's Magazine*, LXVII (1797), 496; *Monthly Mirror*, VIII (1799), 218.

Since this book was sent to the press, there has appeared a new discussion of the Ireland forgeries by D. Bodde, in *Shakespeare and the Ireland Forgeries* (Harvard University Press, 1930).

CHAPTER III

THE POPULAR INTEREST

Attacks on Commentators; Parodies

The popular attitude toward Shakespeare's many commentators during this period is rather amusing. Far back in 1733 David Mallet in a poem, *Of Verbal Criticism*, dedicated to Pope, had more or less led the way:

> But is there no honour due to age?
> No Reverence to great Shakespeare's noble page?[1]

More than fifty years later appeared

The Etymologist

A Comedy of Three Acts
Most Humbly Dedicated

To the Late Dr. S. Johnson's Negro Servant

To the..............Reviewers:

To all the Commentators that ever wrote, are writing, or will write on Shakespear and particularly

To...........................G. S. Esq.

London: Printed for J. Jarvis, 1785.

"G. S." is obviously George Steevens, and he receives the most touching allusions:

---

[1] See also D. Nichol Smith's latest book (*Shakespeare in the Eighteenth Century*, 1928), pp. 45-46, on Fielding's *Journey from this World to the Next* (1743).

Mrs. Drama in I, 3: "Had I chosen reputation as an author, I could have commanded it, by tacking my name, as Mr. Stivens did, to Doctor Johnson's and writing a commentary of Shaksper."

Teague in III, 1: "Master Stavans has used my master main ill in his Shaksper business; he heard all he had to say on the subject, and clapt his own name to half of it."

The Bee in 1791 took occasion to remark that Voltaire's comments on Corneille were like ours on Shakespeare, "verbal criticisms and quaint refinements, extremely strained, and often extremely absurd," following rules and not suited to the genius of these poets;[2] the author of *Canons of Criticism* "lashes Warburton most justly," Mrs. Montagu is too lenient with Voltaire, and Johnson is prejudiced and "too formally scientific."[3] *The Bee's* conclusion was: "Shakespeare has been plyed by commentators and critics more than all the rest of our poets put together. . . . Among the crowd I can distinguish very few."[4]

T. Mathias in 1794 was a little more bitter. He praised Capell as "The Father of all legitimate Commentary on Shakspeare,"[5] but chastised commentators in general for their minute, even indecent, exposition of the poet: "Whole pages are absolutely *filled* with venereal provocatives."[6] Meanwhile William Jackson had announced, in the same vein, that "Many a passage has been criticized into consequence,"[7] with plenty of exemplification of his point.[8]

---

[2] IV (1791), 290.   [3] *Ibid.*, p. 295.
[4] *Ibid.*, pp. 310-11. See also XIV (1793), 303, and II (1791), 198.
[5] *Pursuits of Literature* (7th ed., London: T. Becket, 1798), p. 90 n.
[6] *Ibid.*, pp. 85-86 n.
[7] Properly in 1782, though I am using the 1795 (3rd) ed. of the *Thirty Letters* (London: Cadell and Davies). The page is, in this, 158.
[8] *Ibid.*, pp. 159-63.

Jackson added that a commentator needs two general qualifications: "being versed in the authors of the times—and in the provincial dialects";[9] and that an editor of Shakespeare needs two more: "a poetical imagination—and a discernment to distinguish what is probable from what is merely possible."[10]

Finally, the *Monthly Mirror* in 1798 fired such a parting broadside at Johnson as this: Johnson plays with "trifles" in criticism which would attract no attention whatever without the name of Johnson attached; he produces "fumum ex fulgore," so that "we feel a pride in hurling a stone at the literary Goliah." Such comments as Johnson's, it continues, "merely serve . . . to obscure, not illustrate, the pages of Shakspeare."[11] Even the great and learned Doctor was apparently not to be spared.

Parodies of Shakespeare provide further evidence of popular interest. It has already been pointed out[12] that there were fifty-nine travesties of Shakespeare's plays from 1792 to 1895—five from 1792 to 1808—all of these involving thirteen plays. *Hamlet* had eighteen, *Othello* eight, and *Romeo and Juliet* seven. Curiously enough some of these early parodies were foreign, such as; *Othello*, 1792, Paris, and *Hamlet*, 1798, Vienna.

A more significant point is that the periodicals were publishing many minor parodies of various passages and

---

[9]*Ibid.*, p. 163.

[10]*Ibid.*, p. 164; compare Malone's Preface (1790), I (Part 1), p. liv.

[11]V (1798), 231. For further remarks on the commentators see: *Universal Magazine*, LXV (1779), 263—Shakespeare in the shades meets his critics—a poem; *Hibernian Magazine*, 1783, p. 245—a general article; *Gentleman's Magazine*, LVII (1787), 912—"Shakespeare's Bedside," a poem; *Looker-On*, No. 87, Jan. 18, 1794—"A Criticism after the best Manner . . . of Shakespeare's Commentators"; *Monthly Mirror*, II (1796), 160—Review of a satire: "Familiar Verses from the Ghost of Willey Shakspeare to Sammy Ireland."

[12]R. F. Sharp, "Travesties of Shakespeare's Plays," *The Library*, 4th Series, No. 1 (June, 1920), 1-20.

characters of Shakespeare's plays, rather than whole plays. The *Gentleman's Magazine* easily led in this new popular pastime,[13] though other periodicals had actually anticipated it in the field.[14] Three examples of this activity should suffice:

> I do remember a cook's shop—
> And hereabout it stands—him late I noted
> In tuck'd-up sleeves, with nightcap o'er his brows,
> Cutting up joints. . . .[15]

> O beware, my lord, of conspiracy!
> It is a squint-eyed monster, which doth make
> The ills it feeds on. . . .[16]

> Her father loved me—oft got drunk with me,
> Captain (he'd cry) come tell us your adventures,
> From year to year, the scrapes, intrigues and frolics
> That you've been versed in. . . .[17]

SEQUELS, OPERAS, AND IMITATIONS

Sequels, operas, and imitations developed rapidly through the rising popular interest. The earliest sequel to one of Shakespeare's plays in this period was W. Kenrick's *Falstaff's Wedding*, of which three different copies exist in the McMillan Collection in the University of Michigan.[18] The title-page of the second London text of 1766 is:

---

[13]LXII (1792), 943, 1036, 1132, 1207; LXVIII (1793), 558, 656, 752, 943, 1039, 1135; LXIV (1794), 65, 262, 310, 366, 460; volumes LXV (1795) to LXIX (1799) in the same way. Volumes for this periodical are here given for the two parts together. See also the *Anthologia Hibernica*, I (1793), 152; *Scots Magazine*, LV (1793), 38, 282; LVII (1795), 97, 337, 774.
[14]*London Magazine*, XLII (1773), 253; *Monthly Review*, LX (1779), 232.
[15]*Gentleman's Magazine*, LXII (1792), 943.
[16]*Ibid.*, LXII (1792), 1132.   [17]*Anthologia Hibernica*, I (1793), 152.
[18]The first is dated "London: Printed for J. Wilkie . . . MDCCLX," the

Falstaff's Wedding,

A COMEDY
AS IT IS ACTED AT THE THEATRE ROYAL
IN DRURY-LANE
BEING A SEQUEL TO
THE SECOND PART OF THE PLAY OF
KING HENRY THE FOURTH
WRITTEN IN IMITATION OF SHAKESPEARE
BY W. KENRICK
IN MAGNIS VOLUISSE SAT EST
LONDON: PRINTED FOR L. DAVIS AND C. REYMERS,
MDCCLXVI.

The Advertisement remarks that the author was encouraged to bring it on the stage as a result of "The success, which a juvenile sketch of the Play hath met in publication." This "juvenile sketch" is dated in the Preface (of the Dublin edition) as of 1751, a "poetical exercise." The Preface continues to note that Garrick called the play "a very good imitation of Shakespeare, particularly in the character of Falstaff," but that "it must not be supposed that he [the author] presumes to think it will in the smallest degree contribute to deprive his great master of that honour, which is so justly and peculiarly his due; viz, that of being truly *inimitable.*"

---

second, "Dublin: Printed for James Williams . . . MDCCLXVI," and the third, "London: Printed for L. Davis and C. Reymers . . . MDCCLXVI." The Prefaces seem to be alike (there is none in the second London copy), the one in 1760 being actually dated "Jan. 1, 1766." But the 1760 play is obviously a first version, for it is much shorter, contains far fewer characters than either of the other two, and has no Prologue or Epilogue and only one list of Dramatis Personæ. The last two, of 1766, are practically alike, though the London edition, except for lack of Preface, is probably the better copy. It has eliminated one useless list of Dramatis Personæ which the Dublin copy retains, and it contains both a Prologue and an Epilogue, the latter being absent from the Dublin version.

It will not be necessary to sketch this play here, for such a procedure is beyond the purpose of this book and particularly of this section. That it was popular is evident in the light of the many contemporary reviews of it.[19]

A second interesting development in sequels was Horace Walpole's idea that *The Winter's Tale* represents really the second part of *Henry VIII*.[20] Comment on this novel suggestion appeared in the *London Magazine* in 1768,[21] and as late as 1796 Richard Hole in the Exeter Society *Essays* supported Walpole's thesis in spite of Malone's dating the play as of 1594, a date which Malone himself changed in 1793 to a much later one.[22]

A third was F. Waldron's *The Virgin Queen*, a sequel to *The Tempest*, in 1797. Notices of this production appeared in the *British Critic* in 1798[23] and the *Monthly Mirror* in 1797,[24] the latter offering definite praise.

Of operas there were forty-two based on Shakespeare from 1673 to 1800.[25] The nineteenth century and early twentieth produced sixty-five. During the early period *The Tempest* led with sixteen different versions; *Hamlet* and *Romeo and Juliet* each had eight.

Another popular type of idolatry of Shakespeare in the late eighteenth century was the writing of plays in Shakespeare's general style.[26] However, the critics rather condemned this procedure. Morgann in 1777 announced

---

[19]*Critical Review*, XXI (1766), 149, 319; *Monthly Review*, XXXIV (1766), 240; *Royal Magazine*, XIV (1766), 11; *Scots Magazine*, XXVIII (1766), 95.
[20]*Historical Doubts on the Life and Reign of Richard III* (1768), p. 114.
[21]XXXVII (1768), 86.   [22]P. 260.   [23]XI (1798), 195.
[24]IV (1797), 170. This refers back to II (1796), 161: "a successful imitation."
[25]W. B. Squire, "Shakespearean Operas," in *A Book of Homage to Shakespeare* (ed. Gollancz, 1916), pp. 75-83.
[26]Pope's original ridicule in 1727 of such imitation in the *Memoirs of Martinus Scriblerus*, Chap. IX, "Of Sinking in Poetry" (*Works*, ed. Warburton,

3

flatly his firm conviction that Shakespeare could not be imitated[27] and he also adduced Dryden's comment to the same effect.[28] *The Bee* in 1791 agreed with him: "But none has yet in any degree appropriated the spirit and the manner of Shakespeare."[29] The next year the *Looker-On* descended upon ". . . ridiculous imitations of Shakspeare. . . . It is not by imitating but by emulating this great poet, and by copying unweariedly from the same model which he himself had ever before him, that we can hope to rise to any sort of resemblance."[30] And the *Monthly Mirror* in 1796 gave a final general statement: "The admiration of that figurative style in Shakspere . . . has created a manner of writing consisting entirely of verbage without imagery to sustain it; cold, *altisonant*, gigantesque, shadowy, *inane* and puerile."[31]

Applied to particular imitators this attitude became rather brutal: "Mr. Colman flatters himself he writes like Shakspere. It is a weakness in the poor young man which has often led him astray, and it will undoubtedly be an act of kindness to recall him to sensibility.[32] . . . Rowe

---

1752, VI, 225) should be quoted: "Imitation is of two sorts; the first is, when we force to our own purposes the thoughts of others; the second consists in copying the imperfections or blemishes of celebrated authors. I have seen a play professedly writ in the style of Shakespear wherein the resemblance lay in one single line."

Some imitations of Shakespeare before 1766 include: *Joan of Hedington*, 1712 (in *Useful Miscellanies*); Rowe, *Jane Shore*, 1714; Young, *The Revenge*, 1721; Theobald, *Cave of Shakespeare*, n. d; Philips, *Humphrey, Duke of Gloucester* 1723; Havard, *King Charles I*, 1737; Lillo, *Marina*, 1738; Cibber, *Papal Tyranny in the Reign of King John*, 1745; Shirley, *Edward the Black Prince*, 1750; Lillo, *Arden of Feversham*, 1759.

[27]*Op. cit.*, p. 71.   [28]*Ibid.*, 77 n.   [29]I (1791), 58.
[30]No. 40. See A. Chalmers, *British Essayists* (1823), XXXVI, 72. The *Looker-On* in the same number warns against imitating Shakespeare's style.
[31]II (1796), 232.
[32]*Monthly Mirror*, II (1796), 229. This was a reference to George Colman, Jr.'s *Iron Chest*, p. 7.

once meditated a *Shaksperian* flight, and he produced Jane Shore, but Jane Shore is as far inferior to any play of Shakspere as it is superior to the *Iron Chest*. So much for the imitators of the great bard.³³ . . . Compared indeed with our eagle Shakspere, Rowe was but a wren."³⁴ But finally Harriet Lee, with her *The Mysterious Marriage, or The Hermit of Roselva*, received a modicum of applause: "The style is evidently an imitation of Shakespere—and in some places the resemblance is remarkably striking. By an *imitation* we . . . mean . . . a successful specimen of continued dialogue, which bears the character of his sentiment and structure."³⁵

Modern Characters from Shakespeare, Public Lectures, and Jubilees

Even more intense popular idolatry of Shakespeare in the late eighteenth century was evident in the production of *Modern Characters from Shakespeare*.³⁶ A group of society people assembled at a New Year's Frolic on January 1, 1778, and in the course of the gaiety announced, quite incongruously perhaps, that Shakespeare's "portraits were obsolete, and more of *caricatures* than characters."³⁷ A

---

³³*Monthly Mirror*, II (1796), 230.   ³⁴*Ibid.*, VI (1798), 167.
³⁵*Ibid.*, V (1798), 166. For further comment and material on imitations during this period, consult: J. Armstrong, *Imitations of Shakespeare and Spenser*, 1770; *Gentleman's Magazine*, LI (1781), 16; *Analytical Review*, XI (1791), 427; *Monthly Review, or Literary Journal*, XVIII (1795), 233—on Modern Satirical Imitations of Shakespeare.

³⁶The McMillan Shakespeare Collection in the University of Michigan contains two such anthologies, so to speak, both produced, curiously enough, in 1778: one printed by E. Johnson, London, and the other by D. Brown, London. There must have been others, for the *Anthologia Hibernica* in 1794 wrote about such a collection—III (1794), 268. See also the *Monthly Review*, XVIII (1795), 233. A review of one of the above collections appeared in the *London Magazine*, XLVII (1778), 26.

³⁷Advertisement (March 18, 1778) to *Modern Characters for 1778* (London: D. Brown), p. 7.

nobleman, unnamed but possibly Sir H. B. Dudley, who edited one of these collections, arose to defend Shakespeare, and had the frolickers write names of intimate friends on slips of paper. These he dropped into a Shakespeare Folio, with the astonishing result that Shakespeare's characters matched the modern names that fell by accident opposite them! Such is the irresistible announcement of the Advertisement of one of these collections which appeared in 1778. The same Advertisement summarizes the results of the experiment: "a general Collection of these *Modern Likenesses*, for the amusement of the *Beau Monde*, and proving to the world, that the Characters, drawn by the pencil of Shakespear, are striking copies from the *School of Nature*, and will therefore represent the features of every age, down to the latest posterity."

The general development of these collections may be illustrated by the first two "modern characters" in one of them:

>   Mrs. C[re]we
> Why, if two gods should play some heav'nly match
> And on a wager lay two earthly women,
> And *Portia* one,—there must be something else
> Pawn'd with the other; for the poor, rude world,
> Hath not her fellow—
>
>   *Merch. V.* Act III
>
>   Duke of M[arlborou]gh
> Take physic pomp!
> Expose thyself to feel what wretches feel,
> That thou may'st shake the superflux to them,
> And shew the Heav'ns more just!—
>
>   *Lear*, Act III[38]

---

[38]Both of these are from the D. Brown edition of 1778.

Thus the modern Mrs. Crewe and Duke of Marlborough were aptly "hit off" by Shakespeare's lines written in a quite different age.

At the close of his most recent book Professor Nichol Smith very briefly mentioned an interesting new feature: "the first public lecture on Shakespeare of which we have record,"[39] by William Kenrick, Jan. 19, 1774. Perhaps a few more intimate items here will serve to illuminate Professor Smith's remarks.

Kenrick's title-page was:

INTRODUCTION
TO THE
SCHOOL OF SHAKESPEARE;
HELD ON WEDNESDAY EVENINGS,
IN THE APOLLO, AT THE DEVIL TAVERN, TEMPLE BAR.
TO WHICH IS ADDED
A RETORT COURTEOUS ON
THE CRITICKS
AS DELIVERED AT THE SECOND AND THIRD LECTURES
LONDON: PRINTED FOR THE AUTHOR
[n. d.]

The Advertisement announces that Dr. Kenrick deferred his edition of Shakespeare in favor of Mr. Steevens, but now that "a mutilated *play-house* copy" (Bell's?) has appeared, he will give his textual comment in public lectures. Declamation itself will do much to explain passages. The Lectures will be free to Kenrick's subscribers: "N. B. The Subscribers to Dr. K's Shakespeare will be admitted to the whole course without farther subscription; or, if dissatisfied, may have their former subscription returned."

---

[39]*Shakespeare in the Eighteenth Century* (1928), pp. 90-91.

In conclusion he calls for communications on new "poetical or moral beauties of Shakespeare."

That Kenrick had his troubles with the newspapers is apparent from his reply to a baiting journalist in the *Public Ledger*: "It is this writer who repeatedly informs the publick, that the ladies yawn, as he elegantly expresses it, at my lecture, for want of wit and musick . . . I have too good an opinion of my fair auditors to suppose they cannot be kept, two or three hours, awake, by a comment on Shakespeare, without the aid of a jest or the squeaking of a fiddle."[40] His bitter conclusions on the battle appear at length in his *Addition to the Retort Courteous*: "To the critic of the Publick Ledger I am indebted for the misrepresentation of almost everything he hath noticed; particularly for falsely charging me with adopting the meanings I explode. . . . To the Public Advertiser, Gazetteer, and most of the evening papers I am obliged for their truth, their impartiality and their candour. There is also a morning paper which has honoured me nearly as much by its abuse; but I have too much respect for my auditors to notice any thing inserted in the *Morning Post* . . . as I intend . . . to publish my Introductory Address and Reply to the Criticks in a printed pamphlet, I mean . . . to recite them no more, nor take any farther notice in this place of the news-paper remarks."[41]

The most spectacular popular tribute to Shakespeare in the late eighteenth century was the holding of jubilees, the most significant of which was that in 1769.

Boswell wrote a letter to the *London Magazine* in 1769 describing this famous jubilee,[42] and Arthur Murphy in

---

[40]*Addition to the Retort Courteous*, p. 37.

[41]In the McMillan Shakespeare Collection, Kenrick's *Introduction*, *A Retort Courteous*, and *Addition to the Retort Courteous* are bound together and paged consecutively. This discussion appears, therefore, on pp. 36-39.

[42]XXXVIII (1769), 451.

his *Life of David Garrick* recounted it in detail.[43] A boarded rotunda was built on the banks of the Avon, and the town of Stratford was decorated. On the fifth and sixth of September the crowd assembled; on the seventh occurred public worship, and after it the crowd went to read Shakespeare's epitaph. At three of the same day the throng met for dinner in the rotunda, and at five musical performers sang songs "composed by Garrick." "Garrick closed the whole with his Ode, upon dedicating a building, and erecting a statue to Shakespeare, in his native city." On the eighth a ball was held in the rotunda, and a procession was announced for the ninth, "in which the principal characters of Shakespeare's plays were to be exhibited." But it rained, and "The Jubilee ended abruptly."

In October the celebration was transferred to Drury Lane, where Garrick put on "a comic fable" of his own invention, never published. He used in it "the inferior people of Stratford and the visitors," together with songs and a procession of Shakespeare's plays at the end, with a "train of performers, dressed in character." Mrs. Abington acted as the Comic Muse, "in a triumphal carr," and Dr. Arne's music was used. The piece was repeated one hundred nights, and on "several intermediate nights" Garrick spoke his Ode. Such is Murphy's story.

Meanwhile there had appeared G. S. Carey's *Shakespeare's Jubilee, A Masque*, in 1769, with the Dramatis Personae including Apollo, Tragedy, Comedy, Ceres, Minerva, Hecate, Three Witches, Oberon, Faery Queen, Puck, Fairies, Falstaff and Caliban—truly a motley crew. Oberon came in and announced: "Great Shakespeare's

---

[43] Pp. 297-99. I am using this account, published in Dublin, 1801. For detailed modern descriptions see Miss L. B. Campbell's "Garrick's Vagary," in *University of Wisconsin Studies*, 1916, pp. 215 ff.; and particularly the *London Times Literary Supplement*, April 18 and May 16, 1929.

matchless fame they mean to sing."

George Colman produced his *Man and Wife; or the Shakespeare Jubilee* in 1770.[44] The scene was laid at Stratford, and the second act was followed by "The Pageant—Exhibiting the Characters of Shakespeare." The play is described in F. Gentleman's *Dramatic Censor*,[45] but the most interesting thing to us at present is Gentleman's tremendous worrying over the "most extraordinary madness" of the London crowds for "ninety nights" showing "idolatry" of Shakespeare.[46]

Garrick's *Jubilee* was revived in 1775, 1777, and 1785, and other jubilees appeared: in 1773 at Waterford, and Ritson's *Stockton Jubilee* in 1781. But F. Gentleman's final comment on the early tribute to Shakespeare expressed in Colman's play in 1770 must be quoted in conclusion:

"Oh Shakespeare, Shakespeare, what a spectacle art thou made; how is thy muse of fire *cabin'd, cribb'd, confin'd*, by such mechanical representation; methinks, if thou wert alive again, the shallow justice who prosecuted thee for stealing venison would be sooner forgiven, than those who make thy great name a bait for gudgeons."[47]

Steadily, therefore, throughout the period from 1766 to 1799 both scholarly and popular interest in Shakespeare increased—a development which can be traced statisti-

---

[44]London: Becket, 1770. In Chap. VIII below (on Voltaire and Shakespeare), I quote from this play.

[45]London: Bell, 1770, I, 378 ff. The *Shakespeariana* of the N. Y. Shakespeare Soc., V (1888), 482, denotes F. Gentleman the author of *The Stratford Jubilee* (1769).

[46]*Ibid.*, I, 387.

[47]*Ibid.*, I, 388. Periodical reviews of the Jubilees include: *Critical Review*, XXVIII (1769), 236 (Carey's); *Gentleman's Magazine*, XXXIX (1769), 364, 454; *Ibid.*, XL (1770), 437; *Ibid.*, XLIX (1779), 280; *London Magazine*, XXXVIII (1769). 407, 451, 481 (Garrick's *Ode*); *Monthly Review*, XLI (1769), 238 (Carey's); *Ibid.*, XLI (1769), 394 (Colman's); *Scots Magazine*, XXXI (1769), 387, 397, 449; *Universal Magazine*, XLV (1769), 158.

cally, as has been indicated. It would be logical now to expect the literary criticism of the period to reflect this rising barometer of interest in Shakespeare by casting aside the traditional objections of the early eighteenth century, by carrying on elements of appreciation which had been Shakespeare's meed from the beginning, and by adding new emphases on aspects of Shakespeare's greatness hitherto generally unappreciated. It will be the purpose of the subsequent chapters of this book to trace these three developments, and to link them finally with the eulogies of Coleridge, Hazlitt, Lamb, and other critics of the early nineteenth century as merely culminating echoes of late eighteenth-century idolatry of Shakespeare.

PART II

SHAKESPEARE DEFENDED AGAINST TRADITIONAL OBJECTIONS

CHAPTER IV

THE UNITIES REJECTED

It is well known that from the time of its inception with Ben Jonson, criticism of Shakespeare throughout the seventeenth and eighteenth centuries developed two prominent contentions which persisted even into the nineteenth— namely, that Shakespeare neglected the unities and that he violated decorum. In support of these two fundamental objections arose a warring throng of critics who spoke most loudly in the seventeenth and early eighteenth centuries, but whose cries died down considerably during the latter years of the eighteenth. It will be the purpose of this chapter and those immediately succeeding to show how the last three decades of the eighteenth century practically silenced these two loud outcries against Shakespeare and thus helped prepare the way for Coleridge and the other early nineteenth-century Romantics. Meanwhile, in connection with these two main contentions should be noted some minor objects of attack which are in the same general tradition: Shakespeare's learning and his relation to the ancients, his tragicomedy, his supernatural characters, his blank verse, and his puns.[1]

SHAKESPEARE'S VIOLATION OF THE UNITIES[2]

The most prominent objection to Shakespeare in seventeenth and eighteenth-century dramatic criticism was that

---
[1] For a good composite statement of these objections to Shakespeare in English criticism, see Cuthbert Constable, *An Essay Towards a New English Dictionary*, c. 1720 (excerpts quoted in Maggs Cat., No. 434, pp. 250-52). My Chap. I shows the attitude of the early eighteenth century on these objects of attack.

[2] No use is made in this chapter of the reviews of Johnson's *Preface* (1765):

he violated the unities of time, place, and action.³ It should be perhaps noted that, in general, unity of action implied a beginning, middle, and end; unity of time permitted the play to cover, at most, twenty-four hours; unity of place denied change of scene, except possibly between acts. This chapter will attempt to indicate the reaction of the late eighteenth century against these unities as applied to Shakespeare's plays.

Attacks on Shakespeare for his violation of the unities still persisted after 1766, most of them being rather mild. In 1769 the *Monthly Review* was worried about Shakespeare's neglect of the unities and attributed it to the coarse taste of the time.⁴ A year later, Francis Gentleman announced that "[we are] not . . . the friends of strict

---

i.e., *Gentleman's Magazine*, XXXV, 479; *Critical Review*, XX, 321; *London Magazine*, XXXIV, 529; and *Monthly Review*, XXXIII, 285, 374. For a full discussion of them, and for other material preceding 1766, see Dr. T. M. Raysor's article in *MLN*, XLII (Jan., 1927), 1 ff.; and Dryden's *The Vindication* (1683); Dryden's *Heads of An Answer to Rymer's Remarks* (Post 1678); *The Gentleman's Magazine*, II (1732), 786 ("A Critique"); W. Guthrie's *Essay on English Tragedy* (1747); *Universal Magazine*, VIII (1751), 98 ("Aristotle's definition of Tragedy generally mistaken"); the *Covent Garden Journal* (1752), No. 62, "On Unities in Drama"; W. Wilkie's *Dream* (1759); J. Moor's *On the End of Tragedy According to Aristotle* (1763); *Monthly Review*, XXX (1764), 63 (Review of Moor). See also, for more general material, C. Gildon's *Reflections on Rymer's Short View* (1694); *Tatler*, Nos. 22, 47; *Spectator*, Nos. 39, 40, 42, 44; *Guardian*, No. 110; T. Edwards' *Canons of Criticism* (1748); D. Hume's *Essay on Tragedy* (1757); *Critical Review*, X (1760), 34 (On Tragedy); George Colman's *Critical Reflections on the Old English Dramatic Writers* (1761), etc.

³The greatest individual defense of Shakespeare against this doctrine was made by Samuel Johnson in his *Preface* of 1765, and Dr. Raysor has shown how, subsequent to Johnson, the doctrine lost favor in Shakespearean criticism. However, by necessarily confining himself to books within the limits of a brief article, and neglecting references in periodicals, Dr. Raysor has apparently missed some of the force of the whole reaction against the unities from 1766 to 1799. This reaction, I should say, assumed six more or less distinct aspects, which will appear in this chapter.

⁴XLI (1769), 130. For this note, I am indebted to Miss Edna Richards of the University of Michigan.

limitation, but cannot countenance the introduction of a sea-voyage, where there is no occasion for it."[5] Similar objection appeared in the *Monthly Review's* comments on Dr. Berkenhout's strictures on the unities: ". . . we do not find ourselves disposed to be quite so angry with the *unities* as he is."[6] And the same slightly critical attitude continued in Kemble's *Macbeth Reconsidered* (1786),[7] in the *Universal Magazine* in 1787,[8] and in the *European Magazine* in July, 1789.[9] But one violent attack on Shakespeare was made, in 1774, by Edward Taylor, "an Englishman long domiciled in France,"[10] whose anathemas hurled at Johnson and Shakespeare in general may be indicated by such remarks as: ". . . our excentric English tragedian has presumed to quit the beaten track,"[11] and Shakespeare has "great merit as a comic writer, greater still as a poet, but little, very little as a tragedian."[12] Taylor's book was negligible in its influence on the attitude toward the unities in the late eighteenth-century Shakespearean criticism, and Mr. Haines' comment on it[13] is perhaps the sanest summary of it. Curiously enough the *Critical Review* for August, 1774, approved of it with the astonishing remark that "it would be injurious to tax him [Taylor] with

---

[5]*Dramatic Censor* (London: Bell, 1770), I, 134. He is discussing *Othello*.
[6]LVII (1777), 194.   [7]London: Egerton, 1786, p. 3.
[8]LXXXI (1787), 4.
[9]XVI (1789), 15. The latter is reprinted in the *Hibernian Magazine*, Sept., 1789, p. 470. For other mild rejections of Shakespeare, see Mrs. Griffith, *op. cit.*, p. 2, and Blair, *Lectures on Rhetoric* (1783), Lecture III, vol. I (Philadelphia, 1804), p. 34. Dr. Raysor seems to feel that both Richardson and Whately are mildly anti-Shakespeare on this point, but see below, pp. 48, 52.
[10]Haines, *op. cit.*, p. 47.
[11]*Cursory Remarks on Tragedy, on Shakespear* (London: Owen, 1774), p. 36.
[12]*Ibid.*, p. 37. See, also, pp. 2-6, 8, 9, 26-28, 32-33, 60, 74, 96, 107.
[13]"Taylor represents the last stage of the formalist school, who were now reduced to the attempt to rationalize those rules which in fact rested not upon reason but upon a tyrannical literary tradition,"—*Op. cit.*, p. 47.

being influenced either by prejudice or a spirit of singularity."[14] This was the last loud war cry of the critics favoring the unities.

GENERAL SCEPTICISM CONCERNING THE UNITIES

Among the opposing critics—that is, those defending Shakespeare—appeared early a general scepticism without detailed argument. The *British Magazine* in 1767 announced: "With regard to the Unity of time, which some rigid critics look upon as a matter of such great importance, it [*Julius Cæsar*] is remarkably defective."[15] Horace Walpole's Postscript to *The Mysterious Mother* (1768),[16] in defending Shakespeare against Voltaire, rejected the unities simply as "mechanic," and in 1773 the *Macaroni and Theatrical Magazine* in direct extenuation of Shakespeare contended: ". . . the example of the ancients, upon this point, ought to have no weight with us, . . . our critics are guilty of a mistake in admitting no greater latitude of place and time, than was admitted in Greece and Rome."[17] Two years later the *Universal Magazine* declared that writers who use mechanical methods "are justly denied the palm of genius"; hence critics ought not "to comment by line and rule";[18] and repeated the idea in 1777.[19] William Hodson directly rejected the unities in his *Observations on Tragedy* (1780),[20] and, four years later, William Richardson advocated deviation from the unities,[21] and referred to Aristotle

---
[14] XXXVIII (1774), 119.   [15] VIII (1767), 572.
[16] This Postscript first appeared in J. Dodsley's Edition, 1781.
[17] P. 533. As for maintaining unity of action, "How successfully is this done by Shakespear! in whose works there is not to be found a single barren scene" (p. 533).
[18] LVII (1775), 287.   [19] LXI (1777), 174. Quoting Dr. Berkenhout.
[20] P. 75. [Bound with his play, *Zoraida*].
[21] P. 388 of the 5th ed. (1798) of his *Essays on Shakespeare's Dramatic Characters* (London: J. Murray and S. Highley), which is the edition used *passim*

only twice in his 401 pages of criticism of Shakespeare.[22]

Johnson's Rejection of the Unities

But Johnson's analysis of the unreality of dramatic representation was the starting point of a much more important development throughout the latter third of the century. "It is false," wrote Johnson, "that any representation is mistaken for reality."[23] Hence acceptance, by the imagination, of the first scene at Rome will presuppose acceptance of other scenes elsewhere later in the play. Similarly, "the time required by the fable elapses for the most part between the acts,"[24] and "Time is, of all modes of existence, most obsequious to the imagination."[25] Now if the drama is merely "credited . . . as a just picture of a real original,"[26] then "the action is not supposed to be real, and it follows that between the acts a longer or a shorter time may be allowed to pass."[27]

It has been recently pointed out that Johnson was indebted to his predecessor, Kames, and that Johnson's general destruction of all dramatic illusion was decried by both the *Monthly Review* and Edward Taylor[28]—a point upon which Coleridge later also took issue with Johnson. But the Kames-Johnson ideas were pursued to the close of the century by Mrs. Montagu (1769), William Cooke (1775), Blair (1783), Beattie (1783), *The Bee* (1791), and Belsham (1792).[29] To these important texts should be ad-

---

for Richardson in this chapter. For Richardson's texts, see *JEGP*, XXVIII (Jan., 1929), 117.
[22] P. 170 of the 1784 series, and p. 342 n. of the 1798 edition.
[23] See D. Nichol Smith, *Shakespeare Criticism* (1916), p. 108.
[24] *Ibid.*, p. 109. [25] *Ibid.*, p. 110. [26] *Ibid.*, p. 110. [27] *Ibid.*, p. 111.
[28] See T. M. Raysor's article in *MLN*, XLII (Jan., 1927), 1 ff.
[29] All this has been developed by Dr. Raysor's article. A review of Belsham appeared in the *Critical Review*, LXXIV (1792), 132. Hence Dr. Raysor apparently misdated Belsham as of "1799."

ded a few periodical references which used Johnson's method, if not precisely his ideas. For example the *Macaroni and Theatrical Magazine* in September, 1773, declared that we do not read a narrative poem with our eyes on reality—hence why should we worry about drama?[30] The *European Magazine* followed Johnson in general but insisted that the *single act* should be indivisible.[31] And the *Monthly Review* declared that we put up with Romans in *Cato* speaking English blank verse, Cato in a white wig, and "Porcia" in a fine cap; hence "if we do not desire a unity of language, of dress, and an hundred other unities, which historical truth might require, why should we, on seeing an excellent play of Shakespeare's . . . performed, be angry, because the three unities, prescribed by Aristotle, are not strictly adhered to?"[32] Such a remark as this indicates rather well, in conclusion, the logical application of the Johnsonian psychological method of refutation in the late eighteenth century.

OTHER ARTS AND THE UNITIES

Johnson himself contrasted Shakespeare's composition with "The work of a correct and regular writer," which "is a garden accurately formed and diligently planted," whereas Shakespeare's "is a forest, in which oaks extend their branches, and pines tower in the air, interspersed sometimes with weeds and brambles."[33] This was not written precisely in connection with the unities, but it will serve to introduce the idea that comparison with other arts will perhaps by analogy lead to more indulgence

---

[30] P. 533. [31] XVI (1789), 14-15.
[32] IV (1791), 285. Quoting Dr. F. A. Wendeborn. See also the *Gentleman's Magazine*, XLVII (1777), 64.
[33] All of these quotations are from D. Nichol Smith, *Shakespeare Criticism* (1916), p. 117.

toward Shakespeare with regard to the unities in drama. For example, Mrs. Montagu pleaded in 1769 that poetry should have the same indulgence as painting: "Had Michael Angelo's bold pencil been dedicated to drawing the Graces, or Rembrandt's to trace the soft bewitching smile of Venus, their works had probably proved very contemptible."[34] Mrs. Griffith in direct attack on the unities remarked very aptly that the commentators are unjust to Shakespeare in judging him "by the cold rules of artful construction. Shakespeare's writings resemble the ancient music, which consisted in *melody* alone, without regard to *harmony*, which is a science of much later invention . . . Would they restrain him within the precincts of art, the height, the depth of whose imagination and creative genius found even the extent of Nature too streightly bounded for it to move in? . . . Like an eastern monarch, his word was law . . . But there are certain *mechanists* in criticism, who have no other way of judging, but by applying *rule* and *compass;* like ancient gardeners, who trimmed their forest-trees into cones and cylinders, and reduced winding brooks to square canals."[35]

NATURE GREATER THAN THE RULES

Another method of rejecting the unities in Shakespeare criticism of this period was to argue that nature[36] is greater than rules. On this basis the unities were dismissed as mere pedantry, and the accent was placed on

---

[34] *Essay on the Genius and Writings of Shakespear* (London: Dodsley, 1769), p. 64. See also, for the same point, *Monthly Review*, XLI (1769), 132.

[35] *Op. cit.* (1775), p. 26. ". . . he [Shakespeare] seldom sins against a fourth [unity],' she added, which is "worth them all—namely, that of *character*." (p. 26).

[36] For this sense of the term Nature, see A. O. Lovejoy's article on " 'Nature' as Aesthetic Norm" in *MLN*, XLII (Nov., 1927), 445-47. It is Mr. Lovejoy's No. 14. See also Chap. IX, below.

the magic of the scene and characters as triumphant over all rules. Mrs. Montagu viciously attacked "The pedant who bought at a great price the lamp of a famous philosopher."[37] "Heaven-born genius," she adds, "acts from something superior to rules . . . and has a right of appeal to nature herself."[38] This idea was repeated in the *Monthly Review*,[39] and by Dr. Berkenhout in 1777, who noted that if these rules had been in nature Shakespeare would have found them.[40] Whately put delineation of character far above the unities in importance and added: "Experience has shewn, that however rigidly, and however rightly, the unities of action, time, and place have been insisted on, they may be dispensed with, and the magic of the scene may make the absurdity invisible. Most of Shakespeare's Plays abound with instances of such a fascination."[41] This idea appeared again with even more emphasis, in the *Macaroni and Theatrical Magazine*, September, 1773,[42] and in Mrs. Griffith's remarks, with accent here on character, in 1775.[43] Morgann, two years later, declared Aristotle would have said: "True Poesy is *magic*, not *nature*. . . . To the Magician I prescribed no laws";[44] but the most interesting example of this type of argument is Tom Davies' slightly sarcastic remark in 1784: "Sheffield Duke of Buckingham[shire], observing there was a double plot in this play, sat down to form two tragedies out of one, Julius Cæsar, and the death of Marcus Brutus. Whether they are strictly conformable to the rules of the drama, and observe the unities, I have not so critically examined them as to

---

[37]*Op. cit.* (1769), pp. 5-6.   [38]*Ibid.*, pp. 7-8. See also p. 79.
[39]XLI (1769), 130-31.   [40]See *Universal Magazine*, LXI (1777), 174.
[41]*Remarks on Some of the Characters of Shakspeare*, p. 2, of 2nd ed. (Oxford, 1808), which I am using. In dating Whately (1770?) I am following D. Nichol Smith's text (1916), p. 143 n.
[42]P. 533. See quotation given above, p. 48, n.
[43]*Op. cit.*, p. 26. See quotation given above, p. 51, n.   [44]*Op. cit.*, p. 71.

determine, but he seems to have taken great pains to extinguish the noble fire of the original."[45] All this should enforce the critics' idea that Shakespeare's natural genius was quite sufficient to offset neglect of the unities.[46]

THE HISTORICAL REJECTION OF THE UNITIES

The historical rejection of the unities was suggested by Pope in 1725: "To judge therefore of Shakespear by Aristotle's rules, is like trying a man by the Laws of one Country, who acted under those of another."[47] In the late eighteenth century this form of argument took three more or less related directions: the attempt to show how Aristotle would now regard Shakespeare, the accent upon the uniqueness of the Greek chorus, and the objection to the restraining influence of the unities upon the development of new types of plays since the days of Aristotle. The first and third do not appear as often as the second, but all are of about equal importance.

Morgann, in 1777, put in Aristotle's mouth an interesting remark to show what the Greek would have said now as a modern: "I [Aristotle] . . . knew not that a larger circle might be drawn . . . I see that a more compendious nature may be obtained; a *nature* of *effects* only, to which neither the relations of place, or continuity of time, are always essential."[48] Rymer irritated Morgann greatly: ". . . a fellow, like Rymer . . . charge this great magician . . . in the name of Aristotle, to surrender; whilst Aristotle himself, disowning his wretched Officer, would fall prostrate at his feet and acknowledge his su-

---

[45]*Dramatic Miscellanies*, II, 202-3. Compare *Universal Magazine*, LXXXI (1787), 243.
[46]See Chap. IX, below.
[47]See D. Nichol Smith, *Shakespeare Criticism* (1916), p. 51.
[48]*Op. cit.*, p. 70.   [49]*Ibid.*, pp. 69-70.

premacy—O Supreme of Dramatic excellence! (*might he say,*) not to me be imputed the insolence of fools."[49]

The uniqueness of the Greek chorus was a stock argument from 1769 to the end of the century against modern application of the unities. The *Monthly Review* early restated the general theory: ". . . the common source of false criticism . . . is making the characters and manners of one time and country the test of pieces which exhibit the characters and manners of another."[50] It repeated its point in 1773,[51] and four years later the *Gentleman's Magazine* noted that the Greek chorus was adapted to unity of scene but that even modern operas, if modeled on the Greeks, should adopt change of scene.[52] The *Universal Magazine* declared that Aristotle admitted the constraining influence of the Greek chorus,[53] and Blair developed the same point in his *Lectures* in 1783.[54] Finally the *European Magazine* in 1789 trampled heavily on the Greek chorus as tending to weaken probability and energy, interrupting the "progress of the passions," and confusing the whole.[55]

It was obvious also that adherence to the unities would prevent invention of new types of drama. Here Shakespeare's own initiative was cited, especially with regard to the historical plays. Mrs. Montagu announced quite definitely that the unities should not be applied to the historical plays,[56] and Dr. Berkenhout declared that it was ridiculous to follow the Greek unities, because this pro-

---
[50] XLI (1769), 132.
[51] XLVIII (1773), 388. Quoting T. Hawkins. For this note I am again indebted to Miss Richards.
[52] XLVII (1777), 64-65.   [53] LXI (1777), 6. Quoting Morgann.
[54] Lecture XLV—vol. II (1804), 326-27.
[55] XVI (1789), 14-15. See also W. Cooke, *Elements of Dramatic Criticism* (London: G. Kearsly, 1775), Chap. XI, pp. 89-90.
[56] *Op. cit.*, pp. 55-56. Compare also Johnson in D. Nichol Smith, *Shakespeare Criticism* (1916), p. 106.

cedure would preclude invention of other species of dramatic entertainment—Shakespeare's historical plays, for example.[57] The *Monthly Review* repeated that the unities "should not be suffered to limit the human genius, so as to prevent the invention of other kinds of dramatical productions."[58] So, historically, Shakespeare was again exonerated by virtue of his inventive genius.[59]

Aristotle's Support of the Unities Denied

The final and decisive demolition of the unities came at the end of the century, when Twining in translating the *Poetics* denied Aristotle's support of the unities: ". . . unity of time . . . receives not the least support from Aristotle's authority; . . . place is not once mentioned, nor even hinted, in the whole book"[60] and "he [Aristotle] only refers . . . to the usual practice of the dramatic poets of his time."[61] It is notable that this same idea had appeared in *The Observer* (1785-90), No. 135, and that Tyrwhitt's and Pye's translations in 1795 clinched the matter.[62] The only curious aspect of this whole development is that the *Critical Review* in 1775[63] reviewed a translation of the *Poetics* without hitting upon the above elimination of the pseudo-Aristotelian unities of time and place.

In summing up this whole reaction against the unities from 1766 to 1799, it should be noted that Johnson's great

---

[57]See the *Universal Magazine*, LXI (1777), 174.
[58]LVII (1777), 195. This was applied especially to Shakespeare.
[59]Even E. Taylor exempted Shakespeare's historical plays, "as of an original and peculiar kind" (*op. cit.*, p. 221).
[60]*Monthly Review*, VII (1792), 124.
[61]*Ibid.*, 125. For same point, see W. Hodson, *op. cit.*, p. 75.
[62]See the *Monthly Review*, XVII (1795), 322, 368, and XVIII (1795), 121. This whole development should be compared with the *Universal Magazine*, VIII (1751), 98: "Aristotle's definition of tragedy generally mistaken."
[63]XL (1775), 393.

contribution has somewhat overshadowed the contributions of other critics during the period. Thus more credit for aiding the general reaction should now be given to the various periodicals, and perhaps also certain other prominent individual critics of the period should be emphasized—notably Mrs. Montagu, Morgann, and Mrs. Griffith.

CHAPTER V

SHAKESPEARE'S CLASSICAL LEARNING[1]

Immediately connected with the problem of the unities in Shakespearean criticism is that of Shakespeare's learning, for if Shakespeare knew not the classics, "it would be hard," as Rowe pointed out, "to judge him by a Law he knew nothing of." "Shakespear," says Rowe, "liv'd under a kind of mere Light of Nature, and had never been made acquainted with the Regularity of those written Precepts."[2] So also Pope, as noted above: "To judge therefore of Shakespear by Aristotle's rules, is like trying a man by the Laws of one Country, who acted under those of another."[3] And Johnson: "Those whom my arguments cannot persuade to give their approbation to the judgment of Shakespeare, will easily if they consider the condition of his life, make some allowance for his ignorance."[4]

THE BEGINNINGS OF THE CONTROVERSY

It is possible that Rowe started the controversy over Shakespeare's learning by the above remark.[5] But Fuller several decades earlier had written: "Indeed his Learning was very little,"[6] and so also Edward Phillips in 1675: ". . . probably his Learning was not extraordinary."[7]

---

[1] Most of this chapter has already been published in *PQ*, IX (1930), 116-22. It is reprinted here with permission.
[2] Rowe's *Preface* (1709) quoted in D. Nichol Smith's *Shakespeare Criticism* (1916), p. 35.
[3] Quoted, *Ibid.*, p. 51.   [4] Quoted, *Ibid.*, p. 113.
[5] See D. Nichol Smith, *Eighteenth Century Essays on Shakespeare*, Introduction (1903), p. xxii n. A more detailed modern survey of this field before 1766 appeared in *Anglia*, XXVIII (1905), 457-76, by H. A. Evans.
[6] Quoted in D. Nichol Smith, *Shakespeare Criticism*, p. 11.   [7] *Ibid.*, p. 28.

However, the precise inception is a minor matter. Without doubt the best contemporary survey of the origin of the problem appeared in Richard Farmer's preliminary discussion in his *Essay on the Learning of Shakespeare* (1767).[8] And meanwhile one should not overlook articles in the *Gentleman's Magazine* in 1748,[9] and the *Monthly Review* in 1765[10] as links in the general development before 1766.

The controversy over Shakespeare's learning continued throughout the whole period from 1766 to 1799. In its sanest aspect—that is, the denial of Shakespeare's direct knowledge of the classics—it took two lines of development, which should be followed through at once as the most important features. First, there was the work of Farmer with its subsequent supporters, and, second, there was much comment of the same tenor presented apparently quite independently of Farmer. Nevertheless Farmer occupied the center of this whole picture.

Farmer's Denial of Shakespeare's Direct Knowledge of the Classics

Farmer's first edition in 1767 was a startlingly brilliant piece of work, from an academic point of view. He surveyed his problem carefully, giving first a list of men who denied Shakespeare's learning, that is, Jonson, Suckling, Denham, Milton, Dryden, Fuller,[11] etc., and then the array of upholders of Shakespeare's classical knowledge, for example, Gildon, Sewel, Pope, Theobald, Warburton, Upton, Grey, Dodd, and Whalley.[12] Of the latter he remarked:

---

[8]Pp. 4-8. My pages always refer to the first edition, unless otherwise noted. (1st ed., Cambridge: J. Archdeacon, 1767; 2nd ed., Cambridge, Woodyer, 1767).
[9]XVIII (1748), 25, 48, 113, 126.
[10]XXXIII (1765), 382. Reviewing Johnson.
[11]*Essay on the Learning of Shakespeare*, pp. 4-5 (of 1st ed., which I am using).
[12]*Ibid.*, pp. 5-8.

"These critics . . . have sometimes persuaded us of their learning, whatever became of their Author's."[13] His point of view is quite definite, then: he will defend the former group—he will deny Shakespeare's direct knowledge of the classics.

His devastating argument proceeds in two directions. First he shows, by paralleling mistakes, that Shakespeare used translations—for example, North's translation (1579) of Amyot's Plutarch—rather than the original Greek.[14] Next he studies comparatively the language of Shakespeare's day in order to disprove the poet's supposed use of Greek and cites, for example, B. Heath, to support him in this.[15] The same methods are applied to Latin,[16] and if no translation existed, Farmer points out that Shakespeare used an indirect reference such as might appear in a grammar.[17] He employs the same procedure in attacking Colman's defense of Shakespeare's learning in a *Preface to a Translation of Terence*,[18] and, after discounting Aubrey as a reliable source of Beeston's butcher story,[19] applies his main arguments again to Shakespeare's use of modern languages, Italian, Spanish, and French.[20] In the case of the latter he even proposes possible interpolation,[21] and his general conclusion is quite definite: ". . . his [Shakespeare's] Studies were most demonstratively confined to *Nature*, and *his own language*."[22]

---

[13] *Ibid.*, p. 8.
[14] *Ibid.*, p. 9. Thus Shakespeare made North's mistakes.
[15] *Ibid.*, pp. 12-13. "Haver" and "having" are not from Greek: "This was the common language of Shakespeare's time."
[16] *Ibid.*, pp. 19-21, 25.
[17] *Ibid.*, pp. 26-27. Farmer obviously owes a debt, for his methods, to Johnson's *Preface* [see D. Nichol Smith's *Shakespeare Criticism* (1916), pp. 118-19].
[18] *Ibid.*, pp. 29-32.   [19] *Ibid.*, pp. 36-39.   [20] *Ibid.*, pp. 39-45.
[21] ". . . it is equally probable, that the *French* ribaldry [in *Henry V*] was at first inserted by a different hand"—pp. 44-45.   [22] *Ibid.*, p. 49.

This first edition included fifty pages of text. The second, produced within the same year, apparently as a reply to a criticism in the *Critical Review* for January, 1767,[23] reached ninety-five pages. There were long interpolations—that is, new sections,[24] but there was nothing new in method. Farmer was merely enlarging his quotations from Shakespeare's sources, supplementing his evidence by similar evidence, adding footnotes, or else, occasionally, citing a new authority to support himself.[25] As a whole it was certainly a stronger piece of work than the first edition and deserved its complete reprinting in 1789,[26] as a splendid specimen of sane scholarship.

THE REACTION TO FARMER'S WORK

The most immediate reaction to Farmer's work came obviously from Colman, who in the Appendix to the second edition of his *Translation of Terence*, in 1768, proceeded to announce: "Shakespeare's total ignorance of the learned languages remains to be proved."[27] In general, however, he admitted Farmer's main contention as to Shakespeare's use of translations,[28] but insisted on the poet's knowledge of French and Italian.[29] As his most vicious thrust at Farmer he noted that the latter had said that Shakespeare " 'came out of her [Nature's] hand, *as some one else expresses it*, like Pallas out of Jove's head' . . . It is whimsical enough," he continues, "that this *some one else*, whose expression is here quoted to countenance the general notion of Shakespeare's want of literature, should be no other than myself."[30] Farmer replied by pointing

---
[23]XXIII (1767), 47-50.
[24]Pp. 13-19, 27-32, 36-38, 43-44, 48-56, 57-61, 66-69, 87-88.
[25]For example, Hurd on pp. 40-41.   [26]London: Longman, 1789.
[27]Quoted in Johnson and Steevens' 2nd ed. (1778), I, 102.
[28]*Ibid.*, p. 104.   [29]*Ibid.*, p. 104.
[30]*Ibid.*, p. 104 n. He quoted from p. 29 of Farmer's first edition.

out Colman's utter ignorance of Shakespeare's language and suggested that Colman read a few of the old plays to learn about popular Latin terms.[31] But it remained for an anonymous critic to demolish Colman's brightest quip (noted above), by showing that the *some one else* referred to by Farmer was Dr. Young in the *Conjectures* rather than Colman—"*some one else the second* transcribed it from the author already mentioned."[32]

Otherwise the reaction to Farmer was generally favorable and became more and more so as the century neared its close. At first, of course, there was some surprised dismay: for example, from the *Critical Review* in 1767,[33] to which, as noted above, Farmer replied with his second edition. But the *Critical Review* declared immediately that Farmer had failed to change its point of view.[34] Neutral reviews appeared in the *British Magazine*[35] (which were reprinted in the *London Magazine*),[36] and in the *Gentleman's Magazine*.[37] The *Monthly Review*[38] indeed ventured to approve of Farmer. But it was the more prominent individual critics of the day who finally declared his importance.

Richard Warner in *A Letter to David Garrick*, in 1768, remarked: "Mr. Farmer, in the very ingenious essay on the learning of Shakespear, which he has lately oblig'd us with, has with many seemed to put it out of all doubt, that all his allusions to ancient authors, he took from translations."[39] Mrs. Montagu the next year agreed: "It has been demonstrated with great ingenuity and candour that he [Shakespeare] was destitute of learning."[40] So also assented The Advertisement to the Reader in Johnson and

---

[31] Johnson and Steevens' 2nd ed. (1778), II, 435 n.
[32] Johnson and Steevens' 3rd ed. (1785), I, 107 n.
[33] XXIII (1767), 47-50.
[34] XXIV (1767), 400.
[35] VIII (1767), 5-8.
[36] XXXVI (Feb., 1767), 81-83.
[37] XXXVII (1767), 120.
[38] XXXVI (1767), 153.
[39] P. 9.
[40] *Op. cit.*, p. 285.

Steevens' *Edition* (1773): "The dispute about the learning of Shakespeare being now finally settled" by Mr. Farmer's "very decisive pamphlet." Johnson, in conversation, fairly clinched the matter: "Dr. Farmer, you have done that which was never done before; that is, you have completely finished a controversy beyond all further doubt." "There are some critics," answered Farmer, "who will adhere to their old opinions." "Ah," said Johnson, "that may be true; for the limbs will quiver and move when the soul is gone."[41]

Horace Walpole in a letter May 4, 1781, continued the praise of Farmer.[42] Malone in 1790 enthusiastically noted Farmer's "admirable Essay on the learning of Shakspeare, by which as Dr. Johnson justly observed, 'the question is for ever decided' ";[43] and in his *Letter to the Rev. Richard Farmer* in 1792 reiterated his judgment more forcibly: ". . . the most conclusive Essay that ever appeared on a subject of criticism."[44] And, meanwhile, William Jackson, in his *Thirty Letters on Various Subjects*, had echoed this judgment with the following positive statement, "Farmer's essay is the most satisfactory piece of criticism that has yet appeared on Shakespeare."[45]

---

[41] Boswell's *Life of Johnson* (ed. Hill), III (1776), 38-39 n. Yet, when stirred by Colman's reference to him—"What says Johnson?"—in the *Appendix to the Translation of Terence*, Johnson in some irritation replied to Boswell: "Sir, let Farmer answer for himself: *I* never engaged in this controversy. I always said, Shakspeare had Latin enough to grammaticise his English."—*Ibid.*, IV (1780), 18.

[42] *Letters of Horace Walpole* (ed. Mrs. Paget-Toynbee, 1904), XI, 436. Two years later, in 1783, a Dublin edition of the *Beauties of Shakespeare* praised Farmer, p. 111.

[43] Edition of 1790, Vol. I, Pt. 2, p. 171.   [44] P. 7.

[45] *Thirty Letters* (1782), p. 164, of the 3rd (1795) edition, which I am using. Compare D. Nichol Smith's praise in his most recent book (*Shakespeare in the Eighteenth Century*, 1928), p. 52.

FARMER'S POINT OF VIEW CORROBORATED
BY OTHER CRITICS

Simultaneously, and apparently quite apart from Farmer, comment was appearing that fully supplemented this scholar's point of view. The *Monthly Review* in 1773 noted Shakespeare's probable ignorance of the rules of the ancients.[46] Morgann in 1777 declared that the Latin in "trash" imputed to Shakespeare proves that such "trash" is *not* Shakespeare's.[47] The *Gentleman's Magazine* in 1780 rejected the method of proof by similarity of passages.[48] William Richardson in 1784 doubted Shakespeare's learning,[49] and Tom Davies in the same year declared: "Shakespeare knew little of the antient chorus,"[50] and, rejecting Warburton,[51] pointed out that Shakespeare used Lucian, in *translation*.[52] J. M. Mason in the following year wrote: "Warburton's observations frequently tend to prove Shakespeare more profound and learned than the occasion required, and to make the Poet of Nature the most unnatural that ever wrote."[53] And finally should be quoted a bit of sarcasm—to conclude the point of view and bring us back to Farmer—from the *Gentleman's Magazine* in 1791: "After Dr. Farmer had most satisfactorily proved that Shakspeare was not versed in Greek or Latin, comes a person to shew that he understood *Hebrew!*"[54]

Yet strangely enough, in spite of all this overwhelming evidence and support, the heretics, if they may be called

---

[46]XLVIII (1773), 388. Quoting T. Hawkins. For this note I am indebted to Miss Edna Richards of the University of Michigan.
[47]*Op. cit.*, p. 64.   [48]L (1780), 558.
[49]Fifth edition of *Essays*, p. 388. For Richardson's texts on Shakespeare, see *JEGP*, XXVIII (Jan., 1929), 117.
[50]*Op. cit.*, III, 91.   [51]*Ibid.*, II, 295.
[52]*Ibid.*, III, 20. On this point compare the *Monthly Magazine*, I (1796), 91.
[53]*Op. cit.*, p. 18; see also p. 350.   [54]LXI (1791), 33.

such, still persisted. Capell as early as 1767 had declared that Shakespeare "was very well grounded, at least in Latin."⁵⁵ Even Warner in 1768 compromised: "As on the one hand, I cannot by any means raise his learning to the first pitch, so, neither can I bring it down so low as that gentleman [Farmer] would have it."⁵⁶ Colman has already been noted above. Perhaps the most violent heretic was Dr. Prescot, who in 1773 raptly paralleled Horatio's "It was about to speak when the cock crew" with Prudentius,⁵⁷ lines from *Julius Cæsar* with Seneca and Arrian,⁵⁸ and concluded, vigorously: "It is therefore unwarrantable to ascribe the little Latin we have seen, and the hardly found Greek but to a celerity of apprehension, during his [Shakespeare's] own survey and reading. Renderings scarcely would have spoke the lively and concise sense. . . . He floods deep in Learning."⁵⁹ No one else, apparently, approached such confidence, though even the ubiquitous Morgann had some strange backslidings in this direction: "There is indeed nothing perishable about him [Shakespeare], except that very learning which he is said so much to want. He had not, it is true, enough for the demands of the age in which he lived, but he had perhaps too much for the reach of his genius, and the interest of his fame."⁶⁰ Actually this strange undercurrent persisted to the very end of the century, for the *Universal Magazine* in 1791 declared: ". . . his [Shakespeare's] knowledge of ancient literature was not so confined, as some have represented it to be";⁶¹ the *Monthly Mirror* in 1796 added: "We do not enter the lists with those who contend for or against

---

⁵⁵Introduction to *Edition*, p. 31 n.   ⁵⁶*Op. cit.*, p. 16.
⁵⁷*Letters* . . . *with Additional Classic Amusements* (Cambridge: Archdeacon, 1773), p. 294.
⁵⁸*Ibid.*, p. 290.   ⁵⁹*Ibid.*, p. 291.
⁶⁰*Op. cit.*, pp. 65-66.   ⁶¹LXXXVIII (1791), 285.

the learning of Shakspeare";[62] and in the *Monthly Magazine* in 1799 "N. N." wrote a letter to the editor noting that a recent correspondent declared Shakespeare may have known more than the critics believe, and subjoined two passages to show similarity of Shakespeare to Seneca and Lucretius.[63]

THE LATE EIGHTEENTH-CENTURY POINT OF VIEW

There is, therefore, no conclusion to make beyond the fact that to the late eighteenth century in general, Shakespeare was not at all learned in the classics.[64] One cannot, however, say that the controversy absolutely closed then, for it still exists today.[65] But the point that should primarily be kept in mind is that inasmuch as the late eighteenth century decided against Shakespeare's knowledge of the classics, it, to some extent, as the preliminary quotations of Rowe, Pope, and Johnson suggested, absolved Shakespeare from the neglect of the unities.

---

[62]II (1796), 339.
[63]VIII (1799), 790. Yet he admitted that the similarity to Lucretius is "no more than a coincidence of sentiment between two great geniuses." Compare again the same periodical, I (1796), 91.
[64]For supplementary material on this subject of Shakespeare's learning see: "K. P." [K. Prescot], *Shakespeare, An Essay* [on the Learning of Shakespeare] (Privately printed, 1774).
[65]See Mr. J. C. Collins' articles in the *Forthnightly Review*, April, May, July, 1903; also D. Nichol Smith's Introduction to *Eighteenth Century Essays on Shakespeare* (1903), p. xxvi; J. S. Smart, *Shakespeare: Truth and Tradition*(1928), pp. 149-90; *MLN*, XL (1925), 380-81, 440. I have deliberately neglected W. Maginn's "On the Learning of Shakespeare," in *Shakespeare Papers* (ed. S. Mackenzie, N. Y., 1856—but originally in *Fraser's Magazine*, beginning Sept., 1839) because of its too obvious bias and vicious contentiousness: e.g., "I have always considered Dr. Farmer's 'celebrated Essay' . . . a piece of pedantic impertinence, not paralleled in literature . . . this third or fourth rate scholar" (p. 229). This "quip modest" would perhaps apply much more aptly to Maginn himself.

Shakespeare Above the Ancients

In fact, the late eighteenth century did more than this. It elevated Shakespeare above the ancients[66] and absolved him from the imitation of models. The general revolt against the ancients—a revolt which implied rejection of the rules of the ancients—in the late eighteenth century may be indicated by a few passages. The *Monthly Review* in 1770 deplored "The unreasonable Compliments paid to the Ancients for their Works."[67] Six years later the *Hibernian Magazine* declared that nature did not shape the ancients of better clay than the Moderns: ". . . it is not to be wondered at if we surpass them."[68] In the following year the *Gentleman's Magazine* rather violently decried the Greek chorus: ". . . it seems to me absurd to suppose, that the principal persons of a tragedy would conduct their affairs so badly as to have all their thoughts exposed to the public eye."[69] Then the revolt became even more pronounced, in the *Universal Magazine*,[70] the *European Magazine*,[71] and Blair's Lecture XXXV: "Let us guard, however, against a blind and implicit veneration for the ancients in every thing."[72] The *Lady's Magazine* in 1784[73]

[66]For some material on the ancients versus the moderns, preceding 1766, see: C. Gildon, *Essays* (1694), p. 220; *Comparison between the Two Stages*, 1702; *J. Dennis, *Advancement of Modern Poetry*, 1701; *C. Gildon, *An Essay on the Art, Rise and Progress of the Stage*, 1710; *The Spectator*, Nos. 61, 249, 253; *The Guardian*, Nos. 12, 25; *Gentleman's Magazine*, V (1735), 192; *S. Foote, *The Roman and English Comedy Consider'd and Compar'd*, 1747; *Monthly Review*, XX (1759), 66, 504; XXV (1761), 362; XXVII (1762), 113; *Adventurer*, No. 49; *The World*, No. 137; *Universal Spectator*, III (1756), 127, 257.

Material preceding 1766 on imitation of models is given below. Starred texts above refer more directly to Shakespeare.

[67]XLII (1770), 295. [68]VI (1776), 624. [69]XLVII (1777), 64.
[70]LXXII (1783), 141. [71]III (1783), 27-29.

[72]II (1804), 152. For a fuller statement of Blair's long analysis of the relationship, see V. Knox, *Elegant Extracts*, No. 71. (This note was given me by Mr. A. A. Appleford of the University of Michigan.)

[73]XV (1784), 588-91.

continued the reaction, as did also the *Lounger* (1785-86), No. 73. Finally, the *Hibernian Magazine* in 1794 fired a parting shot at the ancients.[74] All of this material forms an excellent background for the attitude toward Shakespeare as a modern.

In 1767 the *British Magazine* remarked: "This single circumstance would be sufficient to set him [Shakespeare] greatly above any of the tragic poets of antient Greece."[75] Two years later Mrs. Montagu pronounced Shakespeare's dramaturgy superior to the Greek chorus[76] and Shakespeare's praeternatural beings finer than those of the ancients.[77] The *Gentleman's Magazine* noted that Shakespeare's description of night in *Macbeth* "infinitely excels all that have preceded it."[78] Mrs. Griffith preferred her Shakespeare;[79] Cumberland's *Observer* (1785-90) four times promoted Shakespeare above Aeschylus;[80] and the *Analytical Review* twice, in 1788 and 1791, declared Shakespeare eclipsed all three Greek tragedians, Aeschylus, Sophocles, and Euripides.[81] Finally in *The Bee* (1791) Shakespeare was lifted above the moderns themselves: ". . . our moderns . . . can bear no comparison to the old poets, Shakespeare, Johnson, and Fletcher."[82] There is further evidence of this elevation of Shakespeare above the famous Greeks, but the point is now probably sufficiently obvious.[83]

---

[74]Part II, p. 350.
[75]VIII (1767), 620.
[76]*Op. cit.* (1769), p. 179.
[77]*Ibid.*, pp. 152-53, 162-66, 168, 199.
[78]XLIV (1774), 24.
[79]*Op. cit.* (1775), p. 525.
[80]No. 69 (p. 123); 70 (p. 129); 71 (p. 137); 74 (p. 154).—Chalmers, *British Essayists*.
[81]I (1788), 176, and XI (1791), 192. Compare also Malone's *Preface* (1790), p. lxix.
[82]VI (1791), 40. Cumberland put Shakespeare above Johnson in *The Observer*, No. 74, and the *British Magazine* in 1767 (VIII, 620) placed Shakespeare "above the celebrated dramatic authors of France."
[83]See George Colman, *The Gentleman*, No. VI, Dec. 4, 1775; and *Playhouse Pocket Companion*, chap. V, p. 36.

Absolved from the Imitation of Models

Johnson: "Shakespeare engaged in dramatic poetry with the world open before him; the rules of the ancients were yet known to few; the publick judgment was unformed; he had no example of such fame as might force him upon imitation"[84]

Preface (1765)

One of the points critics agreed on in the late eighteenth century, as will appear in Part III below,[85] was that Shakespeare could, and did, imitate nature, in the various senses implied by that most comprehensive term.[86] Hence one cannot say that there was any attack on the doctrine of imitation in general as applied to Shakespeare. Yet from imitation in one of its more objective senses Shakespeare was absolved.

Mrs. Montagu in 1769 attacked imitation of models: "Nothing great is to be expected from any set of artists who are to give only copies of copies. The treasures of nature are inexhaustible, as well in moral as in physical subjects. The talents of Shakespear were universal."[87] T. Hawkins continued her defense in 1773: ". . . it will be sufficient for our purpose to contend, that it [Shakespearean drama] was a distinct species of itself, and not a re-

---

[84]Quoted from D. Nichol Smith, *Shakespeare Criticism* (1916), p. 100. For the *general* background of the attack on imitation of models in the early 18th century I should refer the reader to Professor R. S. Crane's review of Mr. P. Kaufman's "Heralds of Original Genius" in the *Philological Quarterly*, VI (1927), 168-69. Shakespeare himself was defended, before 1766, by E. Young, *Conjectures on Original Composition* (1759), reviewed in the *Monthly Review*, XX (1759), 66, 504; see also *ibid.*, XXIII (1760), 374, quoting Lloyd's "Shakespear; An Epistle to Mr. Garrick." (For this reference I am indebted to Miss Edna Richards of the University of Michigan.)

[85]See pp. 119-23 below.

[86]See A. O. Lovejoy's article in *MLN*, XLII (1927), 445-47.

[87]*Op. cit.*, p. 65. Compare her comment on the "histories, being of an original kind," p. 55.

vival of the *ancient drama*, with which it cannot be compared, and must never be confounded."[88] Two years later again Mrs. Griffith announced flatly that Shakespeare's plays were not "an imitation of the Greek," but rather "a distinct species of Drama."[89] Martin Sherlock continued in 1786: "Shakspeare, . . . disdaining imitation, opened to himself a new road, leaped over it under the wing of genius, and created a species quite new."[90] And *The Bee* in 1791 clinched the matter: ". . . they [Homer and Shakespeare] were generally unassisted by the writings of others.[91] . . . An idea imagined by any other would be inadequate to the grasp of their genius and uncongenial with their usual mode of conception."[92]

Hence the late eighteenth century elevated Shakespeare above even the ancients themselves and at the same time absolved him of copying ancient models. Both of these developments represent reactions supplementary to those of the defense against the unities and the dismissal of his classical learning, which are themselves reactions against traditional objections. It will be appropriate now to turn to two other prominent objections to Shakespeare, his lack of decorum and his eccentricities of style, and note how the late eighteenth century defended him on both of these points, also.

---

[88]Quoted in the *Monthly Review*, XLVIII (1773), 388, from *The Origin of English Drama*.
[89]In her Preface to *op. cit.*, p. vi.
[90]*A Fragment on Shakspeare* (1786), p. 34.
[91]I (1791), 56. [92]*Ibid.*, p. 57.

CHAPTER VI

SHAKESPEARE AND DECORUM;[1] OTHER POINTS OF ATTACK

SHAKESPEARE'S VIOLATION OF DECORUM

The second really great traditional objection to Shakespeare, which went hand in hand with the emphasis on the unities, was the Horatian principle of decorum with its corollary: "inconsistent things must not be joined."[2] The application of this principle led to distaste for Shakespeare's general coarseness, his mingling of social ranks, and his use of tragicomedy and supernatural characters.

Shakespeare's coarseness was excused in at least three ways. F. Gentleman in 1770 attacked the murder of Lady Macduff and son as "farcically horrid,"[3] abhorred "the drunkenness of Cassio,"[4] and called Bianca "a despicable non-essential";[5] but Morgann replied: "Indecorums respect the propriety or impropriety of exhibiting certain actions; not their truth or falsehood when exhibited. Shakespeare stands to us in the place of *truth* and *nature*."[6] A better extenuation, doubtless, is the historical point of view, such as appeared in the *Lady's Magazine*, with the pronouncement that Shakespeare's Romans talked as old

---

[1]This chapter and the next are particularly concerned with elements of taste. *The Spectator* had a paper on "Improprieties on the Stage," No. 141. See also No. 502.
[2]G. Saintsbury, *A History of English Criticism* (1911), I, 15.
[3]*Dramatic Censor*, I, 97.   [4]*Ibid.*, I, 138.
[5]*Ibid.*, I, 145. See also I, 365: ". . . it brings an unnecessary death upon the stage."
[6]*Op. cit.*, pp. 43-44.

Romans did, that is, coarsely;[7] but the third and most interesting defense appeared in *The Bee* (Edinburgh) in 1793:[8] Many passages were not written by Shakespeare; it is hard to separate the tares from the wheat; men who wanted to attract the public interpolated "scenes of ribaldry, and low humour."

As to mingling of social ranks, the *British Magazine* in 1767 voiced the typical complaint: Cicero should not have been introduced in *Julius Cæsar* because Horace has observed that "a god should not be introduced in a tragedy, except upon a juncture important enough to require the presence of a superior being"; and the same is true of "a great personage."[9] The answers to this expression of a general point of view took the form of direct approval of Shakespeare, historical extenuation, and the appeal to nature or real characters again. For example, Morgann remarked: "I have nothing to do with Shakespeare's indecorums in general. That there are indecorums in the Play [*Henry IV*, Pt. 1] I have no doubt: the indecent Treatment of Percy's dead body is the greatest . . . but the admission of Falstaff into the Royal Presence . . . does not seem to be in any respect among the number."[10] Tom Davies in 1784 directly praised Shakespeare for decorum,[11] and *The Bee* enthusiastically agreed: Shakespeare "has drawn low characters and ludicrous scenes with the same unrivalled propriety as the sublime and prophetic."[12]

---

[7] IX (1778), 532. See also for this method: *Monthly Review*, XLI (1769), 131.
[8] XVI (1793), 273-74.
[9] VIII (1767), 572-73. See also F. Gentleman, *op. cit.* (1770) on Macbeth's language, I, "78" [misprint for 99].
[10] *Op. cit.*, p. 43.   [11] *Op. cit.*, II, 156.   [12] XVI (1793), 274.

The Historical Defense

The historical defense appeared, expressly, in the *Lady's Magazine* in 1778: "Was Shakespeare to write now, his conduct in introducing such personages would be inexcusable; but at the time he wrote, it was proper."[13] This same idea was proposed in the *Universal Magazine*, with relation to Shakespeare's audience, together with Dr. Berkenhout's blunt assertion that this idea "ought forever to preclude all attempts to ridicule Shakespeare on that account";[14] and the same periodical repeated the historical defense in 1787.[15] Finally, the appeal to nature, or real characters, was voiced by the *Analytical Review*: "In Shakespeare as in real life, buffoonery is mixed with sublimity. Such is man." . . . A man of any rank expresses passions as do other men; hence Shakespeare lets great men use "low expressions."[16] And so also *The Bee* in 1791: "Shakespeare's low characters have so curious and so perfect a resemblance to nature, that they must always please"; and they "illustrate and endear the great characters."[17] This last excerpt shows immediately how close this defense is to that of tragicomedy.

Tragicomedy Attacked and Defended

The opposition to tragicomedy[18] persisted with considerable vigor, to 1784, and after that quickly lost force, the pendulum swinging far over to defense of Shakespeare.

---

[13] IX (1778), 531. [14] LXI (1777), 174.
[15] LXXXI (1787), 5—quoting H. Blair. [16] V (1789), 568.
[17] IV (1791), 293. On this point see also the *Lady's Magazine*, IX (1778), 531.
[18] For some material on tragicomedy preceding 1766: Attacking tragicomedy (in general): *Spectator*, Nos. 39, 40, 42, 44; *Gentleman's Magazine*, XXII (1752), 163. Favoring Shakespeare's combination: *Rambler*, No. 156 (Sept. 14, 1751); *Monthly Review*, XXXIII (1765), 291.

The early years of the period, however, produced such emphatic criticism as: ". . . it [*Julius Cæsar*] is disgraced by a mixture of low buffoonery, which is altogether unsuitable to the dignity of its subject";[19] and Francis Gentleman's attack on Shakespeare for introducing the porter scene in *Macbeth*.[20] Colman in his *Man and Wife; or, The Shakespeare Jubilee* (1770) let one character speak the general point of view of the period: "as uncouth a medley to present to this age as a pageant or a puppet-show."[21]

But the most violent enemy of Shakespeare in this matter appeared in 1774 in the person of Edward Taylor. Taylor's critical temper has already been suggested above,[22] but a few further remarks of his apropos of tragicomedy might be quoted now: ". . . there are parts of nature that require concealment[23] . . . Shakespear abounds in the true sublime; but . . . he abounds likewise in the low and vulgar.[24] . . . The scene of the gravediggers in Hamlet is certainly real life . . . yet how misplaced, how unworthy the tragedian."[25] . . . Even in comedy there should be "a certain graceful decorum . . . It is not long ago that even a comedy . . . met with unfavorable reception, on account of a low illiberal dialogue."[26] After Taylor there remained only Blair[27] (1783) and William Richardson[28] (1784) as serious detractors of Shakespeare on this score.

---

[19]*British Magazine*, VIII (1767), 572.
[20]*Op. cit.*, I, 90. Compare also his attack (I, 171) on *Romeo and Juliet*.
[21]P. 18. Compare Chap. VIII, below.
[22]See above, the chapter on the unities.   [23]*Cursory Remarks*, p. 39.
[24]*Ibid.*, p. 42.   [25]*Ibid.*, p. 40.
[26]*Ibid.*, p. 41. See also pp. 44, 52, 58-59, 69, 99. The play referred to is, I believe, Goldsmith's *Good-Natured Man*.
[27]*Lectures on Rhetoric* (1783), Lecture III, vol. I (1804), 35; Lecture XLV, vol. II (1804), 328-29; Lecture XLVI, vol. II (1804), 356. Some of Blair's remarks were reprinted in the *Universal Magazine*, LXXXI (1787), 4-5.
[28]Richardson, *Essays* (5th ed., 1798), pp. 365, 377, 380-91. Richardson

The defenders of Shakespeare had meanwhile appeared early in the period and their methods of defense became more and more diverse. Mrs. Montagu voiced an historical point of view in 1769: To the French "a tragi-comedy of this kind will be deemed a monster . . ." but "From some peculiar circumstances relating to the characters in this piece [*Henry IV*, Pt. 1], we may, perhaps, find a sort of apology for the motley mixture thrown into it. We cannot but suppose, that at the time it was written, many stories yet subsisted of the wild adventures of this Prince of Wales and his idle companions"; but as the prince later became a popular hero, Shakespeare could not put his follies in "a piece entirely serious."[29] This historical method was carried on from another point of view by M. Sherlock in 1786: "The only view of Shakspeare was to make his fortune, and for that it was necessary to fill the play-house . . . Shakspeare forced his sublime genius to stoop to the gross taste of the populace."[30] Molière did the same thing, he continues, supporting plays with farces much longer than Shakespeare's interpolated scenes; hence "for this single scene [the grave-diggers], which takes up eight minutes in the representation, the enlighted critics of this age have condemned ten volumes of the plays of Shakspeare. . . . The master of Shakspeare and Molière was the people, a foolish and fantastic monster."[31] Even so (continues Sherlock) Raphael violated his Transfiguration with two Dominicans, against both good sense and the unities, to please his master because he "wanted to be a cardinal."[32]

Pilon in 1777 noted compensations for the evils of tragi-

---
declares there is no such mixture in painting or music (p. 381). W. Cooke's attitude in 1775 (*Elements*, chap. XIV) was rather general.
[29]*Op. cit.*, pp. 101-2.   [30]*Op. cit.*, p. 35.
[31]*Ibid.*, pp. 36-37.   [32]*Ibid.*, pp. 36-37.

comedy: "The opening of the fifth act [of *Hamlet*] is stained with low ribaldry, but so intimately connected with striking beauties, that it would be impossible to expunge the one without losing the other."[33] Tom Davies similarly defended the same scene in *Hamlet*[34] and remarked further, with reference to Shakespeare's tragicomedy in general: ". . . the excellency of Shakspeare's genius has fixed it on us[35] . . . Ben [Jonson] understood not the art of blending them [comedy and tragedy] so happily as not to destroy the effect of either."[36]

THE APPEAL TO NATURE

But the strongest argument of all was the appeal to nature, real life, the original Johnsonian defense.[37] In 1775 Mrs. Griffith wrote: ". . . his Plays cannot properly be stiled either Tragedies or Comedies, but are, in truth, a more natural species of composition than either."[38] The *Critical Review* continued this support in reviewing Richardson,[39] and Colman repeated the idea: ". . . *the natural, though mixt Dramas*, of Shakespear."[40] In 1787 the *Universal Magazine* pointed out that Shakespeare's combination followed nature, which does not impose restraint of attention fixed to one point, and further, "our *real character* is best shewn in our unguarded moments."[41] The *Analytical Review*, as noted above,[42] declared: "In Shakespeare, as in real life, buffoonery is mixed with sublimity. Such is

---

[33]*An Essay on the Character of Hamlet* (London: Flexney, 1777), p. 22.
[34]*Op. cit.*, III, 131-32.   [35]*Ibid.*, I, 240.   [36]*Ibid.*, II, 24.
[37]See D. Nichol Smith, *Shakespeare Criticism* (1916), pp. 97-98; and Lovejoy, *MLN*, XLII (1927), 445-47.
[38]*Op. cit.*, p. 172.   [39]LVII (1784), 107.
[40]In "Notes on the Art of Poetry," in *Prose on Several Occasions* (1787), III, 105.
[41]LXXXI (1787), 243.
[42]Under section on mingling of social ranks, in this chapter, p. 72.

man";[43] and the *European Magazine* repeated this idea.[44] So Johnson's original suggestion kept accumulating force throughout the century, even as his hint to Farmer was picked up and supported more and more vigorously. In concluding the subject of tragicomedy, only one further item of defense need be noted—and this is the most interesting of all—from *The Bee* (Edinburgh) in 1791: ". . . for besides the humour that is thereby produced, it [tragicomedy] elucidates the subject, by placing it in a variety of lights."[45] By the end of the century, therefore, tragicomedy was no longer on the defensive—it was now an *improving* agent: certainly a most interesting shift.

SUPERNATURAL CHARACTERS ATTACKED AND DEFENDED

Another aspect of decorum, distinctly minor, was the objection to supernatural characters.[46] In 1783 Blair stated the general classical theory that "wild or romantic circumstances . . . check passion in its growth."[47] But the late eighteenth century also defended Shakespeare on this point.

Mrs. Montagu in 1769 devoted one whole chapter to praise for Shakespeare's "Praeternatural Beings,"[48] placing them, as already indicated, above those of the ancients. The *Monthly Review* in the same year praised Shakespeare's fairies.[49] F. Gentleman approved of Shakespeare's witches in *Macbeth* as *characters* though he decried their effect.[50] Even Edward Taylor admitted that Shakespeare's supernatural beings were "Sanctified by tradition and vulgar credulity"[51] and voiced strong approval of the Ghost in

---

[43] V (1789), 568.   [44] XVI (1789), 15.   [45] I (1791), 59.
[46] For material preceding 1766 on this subject: *Spectator*, No. 419—Addison praises Shakespeare's art in the supernatural.
[47] *Op. cit.*, Lecture XLV, vol. II (1804), 323.   [48] *Op. cit.*, pp. 133-69.
[49] XLI (1769), 140.   [50] *Op. cit.*, I, 79.   [51] *Op. cit.*, p. 44.

Hamlet.[52] This same historical extenuation appeared in Blair in 1783: "strongly founded on popular belief."[53] Meanwhile Morgann had written a long note[54] defending such characters in general as based upon *magic* as compared with *nature*, with specific praise for *Macbeth* and *The Tempest*,[55] Caliban,[56] the ghosts,[57] and the writing "which holds a middle place between nature and magic" (i.e., the combination of Lear, Edgar, and the Fool).[58] In 1784 Tom Davies praised the Ghost in *Hamlet*[59] and Shakespeare's supernatural characters in general.[60] William Richardson, in the same year, approved of the ghosts in *Richard III*;[61] and finally the *Monthly Mirror* gave important historical analysis of Shakespeare's ghosts in *Hamlet* and *Macbeth*.[62] All this should be sufficient evidence to prove that Shakespeare's lack of decorum with reference to supernatural characters was not a matter of great moment to the critics of the late eighteenth century.

In all these aspects of decorum, therefore, Shakespeare has been ably defended by the late eighteenth century. And the credit for this defense goes most properly to the various periodicals mentioned above, particularly to *The Bee* (Edinburgh), and also to such individually prominent critics as Maurice Morgann, Tom Davies, and Mrs. Elizabeth Montagu.

---

[52]*Ibid.*, p. 45. George Colman declared in 1775 that "Caliban is as natural as Hamlet."—*The Gentleman*, No. VI.

[53]Lecture XLV, vol. II (1804), 323. See also Lecture XLVI, vol. II (1804), 357.

[54]*Op. cit.*, pp. 71-77 n.   [55]*Ibid,*, p. 74 n.

[56]*Ibid.*, p. 75 n. Compare the *British Magazine*, Jan., 1766, on Caliban.

[57]*Ibid.*, p. 76 n.   [58]*Ibid.*, p. 75 n.

[59]*Op cit.*, III, 24.   [60]*Ibid.*, II, 114-15, 178.

[61]*Op. cit.* (5th ed., 1798), p. 239.

[62]V (1798), 110, 170, 301. To be discussed in Chap. XIII, below.

Puns[63] and Blank Verse Accepted

Johnson remarked rather conclusively in 1769 that "Shakspeare never has six lines together without a fault,"[64] but Mrs. Montagu vigorously defended Shakespeare's use of puns, for example, as merely peculiar to the age of Elizabeth: ". . . our author was sensible it was but a false kind of wit, which he practiced from the hard necessity of the times: for in that age, the professor quibbled in his chair, the judge quibbled on the bench, the prelate quibbled in the pulpit, the statesman quibbled at the councilboard: nay even majesty quibbled on the throne."[65] This defense of Shakespeare's language the *Monthly Review* continued five years later: ". . . his 'most regular pieces produce some scenes and passages, highly derogatory to his incomparable merit, . . . he frequently trifles, is now and then obscure and sometimes, to gratify a vitiated age, indelicate.' It is, further, with equal truth remarked, by way of apology for the faults of this wonderful genius, that they 'may justly be attributed to the loose, quibbling licentious taste of his time; and that he, no doubt, on many occasions wrote wildly, merely to gratify the public; as Dryden wrote bombastically, and Congreve obscenely, to indulge the humours and engage the favour of their audience'."[66]

Morgann in 1777 returned to the defense of Shakespeare's punning: "The censure commonly passed on

---

[63]For early eighteenth-century reference to Shakespeare on this see the *Spectator*, No. 61.
[64]Boswell, *Life* (ed., Hill), II, 96. Compare Blair's *Lectures* (1783), Lecture III, vol. I (1804), 34-35.
[65]*Op. cit.*, p. 108.
[66]*Monthly Review*, L (1774), 187. The periodical is using Bell's Advertisement. (For this note I am indebted to Miss Louisa Soukup of the University of Michigan.)

Shakespeare's puns, is, I think, not well founded. I remember but very few, which are undoubtedly his, that may not be justifyed; and if *so*, a greater instance cannot be given of the art which he so peculiarly possessed of converting base things into excellence."[67] But the *Monthly Magazine* as late as 1797 was still worried by Shakespeare's puns,[68] and for that matter the idea is not by any means forgotten today.[69]

The support of blank verse[70] in drama was generally strong. Mrs. Montagu was the most eloquent apologist: "The charm arising from the tones of English blank verse cannot be felt by a foreigner.[71] . . . It rises gracefully into the sublime; it can slide happily into the familiar; hasten its career if impelled by vehemence of passion; pause in the hesitation of doubt; appear lingering and languid in dejection and sorrow; is capable of varying its accent, and adapting its harmony, to the sentiment it should convey, and the passion it would excite, with all the power of musical expression."[72] In 1773 the *Monthly Review* reviewed a poem in eulogy of blank verse and disparagement of rhyme,[73] and even Taylor the next year remarked: "By a parity of reasoning the absurd method of writing tragedies in rhimed verse might be defended."[74] In 1776 the *Gentleman's Magazine* attacked a "pedant rhimer,"[75] and in 1789

[67]*Op. cit.*, p. 105 n.

[68]III (1797), 275: "We are displeased, when Shakspeare intrudes a pun in the midst of his noble flights of fancy or tender strokes of passion." William Jackson in 1782 had assailed Shakespeare's use of alliteration and parenthesis—*Thirty Letters*, pp. 200-1 and 53-55 (of the 3rd ed.).

[69]See *Cornhill*, March, 1928, p. 318.

[70]For some material before 1766: *Monthly Review*, XIII (1755), 95; *British Magazine*, III (1762), 310; D. Webb, *Remarks on the Beauty of Poetry* (1762), with reference to Shakespeare, pp. 36 ff; Dryden as Neander in the *Essay of Dramatic Poesie* led the attack on blank verse.

[71]*Op. cit.*, pp. 211-12.   [72]*Ibid.*, p. 210.

[73]XLVIII (1773), 145. On blank verse in general.

[74]*Op. cit.*, Introduction, p. 9. See also pp. 61-62.

[75]XLVI (1776), 556. See also *Monthly Review*, LXX (1784). 22-3.

the *Analytical Review* declared rhymes in French drama "destroy entirely all representation of real life."[76] *The Bee* noted that whenever Shakespeare tried rhyme "he sunk greatly below the meanest poetaster of the present day,"[77] and suggested that the rhyming parts might be interpolations. Finally, perhaps the most vicious attack on rhyme appeared in the *Monthly Magazine* in April, 1797, when that periodical declared that rhyme was "a still lower species of wit" than Shakespeare's puns and that to deck tragedy in rhyme was absolutely absurd.[78] Hence there is no particular doubt that the alternative, blank verse, especially Shakespeare's, was generally accepted in this period as a matter of course.

The methods by which the late eighteenth century defended Shakespeare vigorously against all the traditional objections to his claims to dramatic excellence have now been indicated. Probably the most important of these several programs of defense was the criticism supplementary to Johnson's apology for Shakespeare's neglect of the unities. Next to that should come the fairly definite settling of the question of the poet's knowledge of the classics by the monumental work of Dr. Farmer. Other individual critics of prominence in this crusade of defense were, in order of importance, Maurice Morgann, Tom Davies, Mrs. Montagu, Mrs. Griffith, Martin Sherlock, and William Richardson. But the most effective work was really done by the many periodicals then flourishing, particularly by the *Universal Magazine, Monthly Review, The Bee* (Edinburgh), *Gentleman's Magazine,* the *Analytical Review,* and

---

[76] V (1789), 568.
[77] XVI (1793), 274. This same idea had already appeared in the *Lady's Magazine,* IX (1778), 531. *The Bee* also attacked rhyme in general—IV (1791), 291-95.
[78] III (1797), 273-78.

the *London Magazine*. It will now be appropriate to show how the late eighteenth century confirmed its point of view in defense by its attitude toward alterations of Shakespeare's plays made to comply with the "rules"; and, second, to summarize, compositely, this whole rejection of the traditional objections by following briefly the reaction of the English critics in the years 1766 to 1799 to the attacks on Shakespeare by the most prominent, and perhaps the most prejudiced, classicist of all, Voltaire.

CHAPTER VII

THE ATTACK UPON ALTERATION OF PLAYS

In the light of the traditional neo-classic objections to Shakespeare's plays, it is obvious that many dramatists of the seventeenth and eighteenth centuries would attempt to revise or adapt them to suit the taste of the new age and the new point of view.[1] That this happened rather often will be apparent from the enumerations listed below, but this chapter attempts simply to show how the late eighteenth century reacted in opposition to these many perversions.

Recent scholarship seems to be extremely interested in this one aspect of the attitude of the Restoration and eighteenth century toward Shakespeare, for within the last nine years three books and one pamphlet have appeared on the subject, and another book has devoted a chapter to the matter.[2] Each editor or critic has had his own ideas as to why there were so many alterations: Professor A. Nicoll in 1921 gave eight reasons[3] and in 1923 gave five;[4] Mr. H. B. Wheatley in 1913 gave four;[5] and Professor Nichol

[1]This chapter has nothing to do with travesties upon or operas from Shakespeare's plays (see Chap. III above). Most of it has already been published in *MLN*, XLV (1930), 446-51. It is reprinted here with permission.
[2]G. C. D. Odell, *Shakespeare from Betterton to Irving* (1921); A. Nicoll, *Dryden as an Adapter of Shakespeare* (1921), Shakespeare Assoc. Pamphlet, No. 8, 1922; M. Summers, *Shakespeare Adaptations* (1922); H. Spencer, *Shakespeare Improved* (1927); A. Nicoll, *A History of Restoration Drama* (1923), chap. II, sec. VI. See also his histories (published in 1925 and 1927) of drama from 1700-1800 (Titles in Appendix B).
[3]*Dryden as an Adapter of Shakespeare*, Preface, pp. 11-12.
[4]*A History of Restoration Drama*, p. 165.
[5]"Post-Restoration Quartos of Shakespeare's Plays," *The Library*, Third Series, IV (July, 1913), 238 ff. His four types of alterations appear on p. 244.

Smith as early as 1903 gave two.[6] But the fact remains that probably the general neo-classic reaction is the basic source, or as Professor Nichol Smith himself put it: "The one [type of alteration] respected the rules of classical drama, the other indulged the license of pantomime," the "improvisation of the theatre manager."[7]

THE POPULARITY OF ALTERATIONS

The number of these alterations provides considerable interest and apparently plenty of material for debate. It is not at all necessary here to enter the lists in this matter, but it will be sufficient merely to give a few figures in order to indicate the great popularity of this sort of dallying with Shakespeare. Johnson and Steevens' second edition, in 1778, has a short list,[8] but their fourth edition, in 1793, prints a list of seventy alterations, involving thirty-one plays, from 1669 to 1786.[9] This summary eclipses that in Malone's Preface of 1790, which noted sixty-six alterations, involving thirty plays from 1669 to 1777.[10] Hence Shakespeare was tampered with steadily from 1660 to 1800, and

---

[6]Introduction to *Eighteenth Century Essays on Shakespeare*, p. xii.
[7]*Ibid.*, p. xii.   [8]I, 242-47.   [9]I, 454-62.
[10]I, Part 1, pp. 236-42. Modern scholarship has produced conflicting figures. *Notes and Queries*, March 19, 1864, printed statistics of alterations extending from 1650 to 1800 as follows: 1650 to 1700—16 alterations; 1701-10: 6; 1711-20: 8; 1721-30: 1; 1731-40: 7; 1741-50: 2; 1751-60: 8; 1761-70: 6; 1771-80: 8; 1781-90: 2; 1791-1800: 3. The total here is 67 alterations from 1650 to 1800, which should be compared with Johnson and Steevens' summaries. Wheatley's article in 1913 listed 52 alterations, involving 28 plays, from 1660-1800. Professor A. Nicoll's *Dryden as an Adapter of Shakespeare* (1921) noted 28 alterations, involving 23 plays, from 1660 to 1700, and his recent book, *A History of Late Eighteenth Century Drama* (1927), dealing with the period from 1750 to 1800, tabulates 33 adaptations, involving 14 plays, from 1754 to 1798 [pp. 56-57, 111-12]. The excitement over these non-checking figures should be dedicated to some of the more brilliant mathematicians. Meanwhile, the point is amply proved: Shakespeare was rather badly mangled all the way from 1660 to 1800.

not necessarily the least in the closing decades of the eighteenth century. For detailed analysis of these tamperings, the reader should consult John Genest, *Some Account of the English Stage . . . from 1660 to 1830*.[11] The task now is simply to note the reaction of the late eighteenth century to all this manhandling of Shakespeare.[12]

Opinion favorable to alterations of Shakespeare proceeded, with some opposition, to about 1775, and after that generally disintegrated. The chief alterer from 1750 to 1775 was Garrick,[13] and the chief proponent of these adaptations was F. Gentleman, who was quite agreeable to Garrick's manipulations as well as those of all others.[14] The plays most generally changed were *Richard III, Timon of Athens, King Lear, Romeo and Juliet, Cymbeline*, and *Hamlet*. It will be best to take up the current in favor of alterations first.

---

[11]For example, Genest analyzes Tate's *Lear* and Colman's *Lear* in vol. V, 194-201; Cumberland's *Timon of Athens*, V, 316-21; Garrick's *Hamlet*, V, 343-47; Kemble's *The Tempest*, VI, 575-78; etc.

[12]For some interesting periodical material on this subject preceding 1766, see: *Spectator*, No. 40—on Tate's *Lear;* H. Fielding, *Historical Register* (1736) —versus Cibber; *Universal Magazine*, XVII (1755), 126—on Garrick's Song for the W. T.; **Critical Review*, I (1756), 144—on the "Absurdity of altering his plays." (Reviewing Marsh's *Winter's Tale*); *Monthly Review*, XIV(1756), 270—on *Catherine and Petruchio*, and Marsh's *Winter's Tale; Ibid.*, XX (1759), 462—on W. Hawkins' *Cymbeline; Ibid.*, XXVI (1762), 151—on Garrick's *Florizel and Perdita; Critical Review*, XIII (1762), 157—on Garrick's *Florizel and Perdita; Theatrical Review*, March 1, 1763 (p. 107)—on Shakespeare and Garrick.

[13]Alterations were also deliberately attacked before 1766 by Upton, *Critical Observations* (1746), pp. 14 n., 16; by the author of *Miscellaneous Observations on the Tragedy of "Hamlet"* (1752), Preface, pp. xi-xii; by Goldsmith, *Enquiry* (1759), chap. xi, "The Stage." Garrick's alterations include: *Romeo and Juliet*, 1750; *M. N. D.*, 1755, 1763 (with Colman); *The Tempest*, 1756; *King Lear*, 1756; *Catherine and Petruchio* (*T. of S.*), 1756; *Florizel and Perdita* (*W. T.*), 1756, 1758; *Antony and Cleopatra*, 1758 (with Capell); *Cymbeline*, 1761; *Hamlet*, 1771.

[14]See below in this chapter, p. 85.

The *British Magazine* in 1767 praised Cibber's adaptation of *Richard III*: "The late laureat has . . . made up a compleat tragedy of Richard the Third, which may vie with the best pieces of our great dramatic poet."[15] Similarly, the *Monthly Review* in 1768 approved Dance's alteration of *Timon of Athens*[16] and in 1771, Cumberland's.[17] Francis Gentleman in 1770 applauded Tate's *Lear*[18] (rejecting Colman's[19]) and offered some suggestions himself for further alteration;[20] he also accepted Cibber's *Richard III*[21] and Garrick's *Romeo and Juliet*[22] and *Cymbeline*.[23] Two years later the *Macaroni and Theatrical Magazine* approved Garrick's adaptation of *Hamlet:* "To clear this piece of these charges (which were in part not ill-founded) has been the task of the present revisor [Garrick]: how far he has succeeded, the applauses of a crowded and judicious audience have already testified."[24] Bell's *Edition* of Shakespeare, 1774, followed the theaters in expunging "obscure, indelicate"[25] passages, and finally Mrs. Griffith in 1775 may be cited as a feminine representative of this waning point of view: Tate's *Lear* is better because "our feelings are often a surer guide than our reason."[26] This date practi-

---

[15] VIII (1767), 627.
[16] XXXIX (1768), 81: "The play, however, in this its new form is, in some respects, better fitted for the stage, than it is in the original."
[17] XLV (1771), 507: "This performance hath now more regularity and decorum [Note these two Neo-classic points] to recommend it to the taste of the present age, than it could boast in the wild and rough state in which it was left by its great Author."
[18] *Op. cit.*, I, 352, 353, 366. "We can by no means agree with the last mentioned gentleman [Colman] that the love episode of Edgar and Cordelia is superfluous or unaffecting" (p. 353).
[19] *Ibid.*, I, 360-62, 365-66, 368.
[20] *Ibid.*, I, 359. He did the same thing in I, 178-79 for *Romeo and Juliet*.
[21] *Ibid.*, I, 3-4: ". . . much indebted for its variety, compactness, and spirit, to the late Colley Cibber."
[22] *Ibid.*, I, 172. [23] *Ibid.*, II, 76. [24] Dec., 1772, p. 119.
[25] Advertisement, pp. 5-6. [26] *Op. cit.*, p. 351.

cally concludes the critics' approval of the mangling of Shakespeare in this century.

The Growing Disapproval

On the other side is an interesting development, from several points of view. Individual plays are rescued from alterations and restored to Shakespeare; prompter's changes are rejected; Garrick is flayed, and there is also an appeal to retain Shakespeare's original language.[27] As early in this period as 1767 the *British Magazine* declared that the Duke of Buckingham [shire][28] had adapted *Julius Cæsar* "with so little success, that his alterations were never adopted by the stage."[29] In the same year it attacked Otway's manipulation of *Romeo and Juliet:* ". . . the great merit of the piece is evidently proved by Mr. Otway's vain attempt to alter it."[30] The next year the *Monthly Review* trampled on Tate: "The admirers of Shakespeare are obliged to Mr. Colman for having refined the excellent tragedy of *King Lear* 'from the alloy of Tate, which has so long been suffered to debase it.' "[31] In 1774 the same periodical called for the Fool in *Lear*: ". . . it is a matter of great question with us, whether the fool in King Lear was not a more general favorite than the old monarch himself."[32] Two years later the *Universal Magazine* explained, defensively and humorously, Garrick's alteration of *Hamlet*: The gravediggers complain to Garrick about being left out of the play. Garrick answers: ". . . the age does not like to be reminded of mortality: 'tis . . . very disgustful

---

[27]These four developments were occurring almost simultaneously.
[28]For this emendation I am indebted to Professor H. Spencer, *Shakespeare Improved*, p. 375, No. 10.
[29]VIII (1767), 572.   [30]VIII (1767), 622.
[31]XXXVIII (1768), 245.
[32]L (1774), 145. For this note I am indebted to Miss Louisa Soukup of the University of Michigan.

to a well-bred company"; whereupon Shakespeare is allowed to appear in spirit and in imitation of the famous "Angels and ministers of grace defend us" scene, addresses Garrick:

> Freely correct my Page;
> I wrote to please a rude unpolish'd age;
> Thou, happy man, art fated to display
> Thy dazzling talents in a brighter day;
> Let me partake this night's applause with thee,
> And thou shalt share immortal fame with me.[33]

THE TURNING OF THE TIDE

But the most vigorous and comprehensive objectors to alterations of Shakespeare appeared in 1784 and 1791, in Tom Davies and *The Bee*. Davies successively, with some disgust, rejected Cibber's *King Lear*,[34] Davenant's *Macbeth*,[35] Garrick in general and his *Macbeth* in particular,[36] Buckinghamshire's *Julius Cæsar*,[37] Tate's *Lear*,[38] Colman's *Lear*,[39] and Garrick's *Hamlet*.[40] This wholesale overthrow of the alterers turned the tide in favor of Shakespeare, for *The Bee* in 1791 continued the devastation: "Shakespeare said just enough in one significant line [in *Measure for Measure*], which is only spun out, in the five finical modern ones";[41] "with what a disgraceful motely [sic] of nonsense and absurdity has this modern poet [Aaron Hill] confounded the beauties of Shakespeare in this play";[42] "Florizel and Perdita, or the Sheep-Shearing . . . Shakespeare is here mangled as usual";[43] and the final, slashing blow: "Bene-

[33]LVIII (Feb., 1776), 101-2.
[35]*Ibid.*, II, 116-17.
[37]*Ibid.*, 203.
[39]*Ibid.*, 261.
[41]III (1791), 39-40.
[43]V (1791), 78.

[34]*Op. cit.*, I, 64.
[36]*Ibid.*, 118.
[38]*Ibid.*, 261.
[40]*Ibid.*, III, 145-47.
[42]II (1791), 279. (*Henry V.*)

dict was ... grossly injured by Garrick's alterations ... it is impossible both to alter and amend him [Shakespeare]."⁴⁴ This last sweeping statement the *Monthly Mirror* fully corroborated in 1797 by attacking Garrick again: "Shakspere has always suffered from unskilful alterations, as is plainly proved from many vain attempts which are buried in oblivion; and I question whether *Romeo and Juliet* has gained much by the amendments of Mr. Garrick."⁴⁵

Such a rejection of Garrick's adaptations as that just suggested was by no means new. Horace Walpole in 1769 remarked on Garrick's "insufferable nonsense about Shakspeare."⁴⁶ Johnson the same year laughed at Garrick "as a shadow" of Shakespeare, with the addendum that "Many of Shakspeare's plays are the worse for being acted, *Macbeth*, for instance."⁴⁷ In 1785 he attacked Garrick even more vigorously: "He has not made Shakspeare better known,"⁴⁸ and (to Garrick directly): "I doubt much if you ever examined one of his [Shakespeare's] plays from the first scene to the last."⁴⁹ Garrick himself in 1776 was rather dubious about his procedure: "I have ventured to produce *Hamlet* with alterations. It was the most impudent thing I ever did in all my life; but I had sworn I would not leave the stage till I rescued that noble play from all the rubbish of the fifth Act."⁵⁰ And finally his biographer, Arthur Murphy, in 1801 corroborated Garrick's doubt, for he says that Garrick, after altering *Hamlet*, "saw his error" because "he never published his alterations."⁵¹

⁴⁴III (1791), 112.   ⁴⁵IV (1797), 292.
⁴⁶*Letters* (ed. Mrs. Paget-Toynbee, 1904), VII, 325. The date of the letter was Oct. 16.
⁴⁷Boswell's *Life* (ed. Hill), II, 92.   ⁴⁸*Ibid.*, V, 244.
⁴⁹*Ibid.*, 244, n.
⁵⁰*Correspondence* (ed. G. P. Baker, 1907), II, 126. The date of the letter was Jan. 10.
⁵¹*Life of David Garrick* (Dublin, 1801), p. 308.

In conclusion, it might be well to add two minor reactions in this period to the alterations of Shakespeare. Even F. Gentleman, the chief defender of Garrick, abhorred prompter's manipulations: "prompters books such miserable, mutilated objects"[52]—a point of view which W. Kenrick in 1773 repeated: ". . . the greater part of the rest [of the principal parts—that is, characters—in Shakespeare's dramas] injudiciously shortened, with a view to accommodate them to the incapacities of inferior performers."[53] But perhaps the most interesting objection, at least from a modern editor's point of view, is Richard Warner's appeal in 1768: "And I cannot but observe, that if this method should prevail, of changing the language of the age into modern English, our venerable bard may, in time, be made to look as aukward as his cotemporary, Sir Philip Sidney now does, as trick'd out by the hands of his modern tire-woman, Mrs. Stanley."[54] With this remark we may well drop stage alterations—the attitude of the late eighteenth century toward them has become steadily more and more adverse[55]—and turn to the greatest manipulator of Shakespeare's language in the century, and one of the most conspicuous representatives of the neo-classic school.

---

[52] *Op. cit.*, I, 136.
[53] In his *Introduction to the School of Shakespeare* (London: Kenrick, 1773), p. 14.
[54] *A Letter to David Garrick* (1768), pp. 73-74.
[55] For some supplementary material in periodicals on this subject of alterations, from 1766 to 1799, see: *Critical Review*, XXXII (1771), 470—on Cumberland's *T. of A.*; *Monthly Review, or Literary Journal*, III (1790), 347—on Kemble's *Tempest*; *Critical Review*, LXXI (1791), 105—on Kemble's *Tempest*; *Gentleman's Magazine*, LXI (1791), 1098—on Proposal for regeneration and modernizing of Shakspeare.

CHAPTER VIII

THE REACTION AGAINST VOLTAIRE[1]

Modern scholarship has failed to give an adequate survey of the English reaction to Voltaire in the late eighteenth century.[2] It has failed because it has neglected the two aspects of Voltaire which the English writers from 1766 to 1799 damned most vigorously: that is, Voltaire's

[1] This chapter has already been published in *Studies in Philology*, Oct., 1930. For the texts of Voltaire's strictures on Shakespeare, and for secondary material on Voltaire, see T. R. Lounsbury, *Shakespeare and Voltaire* (1902) and C. M. Haines, *Shakespeare in France* (1925); also my own Bibliography in *Studies in Philology*, Extra Series I (May, 1929), 92-94, reprinted now in Appendix B. Mr. Haines' book is the most recent and best brief study of Voltaire's attitude toward Shakespeare and has generally disposed of the disagreeable task of collecting here all Voltaire's animadversions on Shakespeare. But certainly Mr. Haines has some omissions, mainly secondary, which should be pointed out. For example, the following letters deserve a specific reference not to be found in Mr. Haines' book: letter to Thériot, October 26, 1726; letters to George Keate, April 16, 1760, and May 17, 1768. Further, the *Weekly Amusement*, IV (October 12, 1765), 653-54, quotes Voltaire on Shakespeare from the *Essay on the Free Liberty of Genius in a Nation*, and the *Gentleman's Magazine*, XLI (1771), 392, quotes from Voltaire's *Questions Concerning the Encyclopédie* on Shakespeare. Five casual references to Mr. Lounsbury's text seem also a little inadequate (pp. 15, 42, 45, 62, 64). But the most superficial section of Mr. Haines' book bibliographically is its list of secondary material on Voltaire and Shakespeare. None of the magazines listed in my Bibliography (noted above) are cited, and even some of the books are omitted. One particular item that Mr. Haines missed, for example, was Mr. R. S. Crane's "The Diffusion of Voltaire's Writings in England," *Mod. Phil.*, XX (Feb., 1923), 261-74. Certainly my more complete bibliography calls for more study than either Mr. Haines' text or my limited point of view can afford.

[2] Mr. Haines gives only eight pages to it: pp. 16, 44-47, 61, 66-67. Obviously this point was to a large extent outside his picture, but his brilliant handling of Taylor and Rutledge suggested the possibilities of the field, in which this chapter is now involved. And Lounsbury's three chapters (XIV, XV, and XX) are inadequate, as this chapter will show.

envy and mistranslation of Shakespeare.³ Whether the Frenchman deliberately manhandled Shakespeare will be left for the reader to decide after the discussion of the English reaction below, but certainly one example of Voltaire's paraphrasing tendencies will be apropos now.

Voltaire's Mistranslation of Shakespeare

In his *Appel*,⁴ Voltaire starts right off with the remark that Hamlet was far from suspecting that his father had been poisoned *"par eux"*—that is, his father *and mother*.⁵ He then proceeds to telescope Scenes 3 and 4 of Act I and all the Ghost's speeches into *one* speech.⁶ He loses Rosencrantz and Guildenstern in Scene 2 of Act II,⁷ and slips over most of the players—Hamlet part of this scene.⁸ In Act III he skips the whole of Scene 1, which incidentally includes the famous "To be or not to be," and again combines the King and Queen in the guilt: "Ils soupçonnent" and "ils tremblent d'être découverts."⁹ Perhaps his wildest perversion appears at the murder of Polonius: "Hamlet ne doute pas que ce ne soit le Roi qui s'est caché là pour l'entendre."¹⁰ . . . "a tué le Chambellan Polonius . . . en le prenant pour un rat!"¹¹ He next omits the Ghost in the closet scene, jumps the whole first four scenes of Act IV, to Ophelia's death (omitting the plotting of the King and Laertes), and then goes to Act V, Scene 2 to explain

---

³Only twice does Mr. Haines sully Voltaire by reference to his envy of Shakespeare (pp. 59-60, 72), and only three times does he mention the Frenchman's inadequate translation of the English poet (pp. 13, 37, 42).

⁴*Appel à toutes les Nations de l'Europe des Jugemens d'un Écrivain Anglais* (1761). Mr. Haines spends three pages on this text (pp. 37-39). Nowhere in those three pages does he mention Voltaire's fearful mangling of *Hamlet*—he concentrates his attention on the French critic's poetical transliteration and on some of his arguments against Shakespeare.

⁵*Ibid.*, p. 7.   ⁶*Ibid.*, pp. 11-13.   ⁷*Ibid.*, p. 14.
⁸*Ibid.*, pp. 16-17.   ⁹*Ibid.*, pp. 19-20.   ¹⁰*Ibid.*, p. 22.
¹¹*Ibid.*, p. 27.

how Hamlet broke away from Rosencrantz and Guildenstern.¹² He thereupon starts backward to pick up the graveyard scene (almost omitting Horatio, whom he has termed "Le Soldat") and the plotting of the King and Laertes,¹³ and returns to his thread with the announcement that the *King* poisoned the point of the sword: ". . . dont j'ai trempé la pointe dans un poison très subtil."¹⁴ The duel receives considerable attention, though Osric's verbiage and Laertes' confession are both omitted,¹⁵ and finally Voltaire manages to get the ending wrong "Un certain Fort-en-bras, *parent* [my italics] de la Maison qui a conquis la Pologne"!¹⁶ Can one wonder that the English got rather upset over this sort of thing by Voltaire?¹⁷

Yet Voltaire did, rather frequently, praise Shakespeare. In 1733 appeared extravagant eulogy: "Si belles scènes, des morceaux si grands et si terribles"; "des idées bizarres et gigantesques de cet auteur"; "il ne faudrait pas l'imiter";¹⁸ in 1761: "Mais sous ces voiles on découvrira de la vérité, de la profondeur—et je ne sçais quoi . . . C'est un diamond brut";¹⁹ in 1765: ". . . but as soon as they [the English] indulged the free liberty of genius, England produced Spencers [*sic*], Shakespears, Bacons, and at last

---

¹²*Ibid.*, pp. 22-24. ¹³*Ibid.*, pp. 25-26, 28-29, 5. ¹⁴*Ibid.*, p. 29.
¹⁵*Ibid.*, pp. 29-30. ¹⁶*Ibid.*, pp. 30-31.

¹⁷Yet, in his three pages on the *Appel*, Mr. Haines mentions not a word about these perversions. Nor can one accept his generalizations on pp. 43, 46, 47, especially the first: ". . . the historical method of inquiry was totally alien to the abstract rationalism of the eighteenth century." This is an interesting remark in the light of the fact that one of Voltaire's chief criticisms of Shakespeare was that Shakespeare merely rehashed other men's plots; incidentally, too, Voltaire had some idea of the barbarous age of Elizabeth. See below.

¹⁸*Lettres Philosophiques, ou Lettres sur les Anglais*, in *Oeuvres Complètes de V.* (Paris: Garnier, 1879), XXII, 149.

¹⁹*Appel*, p. 38.

Lockes and Newtons";[20] even in 1776, "Shakespeare . . . avait des étincelles de génie."[21] . . . "Je dois dire que parmi ces bizarres pièces, il en est plusieurs où l'on retrouve de beaux traits pris dans la nature, et qui tiennent au sublime de l'art, quoi qu'il n'y ait aucun art chez lui."[22] And finally one Englishman, Martin Sherlock, dragged a comment, à la Boswell, out of Voltaire which may well stand last: "On my observing, That foreign nations do not relish our Shakspeare; 'that,' replied he, 'is true, but they only know him by translations. Slight faults remain, great beauties vanish, and a man born blind cannot persuade himself that a rose is beautiful when the thorns prick his fingers.' A charming expression and worthy of its author," concludes Sherlock.[23] To be sure, but it is magnificent irony in the light of Voltaire's own *Appel*.

Voltaire's Strictures on Shakespeare

It is possible to divide Voltaire's strictures on Shakespeare into two stages, the first extending from 1733 to 1761 and consisting of attacks based upon the unities and decorum, and the second from 1761 to 1776, wherein the same objects of attack appear, plus a few other ideas: that Shakespeare merely rehashed other people's plots, that he wrote blank verse because he was lazy and prose because he could not write poetry. In this second stage, also, Voltaire admitted that Shakespeare's grossness was due largely to the barbarity of the Elizabethan Age. This sum-

---
[20]Quoted in *Weekly Amusement*, IV (October 12, 1765), 653-54.
[21]*Lettre à l'Académie française* [Aug. 25, 1776] in *Oeuvres Complètes de V.*, XXX, 364.
[22]*Ibid.*, p. 365.
[23]*A Fragment on Shakspeare* (1786), pp. 33-34. Mr. G. Hallam comments on Voltaire: ". . . but he imitated Shakespeare . . . and no compliment approaches that of imitation."—*Shakespeariana* of the N. Y. Shakespeare Soc., IX (1892), 38. Mr. Haines seems to neglect this point of view in Voltaire.

mary, though rather obviously simple,[24] will serve as a general background for a few excerpts from Voltaire's texts on Shakespeare. In this procedure merely three texts will be used, dated 1733, 1761, and 1776, as representative.[25] In all three of these it is possible, first, to point out the attack based upon the unities. In 1733 Voltaire remarked that Shakespeare was "sans la moindre connaissance des règles";[26] he praised Cato as "une tragédie raisonnable"[27] and lamented that "Les monstres brillants de Shakespeare plaisent mille fois plus que la sagesse moderne."[28] This point of view is continued in 1761,[29] and in 1776 appears again in these sarcastic quips: "a cinq cents milles sur le continent" and "actions . . . qui furent un demi-siècle."[30] His attack on decorum began in 1733: "sans la moindre étincelle de bon goût,"[31] and "ces bouffoneries,"[32] in 1761: the English genius "ne craint les idées les plus basses, ni les plus gigantesques"[33] in writing for "Les Bourgeois de Londres";[34] in 1776: "Il n'y a point de singe en Afrique, point de babouin, qui n'ait plus de goût que Shakespeare."[35] This grossness of Shakespeare seemed to worry Voltaire considerably, for in a letter to Horace Walpole he regrets that the latter "donne la préférence à son *grossier buffon* Shake-

---

[24]Voltaire's historical excuse for Shakespeare's grossness appeared as early as 1733, for example.
[25]For a generally complete list, see C. M. Haines' Bibliography in *Shakespeare in France*. The three texts for these years have already been cited above. As for the plays, *Othello's* influence is represented by *Zaire*, *Hamlet* by *Semiramis* and *Eriphyle*, *Macbeth* by *Mohamet*, and *Julius Caesar* by *La Mort de César*.
[26]*Op. cit.*, XXII, 149.   [27]*Ibid.*, 154.
[28]*Ibid.*, 156.   [29]*Op. cit.*, pp. 38-39.
[30]*Op. cit.*, XXX, 356.   [31]*Op. cit.*, XXII, 149.
[32]*Ibid.*, p. 150.   [33]*Op. cit.*, p. 37.
[34]*Ibid.*, p. 33.
[35]*Op. cit.*, XXX, 363. Quoting Rymer, with approval. The passage quoted was printed in the *Gentleman's Magazine*, XLVI (1776), 556.

speare sur Racine et sur Corneille";[36] and in another letter Shakespeare is "ressemblant plus souvent à Gilles, qu'à Corneille."[37] Other minor representative thrusts at Shakespeare in passing include: ". . . il faut savoir que Shakespeare avait eu peu d'éducation";[38] ". . . on n'a jamais représenté, sur aucun théâtre étranger aucune des pièces de Shakespeare" [this in 1776];[39] "c'est la lie du peuple qui parle son langage";[40] the Danes are "idolâtres au premier acte" but have "une église et un cimetière" in the fifth;[41] ". . . comment tant de merveilles se sont accumulées dans une seule tête?"[42] With regard to the last question Voltaire answers by noting that all Shakespeare's tragedies are taken from stories or romances.[43] These few quotations, together with the preceding paragraph, will indicate, possibly, how comprehensively Voltaire managed to cover the program of traditional objections to Shakespeare. And his spirit was so bitter that one must expect the reaction against him to be similarly tense.

The Reaction of British Critics

Before 1766 a reaction had already set in against the Frenchman. The *Monthly Review* three times attacked him, in 1755, 1761, and 1764.[44] Foote and Guthrie both flayed him in 1747, and Aaron Hill did not spare him in his Advertisement to his translation of *Mérope* in 1749.[45] In 1759

---

[36]Letter CCLXXXVII, quoted in the *Analytical Review*, V (1789), 567.
[37]Letter CLVII, quoted in the *Analytical Review*, IV (1789), 89.
[38]In *The Bee* (Edinburgh), IV (1791), 293.   [39]*Op. cit.*, XXX, 367.
[40]*Ibid.*, p. 352.   [41]*Ibid.*, p. 355.   [42]*Appel*, p. 31.
[43]*Ibid.*, p. 32. For attack on blank verse, see *ibid.*, pp. 34-37.
[44]XIII (1755), 495; XXIV (1761), *138; XXX (1764), 536. See also *New Memoirs of Literature*, VI (1727), 461; *Caribbeana*, I (1741), 33, 291; *Critical Review*, XVIII (1764), 467; *Gentleman's Magazine*, XXXV (1765), 469.
[45]Lounsbury is excellent on these early attacks on Voltaire: see his

Arthur Murphy prefixed an *Epistle to Voltaire* to his *The Orphan of China*, and Kames continued the war in 1762. Horace Walpole in his Preface to the second edition of *The Castle of Otranto*, in 1765, defended Shakespeare against Voltaire, dubbing the latter's criticisms "effusions of wit . . . rather than the result of judgment," and pointing out Voltaire's misunderstanding of English: "as incorrect and incompetent as his knowledge of our history." Voltaire apparently made "a very civil answer," as Walpole noted later, in 1768, when he decided to drop the subject.[46] Finally Johnson's *Preface* (1765) trampled heavily upon Voltaire,[47] and when Voltaire replied in the *Dictionnaire Philosophique*,[48] Boswell commented: "Voltaire was an antagonist with whom I thought Johnson should not disdain to contend. I pressed him to answer. He said, he perhaps might; but he never did."[49] Nevertheless, Johnson and the rest had cleared the way for the subsequent demolition of Voltaire.

The British reaction against Voltaire from 1766 to 1799 assumed two distinct forms, the first involving the reply to Voltaire on the points of the traditional objections to Shakespeare, in particular the unities, decorum, tragicomedy, and blank verse; and the second developing a direct and violent attack on Voltaire as a critic, as a translator, and as a man, the latter particularly with regard to his envy of Shakespeare. Only one Englishman, apparently, Maurice Morgann, attempted to excuse Voltaire's attitude: "We have been charged indeed by a Foreign

---

chapters VII ("Resentment of the English,") XII ("The Critic Criticized"), XIII ("The Voltaire-Walpole Correspondence"), and XIV ("Two New English Adversaries").

[46]See Walpole's *Short Notes of My Life*, June 20, 1768 (ed. P. Cunningham, 1861), p. lxxv.

[47]See D. Nichol Smith's *Shakespeare Criticism* (1916), pp. 96, 99, 112, 116.

[48]Quoted in Boswell's *Johnson*, (ed. Hill), I, 499 n.   [49]*Ibid.*, I, 499.

writer with an overmuch admiring of this Barbarian";[50] but this charge arises from the fact that the editors "have never undertaken to discharge the disgraceful incumbrances of some wretched productions, which have long hung heavy on his fame."[51] Yet Morgann adds quickly: ". . . this wild, this uncultivated Barbarian, has not yet obtained one half of his fame"[52] and proceeds immediately to write one of the greatest panegyrics of Shakespeare ever produced in the eighteenth century.[53] So Morgann himself had no respect for Voltaire, and as for the rest of the English critics—*verba deficiunt*. Let us take up the above points in order.[54]

BRITISH REPLY TO THE TRADITIONAL OBJECTIONS MADE BY VOLTAIRE

Voltaire's attack on Shakespeare for violating the unities received its most vigorous answer early in this period from Mrs. Montagu: "Heaven-born genius acts from something superior to rules . . . and has a right of appeal to nature herself.[55] . . . Mr. Johnson . . . has greatly obviated all that can be objected to our author's neglect of the unities of time and place. . . ."[56] The poet who bought at a great price the lamp of a famous philoso-

[50]*An Essay on the Dramatic Character of Sir John Falstaff*, p. 61. Compare Jackson's later (*Thirty Letters*, 1782) extenuation of Voltaire's objections to *Paradise Lost* because "they are the objections of a man of taste to the productions of a man of genius." (3rd ed., p. 169.)

[51]*Op. cit.*, p. 64. [52]*Ibid.*, p. 64. [53]*Ibid.*, p. 65. See also p. 68.

[54]Only three chapters of Lounsbury's book touch this reaction (i.e., XIV, XV, and XX) and all these very inadequately, discussing really not much more than Johnson, Mrs. Montagu, E. Taylor, Morgann, and Baretti —the most prominent critics. This chapter is therefore intended to contradict Lounsbury's twentieth chapter: "Indifference of the English."

[55]*An Essay on the Writings and Genius of Shakespear, Compared with the Greek and French Dramatic Poets, with some Remarks upon the Misrepresentations of Mons. de Voltaire* (London: J. Dodsley, 1769), pp. 7-8. Compare p. 79.

[56]*Ibid.*, p. 15. See also pp. 55-56.

pher, expecting that by its assistance his lucubrations would become equally celebrated, was little more absurd than those poets who suppose their dramas will be excellent if they are regulated by Aristotle's clock."[57] But other critics supplemented Mrs. Montagu. Mrs. Griffith in 1775 replied directly to Voltaire: ". . . he [Voltaire] unfairly tries him [Shakespeare] by Pedant laws, which our Author either did not know, or regarded not. His compositions are a distinct species of the Drama; and not being an imitation of the Greek one, cannot be said to have infringed its rules."[58] Tom Davies, in 1784, grew even more violent about "French writers, who are always chewing the husks of the Greek and Roman critics";[59] he goes on to support Morgann's idea that Aristotle would have worshipped Shakespeare,[60] and concludes that foreigners should note that the "English stage was in its infancy" when Shakespeare wrote, that the unities were "almost unknown," and that the writers who used them "had little else to recommend them to their audiences."[61] Three years later the *Universal Magazine* declared that Voltaire could not step out of the line the ancients had chalked up for him and hence had not the strength to comprehend Shakespeare.[62] And finally, both the *Analytical Review* and *The Bee*, in 1789 and 1791, smote the same final blow: Foreign critics judge by *rule* and hence cannot appreciate Shakespeare; the rules may do for French drama, but "Shakespeare's works, thank heaven! are as unlike French drama as possible . . . Who . . . ever saw an eagle taught to dance in a certain round?"[63]

[57]*Ibid.*, pp. 5-6.
[58]In her Preface to *The Morality of Shakespeare's Drama*, p. vi.
[59]*Dramatic Miscellanies*, III, 130.
[60]*Ibid.*, III, 130; see Morgann, *op. cit.*, pp. 69-70.   [61]*Ibid.*, III, 131.
[62]LXXXI (1787), 244.
[63]This quotation is taken from the *Analytical Review*, V (1789), 567, but the

In the matter of decorum Mrs. Montagu is again the chief defender of Shakespeare. "There never was a more barbarous mode of writing than that of the French romances in the last age,"[64] she declares, carrying the battle into Voltaire's own camp; Corneille also "complied with the bad taste of the age."[65] She then further defends Shakespeare's occasional slips by noting the many, and hence extenuating, great passages in his work.[66] The *London Magazine* in 1772 further espoused the historical defense: ". . . the English vulgar love . . . to see princes rail grossly at each other"[67]—which Voltaire himself admitted, as noted also in the *Monthly Review* in 1776.[68] Finally, Tom Davies, in 1784, may be cited: "Voltaire, who in examining the merit of our author's plays, disdains the use of no unfair method to depreciate them, has ridiculed this passage, as if the mention of a mouse [in *Hamlet*] were beneath the dignity of tragedy";[69] Davies defends Shakespeare by emphasizing the tone of the scene and by adducing some of Sophocles' similar "lownesses," and concludes: "Men of solid judgement and true taste despise such refinement."[70]

Minor aspects of decorum also receive some attention from the irritated English critics. F. Gentleman in 1770 disposed, in general, of Voltaire's worry over tragicomedy by the particular remark: "Mr. Voltaire's objections to the first scene of the fifth act [*Hamlet*] . . . are in a great

---

same idea appears in *The Bee* (Edinburgh), IV (1791), 290. The section below on French drama should also be noted in connection with the unities.

[64]*Op. cit.*, p. 5.

[65]*Ibid.*, p. 74. For this historical defense, see also the *Monthly Review*, XLI (1769), 130.

[66]*Ibid.*, p. 79. See also her pp. 2-3, on an English gentleman's taste.

[67]XLI (1772), 494.

[68]LV (1776), 474. And see above: the *Appel*, p. 32.

[69]*Op. cit.*, III, 6.

[70]*Ibid.*, III, 7. See also the *Looker-On* (1792), No. 77 (Chalmers, XXXVII, 154).

measure true, yet the characters are so finely drawn, such pointed satire, and such instructive moral sentiments arise, as . . . raise it far above insipid propriety."[71] The *European Magazine*, using M. Sherlock (with reference to this same scene), recurred to the historical defense again: Voltaire's claim is unfair because Shakespeare wrote to fill his house.[72] But the most interesting, though indirect, reply is that of Mrs. Montagu, who once again leaps beyond mere defense and declares that Voltaire should have applauded Shakespeare for being able to write *both* comedy and tragedy.[73] Blank verse is also defended by Mrs. Montagu: "The charm arising from the tones of English blank verse cannot be felt by a foreigner,"[74] to which should be added her famous eulogy of English blank verse.[75]

British Attacks on Voltaire as a Writer

If Voltaire received rather harsh treatment from 1766 to 1799 for his neo-classic critical tendencies, he accumulated even more vicious thrusts from the English as a critic in general, as a translator of Shakespeare, and as an envious, malicious, treacherous man.

His plays and works were assailed, together with French drama in general, and he was compared deliberately, and unfavorably, with Shakespeare himself. The *London Magazine* in 1767 rejected his attitude toward Terrasson,[76] and Mrs. Montagu dubbed his criticism superficial, mere *beaux mots*.[77] The *Hibernian Magazine* in 1773 hit him harder: "His taste is rather delicate than just; he is a witty satyrist, a bad critic, and a dabbler in the abstracted sciences."[78]

---

[71] *Op. cit.*, I, 49-50. Reprinted in *London Magazine*, XXXIX (1770), 3.
[72] X (1786), 4.   [73] *Op. cit.*, pp. 284-85.
[74] *Ibid.*, p. 211.   [75] *Ibid.*, p. 210.
[76] XXXVI (1767), 628.   [77] *Op. cit.*, p. 17.
[78] Pp. 347-48. The same extract appeared in the *London Magazine*, XLII (June, 1773), 278, and in *Scots Magazine*, XXXV (June, 1773), 304.

An essay by William Jones in the *London Magazine* attacked his tragedy,[79] and the *Hibernian Magazine* in 1781 became even more contemptuous: "Voltaire was a great literary cook. Give him good meats, no man knew better how to dress them. But they must be given him, for he was not rich enough to provide them himself. . . . He took the gold of Shakespeare, Virgil, . . . and the silver of La Fare, Chanlieu, . . . and melted them together. . . . The metal produced . . . was Corinthian brass."[80] Davies flatly rejected his *La Mort de César* in 1784,[81] and Sherlock in 1786 attacked his style in general: "The brilliant, the flowery, the light Voltaire has introduced a fashion, as it were, of reading without attention. This magician has infused into our minds a most pernicious idleness; and a beauty, which is not superficial, now passes unobserved."[82] The *Analytical Review* in 1789 printed essays by the Marquis D'Argenson attacking Voltaire's tragedy again,[83] and *The Bee* continued the attack in 1793.[84] Finally the *Universal Magazine* in 1794 delivered a coup de grace at his philosophy, as inferior to Bolingbroke's.[85] All in all Voltaire's creative activity was rather roughly handled throughout the period.

An attack on Voltaire's drama implied an attack on French drama in general, which may be indicated briefly. Horace Walpole fired a salvo in his Postscript to *The*

---

[79]XLIII (1774), 35. The same extract appeared in *Scots Magazine*, XXXVI (1774), 32.
[80]P. 259. This extract appeared also in the *Lady's Magazine*, XII (1781), 189. It came originally from M. Sherlock's *Letters on Various Subjects*.
[81]*Op. cit.*, II, 204-5.
[82]*Op. cit.*, p. 21. Compare his further attacks on Voltaire in his *Nouvelles Lettres d'un Voyageur Anglais* (1780), letters XXXVIII-XLIV.
[83]IV (1789), 229. They appeared also in the *Literary Magazine*, VIII (1792), 288.
[84]XIV (1793), 158-60. [85]XCIV (1794), 427.

Mysterious Mother (1768).[86] Mrs. Montagu meanwhile had spent a great deal of time and energy in demolishing the French drama of the period: "French Tragedians . . . attend not to the nature of the man whom they represent";[87] "French tragedians . . . deviate . . . even from the general character of the age and country";[88] she also managed to include thrusts at the love element,[89] and put Corneille below Shakespeare.[90] The *Monthly Review* continued the attack on Corneille and referred to Mrs. Montagu for support.[91] Blair added, in 1783, that Shakespeare surpasses the French tragedians because "his scenes are full of sentiment and action,"[92] and finally the *Analytical Review* denounced the "Vapid love and eternal declamation" in Racine and Corneille as *not* real.[93] All this was indirectly derogatory of Voltaire.[94]

But Voltaire himself received some invidious comparison with Shakespeare. In 1767 the *British Magazine* declared that Voltaire followed Shakespeare in *Julius Cæsar*, but his work "is so much inferior to that of Shakespear that whoever compares them will acknowledge that Voltaire, instead of rivaling that great genius, has only shewn him to be inimitable."[95] The *Universal Magazine* pictured Shake-

---

[86]"Enslaved as they are to rules, and modes"—Dublin Edition (1791), p. 101. This postscript first appeared in J. Dodsley's Edition, 1781.
[87]*Op. cit.*, p. 37.   [88]*Ibid.*, p. 45.
[89]*Ibid.*, pp. 81-82.   [90]*Ibid.*, pp. 82-86, 207-42.
[91]LVI (1777), 390.   [92]Lecture XLV, vol. II (1804), 333.
[93]V (1789), 568.
[94]Compare Beattie's vicious attack on French critics in his *Dissertations* (Dublin: Exshaw, Walker, etc., 1783): "Shakespeare's plays must be absurd farces, and their author a barbarian, because they happen to be framed, upon a plan, and in a style which the Criticks of Paris have never acknowledged to be good. Criticism . . . upon this principle . . . is as much beyond the reach, or below the notice, of rational inquiry, as modes of hairdressing, or patterns of shoe buckles."—I, 222.
[95]VIII (1767), 573-74.

speare as the Bay of Naples and Voltaire as the garden of the Tuileries, with distinct preference for the Bay of Naples;[96] and Whiter in 1794 announced particularly: "Mr. Voltaire himself has nothing comparable to the humorous discussion of the philosophic gaoler in *Cymbeline*."[97]

ATTACKS ON VOLTAIRE'S MISTRANSLATION OF SHAKESPEARE

The two most violent attacks on Voltaire, however, are still to be noted. One of these was the generally bitter contempt expressed for his mistranslation of Shakespeare; at times even there is definite implication that such mistranslation was maliciously deliberate, for incidentally Voltaire had reason to fight viciously, after La Place, in 1745-49, and Le Tourneur, in 1776, had introduced Shakespeare into France. The *Gentleman's Magazine* began the attack as early in this period as 1766,[98] and the reaction continued to the end of the century. A condensed sketch of it will sufficiently impress the point of view.

The *Critical Review* in 1768 quoted Voltaire: "This divine Shakespeare introduced my lord Falstaff, the chief justice," and then flayed the French critic for his absurdity in thus mistaking Falstaff merely because he saw the name of Falstaff under the Lord Chief Justice in the Dramatis Personae: "The French translation is grossly false and defective."[99] Mrs. Montagu the following year declared: "Mr. Voltaire formerly understood the English language tolerably well,"[100] yet he now misunderstands such simple words as "course" and "carve," taking them in the literal rather than figurative sense.[101] She cites many other examples,[102] and then using Voltaire's own phrase-

[96]LXXVI (1785), 338.
[97]*A Specimen of a Commentary on Shakspeare* (London: Cadell, 1794), p. 167 n.
[98]XXXVI (1766), 119.   [99]XXVI (1768), 373-74.
[100]*Op. cit.*, p. 282.   [101]*Ibid.*, pp. 212, 213.
[102]*Ibid.*, pp. 198, 215-16, 278-79, 280, 281, 282, 283.

ology calls his work "miserable galimatheus."[103] The *Critical Review* that year, in reviewing Mrs. Montagu, curiously enough remarked that "He" (i.e., Mrs. Montagu, whose name did not appear on the text till the third edition, 1772) attacks Voltaire too carefully, for Voltaire did not know Shakespeare's language and hence could not understand him.[104] And the *Monthly Review* the same year repeated this argument.[105] Even Edward Taylor in 1774, the defender of Voltaire[106] admitted that Voltaire failed, but not because of ignorance—rather "he has translated too literally"[107] and "exact and genuine translations do not exist."[108] Rutledge also "delivered yet another attack on Voltaire as a translator" in 1776;[109] but the *London Magazine* of the same year offered a slightly more pungent allusion: Voltaire either mistranslated or "is a notorious and wilful liar."[110] One does not need to go into detail much further than this. The *Monthly Review* in 1777 continued the attack,[111] and Tom Davies in 1784 grew even more specific: " 'Hamlet', says this writer, 'kills the father of his mistress, on supposition that it was a *rat* which he destroyed.' Had he read the play or understood the text if he had read it, he would have known, that Hamlet imagined the person he killed was the King himself." . . . Voltaire is an "inventor of . . . false criminations."[112] *The Bee* in 1791 may be permitted to conclude the attack with the following characterization: "This feeble translation"—that is, of *Julius Cæsar*.[113]

---

[103]*Ibid.*, p. 214. Compare the *Critical Review* on this term, XXVI (1768), 373-74; and see Voltaire's *Appel*, p. 38.
[104]XXVII see (1769), 350.
[105]XLI (1769), 131. The periodical was using Mrs. Montagu.
[106]Haines, *op. cit.*, p. 47. [107]*Cursory Remarks on Tragedy*, p. 127.
[108]*Ibid.*, p. 131. [109]Haines, *op. cit.*, p. 66.
[110]XLV (1776), 184. [111]LVII (1777), 320.
[112]*Op. cit.*, III, 101-2. [113]IV (1791), 292.

Attacks on Voltaire's Ignorance of Elizabethan Drama

Somewhat connected with this point of view is the English disgust at Voltaire's lack of historical knowledge of Elizabethan drama. Mrs. Montagu in 1769 dubbed Voltaire "a schoolboy critic who neither knows what were the superstitions of former times, or a poet's privileges in all times"[114] and adds that Voltaire should have indicated how much Shakespeare rose above a rude age.[115] But Voltaire did realize, as noted above, that the audience had something to do with Shakespeare's grossness, and to this *The Bee*, apparently upset by sheer hatred of Voltaire, replied: "I venture to aver, on full conviction of my own mind, that these imputations [of Voltaire] are rash, and even grossly false and injurious."[116] Then Richard Hole in the Exeter Society *Essays* in 1796 returned to a more definite and plausible attack, pointing out Voltaire's lack of knowledge of a topical allusion, which Horace Walpole specifically noted.[117]

Attacks on Voltaire as a Man

Finally comes the inevitable reaction against Voltaire as a man—a malicious, envious, jealous, sneering rival. A few scattered and more or less calm rejoinders may be suggested first as a kind of preliminary skirmish, though of course they are by no means all early. They merely represent the more logical attempts to controvert Voltaire. For example, Mrs. Griffith in 1775 cited Abbé Le Blanc's *Let-*

---

[114]*Op. cit.*, p. 199. In defense of Shakespeare's ghosts.
[115]*Ibid.*, p. 20. See also *Monthly Review*, XLI (1769), 130.
[116]IV (1791), 293.
[117]Exeter Society *Essays* (1796), p. 259: "Elizabeth's having delivered a ring to Essex." Compare *All's Well*, V, 4.

ters on the English Nation* to show Voltaire how one of his own countrymen could be decent to Shakespeare.[118] The *Analytical Review* suggested that French critics who praise Milton, Addison, and Pope (Voltaire praised him in the Preface to *Semiramis*), but berate Shakespeare, should remember that *those* men praised Shakespeare;[119] and *The Bee* repeated this idea.[120] Finally Voltaire was attacked, deliberately, as illogical: Voltaire praises the wisdom and philosophy of the English nation, but certainly a nation "which can for two centuries confer universal applause and admiration upon a low buffoon" must lack both of the above qualities;[121] and *The Bee* repeated, two years later, in 1791: ". . . he [Voltaire] singly contradicts the unanimous opinion of all British people for a course of more than two centuries."[122]

The more violent attack on Voltaire's envious disposition was in evidence in 1768 and continued vigorously to the end of the century. The *Monthly Review* in 1768 printed a poem of George Keate, *Ferney, an Epistle to Mr. de Voltaire*, in which appear the following lines:

> Now, chang'd the scene, with poets, poets jar,
> And waste Parnassus is the field of war.
> Yes! jealous wits may still for empire strive,
> Still keep the flames of critic rage alive.[123]

The following year Mrs. Montagu attacked Voltaire for both envy and jealousy,[124] and in 1771 the *Universal Magazine* returned to the fray poetically:

---

[118]*Op. cit.*, Preface, pp. vi-vii. Le Blanc: "He is . . . of all Writers, ancient or modern, the most of an original. He is truly a great genius. . . . Those of our nation who have ever mentioned him have been content to praise *without being capable of judging sufficiently of his merits.*" [His italics]
[119]V (1789), 568. [120]IV (1791), 294.
[121]*Analytical Review*, V (1789), 567. [122]IV (1791), 294.
[123]XXXVIII (1768), 140. [124]*Op. cit.*, pp. 253, 200.

With envy just bursting, with impotent lyes
And sneers, Momus petted the bard of the skies;
Jove kicked the foul critic from Heav'n's azure round,
And, venting his spleen, now at Ferney he's found.[125]

In 1776 both the *London Magazine*[126] and the *Monthly Review*[127] denounced Voltaire's "mean behaviour," and the former also suggested "his licentiousness as a moralist."[128] The writer of the Preface to the English translation[129] of the *Letter to the French Academy* in 1777 sarcastically announced: The same man "who first made Shakespeare known in France" now berates him—"are we to suppose him grown jealous?" Beattie continued the attack in 1783,[130] and Sherlock in 1786 grew vociferous: "Voltaire is no less celebrated for the extent and variety of talents, than for his dishonesty, and for his practices of first pillaging and afterwards calumniating all the living and the dead. . . . The highwayman who robs has strong reasons afterwards to murder."[131]

The *Analytical Review* in 1789 pointed out that Voltaire was coarse in characterizing Shakespeare, and yet Voltaire was supposed to be a great man.[132] In 1791 *The Bee* twice attacked Voltaire, once for his "remarkably partial prejudice against the English Poet,"[133] and second, for his foppishness: It is not surprising that Voltaire could not put up with Shakespeare because "They were most perfect opposites, as a man of profound abilities and wisdom, is opposite to a pleasant superficial fop."[134] The *Gentleman's*

---

[125]XLVIII (1771), 98.   [126]XLV (1776), 183.   [127]LV (1776), 474.
[128]XLV (1776), 310.   [129]London: J. Bew, 1777.
[130]*Dissertations Moral and Critical*, chap. IV, p. 222 n.
[131]*Op. cit.*, p. 33. Compare George Steevens: "In short, the author of *Zayre*, *Mohomet*, and *Semiramis*, possesses all the mischievous qualities of a midnight felon, who, in the hope to conceal his guilt, sets the house which he has robbed on fire."—*Edition* (1778), X, 423.
[132]V (1789), 568.   [133]IV (1791), 291.   [134]III (1791), 79.

Magazine in 1794 appeared with the awful pronouncement that "the flimsy writings of that wretched caviller Voltaire have *UNDONE* France,"[135] and repeated the anathema in 1796.[136] But though this would make an excellent place to conclude the British characterization of the Frenchman, one cannot resist going back to 1776 to read again from the *Gentleman's Magazine*, in summary of Voltaire: "the malice of a monkey, the cunning of a fox, and the traitorous disposition of a cat.'"[137]

Mrs. Montagu and the Reaction Against Voltaire

As a fitting conclusion to this chapter, Mrs. Montagu's *Essay* (1769) should be rescued, if possible, from the castigations of modern critics.[138] It is customary, of course, to use Johnson against this leader of the Bluestockings: " 'Sir, I will venture to say there is not one sentence of true criticism in her book.' Garrick: 'But, Sir, surely it shews how much Voltaire has mistaken Shakspeare, which nobody else has done.' Johnson: 'Sir, nobody else has thought it worth while. And what merit is there in that? You may as well praise a schoolmaster for whipping a boy who has construed ill.' "[139] Yet Johnson himself was more friendly in 1780.[140]

[135] LXIV (1794), 251.   [136] LXVI (1796), 479.
[137] XLVI (1776), 556-57. This is quoted by W. Kenrick from a French characterization in his bitter attack on Voltaire's famous *Letter to the French Academy*.
[138] Professor Nichol Smith announced in 1903 that "Little importance attaches to Mrs. Montagu's Essay on the Writings and Genius of Shakespeare (1769). It was only a well-meaning but shallow reply to Voltaire, and a reply was unnecessary."—Introduction to *Eighteenth Century Essays on Shakespeare*, p. xx. So also Mr. Haines is sarcastically inclined: Mrs. Montagu's "judgments were often merely grotesque" (p. 47). Is it possible that these two men are attacking a woman merely because she became a little sentimental at times, meanwhile overlooking the *facts* of her arguments?
[139] Boswell's *Life* (ed. Hill), II (1769), 88.
[140] Letter to Mrs. Thrale, April 11, 1780. And see further, for Johnson's

Contemporary opinion of Mrs. Montagu was generally a consistent series of laudations. Beattie, James Harris, and Morgann all praised her.[141] Mrs. Griffith in 1775 remarked: ". . . a Lady [in footnote, p. vii, "Mrs. Montagu"] of distinguished merit has lately appeared a champion in his [Shakespeare's] cause, against this *minor critic*, this *minute philosopher*, this *fly upon a pillar of St. Paul's.*"[142] Horace Walpole approved Mrs. Montagu's "just attack on Voltaire" in a letter, November 28, 1779. Tom Davies in 1784 enthusiastically applauded Mrs. Montagu's "incomparable defence";[143] William Richardson registered approval in 1789.[144] And meanwhile the *Monthly Review* had even gone to the length of printing poetical encomiums on Mrs. Montagu in 1774.[145]

Surely all this contemporary approval cannot be wholly misdirected. And if one merely stops to analyze Mrs. Montagu's contributions to the reaction against Voltaire *alone*, the result is somewhat astonishing. In the several types of argument indicated above in this chapter, Mrs. Montagu is represented *nine* times—that is, she has proposed nine *different* arguments against Voltaire. They need no repetition here—they have all been listed above—but the fact remains that Mrs. Montagu, with all her natural feminine sensibility, or possibly sentimentality, was sane enough to propose more arguments against Voltaire than any two or three male critics combined.[146]

The most interesting summary of and retort upon Voltaire's criticism of Shakespeare appeared in George Col-

---

friendliness, O. Elton, *A Survey of English Literature, 1730-1780* (1928), I, 81.
[141] Professor Nichol Smith himself admits this in his Introduction (1903), p. xx.
[142] *Op. cit.*, Preface, p. vii.   [143] *Op. cit.*, III, 102.
[144] *Essays* (1789), p. 61 n. See also the *European Magazine*, XII (1787), 398.
[145] LI (1774), 390.
[146] And Mrs. Montagu is not absent from the other parts of this book.

man's *Man and Wife; or, The Shakespeare Jubilee, A Comedy, of Three Acts* in 1770:

"Marcourt: '. . . his [Shakespeare's] absurdities. A baby in the first act becomes a grown person in the last—plays made out of half penny ballads—ghosts and gravediggers, witches and hobgoblins—Brutus and Cassius conversing like a couple of English Commoncouncilmen—Hamlet killing a rat—and Othello raving about an old pocket-handkerchief—There's your Shakespeare for you.'

"Kitchen: . . . 'This is a mere hash of foreign criticism, as false as superficial, and made up of envy and ignorance—Shakespeare, Mr. Marcourt—Shakespeare is the Turtle of Literature. The lean of him may perhaps be worse than the lean of any other meat;—but there is a deal of green fat, which is the most delicious stuff in the world.' "[147]

---

[147]Pp. 18-19. On these great speeches F. Gentleman remarked: Marcourt is "a coxcomb of the current year" (*Dramatic Censor*, I, 381); Kitchen is "a third gallant" (I, 382); this "passage . . . has as much merit as any one of equal length we ever met with" (I, 383).

For a contemporary book in French on Shakespeare and Voltaire see J. Baretti, *Discours sur Shakespeare et sur Mons. de Voltaire* (1777).

PART III

THE OLDER EULOGY DEVELOPS NEW EMPHASES

CHAPTER IX

THE PERSISTENCE OF THE OLDER EULOGY

Whereas, in the chapters immediately preceding, Shakespeare has been defended by the late eighteenth century against the traditional objections, the present chapter will point out the continuation of traditional aspects of eulogy throughout the years 1766-1799; and in the course of this development an attempt will be made to show, also, what possibly new characteristics appeared in the application of these old forms of eulogy.

SHAKESPEARE AS POET

That Shakespeare could write great poetry was an idea most readily accepted and carried on by the late eighteenth century.[1] His "exquisite poetry" pleased the *British Magazine* in 1767,[2] and Mrs. Montagu fully agreed.[3] Such "strength of versification," announced F. Gentleman the next year,[4] as did Kenrick in 1773.[5] Bell's Edition (1774) praised Shakespeare's "muse of fire,"[6] and Mrs. Griffith exclaimed: "Our Author's poetical beauties . . . are . . . so striking as scarcely to require the being particularly pointed out."[7] Morgann in 1777 was impressed by Shakespeare's "True Poesy,"[8] and three years later the *Monthly Review* became very eulogistic: "A thousand instances

---

[1] It is probably unnecessary to refer definitely to material preceding 1766 on this well accepted dictum. A glance at the earlier texts in D. Nichol Smith's *Shakespeare Criticism* (1916) will establish the point.
[2] VIII (1767), 572.   [3] *Essay*, pp. 59, 196, 275.
[4] *Dramatic Censor* (1770), I, 113. And see I, 376.
[5] Introduction, p.3.   [6] Advertisement, p. 7.
[7] Preface, p. xii. Compare also pp. 497, 525.
[8] P. 71. Compare *Universal Magazine*, LXI (1777), 6.

8

might be given of this, if it were necessary, to prove Shakespear's superiority to his contemporary poets in that which is the very first excellence of dramatic composition—an irresistible force of language."[9]

William Jackson in 1782 noted the critics' general praise of Shakespeare's verses and commented rather pointedly: "I dare say they are very perfect; but when reading this divine poet, it is as much out of my power to think upon the art of verse-making, as it is to consider the best way of twisting fiddle-strings at a concert."[10] Tom Davies continued the panegyric in 1784,[11] but Martin Sherlock grew a little more rhapsodic: "In the poetry of Shakspeare we find all the sources of poetical beauty that are known to all other poets, and an infinity of new sources of which they were ignorant.[12] . . . With other poets a simile is a principal beauty: in Shakspeare the most beautiful similes are frequently lost in a croud of superior beauties."[13] This latter eulogy the *European Magazine* exemplified with: "They [the princes] are soft as the zephyrs which blow on the violet without moving its fragrant head; but, when their royal blood is kindled, they are furious as the storm which seizes by the top the mountain pine and makes it bend to the valley."[14]

The last decade of the century could hardly improve on all this. But the *Universal Magazine* enjoyed "the sublimity of his language" in 1791[15] and added: ". . . no bard ever answered more the fine character of the poet than did Shakspeare himself."[16] *The Bee* in 1793 announced that "few writers have ever equalled Shakespeare in regard to

[9] LXII (1780), 418.
[10] *Thirty Letters*, p. 94, of the third (1795) edition.
[11] *Dramatic Miscellanies*, I, 80.   [12] *A Fragment* (1786), p. 22.
[13] *Ibid.*, p. 15.
[14] X (1786), 282. The periodical is quoting M. Sherlock.
[15] LXXXVIII (1791), 59.   [16] XC (1782), 432.

the rhythmical flow of poetic cadence,"[17] and Whiter may be allowed to close the chorus: "It was reserved for the knowledge of the present age, to discover that Shakspeare has enriched and ennobled our poetry with new forms of language, rythm, fiction, and imagery, which we know that he first invented, and believe that he has finally completed."[18]

If the age was agreed on the general poetical value of Shakespeare, it was but a natural step to point out particular scenes of beauty throughout his work and then ultimately gather them into collections. A brief sketch of this inevitable development will suffice.[19]

In 1767 the *British Magazine* applauded several passages in *Julius Cæsar:* for example, "The scene in which the conspirators meet, has in it something extremely awful and solemn."[20] The same periodical in the same year pointed to *Romeo and Juliet:* "There cannot be a scene produced in the works of that poet [Racine], or any other, more affecting than that in which Romeo laments his unhappy fate, in being separated from Juliet";[21] and strongly approved, also, Mercutio's Queen Mab speech.[22] In *Richard III*, says the same periodical, still in 1767, the horror of the tent scene "is not to be matched by any other poet";[23] and two other scenes receive great praise.[24]

Mrs. Montagu in 1769 persistently lauded particular

---

[17] XVI (1793), 274.

[18] *Specimen* (1794), pp. 74-75. For supplementary material see *The Trifler* (1788), No. 25—On "Ease in Poetry."

[19] For some material on this preceding 1766 see: T. Reresby, *Miscellany* (1721), 340—"Of Man in Miniature—by Shakespear"; *Caribbeana*, II (1741), 252—"What S. said of the Frailty of Human Nature"; *Monthly Review*, XXXIII (1765), 460—Beautiful Passages. Also D. Nichol Smith's latest book (1928), p. 67, for the general background of this movement.

[20] VIII (1767), 573.   [21] VIII (1767), 620.
[22] *Ibid.*, 621.   [23] *Ibid.*, 626.
[24] *Ibid.*, 625, 626.

scenes and passages in the plays,[25] as did also F. Gentleman in 1770: for example, "as concise and beautiful delineation of human nature as thought can conceive, or words express."[26] The *London Magazine* approved the "remarkable soliloquy . . . which closes the second act" of *Hamlet*,[27] and Kenrick pointed out "a celebrated passage" in *Macbeth* in 1773.[28] This procedure was echoed by Mrs. Griffith's whole book in 1775, by Morgann in 1777,[29] by George Colman's *Remarks on Shylock's Reply to the Senate of Venice*,[30] by Blair in 1783,[31] by Tom Davies repeatedly in 1784,[32] by George Anne Bellamy in 1785,[33] and finally, for example, by J. M. Mason in his attack on Steevens and Chesterfield over the lines in the *Merchant of Venice*, "The man that hath no music," etc. Mason says Steevens decried this passage and adduced Lord Chesterfield's *Letters*, "a book," continues Mason, "of slender authority indeed, where human nature is the subject in question: For . . . his lordship . . . was one of the most affected characters of the age. . . . There cannot be a stronger proof of his contempt of nature than this well-known fact, that he preferred the rhyming tragedies of Dryden, to the noblest productions of Shakspeare. . . . I think the language truly poetical," concludes Mason, "and the sentiment founded in truth and nature."[34]

Without going into further detail, one might note that the last decade of the century was conspicuously crowded

---

[25]*Op. cit.*, pp. 36, 61, 70-71, 97, 115, 118-19, 124, 141, 166-67, 180-82, 184, 188-89, 192, 202, etc.
[26]*Op. cit.*, I, 42. See also I, 37, 38, 39-40, 41, 44, 45, 46-47, etc., etc.
[27]XLI (1772), 579.   [28]*Retort Courteous*, p. 23.
[29]*Op. cit.*, 104-5, for example, on Falstaff's "death."
[30]*Prose on Several Occasions* (1787), II, 189.
[31]Lecture XLVI, vol. II (1804), 356.
[32]*Op. cit.*, I, 11, 51, 158, 262, 304, 383, 406; II, 166; III, 28, 45, 73, etc.
[33]*An Apology of the Life of G. A. B.*, V, 127.
[34]*Comments on the Last Edition* (1785), pp. 77, 79.

with encomiums of particular passages and scenes of Shakespeare. For consider the list from merely a single periodical, the *Universal Magazine*. In 1791 it commented favorably on the first ghost scene in *Hamlet*, on Polonius' precepts, on "To be or not to be," on the King's soliloquy at prayer,[35] on passages in *Cymbeline*, on *As You Like It*, and on *The Tempest*;[36] in 1792 on *Lear*: "Shakspeare has nowhere exhibited more inimitable strokes of his art than in this uncommon scene" ["Blow, winds, and crack your cheeks," etc.];[37] on passages in *Othello* and on *Midsummer Night's Dream*;[38] in 1793 on *Measure for Measure*,[39] on *Romeo and Juliet*, and on *The Winter's Tale:* "The reader, who overlooks these minutiae of Shakspeare, sees not half his greatness";[40] in 1794 on *Richard II*, on *King John*,[41] and on *Henry IV*, Part 1;[42] in 1795 on *Henry IV*, Part 2, especially the passage on Sleep,[43] on *Henry VI*, Parts 1, 2, and 3, and on *Henry V*;[44] in 1796 on *Richard III*,[45] on the *Merchant of Venice*, and on *Julius Cæsar*.[46] And all these, to repeat, are from merely one periodical.

The next step was to collect these passages into books labelled "The Beauties of Shakspeare." The origin of this procedure Professor Nichol Smith has suggested in his latest book,[47] but possibly he should have mentioned T. Hayward, *The British Muse* (London, 1738). The Rev. William Dodd was obviously, however, the greatest indulger in the diversion in the period, and his anthology went through several editions, 1752, 1757, 1773, 1780, 1782,

---

[35] LXXXIX (1791), 114, 117, 277, 437.
[36] LXXXVIII (1791), 351-55, 220, 59-61.
[37] XCI (1792), 107, 184, 270.   [38] XC (1792), 34, 171, 346-50.
[39] XCII (1793), 244.   [40] XCIII (1793), 44, 196, 292,
[41] XCIV (1794), 406, 111.   [42] XCV (1794), 178.
[43] XCVI (1795), 34, 107.   [44] XCVII (1795), 327, 203.
[45] XCVIII (1796), 186.   [46] XCIX (1796), 252, 78.
[47] *Shakespeare in the Eighteenth Century* (1928), p. 67.

etc.⁴⁸ There was also an anonymous selection in 1777: *The Beauties of the English Drama* [including Shakespeare, Jonson, Dryden, etc.]. J. A. Croft's *A Select Collection of the Beauties of Shakspeare* was published in 1792, and, following this, there were other collections by C. Taylor in 1778, 1783, and 1792.

In conclusion, a comment by the *Monthly Review* in 1783 on this general procedure is interesting: Gildon made a selection called *Shakespeariana* and affixed it to his *Complete Art of Poetry*.⁴⁹ The arrangement was "under distinct heads." Dodd "culled out what he thought the more striking passages, and placed them in the order in which they occur in the plays, without any regard to alphabetical distinction." This more recent book [now being reviewed, and published by Kearsley] follows Gildon's idea: "how Shakespeare hath expressed himself on various subjects which relate to the passions and pursuits of men, and the events of human life."⁵⁰

The contribution of the late eighteenth century to all this eulogy of the poetry of Shakespeare was undoubtedly the increased emphasis on particular passages, with the accompanying publication of such passages in anthologies. For the first step in this development the periodicals were mainly responsible, and for the second William Dodd should be given the greatest credit. Nevertheless other critics deserve some attention for their labors in behalf of the eulogy of Shakespeare's poetry, and among these should undoubtedly be noted Mrs. Elizabeth Montagu, Francis Gentleman, and Tom Davies.

---

⁴⁸In the nineteenth century this was reprinted in 1810, 1818, 1820, 1821, 1823, 1824, 1825, 1827, 1831, 1835, 1837, 1839, etc. The McMillan Collection in the University of Michigan contains Dodd's first and third editions and also a Dublin edition of 1783.

⁴⁹London: C. Rivington, 1718. ⁵⁰LXIX (1783), 263.

Shakespeare as Poet of Nature[51]

The late eighteenth century continued to recognize the reality of Shakespeare's imitations.[52] Mrs. Montagu noted it in 1769 with her reference to "human nature, of which Shakespear's characters are a just imitation."[53] Two years later appeared a poem in the *Universal Magazine*:

When Nature to Athens and Rome bid adieu
To Britain the Goddess, with extasy flew;

. . . .

On Avon's fair banks, now the subject of Fame
She brought forth a boy, and Will Shakespeare his name;
Not egg was to egg more alike, than in feature,
The smiling young rogue to his Parent, dame Nature.[54]

In 1772 the *Gentleman's Magazine* announced: "Nothing less than general Nature, such as she has been from the first formation of society, and will remain for ever, could satisfy the comprehensive mind of Shakespeare."[55] Morgann continued the theme in 1777,[56] and Johnson repeated his dictum in a letter to Mrs. Thrale in 1780:[57] "the pure voice of Nature." The eulogy then proceeded through the *Monthly Review* in 1784,[58] J. M. Mason in 1785,[59] the *Ana-*

[51]See A. O. Lovejoy, " 'Nature' as Aesthetic Norm," *MLN*, XLII (1927), 445-47, for the various implications of the term, "nature," as used in this chapter.
[52]Mr. Lovejoy's No. 1. See Johnson's *Preface* (1765), p. viii.
[53]*Op. cit.*, p. 112. Compare also pp. 17-18, 184. The whole of Chaps. XI and XII below should be read as supplementary, therefore, to this paragraph.
[54]XLVIII (1771), 97-98.
[55]XLII (1772), 522. Compare also F. Pilon, *An Essay on the Character of Hamlet* (1777), p. 22: "the genius of Shakespear penetrated all nature." And Mrs. Griffith, Preface, p. vi.
[56]*Op. cit.*, pp. 43-44. [57]April 11, 1780. See *Preface* (1765), p. viii.
[58]LXX (1784), 182-83, 337. The periodical is reviewing Blair and Ritson and uses Dryden. Compare Richardson, *Essays* (5th ed., 1798), p. 377.
[59]*Op. cit.*, (1785), p. 77. Compare the *Universal Magazine*, LXXXI (1787), 5.

lytical Review in 1789[60] ("Shakespeare seizes Nature herself, and not her veil"), and *The Bee* in 1791: "true pictures of nature."[61] Finally the Exeter Society essayist, Richard Hole, in 1796 wrote: ". . . our bard is universally allowed to be a copyist of nature."[62]

But "nature" was also being applied more and more to Shakespeare in the senses of freedom from the influence of convention and rules, and freedom from reflective design—that is, artlessness.[63] For example, two poetic excerpts appeared in the *Monthly Review* and *Universal Magazine* in 1768 and 1769:

> Our Shakespeare yet shall all his rights maintain
> . . . .
> Above controul, above each classic rule,
> His tutress Nature, and the world his school.[64]

> Where Nature led him by the hand,
>   Instructed him in all she knew
> And gave him absolute command.[65]

Mrs. Montagu emphasized Shakespeare's "amazing force of nature . . . what no rules can teach."[66] And J. M. Mason wrote in 1785: "Warburton's observations frequently tend to prove Shakespeare more profound and learned than the occasion required, and to make the Poet of Nature the most unnatural that ever wrote."[67] Further emphasis on this point of view has already appeared above

---

[60] V (1789), 568.
[61] IV (1791), 291. Compare the *Universal Magazine*, LXXXVIII (1791), 60.
[62] Exeter Society *Essays*, p. 262.
[63] That is, Mr. Lovejoy's No. 14 and No. 15. See Farmer's *Essay on the Learning of Shakespeare* (1st ed., 1767), pp. 5, 49, for a background of this development.
[64] *Monthly Review*, XXXVIII (1768), 140.
[65] *Universal Magazine*, XLV (1769), 154.   [66] *Op. cit.*, p. 11.
[67] *Op. cit.* (1785), p. 18. See also p. 350.

in the chapters on the unities and Shakespeare's learning.[68] Shakespeare's artlessness was pointed out by Mrs. Montagu in 1769: ". . . nature, which speaks in Shakespear, prevails over them all [that is, 'rules of art,' which she has just mentioned]."[69] Morgann maintained in 1777 that Shakespeare went even beyond nature to magic;[70] the former being "felt propriety," and the latter "a like feeling of propriety and truth, supposed without a cause."[71] Johnson remarked in a letter to Mrs. Thrale in 1780: ". . . like Shakespeare's works, such graceful negligence of transition."[72] And the *European Magazine* printed "Stanzas, on Seeing Mr. Garrick's Picture placed near a Bust of Shakespeare," by Dr. Harrington, of Bath:

> Art may express yon venerable bust,
> And form each feature to resemblance just;
> But Nature, pleas'd with choicest tints design'd
> Thee! happy symbol of her Shakespeare's mind.[73]

Finally the *Gentleman's Magazine* in 1799 quoted from Mrs. West's *Poems and Plays:*

> And shall fastidious Taste refuse
> The pages of Shakspeare to peruse,
> Though Nature's suppliant voice thy fixed attention craves?[74]

---

[68]Contrast Richardson in 1784: "All these things . . . may be termed natural. Yet, I conceive that the solemn, in dramatic composition, should be kept apart from the the ludicrous."—5th ed., p. 380.
[69]*Op. cit.*, p. 79. Compare *Scots Magazine*, XXXV (1773), 435:
> "Exalted Shakespeare, with a boundless mind,
> Rang'd far and wide, a genius unconfin'd,
> The passions sway'd, and captive led the heart,
> Without the critic's rule, or aid of art."

[70]*Op. cit.*, p. 71. Compare pp. 58-62 n. and p. 60.
[71]*Ibid.*, p. 72 n. [72]April 11, 1780.
[73]XII (1787), 424. For this note I am indebted to Miss Mary C. Roach of the University of Michigan.
[74]LXIX (1799), 882.

Other aspects of the term "nature" appeared more sporadically in application to the natural qualities of Shakespeare's genius. Mrs. Montagu mentioned the "proud irregularity of greatness,"[75] and she came fairly close to primitivism with her characterization of Shakespeare's power as "wild nature's vigour working at the root."[76] But perhaps the most interesting minor application during the period was the recognition of nature's fullness, or variety in Shakespeare,[77] as it appeared in Martin Sherlock's tremendous eulogy: "It is she [Nature] who was thy book, O Shakspeare; . . . it is she from whom thou hast drawn those beauties which are at once the glory and delight of thy nation . . . thy variety is inexhaustible. Always original, always new, thou art the only prodigy which Nature has produced. . . . The reader who thinks this elogium extravagant is a stranger to my subject. . . . But, say you, we have never seen such 'a being.' You are in the right; Nature made it, and broke the mould."[78]

A conclusion should point out again both the continuity of the traditional eulogy of Shakespeare as poet of nature and the growth of a varied application of the term to his plays within the limit of the years 1766-1799. In the case

---

[75] P. 11. Mr. Lovejoy's No. 11. Compare Pope's *Preface* (1725) in D. Nichol Smith's *Shakespeare Criticism* (1916), p. 56.

[76] P. 203. Mr. Lovejoy's No. 16. She is applying line 184 of Pope's Epistle Two of the *Essay on Man* to Shakespeare. Compare *Scots Magazine*, XXXIII (1771), 656:

"So Shakespear's page, the flower of poesie,
Ere Garrick rose, had charms for ev'ry eye:
'Twas Nature's genuine image, wild and grand."

[77] Mr. Lovejoy's No. 12. Dryden, Pope, and Theobald had all applied this to Shakespeare. See also Gray's Letter to West, c. 1742, on Shakespeare's language.

[78] *Op. cit.* (1786), pp. 13-14. Compare Ritson: "Shakspeare is the *God of the writers idolatry* . . . darling child of nature and fancy, whom *age cannot wither*, and whose *infinite variety custom cannot stale.*"—*Remarks* (1783), Preface, p. vi.

of the former perhaps it was natural that the periodicals should carry on the tradition, while the greater variety of application was made generally by more prominent individual critics such as Mrs. Griffith, Mrs. Montagu, Morgann, Ritson, and Martin Sherlock. The versatility of Mrs. Montagu in this field of activity is interesting. As Pope in the *Essay on Criticism* confusedly attempted to synthesize, so she seems to have jumbled together several different implications of the term "nature" within her three hundred pages of criticism.

Shakespeare, Original Genius

The late eighteenth century not only continued the eulogy of Shakespeare as poet of nature, but proceeded to rationalize and advance his status in terms of the developing idea of the "original genius."[79] Throughout the century Shakespeare remained a genius, but the earlier application of the term as a mere explanation of his triumph over the "rules" became, in the course of the later decades, a paean of praise in terms of the intrinsic superiority of original genius itself.

Mrs. Montagu in 1769 continued the general apostrophizing of Shakespeare's genius: "The genius of Shake-

---

[79] For some material preceding 1766 on this see: *Tatler*, No. 68; *Spectator*, No. 160; *Guardian*, No. 144; William Sharpe's *Dissertation on Genius*, 1755; E. Young, *Conjectures*, 1759; *Critical Review*, XI (1761), 164.

A history of the development of the term, "Original Genius" is given in Mr. P. Kaufman's "Heralds of Original Genius," in *Essays in Memory of Barrett Wendell* (Harvard University, 1926). This article is reviewed by Professor R. S. Crane in the *Philological Quarterly*, VI (April, 1927), 168-69.

Mr. Kaufman's texts should be supplemented by a few periodical references subsequent to 1766: *Universal Magazine*, XLVIII (1771), 228; *Universal Magazine*, LXVII (1780), 193 (Quoting Donaldson's *Elements of Beauty*); *Universal Magazine*, LXXVII (1785), 33 (Quoting Hannah More's *Preface* to Ann Yearsley's Poems); *The Bee*, V (1791), 177.

spear is so extensive and profound."[80] So also did Garrick's excerpts in his *Testimonies to the Genius and Merits of Shakespeare*, and the *Critical Review* in the same year.[81] In 1773 Kenrick maintained "his superiority of genius,"[82] as did W. Richardson in 1774[83] and Tom Davies in 1784.[84] And this same general eulogy appeared in the *Universal Magazine* in 1777, 1787, and 1792,[85] and *The Bee* in 1791 and 1793,[86] proceeding, therefore, to the close of the century.

But in 1767 the *British Magazine* had made a fundamental distinction: "Genius and Wit . . . were united in Shakespear almost in an equal measure."[87] Mrs. Montagu two years later emphasized the spontaneity of genius: "Heaven-born genius acts from something superior to rules . . . and has a right of appeal to nature herself";[88] and ". . . genius, powerful genius only . . . could have produced such strong and original beauties."[89] Prescot in 1773 wrote: "Trace lightning, answers my friend, that cannot be. Why not is the reply: why not, as well as the flashes of genius: why not as well as the flashes of the genius of Shakespear?"[90] And even Taylor the next year agreed: ". . . but our English poet will be found to assume any shape at will, and in whatever figure, whatever dress he may appear, it will sit easy on him, it will seem natural to him."[91] Mrs. Griffith's tremendous eulogy in 1775 has already been noted above in the chapter on the unities, but part of it should be repeated here: "Would

---

[80] *Op. cit.*, p. 288. See also pp. 16, 20-21. [81] XXVII (1769), 351.
[82] Introduction, p. 2. Compare also *Scots Magazine*, XXXV (1773), 435: "a genius unconfin'd."
[83] *Op. cit.*, 5th ed. (as always), pp. 31, 156. [84] *Op. cit.*, II, 6.
[85] LXI (1777), 6; LXXXI (1787), 243; XCI (1792), 23.
[86] IV (1791), 290; XIV (1793), 303.
[87] VIII (1767), 235. Compare also p. 574. [88] *Op. cit.*, pp. 7-8.
[89] *Ibid.*, p. 203. [90] *Letters*, p. 289.
[91] *Cursory Remarks*, p. 75.

they restrain him within the precincts of art, the height, the depth of whose imagination and creative genius found even the extent of Nature too streightly bounded for it to move in?"[92]

Blair in 1783 applied Gerard's modification of taste[93] to Shakespeare as a genius: Shakespeare is "a great but incorrect genius[94] . . . it is genius shooting wild; deficient in just taste, and altogether unassisted by knowledge or art."[95] Two years later the *Universal Magazine* was again apostrophizing Shakespeare's "own divine and incomprehensible genius,"[96] and M. Sherlock carried on: "Shakspeare . . . disdaining imitation . . . leaped over it under the wing of genius and created a species quite new."[97] *The Bee*, in 1791, in comparing Homer and Shakespeare, continued that "The genius of both poets was then of undoubted originality."[98] And finally in 1797 the *Monthly Mirror* printed an article entitled "The Genius of Shakspeare," which struck precisely the Blakeian note: "It is now more than thirty years that the thermometer of Shakspeare's glory, which is graduated to the end of time, has been consistently rising. . . . It is in genius, in that divine emanation, which in its nature is inexplicable."[99]

The conclusion has already been suggested: namely, that the early eighteenth-century explanation of Shake-

---

[92] *Op. cit.*, p. 26.
[93] See Mr. Kaufman's article cited above for Gerard's use of taste as a guide to genius.
[94] *Lectures* (1783) in I (1804), 62.
[95] *Ibid.*, II (1804), 356. Compare Chap. X, below. Jackson had already rejected this modification—i.e., this plea for taste to guide genius: Taste represses genius—i.e., "force and sublimity"—and encourages "correctness and elegance."—*Thirty Letters* (1782), in 3rd ed. (1795), p. 173 (Letter XXIII).
[96] LXXVII (1785), 33. Quoting Hannah More.
[97] *A Fragment*, p. 34. Compare p. 13.   [98] I (1791), 56-57.
[99] III (1797), 147-48. Compare Mr. Kaufman's article on this note.

speare's eccentricities as those of a poet of nature became by the end of the century a glorification of Shakespeare *in toto* in terms of the rising deification of original genius as such. And this was undoubtedly one of Shakespeare's greatest triumphs in the period.

CHAPTER X

NEW EMPHASES: SHAKESPEARE AS CONSCIOUS ARTIST AND AS MORAL PHILOSOPHER

Not only did the late eighteenth-century critics overthrow the traditional objections to Shakespeare and continue the traditional forms of eulogy, but meanwhile also they were evolving new emphases of their own in their attitude toward the poet. In accordance with the purposes of this book, emphasis has been placed upon the results of these new developments within the period studied rather than upon the beginnings (though in each section some of the material preceding 1766 is suggested);[1] and these results appear in this chapter and in those immediately following.

SHAKESPEARE AS CONSCIOUS ARTIST WITH JUDGMENT EQUAL TO HIS GENIUS

The final step in emancipating Shakespeare from the traditional objections to his plays was to grant him judgment. The late eighteenth century had defended his decorum[2] and offered him obeisance as an original genius,[3] but its final, climactic tribute in this field of its criticism was to announce that he possessed judgment—conscious artistry. It is true that the greatest credit for inaugurating this new emphasis belongs to a man who precedes 1766—

---

[1]That is, the material particularly in periodicals. See Chapter I above for the general developments before 1766, especially during the transitional period from 1730 to 1765. The "New Emphases" to be discussed now are generally full developments of the hints suggested by this directly preceding period.
[2]See Chap. VI, above.   [3]See Chap. IX, above.

that is, Daniel Webb[4]—but the successors of Webb were many, and the rising tribute to Shakespeare's judgment proceeds quite steadily throughout all the last four decades of the eighteenth century.

In 1769 Mrs. Montagu praised Shakespeare's art: "Such appearances, says he [Horatio], preceded the fall of mighty Julius, and the ruin of the great commonwealth; and he adds, such have often been the omens of disasters in our own state. There is great art in this conduct. The true cause of the royal Dane's discontent could not be guessed at."[5] She also attributed to him the "sagacity of a Tacitus":[6] "Poor Shakespear from the wooden images in our mean chronicles was to form his portraits. What judgment was there in discovering, that by moulding them to an exact resemblance he should engage and please";[7] . . . "With great judgment the poet has given to Macbeth the very temper to be wrought upon by such suggestions."[8] F. Gentleman in the following year exclaimed: "The entrance of Macbeth, his high-wrought confusion, and every syllable of the ensuing scene, exhibit an unparalleled combination of judgment and genius."[9] So also Whately: ". . . the character of Macbeth is much more complicated than that of Richard; and therefore, when they are set in opposition, the judgment of the poet shews itself as much in what he has left out of the latter, as in what he has inserted."[10]

Morgann in 1777 declared that "he boldly makes a character act and speak from those parts of the composi-

---

[4]*Remarks on the Beauty of Poetry* (1762), pp. 31-55. See also Pope's *Preface* (1725) quoted in D. Nichol Smith, *Shakespeare Criticism* (1916), pp. 55-56.

[5]*Op. cit.*, p. 165. Compare p. 162: "And the slight fairies, *weak masters though they be,* even in their wanton gambols and idle sports, perform great tasks by *his so potent art.*"

[6]*Ibid.*, p. 94.   [7]*Ibid.*, p. 68.

[8]*Ibid.*, p. 176. See also p. 183.   [9]*Op. cit.*, I, 89.   [10]*Op. cit.*, p. 90.

tion, which are *inferred* only, . . . And this is in reality that art in *Shakespeare*, which . . . we more emphatically call *nature*";[11] thus ". . . with an art not enough understood, he most effectually preserves the real character of *Falstaff* even in the moment he seems to depart from it."[12] Both Morgann and Whately, therefore, had much the same idea about Shakespeare's art.

"The perusal of these old plays [Nichols' *Six Plays*]," announced the *Monthly Review* in 1779, "will . . . shew that the delicacy of his [Shakespeare's] taste and the soundness of his judgment were almost as remarkable as the richness of his fancy."[13] Five years later Tom Davies praised Shakespeare's[14] art and added: "What affords the most evident proofs of our author's infallible judgment and sagacity is, that, notwithstanding the great alteration and improvement in the public taste . . . these characters and scenes never fail to produce the same effect at this day."[15]

Richardson continued the applause in 1789: "Here the poet's good sense, his sense of propriety, his judgment, and invention, are indeed remarkable."[16] *The Bee* announced Shakespeare's "native genius and judgment,"[17] and the *Universal Magazine* praised Shakespeare's judgment four times in 1791-1792: "Shakspeare shows the greatest judgment";[18] ". . . and the judgment with which he repre-

---

[11]*Op. cit.*, p. 62 n.   [12]*Ibid.*, p. 143.
[13]LXI (1779), 296.   [14]*Op. cit.* (1784), I, 406.
[15]*Ibid.*, II, 23-24. Compare also the *Monthly Review*, LXX (1784), 22: "These anecdotes . . . shew with what taste and judgment Shakespeare adopted historical circumstances." For this note I am indebted to Mr. R. C. Chapman of the University of Michigan. Dr. Raysor has pointed out the *Lounger's* (1785-86) references to Shakespeare's "art" and "skill" in Nos. 68 and 69 (XXXI, 109, 113 of Chalmers), and judgment—i. e. "good sense"—in No. 68 (XXXI, 109 of Chalmers).
[16]*Essays* (1798), p. 281.   [17]IV (1791), 291.
[18]LXXXVIII (1791), 60.

sents the distinguishing traits of his character . . . is among the most striking proofs of his abilities as a dramatic writer";[19] "There is nothing in this tragedy in which Shakspeare has more displayed his judgment, than in the circumstance of the handkerchief";[20] "Our poet's representation of the origin and progress of the distraction of Lear, exhibits the greatest judgment and skill."[21] Finally the *Anthologia Hibernica* in 1794 exclaimed: "Shakespear makes his very bombast answer his purpose by the persons he chuses to utter it."[22]

So the wheel has come full circle: Shakespeare has decorum, original genius, and judgment. The way is now clear for Coleridge's later and more ecstatic emphasis.

Shakespeare as Moral Philosopher

Johnson in 1765 wrote: "He [Shakespeare] sacrifices virtue to convenience, and is so much more careful to please than instruct, that he seems to write without any moral purpose. From his writings indeed a system of social duty may be selected, for he that thinks reasonably must think morally; but his precepts and axioms drop casually from him."[23] Then he proceeded to criticize Shakespeare for failure to respect poetic justice.

The late eighteenth century, however, became increasingly interested in the spectacle of Shakespeare as a moral philosopher.[24] Ultimately, this might come down to the

---

[19] LXXXVIII (1791), 351. Compare also p. 352.
[20] XC (1792), 172. Contrast Rymer, *A Short View of Tragedy* (1693), on this.
[21] XCI (1792), 183.   [22] III (1794), 17.
[23] This whole quotation is from D. Nichol Smith, *Shakespeare Criticism* (1916), p. 102.
[24] For some material preceding 1766 see the *Tatler* No. 111; The *Gentleman's Magazine*, VII (1737), 558—on the Moral of a Play of Shakespeare; the same periodical, XVIII (1748), 503, 553.

poet's use, or misuse, of poetic justice, and in such a narrowing of the field Johnson would come to the fore, as just noted—with his horror over the death of Cordelia, for example.[25] But there was actually more to the matter than simply poetic justice. The new interest involved the question as to whether Shakespeare provided a good book of moral etiquette as a whole, and in this discussion the speakers went far beyond Johnson's grudging admission.

In 1767 the *Gentleman's Magazine* attempted to defend Shakespeare's morality,[26] and two years later Mrs. Montagu became rhapsodic on the matter: "We are apt to consider Shakespear only as a poet; but he is certainly one of the greatest moral philosophers that ever lived . . ."[27]— a statement which the *Monthly Review*[28] endorsed. F. Gentleman in 1770 stated his premise: ". . . it becomes necessary to enquire for the moral, without which no dramatic piece can have intrinsic worth,"[29] and immediately proceeded to go straight through the plays of Shakespeare, drawing general morals right and left; for example, on *Hamlet:* ". . . all the moral we can deduce is, that murder cannot lie hid, and that conscience ever makes a coward of guilt."[30]

Kenrick in 1773 rivalled Mrs. Montagu in panegyric of Shakespeare: ". . . a *moral philosopher;* his works containing a practical system of ethics . . . have perhaps contributed more to form our national character . . . than all the theoretical books of morality which have ap-

---

[25]*Ibid.*, p. 137.
[26]XXXVII (1767), 123. For this note I am indebted to Miss Gladys A. Gray of the University of Michigan.
[27]*Op. cit.*, p. 59. See also pp. 61, 68, 196.
[28]XLI (1769), 135. With some qualifications.
[29]*Op. cit.*, I, 9.
[30]*Ibid.* I, 59. Compare I, 9 (*Richard III*), 104 (*Macbeth*), 150 (*Othello*), 188 (*Romeo and Juliet*), 285 (*Merchant of Venice*), etc.

peared in our language."[31] E. Taylor was not so well satisfied, though as a general detractor of Shakespeare he showed amazing compliance here: "The morals of Shakespear's plays are in general extremely natural and just; yet why must innocence unnecessarily suffer?"[32] But the male moralist, par excellence, of this period, was William Richardson, whose method through three series of essays (1774, 1784, 1789)[33] echoed and reëchoed that of F. Gentleman: "Moralists of all ages have recommended Poetry as an art no less instructive than amusing. . . . The propriety of bestowing attention on the study of human nature, and of borrowing assistance from the poets, and especially from Shakespeare, will be more particularly illustrated in the following remarks."[34] ". . . An exercise no less adapted to improve the heart, than to inform the understanding."[35] In application this great ethical purpose becomes (at the end of the 1774 essay on Imogen): "We ought, therefore, to beware of limiting our felicity to the gratification of any particular passion. Nature, ever wise and provident, has endowed us with capacities for various pleasures, and has opened to us many fountains of happiness: 'let no tyrannous passion, let no rigid doctrine deter thee; drink of the streams, be moderate, and be grateful.' "[36] This point of view follows straight through 1774 and 1784, until at the very end of his last series, 1789, he states the irresistible conclusion: "Thus the moralist becomes a critic: and the two sciences of ethics and criticism appear to be intimately and very naturally connected. In truth no one who . . .

[31] Introduction, p. 15. He applauds Mrs. Montagu on this subject, p. 15.
[32] *Cursory Remarks* (1774), p. 45. In reference to Cordelia. Compare Johnson, above.
[33] I am using the dates in the McMillan Collection.
[34] *Essays* (1798), pp. 1-3.   [35] P. 33.
[36] P. 196. Compare p. 120 on Hamlet, and p. 168 on Jacques. All pages noted refer to the fifth ed., always, unless otherwise stated.

entertains improper notions of human conduct, can discern excellence in the higher species of poetical composition."[37]

Mrs. Griffith, Richardson's feminine compeer, wrote a whole book, in 1775, entitled *The Morality of Shakespeare's Drama*, in pursuance of the thesis stated in her Preface that in improving our minds, "no one so . . . universally succeeded, as . . . our greatest Poet, Shakespeare.[38] . . . I have ventured," she continues, "to assume the task of placing his Ethic merits in a more conspicuous point of view, than they have ever hitherto been presented in to the Public."[39] Her method, in its general aspects, is essentially the same as that of Gentleman and Richardson, though she makes no reference to either: "From this short story [*The Tempest*] I think the following *general moral* will naturally result."[40] But she has an additional little twist which is more specific: "Let us now proceed to the particular maxims and sentiments which occur from the several parts of the Dialogue."[41] Her final note of praise echoes Kenrick's: The dramatic moralist is better than the doctrinal.[42]

Johnson in 1776 lauded the morality of *Othello*,[43] Morgann declared Shakespeare exercised poetic justice rightly on Falstaff in *Henry IV*, Part 2,[44] and Tom Davies approved the poet's morality in *Henry VIII* and *Hamlet*.[45] In 1786 Sherlock wrote that the Greek poets excel in morali-

---

[37] Pp. 398-99. For 1784 see pp. 138 n., 132, 208, 373, etc. For 1774 see pp. 40, 49, 85, etc. For 1789 see pp. 359, 281, 286, etc. On his desire for poetic justice see pp. 118-19, 198-99, 281. There was, of course, a new essay on Fluellen in the 1812 (6th) ed.

[38] P. v.   [39] P. ix.

[40] P. 3. She praises Johnson on the matter, pp. viii-ix of the *Preface*, and quotes Shaftesbury, pp. xi-xii, and p. 516.

[41] P. 4. Compare pp. 6, 7, 11, 62, 109, etc.   [42] P. 526.

[43] Boswell's *Life* (ed. Hill), III (1776), 40.   [44] *Op. cit.*, p. 179.

[45] *Op. cit.*, I, 339 and III, 148. Compare also the *Universal Magazine*, LXXIV (1784), 15.

ty, but that "Shakspeare has more morality than they";[46] and J. P. Kemble took up the cry with the statement: "Plays are designed . . . to have a good influence on the lives of men. . . . This essay . . . concerns itself only with the sentiments of the hero of it [Macbeth], presuming they will . . . effectually serve ethicks."[47] The *Universal Magazine* noted Shakespeare's "instructive lessons,"[48] as did also *The Bee*,[49] and in 1792 the *Universal Magazine* repeated the note of both Kenrick and Mrs. Griffith: "A scene, like this [in *Othello*], exhibits a more instructive lesson against drunkenness than the most laboured dissertations, or the most studied harangues."[50] Finally, in 1796, both the Exeter Society essayist, Richard Hole,[51] and the *Scots Magazine*[52] contributed to the general acclaim, prevalent since 1767, that Shakespeare was a great moralist as well as a great genius.

There is no doubt, therefore, that Johnson's grudging admission in 1765 was taken up and pursued vigorously throughout the rest of the century. The chief contributors to this panegyric of moralism were undoubtedly Francis Gentleman, William Richardson, and Mrs. Griffith. Mrs. Griffith in particular received complimentary reviews in the *Critical Review* and the *Monthly Review*,[53] and the *Universal Magazine* honored her even more, and Shakespeare by implication, by printing her book serially.[54] So Shakespeare, mainly through the efforts of a woman, reached the heights as a moral philosopher at the close of the eighteenth century.[55]

[46]*Op. cit.*, p. 14.   [47]*Macbeth Reconsidered* (1786), pp. 3-4
[48]LXXXVIII (1791), 59.   [49]I (1791), 58.
[50]XC (1792), 37. See also p. 171.   [51]P. 572.   [52]LVIII (1796), 461-63.
[53]*Critical Review*, XXXIX (1775), 203; *Monthly Review*, LII (1775), 465.
[54]*Universal Magazine*, LV (1774), LVI (1775), LVII (1776), LVIII. (1777), etc.

[55]For some further supplementary periodical material on this chapter: *Analytical Review*, II (1788), 458-59—"Shakespear's Morality Commended." (Quoting W. Richardson).

CHAPTER XI

APPRECIATION OF CHARACTERS

Applause for Shakespeare's powers of characterization appears all the way from 1767 to the close of the century.[1] In 1767 the *British Magazine* took up the program of praise: "The characters are all so admirably drawn that the true spirit of the Romans seems to breathe in them."[2] Mrs. Montagu two years later added: "In delineating characters he must be allowed far to surpass all dramatic writers, and even Homer himself.[3] . . . Shakespear seems to have had the art of the Dervise, in the Arabian tales, who could throw his soul into the body of another man, and be at once possessed of his sentiments, adopt his passions, and

---

[1]Though this chapter is not concerned with "The Study of Shakespeare's Characters" before 1766, possibly it should suggest the inadequacy of work done on this period. Dr. T. M. Raysor has pointed out four critical excerpts on Shakespeare's characters before 1766: Dryden's Preface to *Troilus and Cressida* (1679), John Hughes' essay on *Othello* in *The Guardian* (No. 37, 1713), Joseph Warton's *Adventurer Essays* (1753-54), and Johnson's *Preface* (1765)—all these in *MLN*, XLII (1927), 495-500. He remarks, after mentioning Hughes, that there "seems to be no evidence . . . for another half century" (p. 496). But Prof. Nichol Smith in his latest book, *Shakespeare in the Eighteenth Century* (1928), has suggested several further items: e.g., *The Censor*, Nos. 7 and 15 (1718), on King Lear; *The Prompter*, May 27, 1735, on Polonius; and *The Prompter*, No. C (Oct. 24, 1735), on Hamlet. To these studies of Shakespeare's characters might be added the following: *Tatler*, No. 8—on Shakespeare's "noble characters"; *Spectator*, No. 238—Malvolio a Mixed Character; Corbyn Morris' *An Essay towards Fixing True Standards of Wit* (1744—on Falstaff); *Gentleman's Magazine*, XVIII (1748), 553—on Shakespeare's women; *The Diverting History and Droll Adventures of Sir John Falstaff* (1750); *Gentleman's Magazine*, XXII (1752), 458-59—on Macbeth and Falstaff; the *Monthly Review's* comments on *Miscellaneous Observations on "Hamlet*," VI (1752), 76; and the *Gentleman's Magazine*, XXIV (1754), 311—on Shylock. And see my Chap. I.

[2]VIII (1767), 572. [3]*Op. cit.* (1769), p. 20.

rise to all the functions and feelings of his situation."[4] F. Gentleman agreed: ". . . our author had when he pleased an almost magic power over the human heart."[5] In 1773 W. Kenrick showed how a fine actor "might discover . . . many exquisite strokes of character, passion, and humour, evidently designed by the poet, which yet would otherwise escape the notice of the mere literary critick,"[6] and applauded Mrs. Montagu's use of the "Dervise." Even Edward Taylor, the great detractor of Shakespeare,[7] was interested: "Fired with the exalted sentiments of his heroes, from whose mouths virtue herself seems to dictate to mankind, we feel our hearts dilate, the current of our blood flow swifter in every vein, and our whole frame wound up to a pitch of dignity unfelt, unknown before."[8] Mrs. Griffith continued the praise the following year (1775),[9] as did Morgann in 1777, with a more resonant note: ". . . they are struck out *whole*, by some happy art which I cannot clearly comprehend, out of the general mass of things, from the block as it were of nature."[10]

This panegyric kept on through the *Universal Magazine*,[11] the *Lady's Magazine*,[12] Colman's *Preface to the Works of Beaumont and Fletcher* (1778),[13] William Jackson's *Thirty Letters*

[4] *Ibid.*, p. 37. See also pp. 65, 68, 81, 92, 111, 192.
[5] *Op. cit.* (1770), I, 147. See also I, 387.
[6] *Introduction to the School of Shakespeare* (1773), p. 9. Compare also pp. 13, 14.
[7] See Chaps. IV and VIII above.
[8] *Op. cit.* (1774), p. 43. Compare W. Richardson in his first series of essays published the same year: "He [Shakespeare] thus unites the two essential powers of dramatic invention, that of forming characters; and that of imitating, in their natural expressions, the passions and affections of which they are composed." (5th ed., 1798, p. 33). For the texts of Richardson's criticism of Shakespeare, see *JEGP*, XXVIII (Jan., 1929), 117.
[9] Preface to *op. cit.* (1775), p. x, and pp. 26, 167, 357, etc. She quotes Lyttelton's praise: "He [Shakespeare] painted all characters . . . with equal truth, and equal force" (p. x).
[10] *Op. cit.* (1777), p. 154, and compare p. 155.   [11] LXI (1777), 6.
[12] IX (1778), 531.   [13] *Prose on Several Occasions* (1787), II, 154.

(1782,)[14] Blair's *Lectures* (1783),[15] Beattie's *Dissertations* (1783),[16] and Tom Davies' *Dramatic Miscellanies* (1784): "It is the peculiar privilege of Shakspeare to draw characters of the most singular form, and such as, though acknowledged to come from nature's mint, had never entered the mind of any other writer, antient or modern."[17] Richardson's second series of Essays (1784)[18] continued the praise, and the *Lady's Magazine* in the same year announced: ". . . we always behold the portrait of living nature and find ourselves surrounded with our fellows."[19] So also agreed the *Universal Magazine*,[20] Martin Sherlock's *Fragment* (1786),[21] Richardson's third series (1789),[22] the *Lady's Magazine*,[23] and *The Bee* in 1791 and 1793:[24] "A talent for discriminating human characters . . . Shakespeare . . .

---

[14] Letter XIV, p. 93 of 1795 (3rd) ed.: "Shakespeare's characters, have that appearance of reality which always has the effect of actual life."

[15] Lecture III, I (1804), 35: Lecture XLVI, II (1804), 347, 356. "He [Shakespeare] is more faithful to the true language of nature, in the midst of passion, than any writer." (p. 347). See review of Blair in *Monthly Review*, LXX (1784), 182-83.

[16] Part I, Chap. III, pp. 186-87: "In observing the characters of men . . . he must have been indefatigable."

[17] II, 288.

[18] 5th ed. (1798), pp. 125, 210, 222, 226, 293, 364, 379-80, etc. Compare also the 6th ed. (1812) on Fluellen, pp. 374 ff.

[19] XV (1784), 208.

[20] LXXVII (1785), 119—from *Letters of Literature by Robert Heron* (by J. Pinkerton).

[21] P. 22. Tacitus has drawn great characters, but "Shakspeare has drawn them better than Tacitus." See also pp. 15, 32. Compare *European Magazine*, X (1786), 282, and the *Universal Magazine*, LXXXI (1787), 5: ". . . he pleases us by his animated and masterly representations of characters."

[22] P. 286: "Shakspeare, whose morality is no less sublime than his skill in the display of character is masterly and unrivalled."

[23] XXI (1790), 630: "Shakespeare makes no character speak what is not perfectly natural to it."

[24] III (1791), 232: "The genius of Shakespeare formed natural characters." See also p. 310. IV (1791), 291: Shakespeare's "wonderfully various and natural characters." See also I (1791), 58.

possessed this happy talent in a degree superior to that of any other of the sons of men who have yet appeared on the globe."[25]

HISTORICAL CHARACTERS

To turn from general to more particular reference, the historical characters received praise from Mrs. Montagu in 1769,[26] and her judgment was approved by Blair in 1783.[27] Tom Davies devoted one whole volume to them,[28] and Richard Hole, "T. O.," of the Exeter Society *Essays* exclaimed in 1796: ". . . the historical dramas of Shakspeare. The wonder-working power of the poet's pen is there most eminently displayed. . . . His characters . . . are such genuine copies from life, that we must suppose the originals acted and spoke in the manner he represents them."[29]

SHAKESPEARE'S WOMEN

Shakespeare's women were applauded quite fulsomely by Francis Gentleman in 1770[30] and by the woman author of *The Correspondent, an Original Novel:* ". . . he is the only poet (that I know of) who has delineated to perfection the character of a *female* friend."[31] Tom Davies remarked: "I

---

[25] XIV (1793), 302-3.
[26] *Op. cit.*, pp. 58-59, 68-69, 86, 89, and her whole third chapter.
[27] Lecture XLVI, II (1804), 357 n.
[28] *Op. cit.*, Advertisement, pp. vi-vii; the whole of vol. I, esp. p. 352. For individuals, for example, note Lady Constance (I, 33-37), Stephen Langton (I, 42 ff), Cæsar (II, 227), etc., etc.
[29] P. 250. See also pp. 251, 270. For reviews of this essay see *Lady's Magazine*, XXVIII (1797), 589, and *Hibernian Magazine*, 1798, pp. 387, 489. For the supernatural characters see Chap. VI, above.
[30] *Op. cit.*, I, 460-79. One must recall that W. Collins, far back in 1743, had rejected Shakespeare's women in his *Epistle to Sir Thomas Hanmer*, lines 57-66. But compare *Gentleman's Magazine*, XVIII (1748), 553.
[31] Quoted in *Monthly Review*, LII (1775), 433. Compare also, the poetic

believe it will be difficult to find, in any other author, such abundant and varied originality, in women's characters, as in Shakspeare";[32] and the *Analytical Review* declared "Shakespear not deficient in delineating female characters."[33] William Richardson's third series of 1789 devoted a whole essay to praise for Shakespeare's "Female Characters" and summarized: ". . . there is not only as much variety in Shakespeare's female characters as we have any title to demand; but . . . they are distinguished with peculiar and appropriated features."[34] The *Lady's Magazine* one year later noted that "Shakspeare evidently was no enemy to the fair sex,"[35] and finally the *Female Mentor* praised Shakespeare's women, with particular reference to Imogen.[36]

Minor Characters

Praise of the minor characters appeared in the *British Magazine*, January, 1766 (on Caliban)[37] and in the *Gentleman's Magazine* in the same year.[38] Mrs. Montagu declared that "Mine hostess Quickly is of a species not extinct. It may be said, the author there sinks from comedy to farce,

---

extract in the *Monthly Review*, XLVII (1772), 410:
        "Oh, matchless Shakespeare! thine it was to know
        The worth of woman, and the joys that flow
        From her soft excellence."
[32]*Op. cit.* (1784), II, 363.
[33]II (1788), 458-59. The periodical is using W. Richardson.
[34]Pp. 344-59, 362. The quotation in the text is from p. 344. 5th ed. (1798) used *passim*.
[35]XXI (1790), 630.
[36]I (1793), 212-35. Compare also the *Hibernian Magazine*, 1791, Part I, p. 118—"Gallantry of Shakspeare."
[37]For this reference I am indebted to Prof. Nichol Smith, *Shakespeare in the Eighteenth Century* (1928), p. 84 n. (The vol. for 1766 was not available in Chicago). Compare Joseph Warton's essays in the *Adventurer* (1754), No. 93, 97.
[38]XXXVI (1766), 405,—on Shakespeare's clown [in *Twelfth Night*].

but she helps to compleat the character of Falstaffe, and some of the dialogues in which she is engaged are diverting."[39] Francis Gentleman in the following year devoted many pages to minor characters while discussing individual plays,[40] and Mrs. Griffith in 1775 remarked that "Shakespeare's fools are not those of *modern times*, but speak a great deal of good sense throughout all his Plays."[41] Similarly both William Richardson[42] and Tom Davies[43] in 1784 discussed many minor characters in the course of their exhaustive studies. Davies' comment on Polonius is particularly interesting: "About five and twenty years since, Mr. Garrick had formed a notion . . . that he [Polonius] was not designed by the author to excite laughter, and become an object of ridicule. . . . Full of this opinion Mr. Garrick persuaded Woodward . . . to put himself in the part of Polonius. And what was the consequence?— The character, divested of his ridiculous vivacity, appeared to the audience flat and insipid."[44]

Iago and Shylock

Both Iago and Shylock, though still essentially minor characters in this period, provided some spirited discussion. Martin Sherlock in 1786 declared that "Tacitus and

---

[39]*Op. cit.*, p. 123. On Hotspur (pp. 91-92), Henry IV (pp. 95, 103-4), Shallow (p. 117), Pistol (pp. 122-23). On minor characters in general, p. 15.

[40]On Shylock and Co. (*op. cit.*, I, 278-98), Romeo and Juliet and Co. (I, 171-93—*Garrick's Alteration*), Cymbeline and Co. (II, 77-101—again Garrick's alteration), Julius Cæsar and others (II, 1-19), characters in *Much Ado* (II, 307-22), Henry V and all (II, 351-64), Henry IV and all (II, 384-98), King John and others (II, 155-73), the Othello group (I, 131-55), etc.

[41]*Op. cit.*, p. 357.

[42]Anne (*op. cit.*, p. 210), Buckingham (p. 220), Timon (whole chapter), etc. He had already discussed Jacques and Imogen at length in 1774.

[43]For example, Parolles (*op. cit.*, II, 40), Kent (II, 289), Polonius (III, 37-42), etc.

[44]*Ibid.*, III, 41-42.

Machiavel together could not have painted or supported the character of a villain better than that of Iago."[45] Ten years later Richard Hole, in the Exeter *Essays*, came to the defense of Iago: "The latter [Colley Cibber] was often in former times Iago's theatrical representative; and I do not see why the original is not as deserving of an apology [referring to Cibber's *Apology*] as the copy."[46] He announces then that Iago's character before the play had been good,[47] that Iago had reason to believe Othello had seduced Emelia,[48] and that he suspected Cassio of the same crime and was jealous of Cassio's military promotion.[49] Hole also accounts for Iago's aversion to Desdemona[50] and thus has given Iago plenty of motivation for villainy.[51]

Shylock Hole also defends by adopting a Jew's point of view on the character: We have, because he is a Jew "a prejudice equally unjust and illiberal."[52] . . . We ought not to try Shylock by our laws, but by those of the community to which he belonged."[53] He lists Shylock's injuries from Antonio and declares that a Jewish poet would "convert his story into a deep tragedy."[54] He then gives a fictitious criticism by a Jewish critic, emphasizing "this curious exposition of the Venetian laws"[55] and the fact that no commentator has remarked on "the unjust judge, the injurious merchant, the undutiful daughter."[56] His point of view on Shylock was taken up immediately in the following year by the *Universal Magazine*.[57] Meanwhile, however, a Mr. David Levi had produced *Dissertations on the Prophecies of*

---

[45] *A Fragment*, p. 15.
[46] *Op. cit.*, p. 397.
[47] *Ibid.*, p. 399.
[48] *Ibid.*, pp. 400-1.
[49] *Ibid.*, p. 403.
[50] *Ibid.*, p. 407.
[51] Contrast Coleridge's attitude toward Iago, in Chap. XV, below. In Chap. XVI, the present writer attempts to prove that Coleridge knew Hole's essay.
[52] *Op. cit.*, p. 553.
[53] *Ibid.*, p. 555.
[54] *Ibid.*, p. 566.
[55] *Ibid.*, p. 570.
[56] *Ibid.*, p. 571.
[57] CI (1797), 124 ff.

the Old Testament (1793-6), in which Shakespeare's depiction of Shylock was now viciously attacked by a *real Jew*—so viciously, in fact, that the *British Critic* rose in vigorously sarcastic defense of Shakespeare: ". . . he [Mr. Levi] dares to stigmatize . . . the greatest poet, that England ever knew. Yet . . . he admits, that the detestable portrait of Shylock was drawn by the hand of *a great master of nature*. . . . If Shakespeare were indeed 'a great master of nature,' there is some degree of probability that the character he has pourtrayed is not altogether unnatural."[58] Thus the battle over Shylock began.

It will be well now to turn to the particular major characters which most interested the late eighteenth century: namely, Lear, Macbeth, Richard III, Falstaff, and Hamlet.[59]

KING LEAR

The source, temper, and progress of Lear's madness greatly interested the late eighteenth century. Horace Walpole wrote in the *Postscript* to his *Mysterious Mother* (1768): "The finest picture ever drawn of a head distem-

---

[58]XII (1798), 45. The *British Critic* also has comments on Shylock in IX (1797), 362. For further material on Othello and his group (rather subordinate characters in late eighteenth-century criticism) see: *The Bee*, I (1791), 56, 87, 132, 176 (by W. N. Anderson); *Gentleman's Magazine*, LXI (1791), 225—Othello misrepresented; W. Parr, *Story of the Moor of Venice*, 1795 [Reviewed in *Analytical Review*, XXI (1795), 63.]; *Monthly Review*, XXII (1797), 7—Apology for Iago [on Exeter *Essay*]. Further comments on relatively minor characters appear in V. Knox, *Winter Evenings*, (1787), No. 50—on Julius Cæsar; *The Mirror* (1779-80), No. 100—on Edgar; *Lounger* (1785-86), No. 91—on Timon and Jaques; *The Bee*, III (1791), 112—on Benedick; *Monthly Review*, XXII (1797), 9—Apology for Shylock [on Exeter *Essay*]; *Monthly Mirror*, V (1798), 110, 170, 301—on Shakespeare's ghosts.

[59]Most of the material preceding 1766 on these characters has already been given in this section. Warton's *Adventurer* essays No. 113, 116, 122 on Lear were noted by Dr. Raysor, and D. Nichol Smith has proposed *Gray's Inn Journal* (1756), No. 65, 66, and 87 on Lear [p. 83 n. of his latest (1928) text]. These discussed the origin of Lear's madness.

pered by misfortune is that of *King Lear*."⁶⁰ The *Monthly Review* remarked: "Lear is a good man but choleric, subject to sudden and violent anger, but not capable of deliberate malice, much less of impiety. That in the bitterness of his soul he should conceive, and even express, the horrid curse of his daughter and her offspring, is consistent with his character and his situation."⁶¹ In 1770 Francis Gentleman gave further study, but it must be remembered that this was not Shakespeare's *King Lear* which the *Dramatic Censor* was reviewing.⁶² W. Richardson in 1784 traced King Lear's madness and summarized: "Shakespeare . . . has exhibited in his Dramatic Character of King Lear the man of mere sensibility."⁶³ Meanwhile in 1782, Jackson had announced conclusively: "The characters of Lear or Falstaffe, tho' as great contrasts as can be found in the whole range of human nature, are both formed upon general principles, so that they are equally excellent now, as when they were first exhibited, and they will produce the utmost effect of tragedy and comedy as long as our language endures."⁶⁴ And the *Universal Magazine* in 1792 concluded: "Our poet's representation of the origin and progress of the distraction of Lear, exhibits the greatest judgment and skill."⁶⁵

[60] P. 99 of Dublin (1791) Edition. This postscript first appeared in 1781, in J. Dodsley's Edition.
[61] LXI (1769), 143.
[62] *Op. cit.*, I, 369-76: ". . . this natural struggle between vanity, and debilitation." (I, 369-70). Dr. Hanawalt of the College of the City of Detroit has kindly informed me that Thomas Hull praised Lear in his preface to *Henry II* (1774).
[63] *Op. cit.*, p. 293. See also p. 312. This repeats J. Warton's analysis of Lear as "an aged monarch of strong passions and quick sensibility."—*Adventurer*, No. 113, Dec. 4, 1753. And both men trace the "progress of the distraction of Lear."
[64] Letter VII, pp. 46-47 of the 3rd ed. (1795) of the *Thirty Letters*. See Appendix A.
[65] XCI (1792), 183.

Macbeth

One of the greatest problems the critics tried to solve was whether Macbeth was as courageous as Richard III. Opinions fluctuated persistently throughout the period. Mrs. Montagu in 1769 was not particularly worried, for she called Macbeth "a man of courage."[66] F. Gentleman praised *Cibber's* Richard III,[67] but with regard to Macbeth remarked: ". . . the author meant to draw him a detestable monster."[68] The battle of Whately (1770) and Kemble (1786) on the subject should be reserved to the chapter below on psychologizing, where it essentially belongs.[69] Meanwhile Morgann in 1777 praised the delineation of Macbeth,[70] and Richardson took up Richard III in 1784, having discussed Macbeth in 1774. Richardson's observations also belong primarily to the chapter on psychologizing, but it may be interesting to note here that Richardson assigns to Macbeth "an amiable temper"[71] whereas he regards Richard in quite a different light.[72] Tom Davies gave Macbeth courage,[73] but the *European Magazine* leaned hesitatingly toward Whately—against courage—in 1787.[74] Two years later the *Monthly Review* reversed the verdict again and, following Kemble, cited Malone to show that Shakespeare did not mean, in Macbeth, to give

---

[66]*Op. cit.*, p. 192. See also p. 183 and compare p. 176 on Richard III: "The bad man is his own tempter."
[67]*Op. cit.*, I, 3-14.   [68]*Ibid.*, I, 83.
[69]The reader may compare reviews of them now, if he wishes, in the *Critical Review*, LXI (1786), 302, and LXIX (1790), 116. Whately denied Macbeth courage. See Appendix A.
[70]*Op. cit.*, p. 69.   [71]*Op. cit.*, p. 68.
[72]*Ibid.*, p. 204: ". . . great intellectual ability employed for inhuman and perfidious purposes." Compare p. 201.
[73]*Op. cit.*, II, 191.
[74]XI (1787), 227. Compare also *The Lounger* (1785-86), No. 69.

an example of cowardice.⁷⁵ Finally, Richard Hole, the Exeter Society essayist, in 1796 gave Richard III some strong coloring: "I conceive that the crimes of Iago, when fairly compared with those of Richard, will fade, like the new moon overpowered by meridian splendor . . ." Richard has "Pharisaic hypocrisy" and the "cruelty of a Borgia."⁷⁶ So opinion vacillated and this vacillation continued into the early nineteenth century.

FALSTAFF

Falstaff also furnished a field for general combat on the subject of his cowardice, although not all critics, of course, entered the lists. Mrs. Montagu in 1769 accepted him without question as "cowardly";⁷⁷ yet he was "the best calculated to raise laughter of any that ever appeared on a stage."⁷⁸ The *Universal Magazine* discussed his historical background,⁷⁹ and William Kenrick in 1773 pugnaciously replied to the *Public Ledger's* attack on him for "clearing the character of Sir John Falstaff of imputed malignity of disposition, and . . . describing him as a *harmless, inoffensive, jocular* creature" with "I left him in full possession of his character for gluttony, lying, cowardice, and theft."⁸⁰ Mrs. Griffith gave Falstaff great praise, without mention of his cowardice, though she did insist that he lacked "virtue."⁸¹

---

⁷⁵LXXX (1789), 553.
⁷⁶*Op. cit.*, pp. 397-98. See also p. 409: Richard is classed with Aaron. Dr. Raysor mentions these Exeter essays but apparently overlooked this analysis of Richard III. For supplementary material on Richard and Macbeth see: *The Observer* (1785-90), Nos. 69, 70, 71, 72—on Macbeth and Richard; *Gentleman's Magazine*, LIX (1789), 20—on Macbeth; *Monthly Mirror*, V (1798), 170—on Macbeth.
⁷⁷*Op. cit.*, p. 103. Compare, also, pp. 102, 106-8.
⁷⁸*Ibid.*, p. 106.   ⁷⁹LI (1772), 62.
⁸⁰*Retort Courteous*, pp. 28-29.   ⁸¹*Op. cit.* (1775), p. 228.

It was Maurice Morgann who in 1777 startled the critics with his absolution of Falstaff: "I do not conceive Shakespeare ever meant to make Cowardice an essential part of his constitution."[82] . . . Cowardice *is not* the *Impression*, which the *whole* character of Falstaff is calculated to make on the minds of an unprejudiced audience."[83] Morgann's nice distinction between the impression and the understanding belongs, of course, in the chapter below on the psychologizing of Shakespeare, but once grant him that distinction and his conclusions follow readily enough: ". . . the leading quality in Falstaff's character . . . is a high degree of wit and humour, accompanied with great natural vigour and alacrity of mind[84] . . . strong, natural constitutional Courage."[85] He even attacks Mrs. Montagu[86] and declares that the players by "low buffoonery" make Falstaff appear a coward.[87] For Shakespeare himself he has nothing but praise: "The progressive discovery of Falstaff's character is excellently managed";[88] Shakespeare shows both "address" and "art."[89] All this was very brilliant, but Johnson's comment on it is amusing: "Why, Sir, we shall have the man come forth again; and as he has proved Falstaff to be no coward, he may prove Iago to be a very good character."[90]

General appreciation of Falstaff appeared in Jackson's *Letters*,[91] in Tom Davies' *Dramatic Miscellanies* (1784,)[92] and in *An Apology for the Life of George Anne Bellamy* (1785).[93] Cumberland in his *Observer* in 1786 returned to the empha-

---

[82]*Op. cit.*, p. 2. Morgann's *Essay* was written as early as 1774.
[83]*Ibid.*, pp. 4-5. Compare p. 11.   [84]*Ibid.*, pp. 17-18.
[85]*Ibid.*, p. 97.   [86]*Ibid.*, p. 111-12.   [87]*Ibid.*, p. 127.
[88]*Ibid.*, p. 129.   [89]*Ibid.*, p. 143.
[90]Boswell's *Life* (ed. Hill), IV (1783), 192 n. Compare also the rather sceptical review in the *Critical Review*, XLIII (1777), 397.
[91]Letter VII, pp. 46-47 of the 3rd ed. (1795).
[92]I, chaps. XI-XVI, especially pp. 202-3, 278.   [93]IV, 181.

sis on Falstaff's cowardice,[94] but Mackenzie in the *Lounger* (1786) was loth to forget Morgann: "Falstaff's cowardice is only proportionate to the danger . . . not so much a weakness as a principle,"[95]—though both admitted that he was a great source of laughter.[96] The latter even compared him with Richard III.[97] Then came the Rev. Mr. Richard Stack with his Examination of Morgann's Essay in the *Transactions of the Royal Irish Academy* in 1788, flatly saying that Falstaff was a coward, in direct contradiction of Morgann.[97a] Stack emphasized mainly the first scene, and the *Monthly Review*, reviewing his work in 1792, largely agreed with him: "We think, a general coward, with an occasional semblance of courage."[98] The *Monthly Review* critic was apparently trying to steer something of a middle course, for he remarked immediately after: ". . . is it not possible that there should be many inconsistencies in Shakespeare's drawing of Falstaff's character?"[99]

Meanwhile had appeared William Richardson with an essay on Falstaff in his third series (1788-9). Richardson is rather puzzling, for he seems to wander around somewhat aimlessly on both sides of the argument. He refers definitely to Morgann's essay in a footnote of this text,[100] and some of his ideas echo Morgann: "In what follows of this Essay, therefore, I shall first exemplify some of the baser, and

---

[94]No. 73. Chalmers, *British Essayists*, XXXIII, 146.
[95]No. 69. Chalmers, XXXI, 112.
[96]*Lounger*, No. 68; *Observer*, No. 73.   [97]*Lounger*, No. 69.
[97a]. . . a *constitutional courage* does not seem to me any part of the *impression* which Shakespear designed to give of Falstaff's character . . . Shakespear has designed cowardice . . . to be a part of Falstaff's real character."—*Transactions*, II (1788), 4-5. The whole paper occupied pp. 3-37.
[98]VII (1792), 63.
[99]*Ibid.*, p. 63. For these last two notes I am indebted to Mr. D. L. King of the University of Michigan.
[100]P. 14. The edition in the McMillan Shakespeare Collection in the University of Michigan is dated "1789."

then some of those agreeable parts of the character that reconcile our feelings but not our reason, to its [the character's] deformity.[101] . . . Thus his cowardice seems to be the result of deliberation, rather than the effect of constitution";[102] yet he deliberately announces Falstaff's cowardice at least twice.[103] The *Monthly Review* in 1789 rejected his harking back to Morgann and pronounced Falstaff definitely a coward.[104]

All these critics, while arguing over the one point, agreed on the great humor of the character, and perhaps White's hoax of the *Original Letters of Sir John Falstaff* (1796) should be noted in conclusion to emphasize this idea, for White in his Preface applauded Falstaff's "bursts of humour . . . his quips and his gybes."[105] The letters themselves illustrate Falstaff's character and include those written (presumably) by Prince Hal, Justice Shallow, Pistol, Nym, Mrs. Ford, Mistress Quickly, Slender, Sir Hugh Evans, Davy, and Captain Fluellen.[106]

Hamlet

The Hamlet problem was not first proposed by William Richardson,[107] nor by George Steevens.[108] Francis Gentle-

---

[101] 5th ed. (1798), p. 249. (This is the edition used *passim* for Richardson).
[102] *Ibid.*, p. 251.
[103] *Ibid.*, pp. 255, 281. There is some good appreciation of Falstaff in pp. 276-77.
[104] LXXXI (1789), 54.
[105] P. xiv. Dr. Raysor apparently misdated this book 1789.
[106] Reviewed in *Monthly Review*, XX (1796), 356. For further material on Falstaff see: *Weekly Amusement*, I (1765-66), 345—Life of Sir John Oldcastle; *Critical Review*, LXVI (1788), 542—rev. of Richardson; *Analytical Review*, II (1788), 457—rev. of Richardson; *Hibernian Magazine*, 1789, p. 24—rev. of Richardson; *European Magazine*, XIV (1788), 422—rev. of Richardson; *Analytical Review*, VII (1790), 406—rev. of Stack.
[107] See *JEGP*, XXVIII (Jan., 1929), 136. But see footnote 140 of this article.
[108] Professor Nichol Smith suggests this in his latest text (1928), p. 88.

man complained in 1770, three years before Steevens: "In respect of characters, we are to lament that the hero, who is intended as amiable, should be such an apparent heap of inconsistency; impetuous tho' philosophical; sensible of injury, yet timid of resentment; shrewd, yet void of policy; full of filial piety, yet tame under oppression; boastful in expression, undetermined in action; and yet, from being pregnant with great variety, from affording many opportunities to exert sound judgement and extensive powers, he is as agreeable and striking an object as any in the English drama."[109] No better summary of Hamlet's inconsistency, yet general appeal, appeared in any later critics in the eighteenth century.

Three years later George Steevens attacked:

> Hamlet . . . makes but one effort to keep his word [to the Ghost] . . . defers his purpose . . . the execution of Rosencrantz and Guildenstern . . . gives him no concern. . . . He is not less accountable for the distraction and death of Ophelia . . . he kills the king at last to revenge himself, and not his father.
>
> Hamlet cannot be said to have pursued his ends by very warrantable means; and if the poet, when he sacrificed him at last, meant to have enforced such a moral, it is not the worst that can be deduced from the play.
>
> I have dwelt the longer on this subject, because Hamlet seems to have been hitherto regarded as a hero, not undeserving the pity of the audience, and because no writer on Shakespeare has taken the pains to point out the immoral tendency of his character.[110]

Richardson added in 1774: "His [Hamlet's] amiable hesitations and reluctant scruples lead him at one time to

---
[109] *Op. cit.*, I, 55.   [110] 1st ed. of *Works* (1773), X, 343-44 n.

indecision; and then betray him . . . into acts of rash and inconsiderate violence."[111] But Pilon in 1777 is much more sane: "The character of Hamlet, though not the most finished, is certainly one of the most splendid efforts of Shakespeare's genius";[112] Pilon goes on to admit the importance of Hamlet's doubt of the Ghost[113] and violently attacks Henderson's omission of Hamlet's reason for not killing the King at prayer: "for Hamlet's continuing to procrastinate, he appears weak and inconsistent, during the last two acts,"[114] that is, *simply because Henderson left out that important speech.*

But Pilon was unable alone to stem the tide of the reaction against Hamlet. Steevens returned to the attack in 1778 with the help of Akenside.[115] Mackenzie contributed further to the disintegration of Hamlet in 1780: "With the strongest purposes of revenge he [Hamlet] is irresolute and inactive,"[116] which Richardson repeated almost verbatim in his second essay on Hamlet in 1784: "In the conduct, however, which he displays, in the progress of the tragedy, he appears irresolute and indecisive."[117] Meanwhile Rit-

---

[111] P. 119 of fifth edition.

[112] *Op. cit.* (1777), p. 3. See also p. 4. This critic is not mentioned by Professor Nichol Smith.

[113] *Ibid.*, p. 19. A fundamental argument of modern historical defenders of Shakespeare on Hamlet.

[114] *Ibid.*, p. 19. Once again a sane historical point of view. His attitude should be flatly contrasted with Richardson's romantic horror over the same speech (p. 131 of 5th ed.).

[115] X, 412 n. "The late Dr. Akinside once observed to me [Steevens], that the conduct of Hamlet was every way unnatural and indefensible, unless he were to be regarded as a young man whose intellects were in some degree impaired by his own misfortunes." This paragraph Steevens inserted between the second and third given above for 1773.

[116] *The Mirror*, No. 99, Chalmers, XXIX, 249. See also No. 100.

[117] P. 123 of 5th edition. The *Critical Review*, in discussing Richardson—LVII (Feb., 1784), 102—admitted Hamlet's inconsistency.

APPRECIATION OF CHARACTERS   151

son had in 1783 replied to Steevens' attack[118]—incidentally, Ritson was astonished at Steevens' bitterness and for eight pages[119] followed Hamlet all the way through the play to refute the point Steevens made, which was really a little different from the general trend of the Hamlet attack: "no writer on Shakespeare has taken the pains to point out the immoral tendency of his [Hamlet's] character."[120] Ritson is said to have been "followed by Thomas Davies in his *Dramatic Miscellanies*,"[121] but this is a rather ambiguous statement which finds corroboration only in chronology (1783 to 1784) and the fact that Davies notes no particular indecision in Hamlet;[122] nevertheless Davies is a perfect echo of Richardson on the speech of Hamlet over the king at prayer: "not only shocking but highly improbable."[123]

Meanwhile, however, there was James Harris' dismay over Hamlet as quoted in the *London Magazine* in 1781: "But should the same Hamlet by chance kill an innocent old man, an old man from whom he had never received offence, and with whose daughter he was actually in love; —what should we expect then? . . . Should we not be shocked . . . were he to be *brutally jocose?* Here the MANNERS are *blamable*, because they are inconsistent; we should never conjecture from Hamlet anything so unfeelingly cruel."[124]

The attack on Hamlet continued in Richardson's second

---

[118]Professor Nichol Smith notes this in his *Shakespeare in the Eighteenth Century* (1928), p. 89.
[119]*Remarks, Critical and Illustrative* (1783), pp. 217-24.
[120]See text above. It is true that Steevens also said that Hamlet "defers his purpose." (Nichol Smith does not note this difference.)
[121]By Nichol Smith, *op. cit.* (1928), p. 89.   [122]*Op. cit.*, III, 143.
[123]*Ibid.*, III, 101, and Richardson, p. 131 of 5th ed. Contrast Pilon above.
[124]L (1781), 534, from Harris' *Dramatic Speculations*. Professor Nichol Smith fails to note this criticism.

essay in 1784,[125] and J. M. Mason the following year repeated the general lamentation: "I cannot read it [Johnson's characterization of Polonius] without heartily regretting that he did not exert his great abilities and discriminating powers, in delineating the strange, inconsistent, and indecisive character of Hamlet, to which I confess myself unequal."[126] Nor can one overlook Craig's article on misanthropy in the *Lounger* (1785-87), No. 91: Hamlet "is endued with the most exquisite sensibility ... he is hurt in his soul's tenderest part, he is unhinged in his principles of action."

Thomas Robertson pursued this rapidly developing tradition with his essay on Hamlet, which appeared originally in the *Transactions of the Royal Society of Edinburgh* in 1790. Here again are noted "high elevation of soul, an exquisite sensibility." But Robertson's chief emphasis is on Hamlet's "extreme gentleness of spirit and sweetness of disposition"; and the critic is greatly interested in the "antic disposition" and the pre-murder as compared with the post-murder Hamlet.[127] In 1793 an anonymous critic was also worried by the antic disposition and blamed Hamlet for not killing the King at prayer and for exercising wit over the body of Polonius.[128] Finally Goethe's *Wilhelm Meister* idea of Hamlet as a flower-in-a-vase appeared, with sympathetic reception—the way had been amply prepared—at the close of the century, and was translated in the *Monthly Review* in 1798: "Shakespeare designed to exhibit *a great deed imposed upon a mind which was not fitted for*

---

[125] See quotation above in connection with Mackenzie. The page in Richardson was 123.
[126] *Op. cit.* (1785), p. 380.
[127] *Transactions*, II (1790), 254-57. The whole paper occupied pp. 251-67. Reviewed in the *European Magazine*, XVIII (1790), 170, 265, 349.
[128] *Anthologia Hibernica*, II (1793), 36—by "W." See reply by "R. A. H.," p. 254.

the commission."[129] Thus the Romantic sentimentalizing of Hamlet was completed by the Germans and made fully ready for further development by Coleridge and the rest of the early nineteenth-century Romantics. The only counterpart of Pilon's sane criticism throughout this development was James Plumptre's attempt in 1796[130] to find an historical basis for Hamlet in the murder of Mary Queen of Scots' husband, Lord Darnley, on the same day of the week (Monday) as that of the elder Hamlet. Hence, says Plumptre, Shakespeare was offering the play as a tribute to Elizabeth. But the *European Magazine* promptly rejected the idea.[131] Then Plumptre produced more evidence in 1797[132] and in 1799 got the *European Magazine* to print a letter from him, dated "April 10, 1799," pointing out that Captain Blackadder was executed for the murder of Darnley, and that the ghost in *Hamlet* makes an allusion to the fact that a *serpent* stung him.[133] Here, then, is a definite attempt at historical criticism, and though perhaps a bad one, it is not yet forgotten today.[134]

---

[129] XXVII (1798), 545 ff. The present quotation is from p. 547.
[130] *Observations on "Hamlet"* (Cambridge: Lunn, 1796).
[131] XXXII (1797), 261.
[132] *Appendix to Observations on "Hamlet"* (Cambridge: Deighton, 1797).
[133] XXXV (1799), 244. See also p. 160.
[134] Miss Lilian Winstanley, with similar obsessions (on Hamlet, Macbeth and King Lear), was thus completely anticipated by the late eighteenth century. Compare also Horace Walpole's idea of the *Winter's Tale* as a sequel to *Henry VIII—Historic Doubts* (1768), p. 114 (see pp. 13 ff. above). For some further material on Hamlet, note: *Critical Review*, XLIV (1777), 152—on Pilon on Henderson as Hamlet; [?], *A Short Criticism on the Performance of Hamlet by Mr. Kemble*, 1789; *Hibernian Magazine*, 1790, Part II, p. 543 —Character of Hamlet; *Critical Review*, LXXI (1791), 130—rev. of Robertson; *Analytical Review*, VIII (1790), 266—rev. of Robertson; *Monthly Review*, IV (1791), 421—rev. of Robertson; *Edinburgh Fugitive Pieces*, 1791, No. 45 —on Henderson's Hamlet; *Analytical Review*, XXIII (1796), 391—on Plumptre; *Ibid.*, XXVI (1797), 168—on Plumptre's *Appendix*.

Conclusion

In conclusion one should emphasize the prominence of four late eighteenth-century critics in all this new emphasis on Shakespeare's character portrayal—namely, Mrs. Montagu, Francis Gentleman, Tom Davies, and William Richardson. Even more credit is due, however, to the many periodicals, particularly the *Monthly Review*, the *Critical Review*, and Mackenzie's *Mirror* and *Lounger*. The most important general character study of the period was certainly that of Hamlet, in so far as diversity of interest was concerned, but for individual brilliancy of discussion Morgann's *Essay on the Dramatic Character of Sir John Falstaff*, to be surveyed more carefully in the next chapter, undoubtedly deserves most respect. All this new emphasis on Shakespeare's character delineation should be approached now from another point of view, which was less impressionistic and more analytically psychological—in short, the psychologizing of Shakespeare in the late eighteenth century.

CHAPTER XII

THE PSYCHOLOGIZING OF SHAKESPEARE

Mr. E. Walder wrote one important paragraph in 1895:[1] "This philosophic movement in Shaksperian criticism was undoubtedly brought about by the wider critical movement of which Locke, Berkeley, and Hume are exponents."[2] This is an extremely interesting point which has been generally neglected with regard to Shakespeare from 1766 to 1799. Unfortunately this chapter can do little more than touch upon the background of such psychological criticism in the eighteenth century.

The Background of Psychological Criticism

The interest of this century in psychologizing is too well known to require much illustration, and it will be quite easy to trace the direct influence of Locke and Hume, for example, on some critics just discussed in the preceding chapter.[3] But there are many others who should be projected into this picture of the background of late eighteenth-century psychological criticism of Shakespeare. For example, Kames was proclaimed by the *Monthly Review* in 1777 "one of the first adventurers" in psychological criticism,[4] and Kames' direct follower was J. Priestley, whose *Lec-*

---

[1] Mr. Walder's book was discussed in my Introduction.
[2] *Shaksperian Criticism Textual and Literary from Dryden to the End of the Eighteenth Century* (1895), p. 19. Walder is referring to Morgann and Richardson.
[3] See this present section, below.
[4] LVII (1777), 89. Lord Kames' *Elements of Criticism* first appeared in 1762. The British Museum Cat. lists 2nd ed., 1763; 4th, 1769; 6th, 1785; 7th, 1788; and 8th, 1807. In 1807 also appeared A. F. T. Woodhouseles' *Memoirs of Henry Home of Kames*.

tures on Oratory and Criticism appeared in 1777.[5] Now whether Kames was the originator of this criticism or not is by no means a matter of moment here, but the fact remains that Kames' *Elements of Criticism* (1762) certainly did have influence on the criticism of William Richardson, who refers directly to the book several times[6] and echoes it verbally over and over again.[7] And Kames' psychological involutions are easily perceptible in his chapter heads: "Perceptions and Ideas in a Train," "Emotions and Passions," "Beauty," "Grandeur and Sublimity," "Novelty," "Uniformity and Variety," "External Signs of Emotions and Passions," "Ridicule," "Wit," etc., etc.

Burke is another man[8] who must be noted in the background of psychological criticism before 1766, for his *Enquiry into the Origin of our Ideas of the Sublime and Beautiful* (1757) also affected later Shakespeare criticism, notably Richardson's again.[9] Burke's psychological tendencies appear in such section heads as: "Novelty," "Pain and Pleasure," "Joy and Grief," "Of Beauty," "Sympathy," "Imitation and Ambition," "Terror," "Power," "Privation," etc., etc.

But the truth is that, quite apart from individual writers, there was a tremendous general background of psychologizing in the early eighteenth century which amply prepared the way for the psychologizing of Shakespeare at the close

---

[5] See *Monthly Review*, LVII (1777), 89 ff.

[6] *Op. cit.* (5th ed., 1798), pp. 30, 66, 265. For a detailed list of Richardson's texts on Shakespeare see *JEGP*, XXVIII (Jan., 1929), 117.

[7] *Ibid.*, pp. 3, 30, 33, 66, 265, 307-8. For example, Kames writes: "The science of rational criticism tends to improve the heart no less than the understanding" (*Elements of Criticism*, New York, E. Duychinck, 1819, Introd., p. xxiii). And Richardson echoes: "An exercise no less adaptable to improve the heart than to inform the understanding" (p. 33).

[8] One might also suggest T. Reid, *Inquiry into the Human Mind* (1764).

[9] See this chapter, below, pp. 162-63.

of the century. It will be appropriate here to suggest in a note merely a brief representation of such material as it appeared, particularly in periodicals, from the beginning of the century to 1766.[10] The psychologizing of Shakespeare from 1766 to 1799 may be divided into two types: the analysis of Shakespeare's interpretation of the passions, and the application of the concept of association to aspects of Shakespeare's art. The first becomes an analysis of Shakespeare's character portrayal in terms of the current psychology of various emotions good and bad; the second implies an explanation, by means of the concept, of obscure and apparently unrelated features of Shakespeare's ideas and language. It must be noted that this psychologizing tendency, here indicated in merely two phases of Shakespearean criticism, spreads over several other related fields in the late eighteenth century. It has appeared also in very direct form in the discussion of the unities, tragicomedy, nature, and original genius, in connection with Shakespeare's plays.[11] In short, it is a very important, though hitherto neglected, factor in the late eighteenth-century criticism of the poet.

---

[10]*History of the Works of the Learned*, I (1699), 261—on the Passions; X (1708), 97—definition of the Passions; T. Reresby, *Miscellany* (1721), 357—Melancholy Ideas Give Pleasure; *C. Morris, *An Essay toward Fixing the True Standards of Wit and Humour*, 1744. (Starred material is more directly concerned with Shakespeare.) D. Hume, *Essay on Tragedy*, 1757; *Monthly Review*, XXVI (1762), 413—review of Kames; *XXVII (1762), 13, 105—review of Kames; *XXVII (1762), 21—Shakespeare superior in delineating passions; XXX (1764), 370—attacking Hume on human nature (Reid's *Enquiry*); *Critical Review*, V (1758), 161—psychological inquiries; X (1760), 368—human nature delineated; XIII (1762), 77—on the passions; *XIII (1762), 185, 285, 365—review of Kames; *Dublin Magazine*, I (1762), 237—review of Kames; *Gentleman's Magazine*, XXXII (1762), 147—notice of Kames.

[11]Chaps. IV, VI, and IX. See also Chaps. VIII and XIII.

Shakespeare's Depiction of the Passions

The procedure applied *passim* by the critics in analyzing Shakespeare's characterization psychologically with regard to the passions is first to describe the passion in general and then to apply this description to a Shakespearean character. For example, all aspects of ambition are explained carefully, whereupon Macbeth is examined for evidence of such aspects, and the critic comes to the conclusion that inasmuch as Macbeth possesses the currently accepted psychology of ambition, he must be an ambitious character and hence represent ambition. But the process is of course by no means always so simple.

Mrs. Montagu in 1769 wrote: "The unhappy and disconsolate state of the most triumphant villainy, from a consciousness of the internal detestation of mankind to that flagitious greatness to which they are forced to pay external homage, is finely expressed in the following words [of Macbeth]."[12] This is fairly typical of the method, though her analysis and application of pity, terror, and ambition are perhaps more to the point.[13] Whately in the following year[14] pursued the method: men differ in minds as in faces—in general the marks of distinction are quickness, severity, etc. "But no assemblage of these will together form the character of any individual: for he has some predominant principle; there is a certain proportion in which his qualities are mixed; and each affects the other, Those qualities check that principle, though at the same time they are themselves controlled by it: for nothing is

---

[12] *Op. cit.* (1769), pp. 193-94. Compare also pp. 179, 183-84, 191, 197, 200, etc.

[13] *Ibid.*, p. 177.

[14] In dating Whately as of 1770 I am following Professor Nichol Smith, *Shakespeare Criticism* (1916), p. 143 n.

absolutely pure and simple in his composition; and therefore if his peculiarities do not appear, no resemblance of him can be seen."[15] So character *directs* passions—gives them a particular turn. Passions must be "accommodated to the character of the person supposed to feel them."[16] Most dramatic writers of tragedy have used only *general* character—hence only "distant resemblance."[17] But a villain differs from others of his type as much as he does from a saint. So Shakespeare (at last Whately has got to him), beyond all other dramatists, *knew* the human heart "and he had a genius to express all that his penetration could discover."[18] His characters "are masterly copies from nature; differing each from the other, and animated as the originals though correct to a scrupulous precision."[19] Hence this type of criticism, concludes Whately, is valuable, though one cannot lay down general rules for it as one can for the fable. It will promote judgment as to real characters, as well as dramatic ones. "To give the mind this turn is the design of the following pages."[20]

William Richardson as Psychological Critic of Shakespeare

But Whately was by no means as intensely analytical as William Richardson, probably the foremost psychological critic of Shakespeare in the late eighteenth century.[21] Richardson's analysis of the passions runs consistently and persistently through all three series of his essays. It reads something like this: "A system of conduct, founded on the

---

[15]Introduction, pp. 4-5. My pages in Whately all refer, as usual, to the 2nd ed. (1808), of the *Remarks*.
[16]*Ibid.*, p. 5. [17]*Ibid.*, p. 6. [18]*Ibid.*, p. 8.
[19]*Ibid.* [20]*Ibid.*
[21]On Richardson's criticism of Shakespeare, see *JEGP*, XXVIII (Jan., 1929), 117-36.

opinion of others, is . . . unstable"[22] [illustrated by Macbeth's operations]; "A passion, when gratified, ceases to operate; it no longer exists; and the mind is left vacant"[23] [also illustrated by Macbeth]; "Sensibility . . . disposes us to benevolence; but, in corrupted minds, by infusing terror, it produces hatred and inhumanity"[24] [Macbeth again]; "The tendency of indignation . . . is to inflict punishment on the offender"[25] [this in explanation of Hamlet's manhandling of Ophelia]; etc., etc. This might be kept up indefinitely,[26] but one should note Richardson's application of it all to Shakespeare in general: "He [Shakespeare] thus unites the two essential powers of dramatic invention, that of forming characters; and that of imitating, in their natural expressions, the passions and affections of which they are composed."[27] "Shakespeare . . . is most eminently distinguished . . . by imitating the passion in all its aspects, by pursuing it through all its wanderings and labyrinths, by moderating or accelerating its impetuosity according to the influence of other principles and of external events, and finally by combining it in a judicious manner with other passions and propensities, or by setting it aptly in opposition."[28]

This last quotation leads to an interesting refinement; both Richardson and Whately are inclined to evolve a *ruling* passion: ". . . his [Richard III's] ruling passion is the lust of power," declares Whately;[29] and Richardson:

---

[22] *Op. cit.* (5th ed., 1798), p. 53. This edition is used *passim*, unless otherwise stated.
[23] *Ibid.*, pp. 57-58.   [24] *Ibid.*, p. 65.   [25] *Ibid.*, p. 102.
[26] *Ibid.*, pp. 3, 5-21, 25, 27, 35, 38, 40, 42-44, 45, 54, 55, 60, 76, 125, 135-39, 160, 178, 186, 210, 222, 232-34, 289-90, 295-96, 298-300, 304-6, 359-60, 397, etc., etc.
[27] *Ibid.*, p. 33.   [28] *Ibid.*, pp. 32-33.
[29] *Op. cit.*, p. 28. For the historical significance of this term in the 18th century, see P. Kaufman's "Heralds of Original Genius" in *Essays in Memory of*

"Among the various desires and propensities implanted by nature in the constitution of every individual, some one passion, either by original or superior vigor or by reiterated indulgence, gains an ascendant in the soul and subdues every opposing principle."[30] "A sense of virtue . . . seems to be the ruling principle in the character of Hamlet."[31] "The repulse of a ruling . . . passion [in this case, love] could dispose Imogen to despondency."[32] "The love of distinction is asserted to be the ruling principle in the conduct of Timon."[33] And Richardson goes even further, to explain the fusing of this passion with other subordinate passions: "we must recollect . . . that when different and even opposite feelings encounter one another and affect us at the same time; those that prevail, under the guidance of some vigorous passion, carry the rest along with them; direct them so as to receive the same tendency with themselves, and impelling the mind in the same manner, receive from their coincidence additional power."[34]

It will be well to stop here a moment, and, as suggested in the introduction to this chapter, trace the background of this idea (among others) of Richardson's. The man who was probably responsible for it was Hume, who in his "Essay on Tragedy" (1757) developed a theory of the ruling passion[35] and then explained psychologically the effect of the fusing of opposite passions: "The subordinate movement is converted into the predominant and gives force to it, though of a different and even sometimes of a contrary

---

Barrett Wendell (1926), and Mr. R. S. Crane's review of Kaufman in *PQ*, VI (1927), 168-69.
[30] *Op. cit.*, p. 160.   [31] *Ibid.*, p. 117.   [32] *Ibid.*, p. 194.
[33] *Ibid.*, p. 314. See also pp. 35, 68, 196, 217-18.
[34] *Ibid.*, p. 245. Compare p. 161: "The ruling passion, blended with others, augments their vehemence, and consequently enhances their pleasure."
[35] *Essays Moral, Political and Literary* (ed. T. H. Green and T. H. Grose, London: Longmans, 1888), I, 262.

nature."³⁶ The last quotation from Richardson above directly echoed this, and inasmuch as Richardson definitely referred twice³⁷ to Hume's essay and used the idea of a ruling passion over and over again,³⁸ one might well suspect a direct influence here. As a matter of fact, also, Hume's ideas appear several times elsewhere in Richardson quite unacknowledged.³⁹

Kames' immediate influence on Richardson has already been suggested in the introduction to this chapter. So also Burke's, for that Burke inspired some of Richardson's productions is quite obvious in the light of the letters from Burke attached to the sixth (1812) edition of Richardson's works. And this is not the only evidence, for Richardson refers directly to Burke's first letter,⁴⁰ and to the *Enquiry*.⁴¹ That Burke's psychologizing in this essay influenced Richardson is fairly apparent from Richardson's analysis of taste, for example, with application to Shakespeare. Burke makes a threefold division: "The senses, the imagination; and the judgment";⁴² which in Richardson becomes "feeling," "discernment," and "knowledge."⁴³ And it should be noted that there is no direct reference to Burke here. Hence it may be very possible that Richardson's idea of selective imitation⁴⁴ can also be traced back directly to Burke,⁴⁵ though Burke is not mentioned in that connection

---

³⁶*Ibid.*, I, 262.   ³⁷*Op. cit.* (5th ed., 1798), pp. 201, 245.
³⁸*Ibid.*, pp. 117, 160, 194, 249, 314, etc. See above in this chapter.
³⁹*Ibid.*, pp. 117, 160, 194, 241, 249, 314.   ⁴⁰*Ibid.*, p. 395.   ⁴¹*Ibid.*, p. 97.
⁴²Bohn Edition, I, 54.   ⁴³*Op. cit.*, pp. 366, 368, 399—especially p. 368.
⁴⁴*Ibid.*, pp. 174, 383, 391. For example (p. 391): "In every interesting representation features and tints must be added to the reality; features and tints which it actually possesses must be concealed." Compare also Richardson's article in the *Mirror* (No. 24), entitled: "Advantage which the artist in the fine arts has over Nature in the assemblage and arrangement of objects."
This is more generally Mr. Lovejoy's No. 2—"la belle nature"—*MLN*, XLII (1927), 445.
⁴⁵Bohn Edition, I, 176: "The truth is, if poetry gives us a noble assemblage

at all by Richardson. This sort of general background study should be applied to other critics of the period. Unfortunately it falls outside the scope of this book.

THE REACTION TO RICHARDSON

All of this psychologizing aroused the critics to considerable reflection on Richardson. The *Critical Review* in 1774 hailed Richardson's "excellent observations on the study and nature of the human mind,"[46] but the *London Magazine* was a little dubious; "Macbeth, Hamlet, Jacques and Imogen are the characters here analyzed, with great critical precision and judgment. The author hath studied human nature, and is well acquainted with the passions and combinations of feelings. We think, however, that he is rather diffuse in his investigation and too refined in some of his observations."[47] And the *Monthly Review*, though it received Richardson with open arms, praised his philosophical method, and quoted liberally, remarked with rather comical abruptness at the end, "We are however apprehensive that this method of criticism, while it is the only one that can please the philosopher and man of taste, will be deemed refinement, and unintelligible, by the common tribe of readers."[48]

In 1784 the reviewers became more impatient: The *Monthly Review* objected to Richardson's analysis of Lear as a man of "refined sensibility" and of Timon's ruling passion as "love of distinction";[49] and the *Critical Review*

---

of words corresponding to many noble ideas which are connected by circumstances of time or place or related to each other as cause and effect, or associated in any natural way, they may be moulded together in any form and perfectly answer their end. The picturesque connection is not demanded, because no real picture is formed; nor is the effect of the description at all the less upon this account."

[46]XXXVII (1774), 334.   [47]XLIII (1774), 448.
[48]LI (1774), 13.   [49]LXX (1784), 136.

doubted whether the human mind might be "rendered less intricate . . . by the contemplation of fictitious personages . . . we shall not perceive his [Richardson's] advances in the history of the human mind . . . he analyzes not . . . character . . . but . . . a representation."[50] And in 1789, though it approved in general of Richardson's analysis of Falstaff, the *Monthly Review* suggested that "analyzing of dramatic characters might easily be carried to an extreme."[51]

The Use of the Psychological Method

Yet the method was popular. E. Taylor in 1774 had recourse directly to Locke: When we see Lear in distress, "the mind is rather passive than active; it perceives, and cannot avoid perceiving, as Mr. Locke justly observes, whilst the eyes and ears are open. Now if there is perception, some sensation must be produced in the mind. In the present instance the perception is that of grief, the sensation is that of pity."[52] And similarly, from perception to sensation again: Murder on the stage gives us pleasure "by rousing the mind from indolence and indifference; by exciting the most comfortable ideas of our own present security—This pleasure is farther increased by our sensations of pity and compassion for the unhappy sufferers."[53] But he rather avoids the further discussion of pleasure and pain, only remarking that sorrow may "result from the intimate alliance between pleasure and pain."[54]

Mrs. Griffith wrote in 1775: "I believe that there is nothing which a woman of virtue feels herself more offended

---

[50] LVII (1784), 101-2. This review also attacked Richardson's psychology of Taste.

[51] LXXXI (1789), 56. But in 1796 the *Monthly Mirror* applauded "Mr. Richardson's philosophical and valuable essays on the characters of Shakspere."—II (1796), 486.

[52] *Cursory Remarks*, pp. 20-21.   [53] *Ibid.*, pp. 24-25.   [54] *Ibid.*, p. 25.

at, than defamation or scandal."[55] Hence, she concludes, a passage in Act IV, Scene 3 of *Much Ado About Nothing* is good.

Morgann's famous distinction in 1777 between impression and understanding has already been suggested[56] and will be elaborated below in connection with Falstaff. But Morgann made some interesting general analyses of Shakespeare's characterization. "Shakespeare's characters," he said, are "essentially different from those drawn by other writers . . . in the groupes of other poets the parts which are not seen, do not in fact exist" . . . but "the forms of Shakespeare" have "an independence as well as a relation."[57] "Bodies of all kinds . . . possess certain first principles of *being*. . . . But each particular body . . . has yet some *peculiar* of its own. Shakespeare appears to have considered the being and growth of the human mind as analogous to this system[58] . . . he boldly makes a character act and speak from those parts of the composition which are *inferred* only, and not distinctly seen. This produces a wonderful effect[59] . . . this is . . . that art in Shakespeare, which . . . we . . . call *nature*."[60] Hence Shakespeare's characters may be considered "rather as Historic than Dramatic beings."[61]

A remark from the *Monthly Review* in 1795[62] will serve to conclude this general discussion: "It may not be altogether digressive, in this place, to remark that there is a passion of the mind,—the strength of which is usually commensurable with the progress of our knowledge of human nature, —which delights to observe the *manners;* to investigate the symptoms of character; to infer, from the occasional ac-

---
[55]*Op. cit.*, p. 159. Compare also p. 226.
[56]In Chap. XI, above. How much of this distinction is due to Hume?
[57]*Op. cit.*, p. 58 n.   [58]*Ibid.*, p. 59 n.   [59]*Ibid.*, p. 62 n.
[60]*Ibid.*   [61]*Ibid.*   [62]XVIII (1795), 126.

tions of an individual, the predisposing bent or state of his mind; or, from a preconceived idea of his turn and disposition, to infer his probable conduct in given circumstances, and to compare with these inferences the actual result;—a philosophic passion, which might be named the *ethic* curiosity. Now it will be found to be the characteristic refinement of modern art chiefly to address this passion, and the characteristic excellence of Shakspeare habitually to satisfy it; in so much that those actions of his heroes, which do not at first surprize, and do not seem necessarily to result from the combined impulse of their habits and situation, nevertheless, when analyzed, are found to be the very actions which such men so circumstanced would unavoidably perform."[63] So Shakespeare's characters taken in general satisfied the investigative psychologizing of the late eighteenth century.

Minor Characters

A few applications of all this to individual characters should be made now, some having already been suggested above. First, for minor characters, E. Taylor in 1774, remarked on Lady Macbeth: "Ambition, or at least the desire of grasping crowns and empires, is a passion inherent in few female breasts"; hence "consider . . . the monstrous character of lady Macbeth."[64] The *Universal Magazine* in 1791 commented on the psychology of Miranda,[65] and *The Bee* in the same year psychologized Coriolanus.[66] As a final example of the interest in minor characters the *Universal Magazine* in 1795 accounted for the attitude of Northumberland on the death of his son: ". . . the human mind, when roused by danger, or inflamed with

---
[63] For this valuable note I am indebted to Mr. Howard Simon of the University of Michigan.
[64] *Op. cit.*, p. 66.   [65] LXXXVIII (1791), 60.   [66] II (1791), 157.

passion, is capable of inspiring the brave heart with additional courage."[67]

MACBETH AND RICHARD III

Macbeth and Richard III received considerable psychological consideration during the period. The *British Magazine* as early as 1767 analyzed the different manner in which cruelty and ambition are treated in the characters of Richard III and Macbeth and strongly approved of Shakespeare: "Nothing should give us a higher idea of the genius of a poet than his being able to vary the same subject, and place the same character in various different points of light. This praise no author has a better right to than Shakespeare."[68]

F. Gentleman psychologized Macbeth briefly in 1770,[69] but T. Whately in the same year went into the contrast of the two characters quite profoundly. In similar circumstances, says Whately, these two characters "differ so much in disposition."[70] Shakespeare goes beyond other ordinary dramatists in ascribing opposite principles and motives to the same designs and actions. "Macbeth . . . is . . . represented as a man, whose natural temper would have deterred him . . . if he had not been immediately tempted and strongly impelled. . . . Richard, on the other hand, brought with him into the world the signs of ambition and cruelty: his disposition, therefore, is suited to those symptoms."[71] Whately cites proof from the text to show that Macbeth had feelings of humanity. "A man of such a disposition will esteem . . . all gentle and amiable qualities in another[72] . . . one who has these feelings . . . cannot easily be induced to commit a murder."[73] "Rich-

---

[67]XCVI (1795), 36. [68]VIII (1767), 626-27.
[69]*Dramatic Censor*, I, 83, 99. [70]*Op. cit.*, p. 9 (2nd ed. as always).
[71]*Ibid.*, p. 11. [72]*Ibid.*, p. 12. [73]*Ibid.*, p. 14

ard is in all these particulars the very reverse to Macbeth."[74] He gives evidence again to prove this,[75] and then announces that Macbeth and Richard differ even in the same qualities. For example, ambition: "In Macbeth it proceeds only from vanity . . . in Richard it is founded upon pride; his ruling passion is the lust of power."[76] As for courage: ". . . in Richard it is intrepidity and in Macbeth no more than resolution."[77] Macbeth had "natural timidity,"[78] Richard "refined hypocrisy."[79] "A mind so framed and so tortured as that of Macbeth, when the hour of extremity presses upon him, can find no refuge but in despair; and the expression of that despair by Shakspeare is perhaps one of the finest pictures that ever was exhibited."[80] This Whately contrasts deliberately with Richard's reaction,[81] and concludes: "Thus, from the beginning of their history to their last moments, are the characters of Macbeth and Richard preserved entire and distinct: and though probably Shakspeare when he was drawing the one, had no attention to the other; yet, as he conceived them to be widely different, expressed his conceptions exactly, and copied both from nature, they necessarily became contrasts to each other."[82]

Unfortunately Whately's essay was not published till 1785, and then Kemble proceeded to attack it in *Macbeth Reconsidered* (1786). Kemble indicates at the beginning that he will show Macbeth equal to Richard III in "personal courage"—that is, that he will save Macbeth from "Mr. Wheatley," from whose idea of Macbeth we "can gain no instruction" and hence "shall never be amended."[83] Kemble's methods are perhaps more direct than Whately's.[84]

[74] *Ibid.*, p. 16.
[77] *Ibid.*, p. 32.
[80] *Ibid.*, p. 75.
[83] P. 4.
[75] *Ibid.*, pp. 16-24.
[78] *Ibid.*, pp. 54-55.
[81] *Ibid.*, pp. 83 ff.
[84] For example, pp. 6, 8, 9.
[76] *Ibid.*, p. 28.
[79] *Ibid.*, pp. 60-61.
[82] *Ibid.*, p. 89.

He adduces textual evidence directly, interprets Macbeth's attitude toward Banquo and Fleance decisively, and defends Macbeth's attitude toward Macduff. So far there is little of Whately's indirect psychologizing. But when Kemble turns to Richard, the picture changes: such a statement as "If it is a mark of resolution in Richard that,"[85] becomes Kemble's cry,[86] and this is the regular psychological method. "Superstition may be a sign of timidity,"[87] but Richard is superstitious as well as Macbeth; "intrepidity and sense of danger are by no means incompatible";[88] "Macbeth and Richard are each of them as intrepid as man can be."[89] The difference between them, concludes Kemble, lies in the fact that "Ambition is the impulse that governs every action of Richard's life,"[90] and it is gratified by "dissimulation" and "cruelty";[91] the same vice appears in Macbeth, "but he gratifies it by hypocrisy."[92] In short, "Richard is only intrepid, Macbeth intrepid, and feeling . . . Richard's character is simple, Macbeth's mix'd."[93] Kemble's final tribute to Whately is a model of splendid deference: he "wishes his approbation were considerable enough to increase the celebrity which Mr. Wheatley's memory has acquir'd from a work, so usefully intended, and so elegantly perform'd."[94]

Meanwhile Richardson had psychologized Macbeth in 1774, and in 1777 the *Universal Magazine* had noted Macbeth as a character in progressive change.[95] Finally the

[85] *Ibid.*, p. 23. [86] See *Ibid.*, pp. 24-29 *passim*, etc.
[87] *Ibid.*, p. 32. [88] *Ibid.*, p. 35. [89] *Ibid.*
[90] *Ibid.* [91] *Ibid.* [92] *Ibid.*
[93] *Ibid.*, p. 36.
[94] *Ibid.* Whately's *Remarks* were reviewed in the *Monthly Review*, LXXX (1789), 553 with the rather disparaging comment: ". . . nor does it require such an investigation and analysis of the two several plays, as prevails in the remarker, to discriminate the leading features that distinguish Richard from Macbeth." Kemble's reply was ridiculed on the same page.
[95] LXI (1777), 6.

Monthly Mirror in 1798 suggested: "Let us suppose Shakspeare has a mind to paint the fatal effects of ambition . . . how beautifully from such a wavering character, does the poet let you into the knowledge of the secret springs and motives of human actions."[96]

Falstaff

The most minute psychologizing of Falstaff was produced by Morgann in his famous essay in 1777. "In Dramatic composition the *Impression* is the Fact.[97] . . . I distinguish between *mental Impressions*, and the *Understanding*.[98] . . . There are none of us unconscious of certain feelings or sensations of mind, which do not seem to have passed thro' the Understanding[99] . . . the Understanding and those feelings are frequently at variance[100] . . . hence . . . we often condemn or applaud characters and actions on the credit of some logical process, while our hearts revolt, and would fain lead us to a very different conclusion."[101] The Understanding deals with actions only, but the Impression deals with *"first principles of character,* which seem wholly out of reach of the Understanding."[102] There are "distinct principles of character in every distinct individual.[103] . . . We often love or hate at first sight . . . by some secret reference to these *principles* . . . but the *Impression* is incommunicable."[104] Our Understanding makes us ashamed of these ideas, but *"one man* in the world" might "steal such Impressions on his audience."[105] "It must be a strange art in *Shakespeare* which can draw our liking and good will towards so offensive an object."[106] "Shakespeare . . . has contrived to make secret Impres-

---

[96] VI (1798), 356-57. [97] *Op. cit.*, p. 4. [98] *Ibid.*, p. 5.
[99] *Ibid.* [100] *Ibid.*, pp. 5-6. [101] *Ibid.*, p. 6.
[102] *Ibid.* [103] *Ibid.*, p. 7. [104] *Ibid.*
[105] *Ibid.*, p. 9. [106] *Ibid.*, p. 10.

sions upon us of Courage . . . as Shakespeare is a Name which contains All of Dramatic artifice and genius."[107] Constitutional Courage "extends to man's whole life, . . . is independent of opinion . . . can avail itself of flight as well as of action.[108] . . . That courage . . . Falstaff . . . possessed."[109]

Here, his preliminary psychologizing over, Morgann stops to chastise the players for overacting Falstaff's supposed cowardice and then points out what "Impressions" Falstaff "has made on the characters of the Drama."[110] "Courage is a quality," he continues, "which is at least as transmissable to one's posterity as features and complexion."[111] "*Shakespeare* has so obscured the better parts of Falstaff and stolen them secretly on our feelings, instead of opening them fairly to the notice of our understandings."[112] The critic admits that Falstaff may well have "had his weak moment,"[113] as may all heroes, and then proceeds to analyze minutely the psychological distinction between "the natural Cowardice of the three associates [of Falstaff at Gadshill] and the accidental Terror of *Falstaff*"[114] . . . "we do not see or feel *Falstaff* to be a Coward, much less a boaster; without which even Cowardice is not sufficiently ridiculous"[115] . . . his "lyes are to be derived, not from Cowardice, but from some other part of his character."[116] So "Shakespeare has made certain Impressions. . . . This was a process which required the nicest hand."[117] "In short, we must look to the art of the writer and to the principles of human nature, to discover the hidden causes of such effects";[118] for "Every man . . . has two characters."[119]

[107] *Ibid.*, p. 13.   [108] *Ibid.*, p. 23.   [109] *Ibid.*, p. 24.
[110] *Ibid.*, p. 28.   [111] *Ibid.*, p. 45.   [112] *Ibid.*, p. 56.
[113] *Ibid.*, p. 114. [114] *Ibid.*, p. 126. [115] *Ibid.*, p. 131.
[116] *Ibid.*, p. 133. [117] *Ibid.*, p. 148. [118] *Ibid.*, p. 153.
[119] *Ibid.*, p. 167.

Johnson's and the *Critical Review's* comments on this subtle treatise have been given above,[120] but one cannot resist repeating Johnson's: "Why, sir, we shall have the man come forth again; and as he has proved Falstaff to be no coward, he may prove Iago to be a very good character."[121] And the *Monthly Review* was a little more bitter: ". . . his ingenuity betrays him into false refinements. The plainest propositions may be controverted by subtle disputants. . . . In dramatic writings, especially, the obvious meaning is most probably the true one; and it is surely no great compliment to Shakespeare's admirable delineation of the character of Falstaff, to suppose, that it has hitherto been generally misunderstood."[122]

It is not necessary to carry this psychologizing of Falstaff further, though Richardson in 1788(9) indulged in convolutions similar to those of his earlier essays,[123] to which he added a tremendous moral: ". . . the mean sensualist is irretrievably lost. . . . An important and awful lesson!"[124]

Hamlet

It was inevitable that this psychological approach should also touch Hamlet, the most discussed character of the period. There was little argument about Hamlet, however, for the Romantic attack had set in with a vengeance, as already indicated, and Hamlet presented to these Romantics no such problem—they were all agreed on him—as did Falstaff's cowardice or Macbeth's courage. Richardson was perhaps the only critic who psychologized Hamlet at length—that is, in terms of the method developed in this section.

---

[120] In Chap. XI., p. 146. [121] Boswell's *Life* (ed. Hill), IV (1783), 192 n.
[122] LVII (1777), 80. [123] *Op. cit.*, pp. 241-43, 245, 249.
[124] *Ibid.*, p. 287.

It is true that F. Gentleman at times verged on the regular generalizing psychology of the age: Hamlet's address to the Ghost "rises too suddenly," for "terror does indeed confound reason, but seldom gives birth to a passionate, presumptive effusion";[125] and "Revenge when most provoked, rather violates human feelings," but this, says Gentleman, will not excuse Hamlet's brutal speech over the king at prayer.[126] These, however, are at best merely scattered remarks. It was Richardson who in both 1774 and 1784 applied the typical psychological convolutions of the age to Hamlet.

In the middle of the first essay on Hamlet (1774), page 90, Richardson asks himself the question as to why an "ingenuous temper" like Hamlet's should betray suspicion. "It is the property of the imagination," he begins his explanation, "when governed by any passion or opinion, to follow the impulse it has received, and to diminish or aggrandize any object not perfectly known to us, according to the judgment we may have formed of it." The reader may wonder exactly what connection this remark has with the preceding, but Richardson continues analyzing—let us merely sketch his reasoning: Fear peoples darkness with spectres—that is, we magnify the unknown and minimize the known. We are inclined, therefore, to attribute more to an "object" than it really has, and moreover, as we are naturally inclined to action, we make those attributions quickly. Now our proneness to be convinced of them will be governed by our passion at the moment. "It is also manifest, that, if any object is naturally difficult to be apprehended and is so complex or delicate as to elude the acuteness of our discernment, or the intenseness of our inquiry, we are more liable to errors in cases of this nature than in those things that we perceive distinctly."[127] Rea-

[125] *Op. cit.*, I, 39. [126] *Ibid.*, I, 46. [127] *Ibid.*, p. 93.

soning by analogy we may make these wrong attributions to qualities of the heart also, whether good or bad, and the extent of them again depends on the passion of the moment. *These* particular attributions may also be affected by former affections for the person concerned. "Hence friendship, changed by neglect or ingratitude into indifference, grows into a hatred."[128] By this time Richardson has reached page 95—he began this involved analysis on page 90. Meanwhile where are Hamlet and the original question about suspicion? *Now* he is ready to come back to them. He has built up his psychological foundation and so now concludes, "It is not wonderful, therefore, nor inconsistent with amiable and kind affections, that Hamlet [the first time the name has been mentioned in five pages of psychologizing] moved by an exquisite sense of virtue and propriety, shocked and astonished at the ingratitude and guilt of Gertrude, whom he had revered and believed incapable of any blemish, should become apprehensive of the total degeneracy of her nature and harbour suspicions concerning his father's death."[129] The method should now be obvious. The same thing happened again in 1784, in the second essay on Hamlet.[130]

Meanwhile Pilon had burst into print in 1777 with a critique on Henderson's acting of Hamlet, and the psychological method was now carried over into the acting tradition. "When the mind is strongly agitated," remarks Pilon, "the body is restless and unsettled—therefore Mr. Henderson's walking to and fro during the time he waited to see his father's spirit was extremely natural";[131] and "his [Henderson's] succeeding pause was just and natural;

---

[128] *Ibid.*, p. 95.

[129] *Ibid.* Much of this discussion of Richardson is taken from my own article on his criticism in *JEGP*, XXVIII (Jan., 1929), 117-36. It is reprinted here with permission.

[130] See esp. pp. 124-26 (of the 5th ed., as always).   [131] *Op. cit.*, p. 7.

for terror incites an instantaneous wish for safety."[132] This psychological point of view is repeated throughout the essay.[133]

The *London Magazine* in 1781 quoted from Harris' *Dramatic Speculations:* "If the leading person in a *drama*, for example, *Hamlet*, appear to have been treated most injuriously, we naturally infer that he will meditate *revenge;* and should that revenge prove fatal to those who had injured him it was no more than was probable when we consider the provocation."[134] And finally the *Monthly Mirror* in 1795 gave a last echo: "The predominant passion of Hamlet, through most of the first act, is GRIEF."[135]

THE IMPORTANCE OF THE NEW CRITICISM

All this psychologizing of the passions in Shakespeare should be added indubitably to the appreciation of Shakespeare's characters in the late eighteenth century. The most important texts were obviously Morgann's and Richardson's, the former showing considerably more sophistication. In fact, it was this brilliant psychologizing by Morgann that led modern critics to place him with—if not above— Coleridge and Hazlitt. Richardson's bent, however, was too moralistic to allow him to ascend to Morgann's sphere. Perhaps Kemble and Whately deserve minor notice, and among the periodicals the persistent interest of the *Monthly Review* in this new criticism is most significant. The whole development was extremely important, and probably this chapter should be dedicated to the now forgotten Mr. E. Walder, who gave the first hint of such psychologizing in 1895.[136] It is indeed unfortunate that the scope of this book has prevented more background study, and it is also to be lamented that a great

---

[132]*Ibid.*, p. 8.   [133]*E.g.*, pp. 11, 14, 15-16, 18, 20-21, 22, etc.
[134]L (1781), 534.   [135]I (1795-96), 47.   [136]*Op. cit.*, p. 19.

deal of material subsequent to 1766 remains still untouched, much of which can merely be suggested here in a note.[137]

THE APPLICATION OF THEORIES OF ASSOCIATION TO VARIOUS ASPECTS OF SHAKESPEARE[138]

The psychological process of association[139] was perhaps first applied definitely to interpret Shakespeare in this period by William Richardson in 1774. His Introduction discussed the harmony of composition and imagery. Our imaginations being stimulated, we enter into the char-

---

[137]*Scots Magazine*, XXXII (1770), 15—On Tragedy; *Hibernian Magazine*, 1774, p. 385—On Tragedy; *Critical Review*, XXXIX (1775), 310—rev. of W. Cooke; V. Knox, *Essays Moral and Literary* (1777), No. 84—"On Philosophical Criticism and on the little assistance it gives to genius"; *Monthly Review*, LVII (1777), 89—On Joseph Priestley's *Lectures on Oratory and Criticism*; *Gentleman's Magazine*, XLV (1775), 244—rev. of W. Cooke; *Hibernian Magazine*, 1780, pp. 94, 213—On "Kaims"; *Universal Magazine*, LXXVII (1785), 124—rev. of Kames; *Gentleman's Magazine*, LX (1790), 892—"Character of Kaims as a Critick"; *European Magazine*, XVIII (1790), 323—Account of Kaimes; *V (1784), 44, 113—rev. of Richardson; *XIV (1788), 422—rev. of Richardson (For other reviews of Richardson, see my other chapters.); *Scots Magazine*, LIII (1791), 472—on Kames, (From vol. VIII of *Encycl. Brit.*); *Universal Magazine*, LXXXIX (1791), 7, 128—on Kames (also from *Encycl. Brit.*); *Analytical Review*, XXVII (1798), 498—rev. of A. F. M. Willich's Translation of Kant's *Elements of Critical Philosophy; Critical Review*, XVIII (1798), 445—rev. of Kant's *Elements of Critical Philosophy*. (See above, p. 155 n., for the many editions of Kames.) (Starred texts refer more directly to Shakespeare.)

[138]For some material on this subject before 1766, see: *History of the Works of the Learned*, VIII (1706), 94—on Imagination; *Spectator*, Nos. 411-21—on Imagination; E. Burke, *Our Ideas of the Sublime* (1757), (Bohn ed., p. 144); D. Hume, *Of Association of Ideas* (1757), (Green and Grose, eds., vol. II); *The Idler* (1758-60), No. 82—Reynolds on the True Idea of Beauty; *D. Webb, *Remarks on the Beauty of Poetry* (1762)—reviewed in *Critical Review*, XIII (1762), 401; *Lord Kames, *Elements of Criticism* (1762), chap. I, "Perceptions and Ideas in a Train." (The starred texts are more directly concerned with Shakespeare.)

[139]Detailed explanation of this term appears below in this section in the exposition of W. Whiter's use of Locke.

acter, for it is always so "with people of warm imaginations."[140] The delusion is furthered on the stage by scenery, dress, and action. Thus "our own imaginations contribute highly to the pleasure we receive from works of invention."[141] For the same reason critics differ, and even one critic will give diverse opinions at different times, for the imagination is variable at different periods and the group of images assembled for the moment in the critic's mind colors his decision.[142] Direct references to the term "association" appear specifically twice: "To be acquainted with the nature of any passion, we must know by what combination of feelings it is excited . . . what propensities and what associations of thought either retard or accelerate its impetuosity."[143] And "if we are affected by any violent emotions, we are accustomed to utter them. Consequently, by force of association and habit . . . they will not be arrested by reflection."[144]

In 1784 Richardson developed, as suggested above in this chapter (in connection with the influence of Burke), the theory of selective imitation, which depends indirectly on association for its foundation. That is, Richardson wrote: ". . . objects intended to please, and interest the heart, should produce their effect by corresponding, or consonant feelings. Now, this cannot be attained by representing objects as they appear. In every interesting representation, features and tints must be added to the reality; features and tints which it actually possesses, must be concealed."[145] And Burke, to whom Richardson had dedicated

---
[140] *Op. cit.*, p. 28. Beattie in his *Dissertations* (1783) included "Association of Ideas" under *Of Imagination*.
[141] *Op. cit.*, p. 28.   [142]*Ibid.*, p. 29.   [143]*Ibid.*, pp. 14-15.
[144]*Ibid.*, p. 50. The method is used also, without direct reference, on pp. 41, 173.
[145]*Ibid.*, p. 391. Compare also pp. 174, 383. For example: "But suppose we receive a single perception from an object exceedingly interesting; this single,

the very section from which this quotation is drawn,[146] had written in 1757: "The truth is, if poetry gives us a noble assemblage of words corresponding to many noble ideas which are connected by circumstances of time or place or related to each other as cause and effect, or associated in any natural way, they may be moulded together in any form and perfectly answer their end. The picturesque connection is not demanded; because no real picture is formed; nor is the effect of the description at all the less upon this account."[147]

Meanwhile in 1777 Maurice Morgann had declared: "If the ideas of Courage and *birth* were strongly associated in the days of *Shakespeare*, then would the assignment of high birth to Falstaff carry . . . to the minds of the audience the associated idea of Courage.[148] . . . if *Shakespeare* meant sometimes rather to *impress* than explain, no circumstances calculated to this end, either directly or by association, are too minute for notice."[149]

Beattie, who wrote in *Of Imagination* two chapters on the "Association of Ideas"[150] with direct references to Locke and "Des Cartes,"[151] pointed out that Shakespeare's imagination was greater than that of Dr. Hill,[152] thereby showing Shakespeare's power in the use of association.

---

and even imperfect perception, makes a lively impression, and it becomes the leading circumstance of an assemblage. Though all the subordinate and adventitious images are the mere coinage of fancy; yet, on account of their intimate union with the primary object, they operate on the mind as if their archetype really existed" (pp. 174-75).

[146]"Essay on the Faults of Shakespeare"—"To a Friend," p. 121. See Burke's letters to Richardson printed at the end of the latter's 1812 Edition.

[147]*Our Ideas of the Sublime*, Bohn Edition, I, 176. This was also quoted above.

[148]*Op. cit.*, p. 46. Compare the *Monthly Review*, LVII (1777), 89, on Kames and Priestley.

[149]*Ibid.*, p. 47.   [150]*Of Imagination*, Secs. II and III (in the *Dissertations*).

[151]*Dissertations* (1783), I, 109, 168.   [152]*Ibid.*, I, 93.

But the most conspicuous use of the doctrine during the period appeared in W. Whiter's *A Specimen of a Commentary on Shakspeare* (1794), the title page of which is:

> A Specimen of a Commentary on Shakspeare containing
> I Notes on *As You Like It*.
> II An attempt to explain and illustrate various passages, on a new principle of criticism, derived from Mr. Locke's Doctrine of the Association of Ideas.
> London: Printed for T. Cadell, in the Strand.
> 1794

Whiter's method appears most deliberately in the second section of his work,[153] though use of it is also apparent in the first.[154] He himself in his Preface announces that the notes on *As You Like It* are meant to establish new interpretations or defend an original reading generally rejected. He gives great praise to Malone and assumes for his second part "the merit of Discovery."

He begins this second division with the announcement that his idea has not been used "as a point of taste or as a subject of criticism."[155] But the principle, he insists, "operates on the *writer in the ardor of invention*, by imposing on his mind some remote and peculiar vein of language, or of imagery"[156]—an effect which may be especially studied "in the writings of Shakspeare."[157] He declares he does not mean the faculty of understanding, but that he

---

[153] *Op. cit.*, pp. 61-258.

[154] For example, pp. 12, 34, 44. "If the reader should enquire why a simile, apparently so remote . . . should on this occasion be presented to the mind of our Poet, I will inform him, that the association was derived from the *feats of activity* in which Orlando had just engaged" (p. 12). Mr. Whiter by no means ever blushes with modesty: "Nothing is more certain than this explanation" (p. 17). Compare p. 23.

[155] *Ibid.*, p. 63.   [156] *Ibid.*, p. 64.   [157] *Ibid.*

is following Locke, whose term, *association*, "is understood to express the combination of those ideas which have *no* natural alliance or relation to each other, but which have been united only by chance or by custom."[158] He even quotes Locke in a footnote: "Ideas, that in themselves are not at all of kin, come to be so united in some men's minds, that it is very hard to separate them; they always *keep in company*, and the one no sooner at any time comes into the understanding, but its *associate* appears with it; and if they are more than two which are thus united, *the whole gang* always inseparable shew themselves together."[159]

"I define therefore," concludes Whiter, "the power of this *association* over the genius of the poet to consist in supplying him with words and with ideas, which have been suggested to the mind by a principle of union unperceived by himself, and independent of the subject, to which they are applied."[160] This principle Whiter will use to settle disputed readings.

The method in action, therefore, belongs, in this book, under Part I, the discussion of Shakespeare's text, and it has already been referred to there. But a few examples of Whiter's manipulations deserve notice here, if merely for clarification.

Timon of Athens, IV, 3: "Will put thy *shirt* on *warm?* Will these *moist* trees" . . . Whiter quotes this, noting that editors substitute *mossed* for *moist*.[161] "If therefore I can shew," he continues, "with extreme probability, from some acknowledged principle of the mind, why this peculiar word might be suggested to our Poet, it surely ought to be considered as a valuable touchstone in the *Art* of *Criticism*."[162]

---

[158] *Ibid.*, p. 65.
[159] *Ibid.*, p. 64 n. He gives the source of this as Locke's *Essay* B 2 C33 ¶5.
[160] *Ibid.*, p. 68.   [161] *Ibid.*, p. 81.   [162] *Ibid.*

Both *warm* and *moist* "were the appropriate terms in the days of Shakspeare for what we should now call an *air'd* or a *damp* shirt."[163] Hence "the image of the *Chamberlain* putting the *shirt* on *warm* impressed the opposite word *moist* on the imagination of the Poet."[164] Q. E. D., etc., etc.

So also "*weed* and *suit*, whether in different senses or referring to the same object, appear to have been particularly combined in the imagination of our Bard."[165] And "It will readily be understood and acknowledged, that this propensity in the mind to associate subjects so remote in their meaning, and so heterogeneous in their nature, must of necessity sometimes deceive the ardour of the writer into whimsical or ridiculous combinations."[166] He gives an example from Julius Cæsar I, 2, of the play on the word "colour."[167]

The extent to which Whiter could project himself into his method appears most humorously perhaps in his discussion of the fishmonger passage in *Hamlet*. "Why should Hamlet mistake Polonius for a *Fishmonger?* Though I am not able to inform the reader respecting the full force and nature of the *exquisite reason*, which belongs to this denomination; yet I can certainly convince him that *some* reason (such as it is) existed in the mind of the Poet."[168] He then goes to Jonson's *Christmas Masque*, wherein Venus says she was a *Fishmonger's Daughter;* hence Hamlet mistakes Polonius as a fishmonger, "though I shall leave others to discover the peculiar notion which was attached to this matter. Probably it was supposed, that the daughters of these tradesmen, who dealt in so nourishing a species of food, were *blessed* with extraordinary powers of *conception*."[169]

[163] *Ibid.*, p. 82.   [164] *Ibid.*   [165] *Ibid.*, p. 87 n.
[166] *Ibid.*, pp. 105-6.   [167] *Ibid.*, pp. 106-7.   [168] *Ibid.*, p. 152 n.
[169] *Ibid.*, pp. 152-53 n. For further exemplification of Whiter in action see

T. Mathias commented in 1794 on Whiter's activity: "This is certainly a very learned and sagacious dog. He is out of the actual chace . . . when a new edition of Shakspeare is printed, there should be a selection of notes from his book."[170] The importance of Whiter's work appears further in the reviews in the *Critical Review* and *British Critic* in 1795,[171] and the *Monthly Review* in 1798.[172] In fact, Whiter is easily the chief proponent of this type of psychologizing during the period.[173] This whole development should now be added to the preceding section on the passions as indicative of an important new type of analysis of Shakespeare in the late eighteenth century.

pp. 161, 165 n., 171, 177, 177-78 n., 184, 184-85 n., 189, 195-96, 198, 209, 214-15, 220, 253-55, 257.

[170]*Pursuits of Literature* (1794), p. 99 n. (of 7th ed., 1798).
[171]LXXXIII (1795), 99, and V (1796), 281, respectively.
[172]XXV (1798), 400.
[173]For some further material on this general subject during the period: *Observer* (1785-90), No. 68; *Looker-On* (1792), Nos. 74, 77.

CHAPTER XIII

HISTORICAL CRITICISM IN THE LATE EIGHTEENTH CENTURY

The last aspect of these new emphases in criticism of Shakespeare in the late eighteenth century—that is, historical criticism—is extremely important in the light of modern criticism of the poet. Professor Karl Young used to lament that between Johnson in 1765 and Rümelin in 1866 there was too much of a break, in the course of which the Romantics somewhat overdid Shakespeare.[1] It will be the purpose of this chapter to show that the break Mr. Young lamented was not so complete as hitherto believed.

Following the regular tenets of its type, late eighteenth-century historical investigation[2] of Shakespeare developed six points of view: the study of Shakespeare's language, of his relation to British history, of his subjection to his audience, of his sources, of his comparative rating among Elizabethan dramatists and in Elizabethan dramaturgy, and finally of his place in the history of the English stage. Of these six, obviously the third and fourth are the most important and received the most attention from the late eighteenth-century critics.

---

[1] See the *Sewanee Review*, XXXV (1927), 15.
[2] This chapter is intended, incidentally, as a refutation of Mr. C. M. Haines' remark: ". . . the historical method of inquiry was totally alien to the abstract rationalism of the eighteenth century" [*Shakespeare in France* (1925), p. 43]. To this should be contrasted D. Nichol Smith's more recent pronouncement in 1928: "The advance that was made after Johnson was in historical knowledge" [*Shakespeare in the Eighteenth Century* (1928), p. 49. See also pp. 50-51, 52, 53, 55, 57]. For an excellent recent survey of historical criticism of Shakespeare before 1766 see Professor Karl Young's "Samuel Johnson on Shakespeare, One Aspect," in *Wisconsin Studies*, 1923; also

Shakespeare's Language

The true significance of the tremendous scope of the development of textual study in the late eighteenth century appears in the many editions of the plays during the period.[3] Needless to say, all the editors had to know Shakespeare's language, and hence it will now be appropriate to give merely a few representative suggestions such as appeared in books criticizing the various editions—that is, the productions especially of Warner, Ritson, Mason, and Whiter.

Richard Warner in 1768 set the style in offering a specimen of a glossary to Garrick: "*Authorities* for Shakespeare's use of words in a particular sense will be taken from Authors, chiefly Poets, before or cotemporary with him."[4] Ritson in 1783 over and over again pronounced against modern emendations with remarks such as: "In the two old folios the passage stands, and rightly, thus; . . ."[5] J. M. Mason two years later reiterated the same idea,[6] emphasizing also the First Quarto or First Folio for proper readings.[7] Malone in 1792 explained to Farmer his similar method of collating "with the original and authentick copies."[8] And finally Whiter in 1794 drove home the meth-

---

Chap. I, above. This present chapter shows historical criticism as a "new emphasis" in the sense of a fuller development.

[3]See Chap. II, above.   [4]*A Letter to David Garrick* (1768), p. 82.

[5]*Remarks, Critical and Illustrative* (1783), p. 29. See also pp. 72, 92, 99, 108-9, 111, 112, 171, 172, 174, 187 195 201; and the *Quip Modest* (London: Johnson, 1788), p. 10. Jackson in 1782 (3rd ed., 1795, p. 164) wrote: "Shakespeare appears more like himself in the twenty plays published from the earliest editions."—*Thirty Letters on Various Subjects.*

[6]*Comments on the Last Edition of Shakespeare's Plays* (1785), pp. 75-76.

[7]Compare the attitude of A. W. Pollard and J. Dover Wilson today as discussed in *Studies in Philology*, XXIV (1927), 243 ff (by R. W. Babcock).

[8]*A Letter to the Rev. Richard Farmer,* (1792 and 1792—I am using this 2nd ed.), p. 8. See also pp. 11-18 and Malone's *Preface* (1790), p. xviii.

od psychologically with his remarks on *Timon of Athens*, IV, 3: "Will put thy *shirt* on *warm?* Will these *moist* trees . . ." (cited in the preceding chapter), to prove, by association, that editors were mistaken in changing "moist" to "moss'd."[9] "When Shakspeare wrote," commented the *Looker-On* graciously, "his style was doubtless of the most popular sort . . . we revere it as the rusty armor of our ancestors."[10]

One need not add more to indicate the path the editors were following. Its anticipation of modern emphasis may be a little surprising.

SHAKESPEARE AND BRITISH HISTORY

Shakespeare's relation to the history of his period appeared early in Mrs. Montagu's chapters on his historical plays,[11] and in Mrs. Griffith in 1775 with such a remark as: the "sudden reformation of Henry Prince of Wales . . . is a fact recorded in history."[12] Tom Davies repeatedly made the same sort of allusions to history,[13] and *The Lounger* in 1786 revived the story of the circumstances of composition of the *Merry Wives:* "Queen Elizabeth, with a curiosity natural to a woman, desired Shakspeare to exhibit Falstaff as a lover: he obeyed her, and wrote the *Merry Wives of Windsor.*"[14] Other such historical allusions appeared in the *Hibernian Magazine*, in 1786: ". . . the subject [of *Macbeth*] . . . was considered as a topic the most likely to conciliate the favour of the court";[15] in the

[9]*Specimen of a Commentary on Shakspeare* (1794), p. 82. See also pp. 83-90, and pp. 180-81 above.
[10]No. 40. A. Chalmers, *British Essayists*, XXXVI, 73.
[11]See especially pp. 95, 102, 198 of *op. cit.* (1769).
[12]*Op. cit.*, p. 255. See also p. 315.
[13]*Dramatic Miscellanies*, I, 60, 116-17, 126-28, 154-56, 194 ff., 204, 314, 363; II, 113-14, 179-82; III, 14-15. These are merely a few illustrations.
[14]No. 69. Chalmers, XXXI, 112. See also No. 68 on the origin of Falstaff.
[15]P. 512. The periodical is quoting Malone.

Universal Magazine in 1792: "This confusion of the seasons, which, with various other evils, Titania, the queen of the fairies, imputes to the jealousy of Oberon . . . is no more than a partial account of the weather, which happened in England, about the time the play was published";[16] in the same periodical in 1794: "Shakspeare's character of Henry IV is perfectly agreeable to that given him by historians";[17] and in James White's *Letters of Falstaff:* "The wild and irregular starts of Percy may have been the subject of much talk with the common people."[18] Finally, the Exeter Society *Essays* in 1796 reiterated this historical point with several possible topical allusions: The King's giving the ring to Helen in *All's Well That Ends Well* represents Elizabeth's giving a ring to Essex;[19] and the deaths of Cardinal Beaufort and Gloster in *Henry VI*, Part 2, and the conversation of Henry V and Williams in *Henry V* (IV, 4) may also have had counterparts in history.[20]

Shakespeare and his Audience

That Shakespeare's age and audience determined his plays was one of the two most fully developed historical views of the period,[21] the other being, of course, the recog-

[16] XC (1792), 429.   [17] XCV (1794), 184.
[18] *Original Letters of Sir John Falstaff* (London: G. G. and J. Robinson, 1796), p. 110 n.
[19] P. 259. "T. O.," Richard Hole, takes occasion here to attack Voltaire, who had ridiculed this idea.
[20] *Ibid.*, pp. 263-64. For others see pp. 265-68, and compare James Plumptre's *Observations on Hamlet* (1796), in Chap. XI, above. For further material on this type of historical criticism see: Horace Walpole, *Historic Doubts*, 1768; *Shakespeare's History of the Times*, 1775; Sir John Harington, *Nugae Antiquae*, 1779; *Universal Magazine*, LXXIV (1784), 7—Richard III misrepresented by historians; *History of Sir John Falstaff*, 1789; *Universal Magazine*, LXXXVI (1790), 232—Historical study of Henry V; *The Enquirer*, XII (1797), 377—"of the age of Queen Elizabeth."
[21] For some material preceding 1766 on this subject see: Pope's *Preface* (1725), quoted in D. Nichol Smith's *Shakespeare Criticism* (1916), p. 50;

nition of his sources. In 1769 Mrs. Montagu wrote that Shakespeare's age was devoid of taste,[22] that "wit was unpolished, and mirth ill-bred"[23] amongst an audience that was "fierce and barbarous,"[24] and the *Monthly Review* noted how specifically she applied this background to Shakespeare.[25] T. Whately in 1770 complained mournfully: ". . . the taste of the age in which he wrote, though it may afford some excuse, yet cannot entirely vindicate the exceptionable passages";[26] the "barbarous and credulous taste of the times," echoed Francis Gentleman;[27] "Puns and quibbles were the vicious taste of the times," came from Colman's *Man and Wife* the same year.[28] Four years later, in 1774, E. Taylor became even more vociferous in grudging extenuation: "Perhaps it will be said, that Shakespear wrote, when learning, taste, and manners were pedantic, unrefined and illiberal; that none but such motley pieces, as his are, could please the greater part of his audience, the illiterate, low-lived mechanics; that some of his characters were necessitated to speak their language; and that their bursts of applause were to be purchased even at the expense of decency and common sense."[29] And again came the echo from the *Monthly Review:*

> The rhiming clowns that gladded Shakespear's age,
> No more with Crambo entertain the stage.[30]

Gentleman's Magazine, IX (1739), 245, 588—S. animated his countrymen; Johnson's *Preface* (1765), quoted in D. Nichol Smith's *Shakespeare Criticism* (1916), p. 115.

[22]*Op. cit.*, p. 285. [23]*Ibid.*, p. 10. See also pp. 14, 18-19.
[24]*Ibid.*, p. 150. [25]XLI (1769), 131 ff.
[26]*Remarks on Some of the Characters of Shakspeare*, 2nd ed. (1808), p. 90.
[27]*Dramatic Censor* (1770), I, 80. See also I, 139. [28]P. 18.
[29]*Cursory Remarks*, pp. 37-8. See also pp. 40, 58, 60.
[30]L (1774), 144. For this note I am indebted to Miss Louisa Soukup of the University of Michigan. See also Bell's Edition (1774) in the Advertisement, p. 5: Shakespeare "is obscure, indelicate," to satisfy his audience.

"Shakespeare's fools are not those of *modern times*," declared Mrs. Griffith with perhaps some slight note of sarcasm.[31] "Shakespeare spent his life in writing for such people. Unhappy Shakespeare: who . . . lived in an age unworthy of him," bewailed the *Universal Magazine* in 1776;[32] ". . . he directed his endeavours solely to hit the taste and humour that then prevailed amongst the meaner sort of people, of whom his audience was generally composed," repeated the *Biographia Dramatica* in 1782.[33] Blair in 1783,[34] T. Davies in 1784,[35] J. M. Mason in 1785,[36] the *European Magazine* in 1786,[37] M. Sherlock in 1786,[38] Ritson in 1788,[39] and W. Richardson in 1789[40] all echoed and re-echoed the same note.[41]

A few final quotations from the last decade of the century may throw a slightly different light on Shakespeare's relation to his age—an attempt on the part of critics to explain, more positively, some minor aspects of Shakespeare in terms of customs and beliefs of the Elizabethans. These appear, for example, in the remarks of the *Universal Magazine:* "His *eating no fish* alludes to the time of queen Elizabeth, when the Papists were esteemed . . . to be enemies to the government";[42] "The character of a Bedlam Beggar, which Edgar is thus determined to assume, was well

---

[31]*Op. cit.*, p. 357.   [32]LIX (1776), 191.   [33]I, 402.
[34]Lecture III, vol. I (1804), p. 35; Lecture XLVII, vol. II (1804), p. 371.
[35]*Op. cit.*, I, 283; III, 35, 47.   [36]*Op. cit.*, pp. 61, 302-3, 385-86.
[37]X (1786), 283. The periodical is quoting M. Sherlock.
[38]*A Fragment*, pp. 35-37: "Raphael, Molière and Shakspeare . . . have erred against good taste . . . they sacrificed it to the desire of making their fortunes" (p. 37).
[39]Ritson declared Johnson "ignorant of the manners . . . of Shakspeare's age."—*Quip Modest* (1788), p. 20.
[40]*Essays*, 5th ed. (1798), pp. 270, 339. For the texts of Richardson's Essays on Shakespeare, see *JEGP*, XXVIII (Jan., 1929), 117.
[41]See also the *Universal Magazine*, LXXXI (1787), 5.
[42]XCI (1792), 109. This refers to Kent's remark in *King Lear*.

understood in the time of Shakspeare";[43] "This was a notion prevalent in Shakspeare's time . . . spiders were then esteemed venomous";[44] "It seems, that to pick the teeth was, in Shakspeare's time, a mark of some pretension to greatness and elegance";[45] " 'To scrape a trencher,' in the house of a nobleman, would now have a very uncouth sound; but, in the time of Shakspeare, trenchers were still used by persons of good fashion."[46] But a finer example of this attempt to reconstruct a point of view appeared in Richard Hole's Exeter Society Essay on Shylock, where a supposed Jewish newspaper was allowed to comment on the *Merchant of Venice:* "The plot is borrowed from an old British bard, who flourished about the beginning of the seventeenth century of their era, and who composed it under the influence of the spirit of inveterate malice against our nation, for which, in that and many preceding ages, the Europeans were notorious."[47] All these details represent a magnificent anticipation of modern historical criticism.[48]

Nor is this all that anticipates the twentieth century. The *Monthly Mirror* in 1798 hit upon a point which at least two modern scholars have used effectively to interpret the character of Hamlet historically: namely, the Elizabethan attitude toward ghosts.[49] One can hardly impress

---

[43] *Universal Magazine,* XCI (1792), 188.
[44] *Ibid.,* XCIII (1793), 198 n.   [45] *Ibid.,* p. 293.
[46] *Ibid.,* p. 45.
[47] *Op. cit.,* p. 567. Reprinted in *Universal Magazine,* XI (1797), 127-28.
[48] For example, that of Mr. E. E. Stoll, who has made the same remark about the Elizabethan attitude toward Jews one hundred and fifteen years years later: *JEGP,* X (1911), 236-79; and see his *Shakespeare Studies* (1927).
[49] Prof. G. L. Kittredge in English 2, in Harvard University, and Prof. E. E. Stoll in *University of Minnesota Studies,* No. 7, 1919. Both E. Taylor and H. Blair as noted above in Chap. VI placed Shakespeare's ghosts properly in popular tradition, but neither man deliberately analyzed the public's attitude.

this point too emphatically as the keynote to the ultimate understanding of Hamlet, and it is most interesting to note that the late eighteenth century, which had fully developed the Romantic Heresy of Hamlet, had also, at the same time, found the germ of the argument which would blow this heresy to the four winds. "That Shakspere designed his ghost to be substantially represented there can be no question," wrote an anonymous critic, "Charon," in the *Monthly Mirror* in 1798.[50] He was on the trail of an important historical analysis, and the preceding anonymous remark which had aroused him was even more suggestive: "There is a tradition, that, at one time, a spectre can be only seen by one person" [this to explain Banquo's appearance only to Macbeth].[51] Obviously this is by no means the powerful and brilliant analysis of modern historical experts, but it represents certainly the germ of this study, and it appeared when the very opposite sort of insane romanticizing of Hamlet was reaching its crest. Hence this and Richard Hole's criticism of Shylock are the two most interesting historical developments in the late eighteenth-century criticism of Shakespeare.

Meanwhile the negative point of view continued to the very end of the period: ". . . the public, therefore, alone remains accountable for their present prostitution of the British drama—It was in the same hope of pleasing their auditors, that Shakspere was sometimes prurient, Wycherly [*sic*] licentious, and Vanburgh [*sic*] profane."[52]

---

[50] V (1798), 301.
[51] V (1798), 170—by "A. L." The same application is made on p. 301 to the closet-scene in *Hamlet*.
[52] *Monthly Mirror*, IV (1797), 47.

SOURCES OF SHAKESPEARE'S PLAYS[53]

From Steevens' notation of the source of *King Lear* in his *Twenty Plays* in 1766 to Chalmers' reference in 1799[54] to Marlowe's *True Tragedy of Richard, Duke of York* as the basis of Shakespeare's *Henry VI*, Part 3, the interest in the study of Shakespeare's sources persisted as the most prominent type of historical criticism during the period. This section will not attempt to cover this wide field completely but will suggest at the end a supplementary bibliography of additional material useful for further investigation.

Capell's Introduction to his edition in 1768 gave the origin of Shakespeare's Fables.[55] Farmer meanwhile had suggested a whole multitude of sources: North's *Plutarch*,[56] Painter's *Palace of Pleasure*,[57] W. Warner and Gascoigne,[58] Holinshed,[59] and many others.[60] The next year appeared, anonymously, *A Key to the Drama*, Volume I of which contained the "Life, Character and Secret History of Macbeth," with a Preface noting that the author had spent much time in studying histories of Dramatis Personæ

---

[53] D. Nichol Smith in his latest book (*op. cit.*, 1928) gives a brief survey of early study in this field, pp. 50-51. See also K. Young's monograph listed above. For further material preceding 1766 see: Hypolitus, Earl of Douglas, *Secret History of Mackbeth*, 1708; Cap't Charles Johnson, *A General History of the Lives and Adventures of the Most Famous Highwaymen* [on Falstaff], 1734; *Gentleman's Magazine*, XXIII (1753), 250, 255—rev. of Mrs. Lennox; *Gentleman's Magazine*, XXIV (1754), 221, 311—Source of Shylock; *Monthly Review*, IX (1753), 145, and X (1754), 309—rev. of Mrs. Lennox; XII (1755), 389—Source of *Merchant of Venice*; *Universal Magazine*, XV (1754), 258—Source of a scene in the *M. of V.*; *Connoisseur* (1754-6), No. 16—Source of a scene in the *M. of V.*

[54] Noted in the *Anti-Jacobin Review*, III (1799), 389—from the *Supplemental Apology*.

[55] On pp. 49-71.

[56] *Essay on the Learning of Shakespeare* (1767—1st ed.), p. 10.

[57] *Ibid.*, p. 15.   [58] *Ibid.*, pp. 30-31.   [59] *Ibid.*, pp. 47-48.

[60] *Ibid.*, pp. 16, 19, 22-23, 26-27. See also the *British Magazine*, VIII (1767), 571-2: "he has followed Plutarch step by step."

"especially of those brought upon the stage by the celebrated Shakespear."[61] Mrs. Montagu in 1769 continued the study of sources,[62] as did Whately in 1770,[63] and Morgann in 1777.[64] Then J. Nichols in 1779 printed *Six Old Plays on which Shakespeare founded his Measure for Measure, Comedy of Errors, Taming of the Shrew, King John, King Henry IV and V, and King Lear*. This book aroused considerable interest, for favorable reviews of it appeared in both the *Gentleman's Magazine*[65] and *Monthly Review*.[66] In 1780 the *Mirror* pointed out the source of *Hamlet*,[67] and Malone's *Supplement* of the same year announced the precise sources for both *Romeo and Juliet* and *Hamlet*.[68]

William Jackson wrote in 1782 that Shakespeare's plots were "mostly taken from historical facts, or from novels . . . more or less heightened."[69] Ritson continued the study in 1783,[70] as did Tom Davies in 1784 at much length.[71] The *Monthly Review* in the same year added items.[72] The *Lounger* in 1786 speculated on the source of Falstaff,[73] and the *Hibernian Magazine* in the same year printed the whole story of Saxo Grammaticus;[74] it also published later in the year a comparison of Middleton's *The Witch* with Shakespeare's *Macbeth*, to ascertain sources.[75]

In 1793 the *Universal Magazine* discussed the source of *Measure for Measure*.[76] Whiter the following year remarked: ". . . our Poet has caught many words and even terms of

[61] P. 1.   [62] *Op. cit.*, pp. 275-76.   [63] *Op. cit.*, pp. 10, 16.
[64] *Op. cit.*, pp. 48 n., 50.   [65] *Gentleman's Magazine*, XLIX (1779), 258.
[66] *Monthly Review*, LXI (1779), 296.
[67] No. 99. Chalmers, XXIX, 253-54.   [68] Advertisement, p. 111.
[69] *Thirty Letters*, 3rd ed. (1795), pp. 97-98.   [70] *Remarks*, pp. 13, 47, 73.
[71] *Op. cit.*, I, Chaps. I and II; I, 209, 298-302; II, 21, 198.
[72] LXX (1784), 15, 334. The periodical is reviewing Capell's *Notes* and Ritson's *Remarks*.
[73] No. 68.   [74] P. 351.   [75] Pp. 512-13.
[76] XCII (1793), 348: "The novel of Cynthio Giraldo."

expression belonging to the novel, from which the play [*As You Like It*] was taken."[77] In 1795 the *British Critic* wrote on the source of the idea of Macduff's supernatural birth,[78] and the following year the Exeter Society *Essays* made an important comment on Shakespeare's source material: "Shakspeare . . . drew his characters and incidents from traditionary stories and family anecdotes;—sometimes, probably, from preceding dramas in which they were preserved, and other short-lived publications that have long since perished in the tide of time."[79] White, in the same year, referred to Holinshed.[80] Finally, the *Monthly Mirror* in 1798 gave, in an article entitled "An Apology for Plagiarism," a whole list of sources for Shakespeare's plays in general, which will serve as a fine climax of the persistent interest in Shakespeare's sources all the way from 1766 to 1799.[81]

It must be remembered that in presenting this survey of the great increase in historical source study of Shakespeare's plays this section has only three times touched editions of the poet, for its purpose was to show how all critics, quite aside from editors who had to do this sort of work, were developing this particular historical criticism of Shakespeare. In conclusion, one should recall the contributions of R. Farmer (1767), J. Nichols (1779), and the *Monthly Mirror* (1798) as the three conspicuous landmarks in the fuller development of this type of historical study in the late eighteenth century.[82]

---

[77] *Op. cit.*, p. 8.
[79] *Op. cit.*, p. 255. See also pp. 258, 262.
[81] VI (1798), 40 ff. See also pp. 356-57.
[78] VI (1795), 343.
[80] *Op. cit.*, p. 47 n.

[82] For further material subject to investigation in this field of source study from 1766-99, see: "*Romeo and Juliet*": *comedy . . . by Lope de Vega, built upon the same story* [as S.'s], 1770; *History of Titus Andronicus*, Translated from the Italian; 1780. E. Capell, *The School of Shakspeare*, 1780; *Universal Magazine*, LXXXIII (1788), 182—Shakespeare—"to whom indebted for

Comparative Study[83]

One of the most popular modern points of view in criticism of Shakespeare is comparative study, the application to Shakespeare of the dramatic conventions and general dramatic background of the Elizabethan Age.[84] But modern critics were long ago anticipated by the critics of the late eighteenth century.

Farmer in 1767 remarked: "Nothing but an intimate acquaintance with the Writers of the time, who are frequently of no other value, can point out his [Shakespeare's] allusions, and ascertain his Phraseology."[85] He used Kyd and Dekker, for example, for the former,[86] and referred to the verbiage and imagery of all Elizabethans for the latter.[87] Malone himself in 1792 could not improve on this method and applauded it in his *Letter to Dr. Farmer*.[88]

Mrs. Griffith in 1775 introduced two interesting comparative topics for this type of study, civil war and jealousy in Shakespeare's plays.[89] Morgann two years later compared Falstaff, Parolles and Bobadil[90] and announced a point of view which has been reproduced by modern

---

his Ideas of an Actor in Hamlet"; *Monthly Review*, XIX (1796), 106—Review of the original story of *Othello*.

[83] For some material preceding 1766 see: Dryden's *Heads of an Answer to Rymer's Remarks* (after 1678), *Works*, ed. by Scott & Saintsbury, XV, 381; Pope, *Preface*, (1725), p. vii; *Gentleman's Magazine*, I (1731), 153—Shakespeare & Jonson; XXIX (1759), 231—Shakspeare & Jonson; Kames, *Elements of Criticism* (1762), chap. XXIII.

[84] See the summary of the work of Professors E. E. Stoll and L. L. Schücking in the *Sewanee Review*, XXXV (1927), 15-31.

[85] *Op. cit.*, p. 49.   [86] *Ibid.*, pp. 28-29.   [87] *Ibid.*, p. 21.

[88] P. 10. In 1772 the *Gentleman's Magazine* continued the popular critical pastime of the comparison of Ben Jonson and Shakespeare—XLII (1772), 522: a somewhat different type of comparative study.

[89] *Op. cit.*, pp. 356, 519.

[90] *Op. cit.*, p. 141. See also pp. 148, 166, 176.

scholars with great éclat: Shakespeare's "characters interpret for one another continually"; hence "If Falstaff had been intended for the character of a Miles Gloriosus, his behaviour . . . would have been commented upon by others."[91] One should note again the supreme originality and importance of Morgann in this period.

Davies in 1784 compared Shakespeare with Beaumont and Fletcher and with Calderon.[92] Mason continued the method in 1785,[93] as did Ritson in 1788.[94] Finally Whiter in 1794 may be cited to summarize the point of view. In order to prove that the stage was "hung with black" for tragedy he quoted from Webster's *Vittoria Corombona* (1612) and Dekker's *A Strange Horse Race* (1613).[95] He repeated this precise method with tremendous effect in at least two other places in his text.[96] Modern critics have never improved upon these three notes of this late eighteenth-century critic.[97]

Stage History

This section will point out briefly the interest of the late eighteenth century in the general position of Shakespeare's plays in the history and acting traditions of British drama.[98]

---

[91] *Ibid.*, p. 77. Compare Mr. Stoll.
[92] *Op. cit.*, I, 105, 434. See also I, 203; II, 41; III, 98.
[93] *Op. cit.*, pp. 53, 61, 98.
[94] *Quip Modest*, p. 11—Shakspeare and Spenser.   [95] *Specimen*, p. 156 n.
[96] P. 170 n. & pp. 209-14. I should add R. Hole (Exeter Society *Essays*), p. 409, on Richard III and Aaron.
[97] To all this should be added the fifth argument against the unities in Chap. IV above. For further possible comparative material see: T. Warton, *History of English Poetry*, 1774, 1778; *Monthly Review*, LXIII (1780), 249—State of Drama in time of S; *Universal Magazine*, LXVIII (1781), 230, 354 —A review of T. Warton on Shakespeare and the Poetry of Elizabeth; R. Alves, *Sketches of a History of Literature*, 1794.
[98] For some material preceding 1766 on this see: L. Riccoboni, *Historical and Critical Account of the Theaters*, 1741; D. Garrick, *An Essay on Acting*, 1744;

Mrs. Montagu in 1769 declared that there were only "palpable allegories" in the background of Shakespeare's plays.[99] Francis Gentleman the next year suggested that "every alterer of Shakespeare should remember, there were no female performers in his day."[100] The *Monthly Review* in 1773 gave excerpts from T. Hawkins' *Origin of English Drama*,[101] and the same periodical in 1780 wrote on the "State of the English Drama in his [Shakespear's] Time."[102]

Ritson referred to pageants in 1783: "this sort of procession was the usual recreation of our ancestors at Christmas,"[103] and the *Gentleman's Magazine* in the same year discussed Elizabethan properties.[104] Richardson in 1784 produced a remark on the dramatic history of a Shakespearean character which a modern critic was not slow to turn against him:[105] ". . . every reader and every audience have hitherto taken part with Hamlet . . . and the voice of the people, in poetry as well as politics, deserves some attention."[106]

The same year Tom Davies proposed the use of Elizabethan tapestry pictures of Hamlet, Sr., and Claudius in the famous closet scene,[107] and this tapestry point was picked up by Whiter ten years later: ". . . our old Poets derived many of their allusions and descriptions from *pictures and representations in Tapestry*, which were then equally familiar to themselves and to their readers."[108]

W. R. Chetwood, *A General History of the Stage*, 1749; *London Magazine*, XXXIV (1765), 151—"Origin of the English Stage."
[99]*Op. cit.*, p. 19. See also p. 150.   [100]*Op. cit.*, I, 360.
[101]XLVIII (1773), 388-89.
[102]LXIII (1780), 250. In a review of Malone's *Supplement*.
[103]*Op. cit.*, p. 38.   [104]LIV (1784), 103.
[105]E. E. Stoll, "Hamlet," *University of Minnesota Studies*, No. 7 (1919), 9.
[106]*Op. cit.*, 5th ed. (1798), p. 124.   [107]*Op. cit.*, III, 106.
[108]*Op. cit.*, p. 34.

HISTORICAL CRITICISM 197

Meanwhile the *Lounger* had given an interesting account of the Falstaff acting tradition,[109] and Malone had produced his famous *An Historical Account of the English Stage* in his edition of 1790.[110] Whiter also recurred to the emphasis on pageants in 1794,[111] and as a final citation may be noted the *Anti-Jacobin Review's* quoting from Chalmers' *Apology* on the players and theaters of Shakespeare's time.[112]

A general conclusion should return first to the superpsychological interest of the period and note how it was carried over even into historical criticism. For this let us resort again to Whiter: ". . . but the more curious examples [of the association phenomenon] will be derived from those impressions which are peculiar to the country, the age, and the situation of the writer"; these may be *indirect* as well as *direct* allusions, "trains of thought . . . pregnant with the materials peculiar to his age"; ". . . the critic must exert . . . knowledge in the phraseology and customs belonging to the age of his author," for though the poet may rise to be universal, "Still however, the secret energy of local influence will continue to operate on his mind. . . . In the fictions, the thoughts, and the language of the poet,

---

[109]No. 68, Chalmers, XXXI, 111.   [110]Vol. I, Pt. 2, pp. 1-284.
[111]*Op. cit.*, pp. 78, 199.
[112]III (1799), 388-89. It must be recalled that both F. Gentleman, *op. cit.*, and T. Davies, *op. cit.*, were concerned mainly with the acting traditions throughout their books. A concluding supplementary bibliography of this section would contain: *London Magazine*, XXXVI (1767), 267—Rise of the English Stage; XLII (1773), 632—History of English Drama to Shakespeare; T. Hawkins, *Origin of English Drama*, 1773; *Monthly Review*, L (1774), 144; LIII (1775), 186—Shakespeare's Plays as acted; *Playhouse Pocket Companion* (1779).—Preface is a Critical History of the English Stage from 536 A.D. to present; *Universal Magazine*, LXXXV (1789), 6—Origin of Dramatic Writing; LXXXIX (1791), 3—Origin and Progress of Comedy; Thomas Percy, *Essay on the Origin of the English Stage*, 1793; *Censor Dramaticus, A Complete History of the Drama*, 1793; *Monthly Mirror*, VII (1799), 114, 177, 247, 306, 370—History of the Stage from 1747 on. This is continued in vol. VIII.

you may ever mark the deep and unequivocal traces of the age in which he lived."[113]

But the most conspicuous aspect of this late eighteenth-century historical study of Shakespeare was its essential modernity. Ritson and Mason were busy emphasizing the first quartos and first folio. Richard Hole and the *Monthly Mirror* had anticipated modern historical criticism of Shylock and Shakespeare's ghosts. John Nichols and the *Monthly Mirror* were resuscitating Shakespeare's sources for comparative study. Morgann's idea of Elizabethan character interpretation and *inter alios* commenting, and Whiter's comparative study of Shakespeare with Webster and Dekker had both anticipated modern critics again. Finally Richardson's reference to the stage history of the character of Hamlet has been cited by one modern critic and carried even further by another.[114] Hence Mr. Young need not worry about the long hiatus from Johnson in 1765 to Rümelin in 1866. These late eighteenth-century critics had really anticipated us in about every possible historical aspect of Shakespeare.

---

[113] *Op. cit.*, pp. 71-73. See also above, pp. 184-85.

[114] See Stoll, *op. cit.*, and Roy Mackenzie, *Washington University Studies*, Oct., 1922, pp. 110 ff. I have already mentioned above that James Plumptre's *Observations on Hamlet* (Camb.: Lunn, 1796), anticipated the modern Lilian Winstanley—See above, p. 153 and 153 n.

CHAPTER XIV

IDOLATRY AD ASTRA

To offset the effect of the preceding realistic development this chapter will conclude with a few general apostrophes to Shakespeare from 1766 to 1799,[1] which will emphasize strongly the natural transition from the late eighteenth to the early nineteenth century. "The eighteenth century could almost lose itself in panegyric of Shakespeare," wrote Professor Nichol Smith in 1903.[2] This chapter will attempt to show that Professor Smith apparently made one mistake in his above remark: he should have omitted the word, "almost."

Direct eulogy of Shakespeare appeared in several poetic collections from 1766 to 1799. In Chalmers' *British Poets* will be found many poems, from Beaumont's "On William Shakespeare"[3] straight on down through the eighteenth

---

[1] W. Kenrick's *Introduction to the School of Shakespeare* (1773), pp. 3-5 contains a brief, general survey of eulogy of Shakespeare before 1766. For further material, see the second paragraph of this chapter and: Capell's *edition* (1767) prints 8 poems; David Garrick, "Testimonies to the Genius and Merits of Shakespeare", 1769; E. Young, *An Epistle to the Right Honorable the Lord Lansdown*, 1713; [Moore's?], *Ode to Garrick*, 1749; T. Blacklock, *Poems on Several Occasions*, 1754; J. G. Cooper, *The Tomb of Shakespear*, 1755; *The Visitation* [Ghosts of Shakespeare and Garrick], 1755; *Past Twelve O'clock* [Maggs Catalogue, 1927, No. 640], 1757; J. Huckell, *Avon, a poem*, 1758; R. Lloyd, *Shakespear: an Epistle to Mr. Garrick*, 1760; *Three Conjurors* [Maggs, 1927, No. 723], 1763. In periodicals: *British Magazine*, II (1747), 177; *The World* (1753-6), No. 179—Cento on Shakespeare's Birthday; *Universal Magazine*, XVI (1755), 85—"Epistle to Juliet"; XXXVII (1765), 268—"The Interview, or Shakespear's Ghost."

[2] *Introduction* to *Eighteenth Century Essays on Shakespeare*, p. xii.

[3] VI, 203. Others include Collins' *Epistle to Hanmer*, Moore's [?] *Ode to Garrick*, Lloyd's *Epistle to Garrick*, J. G. Cooper's *The Tomb of Shakespear*, P. Whitehead's *Verses Dropt in Mr. Garrick's Temple of Shakspeare*, etc.

century. Johnson and Steevens' second edition (1778) lists twenty-seven poems on Shakespeare and the third edition (1785) adds seven new ones. Malone's edition (1790) gives thirty-four. Then there are the collections of Prologues and Epilogues, as they appear for example in *The Theatrical Bouquet* (1778)[4] and R. Griffith's *A Collection and Selection of English Prologues and Epilogues Commencing with Shakespeare and Concluding with Garrick* (1779). But even more suggestive are the many individual tributes scattered through the periodicals from 1766 to 1799.

In 1766 the *Monthly Review* noted "The Interview, or Jack Falstaff's Ghost," inscribed to Garrick,[5] and in the same year quoted from Ogilvie's "Elysium of the Poets":

> Here Shakespeare sat in regal glory bright,
>   And mark'd spontaneous flowers around him blow,
> With scenes still shifting sooth'd his raptur'd sight,
>   Or drunk the musick of the lawns below.[6]

Scots Magazine in 1767 printed "A short Encomium on the Inimitable Shakespeare":

> Once in a hundred years the Phoenix dies,
> And a new flame-born bird his place supplies:
> Two hundred years ago great Shakespeare wrote,
> But where's his flame-born son?—Not yet begot.[7]

In the same year the *British Magazine* proclaimed Shakespeare "a master in every species of composition."[8] Mrs. Montagu wrote in 1769: "He was approved by his own age, admired by the next, and is revered and almost adored at present."[9] This year, the year of the great Jubilee, was

---

[4]Maggs' *Shakespeareana* (1927), No. 528.
[5]XXXV (1766), 79. Miss Eleanor Ross of the University of Michigan gave me this note. On this poem see also *Scots Magazine*, XXVIII (1766), 436.
[6]XXXIV (1766), 121.   [7]XXIX (1767), 154.   [8]VIII (1767), 619-20.
[9]*Essay on the Genius and Writings of Shakespear*, p. 10.

of course prolific in poetic eulogy of Shakespeare. First and most important is Garrick's famous *Ode*, lines of which were reprinted in the *Universal Magazine*[10] and the *Monthly Review*:[11]

> The lov'd, rever'd, immortal name
> .   .   .   .   .
>   To him the first of poets, best of men.
>
> Tho' Philip's fam'd unconquer'd son,
> Had ev'ry blood-stained laurel won;
> He sigh'd—that his creative world,
>   (Like that which rules the skies,)
> Could not bid other nations rise,
> To glut his yet unsated sword:
>
>   But when our Shakespeare's matchless pen,
> Like Alexander's sword, had done with men;
>   He heav'd no sigh, he made no moan,
>   Not limited to human kind,
>   He fir'd his wonder-teeming mind,
>   Rais'd other worlds, and beings of his own!

But other poems by "Mr. G" were printed that year in the *Universal Magazine:* "The Country Girl":

> Yet now I call to mind,
>   Our larned Doctor boasted
> One Skispur did, of all mankind
>   Receive from Heav'n the most-head.[12]

---
[10] XLV (1769), 154.
[11] XLI (1769), 235. The final chorus of this *Ode* is:
> Sing immortal Shakespeare's praise!
> The song will cease, the storm decay,
>   But his Name
>   And undiminished fame,
>   Shall never, never pass away.

[12] XLV (1769), 153.

And "Warwickshire, A Song":

> Our Shakespeare compar'd is to no man
> Nor Frenchman, nor Grecian, nor Roman.[13]

And in the same year appeared Richard Berenger's lines:

> Now worthy friends, the cause why we are met
> Is in celebration of the day that gave
> Immortal Shakespear to this favour'd isle.[14]

F. Gentleman in 1770 complained that "the real Jubilee at Stratford . . . deserves no better title than theatrical idolatry";[15] and in 1771 the *Monthly Review* referred to "all the (we had almost said) *devout* reverence in which even the faults of Shakespeare are generally held."[16] In the same year the *Universal Magazine* produced more poetry:

> And when Willy sung, all the Deities swore
> They ne'er heard such warbling, such wild notes before,
>
> . . . .
>
> Ye bards of all ages, yield Shakespeare the bays . . .
> Let Britons, inraptur'd, their thanks swell on high.
> One Shakespeare on earth—one Jove in the sky.[17]

Bell's Edition in 1774 noted Shakespeare as "the god of their idolatry,"[18] and Richardson in the same year became

---

[13] XLV (1769), 152-53. This appeared in *Shakespeare's Garland* (1769), for reviews of which see: *Gentleman's Magazine*, XXXIX (1769), 447; *London Magazine*, XXXVIII (1769), 538.
[14] *Universal Magazine*, XLV (1769), 152.
[15] *Dramatic Censor*, I, 387. Compare also I, 95, 96, 102, 141-42, 388.
[16] XLV (1771), 507.
[17] XLVIII (1771), 97-98. Compare also *Scots Magazine*, XXXIII (1771), 656, Horace Walpole's lines in his letter of Sept. 9, 1771, and the *Monthly Review's* excerpts from "An Essay on Woman," XLVII (1772), 410, quoted above in connection with Shakespeare's women, in Chap. XI, p. 139 n.
[18] Advertisement, p. 5.

very ecstatic: "Shakespeare, superior to all mankind in the invention of character";[19] ". . . the most solemn and striking apostrophe that ever poet invented."[20] Edward Taylor caused some excitement in 1774 by his attack on Shakespeare, for the *Gentleman's Magazine*, in reviewing him, declared that "the enthusiastic adorers of Shakespeare will scarce forgive this sacrilegious attack on that *god of their idolatry* [their italics]."[21] And Mrs. Griffith announced that "He [Shakespeare] is the only Dramatic Writer who ever alike excelled in Tragedy and Comedy."[22] Horace Walpole in 1777 pronounced Shakespeare "superior to all mankind,"[23] and continued his eulogy in 1778, 1779, 1782, 1786, and 1787.[24] Meanwhile Morgann, the cool psychologizer, had written in 1777 some tremendous panegyrics: ". . . we are possessed by him . . . master of our feelings . . . every thing seems superior . . . we are rapt in ignorant admiration, and claim no kindred with his abilities. . . . He at once blends and distinguishes every thing . . . astonishing that a mere human being . . . should so perfectly comprehend the whole . . . he converts every thing into excellence."[25]

In 1778 Colman raptly praised Shakespeare in his *Preface to the Works of Beaumont and Fletcher*,[26] and the *Critical Review* applauded "C. Melmoth's" [S. J. Pratt's] "The Shadows of Shakespeare, a monody occasioned by the death of Mr. Garrick."[27] Four years later the *Biographia*

---

[19]*Essays*, p. 185 (5th ed., 1798).   [20]*Ibid.*, p. 88.
[21]XLV (1775), 90. Taylor's book was *Cursory Remarks on Tragedy, on Shakespear*, etc.
[22]Dedication of *op. cit.* (1775), pp. iii-iv.
[23]*Letters*, X (Nov. 8, 1777), 155.
[24]*Ibid.*, X (Oct. 8, 1778), 329; X (Feb. 1, 1779), 371; XII (1782), 172; XIII (Dec. 12, 1786), 426; XIV (Oct. 14, 1787), 29.
[25]*Op. cit.*, pp. 66-68. Compare also p. 65, quoted below in the text.
[26]*Prose on Several Occasions* (1787), II, 152.   [27]XLVII (1779), 233.

Dramatica wrote: "a mulberry-tree planted upon his estate by the hands of this revered bard, was cut down not many years ago, and the wood, being converted to several domestic uses, was all eagerly bought at a high price, and each single piece treasured up by its purchaser . . . after the seller of it had been driven out of town."[28] And back came Richardson for the second time, in 1784, with: "His merits have never been overrated";[29] "his merits far surpass those of every other dramatic writer."[30] Tom Davies echoed him: ". . . in this wonderful creative faculty he excels all dramatic writers,"[31] and added: "If I could possibly envy the pleasure which the audiences enjoyed in old times, it would be for that inconceivable delight which intelligent auditors must have felt at the first acting of Shakspeare's noblest dramas. Methinks I see and hear the tumultuous joy and thundering applause which the unparalleled character of Falstaff must have afforded at his first representation!"[32]

In 1785 the author of a poem, "The Immortality of Shakespeare," complained: ". . . after the divine Shakespeare, how poor my imagination";[33] and in the same year the *Monthly Review* printed excerpts from "The Immortality of Shakspeare," by a "youth of eighteen."[34] Martin Sherlock's tremendous eulogy in 1786 deserves full reproduction: "It is she [Nature] who was thy book, O Shakspeare; . . . it is she from whom thou hast drawn those beauties which are at once the glory and delight of thy nation. Thou wert the eldest son, the darling child, of Nature; and, like thy mother, enchanting, astonishing, sublime, graceful, thy variety is inexhaustible. Always origi-

---

[28] (1782), I, 404. [29] *Op. cit.*, (5th ed., 1798), p. 364.
[30] *Ibid.*, 392. Compare also pp. 133, 215, 235. [31] *Op. cit.*, II, 288.
[32] *Ibid.*, I, 277-78. [33] *Critical Review*, LIX (1787), 69.
[34] LXXII (1785), 468.

nal, always new, thou art the only prodigy which Nature has produced. . . . The reader who thinks this elogium extravagant is a stranger to my subject. To say that Shakspeare had the imagination of Dante, and the depth of Machiavel, would be a weak encomium: he had them, and more. . . . To the brilliance of Voltaire he added the strength of Demosthenes; and to the simplicity of La Fontaine, the majesty of Virgil.—But, say you, we have never seen such 'a being'. You are in the right; Nature made it, and broke the mold. . . . *Shakspeare possessed, in the highest degree of perfection, all the most excellent talents of all the writers that I have ever known.*"[35]

This apostrophizing continued unabated through the last decade of the century. In 1791 *The Bee* called Shakespeare "Inimitable,"[36] and added:

> Whoe'er attempts like Shakespeare to compose
> Shall certainly his time and labour lose
>
> .   .   .   .
>
> This mighty poet every Key can hit.[37]

In the same year the *Universal Magazine* exclaimed: "The beauties of this first of dramatic poets may be compared to gold, unseparated from its dross; or, rather, to diamonds, lying intermixed with a much larger number of counterfeits";[38] ". . . so apt, so expressive, and so beautiful, that the prolific brain of a Shakspeare could alone give birth to them."[39] The *Anthologia Hibernica* referred to Shakespeare as "their idol,"[40] and *The Bee* announced:

---

[35] *A Fragment*, pp. 13-14. Reprinted in *European Magazine*, X (1786), 282. Compare W. Richardson in 1789, pp. 281, 286, 288, 394 (all of 5th ed.).
[36] I (1791), 58.
[37] II (1791), 355-56. Compare the same periodical, IV (1791), 294-95: "Shakespeare . . . an unrivalled dramatic poet."
[38] LXXXVIII (1791), 59.   [39] LXXXVIII (1791), 127.
[40] II (1793), 277.

"Shakespeare possessed this happy talent ["for discriminating human characters"] in a degree superior to that of any other of the sons of men who have yet appeared on the globe."[41] The next year, in 1794, the *Universal Magazine* continued:

> O sovereign master, who with lonely state
> Dost reign as in some isle's inchanted land.[42]

And again, in 1797, the same periodical wrote on "The Situation of Shakspeare, in the Island of Fancy":

> There up to heav'n a mass of rock was pil'd
> . . . .
> And on its topmost height, the regal throne
> Of this romantic realm, stood Avon's bard alone.[43]

Finally in 1799 the *Gentleman's Magazine* quoted from Mrs. West's *Poems and Plays:*

What tho' the polish'd bards of Greece
With art their tragic temple plann'd
And deck'd the well-connected piece
With ornaments correct and grand;
Shall not the swelling sea amaze,
Shall not the eye enraptured gaze
On Niagara's thundering waves?
And shall fastidious Taste refuse
The pages of Shakspeare to peruse,
Though Nature's suppliant voice thy fixed attention craves?

Oh! master of that airy band
Who round imagination throng,
Grac'd with spirit-stirring wand
That subjugates the power of song!
Who but thyself, Great Bard! could feign

---

[41]XIV (1793), 302-3.   [42]XCV (1794), 442-43.   [43]CI (1797), 430.

The horrors of the murderous Thane?
Who bid Othello's fury swell,
Make us with frantic Lear to weep,
Or call up spirits from the deep
Embody fairy sylphs, or form the wizard spell?⁴⁴

But the most astonishing eulogy of Shakespeare in this whole period comes from the pen of the coolest psychologizer and analytical critic, Maurice Morgann: "When the hand of time shall have brushed off his present Editors and Commentators, and when the very name of *Voltaire*, and

---

⁴⁴LXIX (1799), 882. And this is but the climax of a stream of poetic eulogy flowing steadily from 1766, whose volume and strength have been merely suggested. For consider the following poetry on Shakespeare not hitherto touched upon in this section: J. Jemmat, *Verses on Barry as Othello*, 1766; Edward Thompson, *Trinculo's Trip to the Jubilee*, 1769; Henry Jones, *Ode to Shakespear*, 1769, 1773, 1779; "Sir Nicholas Nipclose," *The Theaters, A Poetical Dissection*, 1772 [Maggs' *Shakespeareana* (1927), No. 718]; William Pearce, *The Haunts of Shakespeare*, 1776, 1778; Dr. Lawrence, *An Ode on the Spirits of Shakespear*, 1776; E. Jerningham, *The Shakespeare Gallery*, 1791; J. Armstrong, *Sonnets from Shakspeare*, 1791; *The Genius of Shakspeare, A Summer Dream*, 1793; A. Harrison, *The Infant Vision of Shakspeare*, 1794 ["Darling of Nature! Britain's proudest boast, And e'en the world's chief pride"]; T. J. Mathias, *The Pursuits of Literature*, 1794-97; T. Bellamy, *The London Theaters*, 1795.

And for some supplementary periodical material: *Gentleman's Magazine*, XXXVII (1767), 324—Epitaph on Shakespeare; *Critical Review*, XXVIII (1769), 231—Garrick's *Ode*; *Universal Magazine*, XLV (1769), 152—Cento on the birthday of Shakspeare; *Gentleman's Magazine*, XXXIX (1769), 446 —Garrick's *Ode*; *London Magazine*, XL (1771), 169—A Poem on Shakespeare; XLII (1773), 511—Ode to Shakespeare; *Gentleman's Magazine*, XLIX (1779), 208—Nonpareil on Shakespeare; *Universal Magazine*, LXV (1779), 263—Shakespeare in the shades; *Critical Review*, LIX (1785), 69— "Immortality of Shakspeare"; *Gentleman's Magazine*, LVII (1787), 912, 1108—"Shakespeare's Bedside"; *Family Magazine*, I (1788)—"History of King Lear and His Three Daughters"; *Universal Magazine*, LXXXVII (1790), 257—Poetical Character of Shakespeare; *Critical Review*, LXXI (1791), 201—"The Shakespeare Gallery"; *Monthly Review*, IV (1791), 332 —"The Shakespeare Gallery"; *Gentleman's Magazine*, LXI (1791), 333— Two Epigrams on Shakespeare; *Anthologia Hibernica*, IV (1794), 298—Ode on Shakespeare.

even the memory of the language in which he has written, shall be no more, the *Apalachian* Mountains, the banks of the Ohio, and the plains of Sciola shall resound with the accents of this Barbarian."[45] Coleridge never improved on this, and yet it comes from the magnificently subtle psychologizer of Falstaff. Incidentally this book is now being written beyond the "Apalachian Mountains" and not far from "the banks of the Ohio." Perhaps the reader will no longer wonder now at the suggestion that Professor Nichol Smith delete his "almost" from his comment in 1903, "The eighteenth century could almost lose itself in panegyric of Shakespeare."[46]

---

[45] *Op. cit.*, p. 65. Reprinted in the *Universal Magazine*, LXI (1777), 5, and the *London Magazine*, XLVI (1777), 313-14. In his "errata" Morgann corrected "Sciola" to "Sciota."

[46] For some supplementary material in prose, see: *Hibernian Magazine*, 1779, p. 221—Eulogium on Shakespeare; *Ibid.*, 1786, p. 567—rev. of Sherlock; *Gentleman's Magazine*, LVI (1786), 779—rev. of Sherlock; *Analytical Review*, VII (1790), 406—Review of *Observations on the first Act of Shakespear's "Tempest,"* by a Dublin undergraduate [which appeared originally in *Transactions of the Royal Irish Academy*, II (1788), 39-53].

PART IV

THE EARLY NINETEENTH CENTURY
AND SHAKESPEARE

CHAPTER XV

THE REFLECTION OF LATE EIGHTEENTH-
CENTURY VIEWS IN COLERIDGE,
LAMB, HAZLITT, AND THE
MAGAZINES

The complete foundation of late eighteenth-century criticism has now been laid, upon which this Part will show the early nineteenth century erecting its codex. Hence the concluding step in this book is now at hand, namely to indicate how very closely early nineteenth-century criticism of Shakespeare imitated that of the preceding period. Obviously, in doing this, one might suggest two lines of proof, one of which is perfectly germane to this book and the other not. The first is to point out in the work of early nineteenth-century critics the direct repetition of the critical dicta of the late eighteenth century. The second is to prove if possible, or at least suggest proof, that these later critics deliberately used their predecessors. This latter line of action is somewhat beyond the pale of this book, which is primarily concerned with the late eighteenth century and the establishment of its critical dicta as the natural basis for the criticism of the succeeding period. In other words, we are not at all interested in determining how much any specific nineteenth-century critic picked up from particular predecessors. That is a task for nineteenth-century specialists to fulfill. All that will be attempted here will be to show the natural flow of critical dicta from the one period to the next. However, having indicated first this perfect transition, from the late eighteenth century to the early nineteenth, this Part will then attempt to point out a few clues which may link specific later critics more definitely with particular predecessors than has possibly been done before. And inasmuch as the early nineteenth century contains more "big names" than the late eighteenth century, it will be sufficient to concentrate on the criticism of Coleridge, Lamb, and Hazlitt, though the footnotes will suggest, throughout, a background of lesser criticism which will supplement the work of these critics so outstanding within their period. The order followed will directly repeat that of earlier chapters.

EDITIONS, CHRONOLOGY, AND SPURIOUS PLAYS

Coleridge attacked Malone's chronology,[1] and Hazlitt attacked the Poems: "In a word, we do not like Shakespear's poems, because we like his plays."[2] Both of them were interested in spurious plays.[3]

---

[1]Pp. 8, 10, 243-51. The text used for Coleridge is T. Ashe, *Lectures and Notes on Shakspere and Other English Poets* (London, 1883). All pages given refer to this unless otherwise noted. For Coleridge's spelling, "Shakspeare," see Nichol Smith, *Shakespeare Criticism* (1916). I regret exceedingly that Professor T. M. Raysor's very important edition of *Coleridge's Shakespearean Criticism* (Constable, 1930), did not appear until after the present book had gone to the press. I was fortunate enough, however, thanks to Dr. Raysor's kindness, to be allowed to see the page proof of this new edition and have interpolated notes from Dr. Raysor's new material (especially the Tomalin Reports) in my own footnotes. I have also surveyed Dr. Raysor's footnotes for H. N. Coleridge's personal interpolations in the *Literary Remains*.

[2]I, 358. The text used for Hazlitt is *The Collected Works of William Hazlitt*, edited by A. R. Waller and A. Glover (London, 1902). All pages given refer to this unless otherwise noted.

[3]Coleridge: pp. 10-11, 27, 246-47, 533. Hazlitt: I, 356-57. As Nichol Smith points out in his *Shakespeare in the Eighteenth Century* (p. 46 n.), the versification tests had begun as early as 1758, with Richard Roderick. Compare Coleridge, pp. 290-91, and Hazlitt, I, 312. For further material, on this first section in general, see: G. Chalmers, *Appendix to Supplemental Apology*, 1800 (On the *Sonnets*); Johnson and Steevens' Fifth Edition, 1803; Lord Chedworth, *Notes upon Some Passages in Shakespeare's Plays*, 1805; A. Chalmers, *Plays of William Shakspeare*, 1805; H. J. Pye, *Comments on the Commentators on*

SHAKESPEARE ILLUSTRATED, CONCORDANCES, GLOSSARIES AND SHAKESPEAREANA (BIBLIOGRAPHICAL)

The early nineteenth century produced the following items: Sir Robert Smirke, *Illustrations to Shakspeare*, 1821-29; J. R. Planché, Books on Costumes of Shakespeare's Plays, 1823-30; *Edinburgh Review*, XVI (1810), 309, 310—on the Shakespeare gallery; F. Twiss, *A Complete Verbal Index to . . . Shakspeare*, 1805; R. Nares, *A Glossary*, 1822, 1825; F. G. Waldron, *Shakspearean Miscellany*, 1802; C. Lofft, *Aphorisms from Shakespeare*, 1812; J. Wilson, *Shakspereana*, 1827.

BIOGRAPHY

Coleridge declared Shakespeare must have been "a very great actor."[4] A. Skottowe wrote a *Life of Shakspeare* (1824) and John Watkins gave some *Characteristic Anecdotes* (1808).[5]

ATTACKS ON COMMENTATORS; PARODIES

Coleridge remarked: "His critics, among us, during the whole of the last century, have neither understood nor appreciated him."[6] There were also a few parodies[7]—for

Shakespear, 1807; J. M. Mason, *Comments on the Several Editions of Shakespeare's Plays*, 1807; C. Lamb, *King Lear*, 1808; J. Croft, *Annotations on the Plays of Shakespear*, 1810; *A Specimen of a New Edition of Shakspeare*, 1819; W. Oxberry, *Hamlet*, 1820; *Macbeth*, 1821; Boswell's Malone Edition, 1821.

[4] P. 9. See also p. 57. Compare the Tomalin Report, in Dr. Raysor, *op. cit.*, II, 89.

[5] For further material on this subject see: *Quarterly Review*, IV (1810), 176—on spelling of name; J. Britton, *Remarks on the Monumental Bust*, 1816; *Gentleman's Magazine*, LXXXVI (1816), II, 110—portrait; W. Rider, *Views in Stratford-upon-Avon*, 1828.

[6] P. 129. See also pp. 125-6, 128. Other material includes: *School for Satire* [on Capell and Malone], 1802; *Edinburgh Review*, XII (1808), 449—Shakespeare "obscured by his commentators"; *Quarterly Review*, XI (1814), 484, 487.

[7] See also R. F. Sharp, "Travesties of Shakespeare's Plays," The *Library*, Fourth Series, No. 1 (June, 1920), 1-20.

example: J. Poole, *Hamlet*, 1811, 1816; *Othello-Travestie: in three acts. With Burlesque Notes, in the manner of the most celebrated commentators* 1813 [Maggs' Catalogue, 1927, No. 636].

Sequels, Operas,[8] and Imitations

In the early nineteenth century appeared the following: R. W. Elliston, *Burletta of Macbeth*, 1809; *Edinburgh Review*, XIX (1811-2), 266—S. "copied by Miss Baillie"; *Quarterly Review*, XI (1814), 189, 190—"Imitation of Shakspeare by Mr. Coleridge."

Modern Characters from Shakespeare, Public Lectures, and Jubilees[9]

With regard to public lectures, only the name of Coleridge need be mentioned. As for jubilees, America had now entered the field: C. Sprague, *Prize Ode . . . at the Shakspeare Jubilee*, Boston, 1824.

The Unities

Coleridge attacked the unities from several points of view. His two main arguments were the historical—that is, the essential *difference* of Greek tragedy,[10] and the Johnsonian analysis of dramatic verisimilitude, though Coleridge persistently attacked Johnson:[11] Johnson "makes no sufficient allowance for an intermediate state."[12]

---

[8]See also W. B. Squire, "Shakespearean Operas," in *A Book of Homage to Shakespeare* (1916), pp 75-83.

[9]I found nothing on modern characters from Shakespeare during this period, though I did not look very deliberately.

[10]Pp. 53-54, 56, 177 n., 193, 235-36, 321, 389. And see Tomalin Report, in Dr. Raysor, *op. cit.*, II, 82-83.

[11]Pp. 53, 123, 204-7, 274.

[12]P. 274. Compare E. Taylor and the *Monthly Review* on Johnson, Chap. IV above. This latter point is repeated *verbatim* in the text printed in Dr. Raysor's article, "Some Marginalia on Shakespeare by S. T. Coleridge"

Coleridge's other remarks included the points that the unities create absurdities[13] and that Shakespeare had founded a new Romantic Drama.[14] In contradistinction to Aristotelian rules, Coleridge threw most of his emphasis, in defending Shakespeare, on unity of feeling or interest,[15] and on the difference between mechanic and organic unity.[16] All of these ideas had been anticipated by the late eighteenth century.[17]

Hazlitt remarked, "The jealous attention which has been paid to the unities both of time and place has taken away the principle of perspective in drama."[18]

SHAKESPEARE'S LEARNING

Coleridge wrote: ". . . though Shakspeare's acquirements in the dead languages might not be such as we suppose in a learned education,"[19] and referred directly to Farmer.[20] Hazlitt agreed: "This play [*C. of E.*] . . . leads us not to feel much regret that Shakespear was not what is called a classical scholar";[21] and also referred directly to Farmer.[22]

[*PMLA*, XLII (1927), 764], and compare Dr. Raysor's Introduction, *op. cit.*, pp. xxxviii-xl; II, 83, 128-29, 129 n., 200 ff.
[13]P. 123.   [14]P. 204. Compare the Tomalin Report, *op. cit.*, II, 84-85.
[15]Pp. 236-37, 321, 389, 464.   [16]Pp. 133, 229.
[17]This chapter assumes comparison with the previous Parts of the book throughout.
[18]I, 230-31. For other attacks on the unities during this period see: A. Murphy, *Life of Garrick* (1801), pp. 232, 360; J. P. Kemble, *Preface* to the 1817 Edition of *Macbeth and Richard III*.
[19]P. 287. Compare the Tomalin Report, *op. cit.*, II, 86-87.
[20]P. 303.   [21]I, 351. Compare I, 287.
[22]II, 188. For other comments on this subject: *Gentleman's Magazine* LXXII (1802), 486; *Edinburgh Review*, XIII (1808-9), 250—"had less scholarship . . . than Burns."

Shakespeare, the Ancients, and Imitation of Models

Coleridge persistently elevated Shakespeare above the ancients.[23] And the *Quarterly Review* in 1809 published an article to prove that Shakespeare was "above all other men, as well the ancients as the moderns."[24]

Coleridge also drew a distinction between "imitation" and "likeness,"[25] and declared, "The plays of Shakspeare are in no respect imitations of the Greeks."[26] He advocated "true imitation of essential principles."[27]

Decorum: Tragicomedy, and Supernatural Characters

Coleridge threw out the porter scene in Macbeth as a vulgar interpolation by actors.[28] Otherwise no one seemed particularly worried now by Shakespeare's possible lack of decorum, in this general sense.

As for tragicomedy, Coleridge applauded "these happy combinations,"[29] because of their "permitting a larger field of moral instruction,"[30] and repeated his approval often.[31] Hazlitt wrote: "Shakespear is blamed for his mixture of low characters. If this is a deformity, it is the source of a thousand beauties."[32]

Coleridge praised Ariel,[33] Caliban,[34] and the Ghost in *Hamlet*.[35] Hazlitt announced: "His [Shakespear's] ideal beings are as true and natural as his real characters,"[36] though he did admit that "the witches of *Macbeth* indeed are ridiculous on the modern stage."[37] Lamb praised the

---

[23] Pp. 100, 194-95, 218, 234.　　[24] I (1809), 273.
[25] P. 122.　　[26] P. 121.　　[27] P. 227.　　[28] P. 368.
[29] P. 133　　[30] P. 201.　　[31] See pp. 207, 377, 464, 486-87, 537.
[32] I, 254.　　[33] P. 140.　　[34] P. 142.
[35] P. 354. Compare his reference to "magic characters" (see Morgann, pp. 71-77 n.) in the Tomalin Report, *op. cit.*, II, 84.
[36] I, 238.　　[37] I, 194. But compare I, 187.

"supernatural elevation"[38] and rescued Shakespeare's witches from the stigma of comparison with those in Middleton's *The Witch*.[39]

SHAKESPEARE'S PUNS AND BLANK VERSE

Both Coleridge and Hazlitt vigorously defended Shakespeare's puns and conceits.[40] On blank verse Coleridge commented: "Shakspeare's blank verse is an absolutely new creation."[41]

ON ALTERATIONS OF SHAKESPEARE'S PLAYS

Coleridge attacked Dryden's alterations[42] and Hazlitt cited Lamb's rejection of Tate.[43] Hazlitt's general conclusion was: "The manner in which Shakespear's plays have been generally altered or rather mangled by modern mechanists, is a disgrace to the English stage."[44] Lamb attacked Garrick viciously: ". . . would any true lover of them [Shakspeare's excellences] have admitted into his matchless scenes such ribald trash as Tate and Cibber and the rest of them . . . have foisted into the acting plays of Shakspeare?"[45]

---

[38]The text used for Lamb is Brander Matthews, *The Dramatic Essays of Charles Lamb* (London: 1891). The present quotation is from p. 189. Lamb's principal essay, "On the Tragedies of Shakspeare," appeared first in Leigh Hunt's *Reflector*, in 1812.
[39]P. 211. For other generally similar comments: A. Murphy, *Life of Garrick* (1801), p. 49; *Quarterly Review*, XIII (1815), 86.
[40]Coleridge: pp. 72-73, 92-93, 118, 150-52, 263. Hazlitt: I, 314, 318.
[41]P. 540. (From *Table Talk*, March 15, 1834.)
[42]Pp. 279, 317. Compare the Tomalin Report, *op. cit.*, II, 97.
[43]I, 270-71 n.   [44]I, 300.
[45]P. 181. See also pp. 186, 191. For other such comments: *Blackwoods*, IV (Nov., 1823), 556. (This reference was given me by Mr. R. de B. Wickersham of the University of Michigan.)

Voltaire

Coleridge was rather brutal: . . . "the judgment of monkeys . . . put into the mouths of people shaped like men"[46] . . . "vulgar abuse of Voltaire"[47] . . . "I say not, the drunken savage of that wretched sciolist."[48] Hazlitt also decried "French poets."[49]

Shakespeare as Poet

Shakespeare's poetry was of course lauded by all three men,[50] and all three greatly loved to point out beautiful passages, especially Hazlitt.[51]

Shakespeare as Poet of Nature

Coleridge remarked: "Shakspeare is the Poet of Nature, portraying things as they exist";[52] and Hazlitt called his portraits "a sort of written nature."[53]

Shakespeare, Original Genius

Apparently both Coleridge and Hazlitt used the term in its late eighteenth-century sense.[54] Coleridge apostro-

---

[46]P. 132.   [47]P. 229. Compare Dr. Raysor, *op. cit.*, II, 18.   [48]P. 230.
[49]I, 246. For more material, see *Edinburgh Review*, XVII (1810-11), 299; XVIII (1811), 285.
[50]Coleridge: pp. 69, 218, 240-41, 493 ff. Hazlitt: I, 206, 242, 251, 286, 306, 315. Lamb: pp. 184, 185.
[51]Coleridge: pp. 138, 143, 230, 266. Hazlitt: I, 176, 181, 190, 268-69, 287, etc. Lamb: p. 169. See also: *Shaksperian Anthology: comprising the choicest passages*, 1830.
[52]P. 180. See also pp. 68, 88, 160, 237, and compare Tomalin Report, *op. cit.*, II, 81.
[53]P. P. Howe, *New Writings of Hazlitt* (second series, 1927), p. 146. See also I, 186, 191, 228. And Lamb, p. 174. All these men seem to follow Johnson.
[54]Coleridge: pp. 67, 223, and many other pages connected with judgment (below). Hazlitt: I, 197, 228. The ensuing quotations are from Coleridge, p. 67 and Hazlitt, I, 228.

phized "the purity and holiness of [Shakspeare's] genius," and Hazlitt declared: "His genius was . . . a match for history."

SHAKESPEARE'S JUDGMENT

Shakespeare's judgment was the particular favorite of Coleridge: "Shakspeare's judgment was, if possible, still more wonderful than his genius."[55]

SHAKESPEARE AS MORAL PHILOSOPHER

Shakespeare's morality was obviously defended by all three men—Coleridge, Lamb, and Hazlitt.[56] Coleridge's method is the most interesting, in the light of the eighteenth-century criticism: "Shakspeare here [in *Richard III*] . . . developes in a tone of sublime morality the dreadful consequences of placing the moral in subordination to the mere intellectual being."[57]

SHAKESPEARE'S CHARACTERS

Coleridge remarked: "The truth is, Shakspeare's characters are all *genera* intensely individualized"[58] . . . "ideal realities"[59] . . . etc. He pointed out Shakespeare's success at contrasts,[60] as did also Hazlitt persistently.[61] Hazlitt used Pope's praise as his motto[62] for the "profound knowledge of character, in which Shakespear could scarcely fail."[63] Lamb declared that "the characters of Shak-

---

[55]P. 127 n. See also the whole section beginning on p. 223, and scattered references on pp. 52, 54, 226, etc. Compare Dr. Raysor's Introduction, pp. xliii-iv.

[56]Coleridge: pp. 22, 24, 76-77, 94, 225, 238-39, 273, 466, 488. Hazlitt: I, 185, 186, 211, 216, 341, 347. Lamb: p. 170.

[57]P. 273. Compare p. 164 on *Hamlet*. For further material: *Quarterly Review*, III (1810), 435—"Moral advantages of his lessons."

[58]P. 282.   [59]P. 124.   [60]Pp. 148, 380-81.

[61]I, 200, 245, 293, 311, 351.   [62]I, 171.   [63]I, 195.

speare are . . . objects of meditation."[64]

Shakespeare's women received fulsome praise from both Coleridge and Hazlitt. The former said, ". . . he [Shakspeare] only has drawn the female character";[65] and Hazlitt: "It is the peculiar excellence of Shakespear's heroines, that they seem to exist only in their attachment to others."[66]

The minor characters were developed *passim* by both Coleridge and Hazlitt[67]—in fact, they seemed to be particularly interested in this phase of Shakespeare's technique. It is interesting to note, perhaps, that the two critics disagreed on Iago,[68] but that both defended Polonius.[69] These two characters are also transformed now from eighteenth-century minor characters to the nineteenth-century major group.

Of Lear Coleridge offered the famous pronouncement, "In Lear old age is itself a character";[70] Lear has "sensibility."[71] Hazlitt also praised Lear,[72] as did Lamb.[73]

To Richard III Coleridge[74] and Lamb[75] both gave intellect, but Macbeth, said Coleridge, "is all-powerful without strength."[76] Coleridge deliberately referred to "Mac-

---

[64]P. 183.
[65]P. 78. Compare p. 278. And see Dr. Raysor, *op. cit.*, II, 206 n.
[66]I, 180. Compare I, 205.
[67]Coleridge: Tybalt (p. 82), Capulet (p. 83), Mercutio (pp. 84-85, 324), Nurse (p. 86), Iago (pp. 147, 384, 388), Polonius (pp. 237-38, 255 n., 354), Kent (p. 336), etc., etc. And see Tomalin Report, *op. cit.*, II, 81.

Hazlitt: Cloten (I, 183), Iago (I, 206), Polonius (I, 237), the Fool in *Lear* (I, 260), Shylock (I, 320-24), Jacques (I, 339), etc. See Coleridge's *Notes on Shakspeare's Plays from English History* for the historical characters (pp. 252-73); and Hazlitt, I, 195, 198, 215, 275, 284, 291, etc.

[68]Coleridge, p. 388, and Hazlitt, I, 206. Coleridge called Iago's activity "motiveless," but in the following chapter I attempt to show that Coleridge may well have known of Hole's defense of Iago.

[69]Coleridge, p. 354, and Hazlitt, I, 237.   [70]P. 337.
[71]P. 329. And see Tomalin Report, *op. cit.*, II, 84.   [72]I, 258.
[73]P. 185.   [74]P. 147.   [75]P. 182.   [76]P. 373.

beth's cowardice,"[77] and Hazlitt declared that "he is as distinct a being from Richard III as it is possible to imagine . . . Richard is cruel from nature and constitution. Macbeth becomes so from accidental circumstances."[78] Coleridge, according to Collier's *Diary*, asserted that "Falstaff was no coward,"[79] but Hazlitt remarked: "He is represented as a liar, a braggart, a coward, a glutton."[80] Both Coleridge[81] and Hazlitt[82] praised Falstaff's wit, but their conclusions on Falstaff were radically different. Coleridge: ". . . this character so often extolled as the masterpiece of humour, neither contains, nor was meant to contain, any humour at all";[83] Hazlitt: ". . . perhaps the most substantial comic character that ever was invented."[84]

Hamlet was pushed to the absolute limit of the Romantic Heresy. Hazlitt: "It is not a character marked by strength of will or even of passion, but by refinement of thought and sentiment. Hamlet is as little of the hero as a man can well be."[85] Coleridge: Hamlet is "a person, in whose view the external world, and all its incidents and objects, were comparatively dim"[86] . . . "he loses the power of action in the energy of resolve."[87] And Lamb echoed: "the shy, negligent, retiring Hamlet."[88]

---

[77]P. 374. [78]I, 192. [79]P. 8. [80]I, 279.
[81]Pp. 268, 487. [82]I, 278. [83]P. 410. [84]I, 277.
[85]I, 233. [86]P. 159. [87]P. 344.
[88]P. 171. For further material during this period on Shakespeare's characters see: *Kemble and Cooke, or a Critical Review*, 1800; C. Lamb, *G. F. Cooke in Richard III*, 1802; *Remarks on Mr. J. Kemble's Performance of Hamlet and Richard III*, 1802; *Monthly Magazine*, XXIX (1810), 204, and XXX (1810), 9, 225 on Falstaff; W. Richardson's 6th ed. (1812), on Fluellen; *Analectic Magazine*, V (1815), 65—Reprint of Lamb; *Quarterly Review*, XV (1816), 126 —Characters; XVII (1817), 448—Characters; J. P. Kemble, *Macbeth and Richard III*, 1817; *Blackwoods*, II (1818), 504—on Hamlet; *London Magazine*, I (1820), 194—rev. of second edition of Morgann's *Falstaff*; IX (1824), 368, 647—on Hamlet.

Psychologizing

Coleridge psychologized the terms, love,[89] avarice,[90] fame and self-love,[91] etc. Some of his general remarks were: "The necessity of loving creates an object for itself in man and woman"[92] [this to explain Romeo's aberration for Rosaline]; "A brave man is never so peremptory as when he fears that he is afraid"[93] [on Francisco in *Hamlet*]; etc.[94] In Hazlitt: The conspiracy fails because of Brutus' overconfidence in the goodness of the cause. "Thus it has always been. Those who mean well themselves think well of others and fall a prey to their security."[95] This is the process applied backward, but Hazlitt also went the normal way, psychologizing first: "Passion, the love and expectation of pleasure, is infinite, extravagant, inexhaustible, till experience comes to check and kill it. Juliet exclaims on her first interview with Romeo,"[96] etc.

Both Coleridge and Hazlitt were also interested in the conception of the ruling passion.[97] In the *New Writings of Hazlitt*, edited in 1925 by Mr. P. P. Howe, appears a whole essay devoted to "The Ruling Passion." And Coleridge proceeded the further step: ". . . the one predominant passion acting, if I may so say, as the leader of the band to the rest."[98]

On association Hazlitt wrote: ". . . so it probably arose in the same manner in the mind of the author, not from design, but from the force of natural association, a

---

[89] Pp. 95-97, 98.   [90] P. 99.
[91] P. 300. Dr. Raysor is inclined to reject this passage from Coleridge's Shakespearean Criticism, *op. cit.*, I, 115 n.
[92] P. 323.
[93] P. 348. Compare the Tomalin Report, *op. cit.*, II, 96; also II, 237-38.
[94] See also pp. 241-42, 394.   [95] I, 198.
[96] I, 249. Compare also I, 215, 232, 273.
[97] Pp. 81, 147, 306, 316; I, 210.   [98] P. 84.

particular train of thought suggesting different inflections of the same predominant feeling, melting into, and strengthening one another, like chords in music."[99] And Coleridge used the same term.[100]

SHAKESPEARE'S LANGUAGE

Coleridge made remarks in the course of his criticism which showed some knowledge of Elizabethan diction,[101] although he was inclined to introduce his "to my ear" method.[102]

SHAKESPEARE AND BRITISH HISTORY

Both Coleridge and Hazlitt pointed out, critically, Shakespeare's knowledge of British history.[103] For example, Hazlitt remarked: "During the time of the civil wars of York and Lancaster, England was a perfect bear-garden, and Shakespear has given us a very lively picture of the scene."[104] And Coleridge referred to the effect of the historical plays upon the people.[105]

SHAKESPEARE AND HIS AGE

Coleridge and Lamb both referred Shakespeare to his age. Coleridge: ". . . times and manners lend their form

---

[99] I, 184. This should be compared with Coleridge's last remark.

[100] Pp. 76, 87. Coleridge also analyzes Wit and Fancy (p. 74), and Imagination and Fancy (pp. 220-22).

[101] For example, pp. 295, 296: "Theobald's etymology of 'cheveril' is, of course, quite right;—but he is mistaken in supposing that there were no such things as gloves of chicken-skin. They were at one time a main article in chirocosmetics" (p. 296).

[102] Pp. 258, 301. See also *British Critic*, XXIX (1807), 38-9. (Mr. Jacob Haas of the University of Michigan gave me this reference.)

[103] Coleridge: pp. 252-73, especially p. 257. Hazlitt: I, 214, 285, 286, 292, 305. See also A. Luders, *An Essay on the Character of Henry V when Prince of Wales*, 1813.

[104] I, 292.   [105] P. 257.

and pressure to genius";[106] Lamb: "The idea of a Jew, which our pious ancestors contemplated with so much horror, has nothing in it now revolting."[107]

SHAKESPEARE'S SOURCES

Coleridge referred to the sources of *Romeo and Juliet*, *Hamlet*, and *Lear*.[108] Hazlitt did the same for *Romeo and Juliet*, *Two Gentlemen of Verona*, *All's Well that Ends Well*, and *Comedy of Errors*.[109]

COMPARATIVE STUDY

Coleridge, Hazlitt, and Lamb all used this method of criticism, particularly the latter two.[110] Lamb, for example, compared Middleton's use of witches with Shakespeare's;[111] Hazlitt compared Shakespeare with Ben Jonson and Chaucer;[112] and Coleridge wrote: "Biron and Rosaline are evidently the pre-existent state of Benedick and Beatrice."[113]

---

[106]P. 233. Compare pp. 9, 54, 179, 487. But Dr. Raysor admits Coleridge's general lack of historical background, *op. cit.*, pp. xliv-v.

[107]P. 200. Compare p. 187. See also: N. Drake, *Shakspeare and His Times*, 1817; N. Drake, *Memorials of Shakspeare*, 1828.

[108]Pp. 12, 163, 330. See also p. 240.

[109]I, 255, 318, 331, 351. See also E. Malone, *An Account of* . . . *Shakspeare's Tempest*, 1808-9; G. Chalmers, *Another Account of* . . . *Shakspeare's Tempest*, 1815.

[110]Coleridge, pp. 283, 410, 416, 449, 537; Hazlitt, I, 224-25, 311 (and see his texts below in these notes); Lamb, pp. 199, 202, 204, 207, 211, 227-28. See also: W. Godwin, *Life of Chaucer*, 1803; O. Gilchrist, *Examination of* . . . *Ben Jonson's Enmity towards Shakspeare*, 1808; *Edinburgh Review*, XII (1808), 65 (For this reference I am again indebted to Mr. Haas); Lamb, *Specimens of the English Dramatic Poets who lived about the time of Shakspeare*, 1808; W. Hazlitt, *Lectures on the English Poets*, 1818; *Lectures on the English Comic Writers*, 1819; and *Lectures on the Dramatic Literature of the Age of Elizabeth*, 1821.

[111]P. 211.   [112]I, 224-25, 311.

[113]P. 283. Compare the Tomalin Report, *op. cit.*, II, 108.

SHAKESPEARE AND STAGE HISTORY

All three men again touched this point of view in criticism;[114] and all three men disliked seeing Shakespeare's plays *acted*.[115] This idea, however, was violently attacked by *Blackwoods* in 1818.[116]

IDOLATRY AD ASTRA

Of course Coleridge was probably the most prominent of the three in romantic eulogy of Shakespeare. Some of his remarks were: "Shakspeare can never die";[117] "the greatest man that ever put on and put off mortality";[118] "Assuredly that criticism of Shakspeare will alone be genial which is reverential";[119] "Merciful, wonder-making Heaven! what a man was this Shakspeare!"[120] But Hazlitt was not far behind: "An overstrained enthusiasm is more pardonable with regard to Shakespear than the want of it; for our admiration cannot easily surpass his genius";[121] "Shakespear was the most universal genius that ever lived."[122]

---

[114]Coleridge, pp. 122, 197-98, 236, 259, 479; Hazlitt, I, 237, 247 (and see his whole criticism of *Richard III*—pp. 298-303); Lamb, The whole essay, "On the Tragedies of Shakspeare."
[115]Coleridge, p. 479; Hazlitt, I, 237; Lamb, p. 168.
[116]III (1818), 607. Mr. Wickersham again provided me with this note. See also, on this general subject: C. Dibdin, *A Complete History of the Stage*, 1800; *Monthly Mirror*, X (1800), 40-42 (Mr. Haas also gave me this reference); A. Murphy, *Life of David Garrick*, 1801; Mrs. Inchbald, *British Theatre*, 1808.
[117]P. 50.   [118]P. 128.   [119]P. 225.
[120]P. 251. Compare also pp. 217, 350, 394, 500. See Dr. Raysor, *op. cit.*, p. xlvii.
[121]I, 174.
[122]I, 238. And compare I, 357. For further idolatry one should note: J. Huckell, *Avon, A Poem* (1811). (First published in 1758); *Edinburgh Review*, XIX (1811-12), 264—S. "furnishes the best model of English tragedy"; *Macbeth, A Poem* (1817); *Blackwoods*, VI (1819-20), 676. (For this reference I am indebted to Mr. Howard Simon of the Univ. of Michigan); America

15

Conclusion

The conclusion is perfectly obvious. Point for point, from all the different angles, the early nineteenth century merely echoed the late eighteenth. In short, if the question were raised as to whether the nineteenth century produced any *new* criticism of Shakespeare, the answer would have to be—no. What these early nineteenth-century critics did was to develop fields of action already prepared in the late eighteenth: for example, Shakespeare's minor characters, idolatry in general, the versification tests, and the comparison with Shakespeare's contemporaries, etc. The only possible new point that might be given them would be Coleridge's emphasis on first scenes,[123] and that is not strictly new.[124] On the other hand, they produced no critic to equal the combined scholarship and brilliancy of Farmer, Morgann,[125] and Malone. If the objection is made that we are applying a program of criticism based upon only eighteenth-century texts, the answer is that, except for modern sceptical criticism, there *is* no further type of Shakespearean criticism, of any value beyond the "twenty-seven articles" listed above. Part III has already indicated[126] that what we think is new today appeared indubitably in the late eighteenth century. Hence Professor Nichol Smith is correct: "The early nineteenth century was too readily convinced by Coleridge and Hazlitt that they were the first to recognize and to explain the greatness of Shakespeare"[127]—a dictum which he repeated

---

was now joining the poetic paean: C. Sprague, *Prize Ode . . . at the Shakspeare Jubilee* (Boston, 1824); see also, more generally, *Monthly Mirror*, XIII (1802), 270-1, and *Blackwoods*, XIII (1823), 547, etc.

[123]For example, pp. 346, 479.   [124]See pp. 115-18 above.

[125]Morgann and Coleridge will be compared more deliberately in the Conclusion.

[126]Chap. XIII.   [127]Introduction (1903), p. ix.

in 1916: "The criticism of Coleridge and Hazlitt is a natural and direct development from earlier English criticism."[128] But a far more interesting comment appears in a contemporary magazine article in *Blackwoods* in 1831: "By much criticism, sincerely or affectedly philosophical, has the genius of Shakspeare been lately belaboured, by true men and pretenders—from Coleridge and Lamb, to Hazlitt and Barry Cornwall. But, after all, with the exception of some glorious things said by the Ancient Mariner and Elia, little new has been added, of much worth, to the Essays of Professor Richardson, a forgotten work, of which a few copies have been saved by thieves from the moths."[129] Perhaps now one should draw a line (possibly a light one) through the fourteen words beginning with "with" and ending with "Elia."[130]

[128] Introduction (1916), p. xxiii n.   [129] XXX (1831), 94.

[130] We should except some of Coleridge's individual analyses, such as those of Lear and the opening of *Hamlet*, and it should also be noted that we are concerned with the plays, not the poems. Contrast Dr. Raysor's Conclusions, *op. cit.* (1930), pp. xxxii-iii, xlviii, lxi. Doubtless the true estimate lies somewhere between our respective conclusions.

CHAPTER XVI

SOME CLUES TO THE DIRECT INDEBTEDNESS
OF COLERIDGE, LAMB, AND HAZLITT
TO EIGHTEENTH-CENTURY
CRITICISM[1]

Once more it should be repeated that the purpose of this book has been to show the genesis of English idolatry of Shakespeare in the late eighteenth century. That purpose was fulfilled with the completion of the preceding chapter, which showed how comprehensively the last thirty years of the eighteenth century had anticipated the early decades of the nineteenth. This chapter is therefore wholly gratuitous and is written merely for the possible assistance of specialists in Coleridge and his contemporaries who may wish a few clues to guide them in tracing back direct influence.

A FIELD OPEN FOR INVESTIGATION

Professors Nichol Smith and T. M. Raysor are both sceptical about the dependence of early nineteenth-century Shakespeare criticism upon that of the late eighteenth century. The former scholar wrote in 1916: "There is nothing greater—perhaps nothing so great—in Coleridge or Hazlitt. [He is referring to Morgann's *Essay*.][2] Forty years were to pass before they gave us the new criticism in all its strength, and they, to their loss, did not know Morgann."[3]

---

[1]This chapter has already been published in *MLN*, XLV (1930), 377-88. It is reprinted here with permission.
[2]*On the Dramatic Character of Sir John Falstaff.*
[3]Introduction to *Shakespeare Criticism*, p. xx.

This judgment he repeated in 1928.[4] And Dr. Raysor is almost as doubtful: "There is no absolute proof that Coleridge was indebted to his English predecessors, but it is highly improbable that a profound student of Shakespeare, who was naturally a voracious reader, could have entirely ignored the character-studies of the preceding period."[5] He declares that Morgann's *Essay* "might easily have escaped his [Coleridge's] notice" but that "Richardson's study of Hamlet might . . . have been known to Coleridge."[6] He admits, however, that, as indicated in this book, "the eighteenth-century critics . . . certainly anticipated both him and the Germans in the new method of character-studies."[7] So the field is thrown open for further investigation.

It will be best for the purposes of this chapter to confine the discussion to the three prominent critics, Coleridge, Lamb, and Hazlitt. But before they are treated in detail, an item of general interest should be noted. Beginning in 1810 the *Monthly Magazine* produced a series of articles on Shakespeare running through five volumes of the periodical and concluding in 1812 with two articles, the last of which was signed "M. M."[8] At first glance "M. M." looks like Maurice Morgann, but unfortunately it is not, for Morgann was dead.[9] The article in Volume XXXI (1811) refers directly to "the late Mr. Morgan," who wrote "A most able analysis" of Falstaff's "natural courage."[10] Further,

---

[4]*Shakespeare in the Eighteenth Century*, p. 87.
[5]*MLN*, XLII (Dec., 1927), 500.
[6]*Ibid.*, p. 500. For Richardson's texts on Shakespeare, see *JEGP*, XXVIII (Jan., 1929), 117.
[7]*Ibid.*, p. 500. Compare his recent (1930) ed. of *Coleridge's Shakespearean Criticism*, p. xxiv.
[8]XXX (1810), 326; XXXI (1811), 112, 210, 322, 410, 422; XXXII (1811), 19, 112, 222; XXXIII (1812), 27, 218.
[9]He died in 1802. [10]XXXI (1811), 211.

the next article in the same volume refers to the "celebrated"[11] essay on Falstaff again. Hence Morgann's essay was apparently well known in the period, though the second edition did not appear till 1820. Now both Hazlitt and Coleridge knew the *Monthly Magazine:* Coleridge contributed poems to it in 1796[12] and 1797[13] and in a letter, December 12, 1796, remarked: "I receive about forty guineas yearly from the *Critical Review* and the new *Monthly Magazine*";[14] and Hazlitt referred to it directly many times.[15] Could *both* of them, then, have missed *both* references to Morgann? At all events, these two direct references would seem to deserve more attention from students of Coleridge and Hazlitt than a mere indication of them here would imply.[16]

Lamb and Hazlitt

To return to the three men Lamb and Hazlitt seem to be open books. Both of them lean frankly and rather heavily on the eighteenth century. Lamb, for example, could hardly have missed knowing both Johnson and Goldsmith, and both of these men disliked the acting of Shakespeare's plays, particularly Garrick's perversions.[17] In the light of this situation, one can hardly give Lamb credit for originality in the main idea of his essay, *On the Tragedies of Shakspeare.* Furthermore, Johnson and Goldsmith were not

---

[11]*Ibid.*, 325.
[12]II (Sept., 1796), 647; II (Oct., 1796), 732. Both signed "S. T. Coleridge."
[13]IV (Nov., 1797), 374. Three sonnets signed "Nehemiah Higginbotham," but see *Letters* (ed. E. H. Coleridge, 1895), I, 251 n.
[14]*Ibid.*, I, 185.
[15]*Works* (ed. Waller and Glover), II, 175, 177, 192; VII, 230; X, 221, 222, etc.
[16]And there may well be references in other periodicals.
[17]See Chap. VII above. I shall not repeat eighteenth-century bibliography in this chapter, except in special instances.

the only critics in the eighteenth century who objected to the acting of Shakespeare. F. Gentleman said the same thing in 1770,[18] and the *Monthly Review* in 1780 produced an article on the "new" distinction of closet drama.[19] The idea was therefore rather prevalent. Nor was Lamb's comparison of Middleton's *The Witch* with *Macbeth*,[20] so praised by Hazlitt,[21] quite original with Lamb. The *Hibernian Magazine* had done it twenty-five years before him,[22] but one cannot say that Lamb saw this periodical. It may merely be suggested that students of Lamb compare the two accounts. However, we shall now drop Lamb from further discussion, with the assumption that, in his principal essay on Shakespeare at least, he was generally indebted to his eighteenth-century predecessors.

The same thing is even more true of Hazlitt. The Index to the Waller and Glover Edition shows that Hazlitt linked with Shakespeare these critics: Addison,[23] Cibber,[24] Colman,[25] Dodd,[26] Farmer,[27] Garrick,[28] Hanmer,[29] *Heron's Letters* (Pinkerton),[30] W. H. Ireland,[31] Johnson,[32] Kemble,[33] Malone,[34] Pope,[35] William Richardson,[36] Ritson,[37] Rowe,[38] Rymer,[39] Steevens,[40] Voltaire,[41] and J. White.[42] And the following periodicals also appear therein: *Anti-Jacobin Review, Critical Review, Gentleman's Magazine, Lady's Magazine, London Magazine, Lounger, Mirror, Monthly Magazine, Monthly Mirror, Monthly Review, Scots Magazine,* and *Wit's Maga-*

---

[18]*Dramatic Censor*, I, 14.   [19]LXII (1780), 186.
[20]Brander Matthews, ed., *The Dramatic Essays of Charles Lamb*, pp. 211-12. This text will be used *passim*.
[21]I, 194.   [22]1786, pp. 512-13.   [23]I, 370, 372.   [24]I, 180.
[25]VIII, 163 [a reference to the translation of Terence].   [26]I, 257.
[27]II, 188.   [28]I, 290.   [29]III, 405.   [30]II, 181.
[31]VI, 354.   [32]I, 174-79, 270, 303, etc.   [33]I, 237, 299.
[34]II, 184.   [35]I, 174, 176.   [36]I, 171.   [37]II, 184.
[38]VIII, 287.   [39]V, 297.   [40]II, 184.   [41]II, 107, 166.
[42]VII, 37. For the works of all these men on Shakespeare, see Appendix A.

zine. This is a whole program of eighteenth-century study in itself, but Hazlitt adds another important man, with an error, however, as to his name: "A gentleman of the name of Mason, the author of a Treatise on Ornamental Gardening (not Mason the poet), began a work of similar kind about forty years ago, but he lived only to finish a parallel between the characters of Macbeth and Richard III, which is an exceedingly ingenious piece of analytical criticism."[43] This man is Thomas Whately.[44]

In the light of these lists one need not question Hazlitt's knowledge of his predecessors. Curiosity will arise, perhaps, as to whether he actually did follow them, and a few examples may suffice. His analysis of Richard III and Macbeth, suggested above, is practically a direct repetition of Whately.[45] Apparently Hazlitt had not seen Kemble's rejoinder[46] at all. His reply to the critic who called Polonius inconsistent is directed, probably, against Richardson.[47] His analysis of Shakespeare's women in general may owe something to Richardson's essay of 1789, and his application of "the very religion of love"[48] to Imogen, in particular, is a distinct echo of Richardson's essay of 1774 on Imogen. Similarly he is apparently trying to rescue Lady Macbeth[49] from Richardson's horror at her, and possibly the description of Hamlet[50] owes something to Richardson. Further, is not Hazlitt directly attacking Steevens

---

[43] I, 171. On this same page is a direct reference to Richardson's *Essays*.
[44] T. Whately, *Remarks on Some of the Characters of Shakspeare*, 1785, 1808, 1839.
[45] *Ibid.* (2nd ed., 1808), pp. 9 ff. See Chap. XII above.
[46] J. P. Kemble, *Macbeth Reconsidered* (1786).
[47] I, 237. For Richardson, see 5th ed. (1798), p. 388, of the *Essays*.
[48] I, 182.
[49] I, 188. See Chaps. XI, XII, and XV, for comparisons now given.
[50] I, 233. For a full discussion of Richardson's criticism of Shakespeare, see *JEGP*, XXVIII (Jan., 1929), 117-36.

when he remarks, with regard to Hamlet: "The moral perfection of this character has been called in question, we think, by those who did not understand it"?[51] Falstaff Hazlitt calls "a coward,"[52] in direct opposition to the Morgann tradition, but perhaps Hazlitt comes closer to Morgann with his appreciation of the distinction between Lear's real and Edgar's assumed madness.[53] His psychologizing, as indicated above, is a direct imitation of Richardson's method. In fact, he seems to be reacting a little against Richardson, for he writes: "It has been observed that Shakespear's characters are constructed upon deep physiological principles,"[54] but "The modern philosophy, which reduces the whole theory of the mind to habitual impressions, and leaves the natural impulses of passion and imagination out of the account, had not then [in Shakespeare's time] been discovered."[55] He even goes out of his way to attack Coleridge, apparently, on the idea that Iago's "villainy is *without a sufficient motive.*"[56] Hence it is fairly demonstrable that Hazlitt reacted on his individual predecessors and even, at times, on his contemporaries.[57]

COLERIDGE

Coleridge presents a different situation, by no means so easy to solve. In T. Ashe's 541 pages, Coleridge links with Shakespeare the following: Johnson (often),[58] Hume,[59] Pope,[60] Warburton,[61] Tyrwhitt,[62] Farmer,[63] Ayscough,[64] Whalley,[65] Cibber,[66] and Steevens.[67] In his *Letters* (now

---

[51]I, 235. Compare Steevens' *Edition* (1773), X, 343-44 n.
[52]I, 279.   [53]I, 260.   [54]I, 244.   [55]I, 250.
[56]I, 206.   [57]Compare his attention to Lamb, I, 194.
[58]T. Ashe, ed., *Lectures and Notes on Shakspere and Other English Poets* (1883), pp. 25, 45, 152, 163, 165, 364, 388, etc.
[59]Pp. 28, 350.   [60]Pp. 52, 278.   [61]P. 295.   [62]Pp. 301, 385.
[63]Pp. 303, 352.   [64]P. 305.   [65]Pp. 409, 410.   [66]P. 447.
[67]Pp. 14, 269.

using the *Index*) he similarly mentions Johnson[68] and William Jackson.[69] The *Letters* also include references to the *Anti-Jacobin Review, British Critic, Critical Review, Monthly Magazine* and some literary periodicals. For example, Coleridge contrasts his *The Friend* with the *Spectator* "and those that followed (Connoisseur, World, Mirror, etc.) [*sic*]."[70] Dr. Raysor, who discovered this reference,[71] mentions only the *Mirror*. It is obvious now that Coleridge knew eighteenth-century Shakespeare critics, but with the exception of the names of Farmer, Steevens, and William Jackson, the men listed above will not help us much in tracing his direct background in late eighteenth-century Shakespeare criticism. Hence Coleridge will have to be approached from other points of view—his interest in periodicals, for example, as indicated above in connection with his contributions to the *Critical Review* and *Monthly Magazine*—and his critical method in general.[72]

First, however, some of Coleridge's possible direct indebtednesses to particular predecessors should be pointed out, and space can be given to only a few representative examples. His reactions to Johnson are too obvious to discuss and do not concern us in this chapter because Johnson is fundamentally outside the scope of it. But when in the Bristol Lectures the remark appears, "The lecturer alluded to the prejudiced idea of Lady Macbeth as a monster,"[73] one becomes suspicious, for both E. Taylor and W. Richardson were guilty of this "prejudiced idea."[74] Again when

[68]II, 663.
[69]I, 309. For the work of all these men on Shakespeare, see Appendix A.
[70]II, 557.   [71]*Loc. cit.*, p. 500.
[72]In his *Letters* he refers directly to the loss of a "Stockdale's Shakspeare" (II, 484), but the notes in this one-volume edition (1784) are of no value in tracing Coleridge's background. They are almost wholly from Johnson and Steevens—i.e., textual.
[73]P. 469. Compare pp. 375-76.
[74]Taylor, *Cursory Remarks*, p. 66; Richardson, *Essays* (1798), p. 66.

Coleridge declares, "The characters of the *dramatis personæ*, like those in real life, are to be *inferred by the reader*,"[75] one cannot help recalling Morgann's words: "he [Shakespeare] boldly makes a character act and speak from those parts of the composition, which are *inferred* only, and not distinctly seen.[76] Then Coleridge adds a few lines about "your impression will be right,"[77] "our passive impressions,"[78] and "prove to our feelings, even before the word is found which presents the truth to our understandings."[79] All of this is a direct echo of Morgann.[79a] Or to turn to Richardson for a moment, Coleridge's original lecture prospectus contained the announcement: "a philosophic Analysis and Explanation of all the principal *Characters* of our great Dramatist."[80] Compare this with the title of Richardson's first series of essays: *A Philosophical Analysis and Illustration of Some of Shakespeare's Remarkable Characters*. It will not be feasible to go into this comparative development further here in detail,[81] but Coleridge's ideas on Shakespeare's women,[82] on psychologizing in general,[83] on morality,[84] Lear,[85] and Polonius[86] should be compared with Richardson's; also, Coleridge's linking of Richard III and Falstaff on the basis of intellect[87] should be referred to a similar comparison in the *Lounger*, No. 69; his remarks on poetical genius[88] seem to echo those in *The Bee*, V (1791),

---

[75]P. 241. The italics are mine.   [76]*Op. cit.*, p. 62 n.
[77]P. 241.   [78]P. 504.
[79]P. 508. Compare p. 507. It will be recalled that Coleridge, like Morgann, declared "Falstaff is no coward" (see Chap. XV).
[79a]Dr. Raysor is apparently puzzled over Coleridge's reference to "magic characters," in the Tomalin Report (*op. cit.*, II, 84). Could this be a definite use of Morgann's long note, pp. 71-77 n.? See Chap. VI above on the supernatural characters.
[80]P. 5.   [81]This is merely an introductory approach.
[82]P. 278.   [83]Pp. 84, 87, 95-97, 225.   [84]P. 273.
[85]P. 329.   [86]Pp. 354-55.   [87]P. 147.
[88]P. 218.

177; and his attack on the porter scene in *Macbeth*[89] should be aligned with F. Gentleman's similar attack.[90] All in all, there seems to be some reason to believe, by virtue of comparative evidence, that Coleridge used several of his predecessors.

But the method of the *Lectures* suggests the debt even more clearly: "It has been stated, from the first, that one of my purposes in these lectures is, to meet and refute popular objections to particular points in the works of our great dramatic poet";[91] "To the objection that Shakspeare wounds the moral sense by the unsubdued, undisguised, description of the most hateful atrocity . . . I . . . answer . . . not guilty";[92] "This part of the scene after Hamlet's interview with the Ghost has been charged with an improbable eccentricity";[93] "Mr. Coleridge combated the opinion held by some critics that the writings of Shakspeare were like a wilderness";[94] "I cannot agree with the solemn abuse which the critics have poured out upon Bertram."[95] But the climax of this method appears in his remark on Hamlet: "The seeming inconsistencies in the conduct and character of Hamlet have long exercised the conjectural ingenuity of critics."[96] Why that "long exercised," which was apparently repeated from the Bristol Lectures, if Coleridge did not know something of the rise of what may be termed the Romantic Heresy of Hamlet, beginning with F. Gentleman, in 1770 and continuing through Steevens, Richardson, Mackenzie, Harris, Craig, Robertson, and the like?[97] Would not some knowledge of this se-

---

[89]P. 368. I cannot resist suggesting also that his defense (pp. 347-48) of "not a mouse stirring" in *Hamlet* and his praise (p. 367) of Act V, Scene 1, of the same play were probably directed against Voltaire.
[90]*Dramatic Censor* (1770), I, 90.   [91]P. 150. Compare pp. 225-26.
[92]P. 379.   [93]P. 357. See also p. 473.   [94]P. 476.   [95]P. 536.
[96]P. 343. The same remark appears on p. 471, in the Bristol Lectures.
[97]It will be recalled that he knew Steevens and the *Mirror* (in which Mac-

quence of writers be inferred from Coleridge's use of the words, "long exercised," twice? In short, the method in itself implies knowledge of the directly preceding criticism, though Coleridge did not, like Hazlitt, directly refer to the critics by name.[98]

And this now leads us back again to the periodicals that Coleridge knew. The most important here are the *Critical Review* and *Monthly Magazine:* "I receive about forty guineas yearly from the *Critical Review* and the new *Monthly Magazine.*"[99] This is December 12, 1796, and in that year at least two poems of Coleridge had been printed in the latter periodical, as indicated above. Three sonnets also were published in it in 1797.[100] Meanwhile in these two particular volumes (II and IV) appeared also notices of White's *Falstaff's Letters*,[101] Plumptre's *Observations on Hamlet*,[102] the Exeter Society *Essays*,[103] the W. H. Ireland *MSS*,[104] Jackson's *Letters*,[105] Plumptre's *Appendix* to his *Observations*,[106]

---

kenzie's articles appeared). And why not also then the *Lounger*, in which Craig's paper (no. 91) was published? F. Gentleman's attack on *Hamlet* appeared in the *Dramatic Censor*, 1, 55. For Harris, see the *London Magazine*, L (1781), 534 (from the *Dramatic Speculations*). Robertson attacked Hamlet in the *Transactions of the Royal Society of Edinburgh* in 1790. See Chap. XI above.

[98] Compare again his obvious attacks (pp. 347-48, 367) on Voltaire, though the Frenchman's name is not mentioned at all. And see Dr. Raysor, *op. cit.* (1930), pp. xxvii, xxviii, xxix, xxx, xxxii.

[99] *Letters*, I, 185. Professor R. D. Havens through A. W. Craver of the Johns Hopkins University has very kindly referred me to G. Greever's publication of four reviews by Coleridge [in the *Critical Review* for Aug., 1794; Feb., 1797; June and Aug., 1798] in *A Wiltshire Parson and His Friends*, London, 1926, pp. 168-200. But there was no important Shakespeare criticism (other than textual) in 1794 and 1795; the volumes of the *Critical Review* for 1798 and 1799 contain nothing of importance; and the volumes for 1796 and 1797 are discussed in a note below.

[100] See above for date.   [101] II (1796), 570.   [102] II (1796), 487.

[103] II (1796), 812. Coleridge therefore probably saw Richard Hole's defense of Iago. Is he reacting against Hole?   [104] II (1796), 488.

[105] IV (1797), 137. Also some "Observations on Shakspeare" (pp. 127-28), with a reference to Dr. Berkenhout.   [106] IV (1797), 511.

and an account of "Kaimes" (the latter in the very month in which Coleridge's sonnets appeared).[107] It is unfortunate that the second of these volumes contains no reference at all to W. Richardson's Fifth Edition, published in 1797, and reviewed that year by both the *Monthly Review*[108] and the *British Critic*.[109] The latter periodical, however Coleridge referred to in 1801,[110] so that it is quite possible that he may have seen its review of Richardson in 1797. The *Critical Review*, also, quite unfortunately, contains no review of Richardson's Fifth Edition, but in the third volume of the *Monthly Magazine* appeared further reference to the Ireland papers,[111] to Chalmers' *Apology*,[112] and another notice of the Exeter Society *Essays*, this time with a direct reference to Iago and Shylock.[113] The inference now is simply this: that Coleridge could hardly have missed all this material, but he never referred to it; hence, he may have known other late eighteenth-century criticism of Shakespeare to which, also, he did not directly refer: it was not apparently his method.[114]

Study of these periodicals should be continued briefly into the early nineteenth century, on the assumption that Coleridge retained his interest in these particular ones, though it is obvious from his remarks already suggested that he was interested also in others. On Feb. 6, 1797, for example, he wrote: "If . . . I could get engaged by any

---

[107]IV (Nov., 1797), 359.   [108]XXII (1797), 101.
[109]X (1797), 86.   [110]*Letters*, I, 350.
[111]III (1797), 58.   [112]*Ibid*.

[113]III (1797), 48. There was also a notice of Plumptre's *Appendix* on p. 468. The *Critical Review* in 1796 and 1797 also had items on W. H. Ireland in LXXXVI (1796), 361; LXXXVII (1796), 131, 235; on W. Parr's *Story of the Moor of Venice* in LXXXVIII (1796), 70; on the Exeter Society *Essays* in LXXXVIII (1796), 273, 397, and XC (1797), 188; and on White's *Falstaff*, XC (1797), 234.

[114]Incidentally how could he have missed Hazlitt's direct reference to Richardson in 1817 (I, 171)?

one of the *Reviews* and the new 'Monthly Magazine.' "[115] The latter in 1803 gave an account of Farmer's *Essay*,[116] in 1807 printed a letter of William Richardson,[117] in 1810 one of Mrs. Montagu,[118] in the same year had three essays on Falstaff signed "A. B. E."[119] (not one of which, unfortunately, mentions Morgann), and began a whole series of articles on Shakespeare in general, which have already been referred to above and which did mention Morgann twice.[120] These essays were largely concerned with Johnson and Warburton and therefore should be closely compared with Coleridge's lectures. No attempt will be made now to follow through the *British Critic* and the *Critical Review*, but inasmuch as Coleridge wrote for one and was interested in the other, they also should be studied carefully throughout the early nineteenth century. The point may now be repeated: namely, that Coleridge must have known a great deal of late eighteenth-century criticism to which he never directly referred. Some of this he apparently incorporated in his own criticism; the rest of it he rejected—all without specific comment.[121]

In conclusion, therefore, the scepticisms of Dr. Raysor and Professor Nichol Smith should probably be respectfully questioned. For is it absolutely certain now that the latter was right when he remarked that "his [Hazlitt's] patriotic task would have been easier, and might even have appeared unnecessary, had he known that many of Schlegel's acute and enthusiastic observations had been anticipated at home."[122] He probably did know it, though he may not have been proud of it, and so, probably, did Coleridge.

---

[115]*Letters*, I, 215.   [116]XV (1803), 35.   [117]XXIX (1807), 223.
[118]XXX (1810), 435.   [119]XXIX (1810), 204; XXX (1810), 9, 225.
[120]XXXI (1811), 211, 325.
[121]That he believed he knew much of it appears from his disgusted remark that "His [Shakspeare's] critics, among us, during the whole of the last century, have neither understood nor appreciated him" (p. 129). No wonder he did not mention them specifically!
[122]Introduction to *Eighteenth Century Essays on Shakespeare*, p. x.

CHAPTER XVII

CONCLUSION

When one looks back over all "these forgotten emanations of the critical mind," as Charles Knight called them, certain texts stand forth like old friends—friends by virtue both of the labor required to analyze and present them to the reader, and of their importance in the period. These friends may be divided into two classes: first, those of some length and dignity who touched many aspects of Shakespeare's critical status in the closing years of the eighteenth century; and second, those of less length but of no less penetration who merely addressed Shakespeare with a single graceful bow.[1]

The periodicals, general and literary, have provided the backbone of the skeleton of this book. Then William Richardson's many essays, in three successive series, have supplied the limbs. Morgann's famous monograph on Falstaff was a more concentrated study, which gave the brain. Tom Davies and Francis Gentleman should be linked together because of their accent on the acting traditions—they supplied a sort of motor touch. Similarly the two prominent women of the period, Mrs. Montagu and Mrs. Griffith, produced long books which served well to enhance Shakespeare's growing glory—the sentimental motif. Farmer's two rapid editions of his great *Essay* were

---

[1] It will be noted that I have not touched in this book the Beauties-Faults method of criticism mentioned now and then by both Professor D. Nichol Smith and Dr. Raysor. This method, as Dr. C. E. Burklund's recent (1928) Univ. of Michigan Thesis on Herder's *Shakespeare-Aufsatz* has clearly pointed out (p. 152), was common to very opposing types of critics; hence my omission.

monumental in clearing for a century one battlefield of Shakespearean criticism, and Dodd's many editions of Shakespeare's beauties carried this particular development far into the nineteenth century. In textual criticism this book has not been greatly interested, but certainly the importance of the work of Ritson, J. M. Mason, Malone, Hurdis, and George Steevens has been respectfully suggested. Finally, even Edward Taylor's rather brutal book in derogation of Shakespeare showed the poet's growing reputation by the very shrillness of its attempt to controvert Johnson. These friends were all of the weightier type, who gave much time and space to presenting their views and hence provided the fundamental substance of this book.

The lighter, but often more penetrating, friends included Kenrick's belligerent *Introduction* and *Retort Courteous*, Sherlock's brief but amazingly idolatrous *Fragment*, Richard Hole's three short Exeter *Essays* with their clever historical ideas, Pilon's splendid though futile attempt to restore Hamlet to the Elizabethans, Whiter's precise psychological *Specimen*, Whately's unfortunately abandoned essays and Kemble's incisive reply to the Macbeth-Richard III comparison, Jackson's two letters, and finally Plumptre's detailed historical investigations. All of these brief pieces helped prepare the way for later and perhaps greater criticism, and were the decorative features of this book.

Nor can certain outstanding ideas of the period be left unrepeated now. The psychologizing of Shakespeare was a very important innovation, as was, to a large extent, the historical point of view in criticism. During these years, also, Shakespeare fully emerged as both a conscious artist and an original genius, and his text received tremendous attention with particular emphasis on the idea of returning to the first quartos and the first folio. In the field of characterization Falstaff's cowardice and Hamlet's inactivity have come down to us today as problems still to be discussed. All of these ideas were permanent contributions of the late eighteenth century to modern criticism of Shakespeare.

The Introduction to this book suggested, with the authority of Professor Karl Young and Mr. A. C. Bradley, the greatness of Morgann as a critic of Shakespeare, and perhaps the reader has now seen how completely Morgann anticipated the main trend of Coleridge's criticism. It is of course a matter of originality in ideas rather than stylistic expression, and in estimating Morgann's general versatility as a critic the reader should recall that the eighteenth-century man was treating but a single character, Falstaff, within 175 pages, whereas Coleridge was lecturing promiscuously, over 541 pages. Admitting that Coleridge touched all twenty-one points of Shakespearean criticism indicated in Parts II and III (it is not fair to either man to add Part I), the amazing thing is that Morgann touched fifteen. In other words, the reader should compare some 175 pages of Coleridge with Morgann's *Essay* and then discover for himself who will carry off the palm of versatility.[2]

It is interesting to note that the topics this book has covered did not die with the eighteenth century—in fact, many are still very much alive today. In 1849 Mr. N. J. Halpin produced a book on *The Dramatic Unities of Shakespeare*. In 1903 Mr. J. C. Collins reopened the question of Shakespeare's learning,[3] and not so long ago the British

---

[2]Mrs. Montagu in 288 pages touched 19. Hence she was almost as versatile as Morgann. By "touched" I mean simply that the critic was *directly used* on the point in the chapter in question above in this book. Otherwise it must be admitted that both Morgann and Mrs. Montagu "touched" more points than the numbers here given them in the text would indicate.

[3]*Fortnightly Review*, April, May, July, 1903. See also D. Nichol Smith,

CONCLUSION 243

New Statesman pointed out that Shakespeare used Ariosto directly.[4] Mr. E. E. Stoll and Mr. E. C. Knowlton have been battling recently over Falstaff's courage, with Morgann as the starting point.[5] And probably the Hamlet Heresy will never die. Historical critics—G. L. Kittredge,[6] J. M. Robertson, Roy Mackenzie, E. E. Stoll, etc.—have done their best to rescue Hamlet from the clutches of these Romantics and restore him to the Elizabethans, where he belongs, so that perhaps we shall not die in the wilderness. But meanwhile Dowden, Bradley, Clutton-Brock, and even more recently Mr. A. Nicoll have persisted in harking back to the Romantic Heresy promulgated by our friends, the critics of the late eighteenth century: F. Gentleman, Steevens, Richardson, H. Mackenzie, Harris, Craig, T. Robertson, etc. Even *Life and Letters,* one of the newest British periodicals, reprinted in June (1928)[7] George Santayana's probably unconscious rewording of Coleridge, Mackenzie, Thomas Robertson, and Bradley. But the most interesting item in the span of a century is one lone voice, crying out when the whirl was worst, *Blackwoods*—damning, in 1828, the romantic critics for undermining the character of Hamlet: "Now surely, feebleness of mind, the fragility of a china vase, lack of power and energy, are not the characteristics of Hamlet. . . . His anguish is stern and masculine. . . . It is not the weight and magnitude . . . of the deed imposed as a duty, that weighs upon his soul . . . but the preternatural contradiction involved in the duty itself, the irregular means through which the duty

---

Introduction (1903), p. xxvi; and *MLN*, XL (1925), 380-81, 440.

[4]In a review of J. S. Smart's *Shakespeare: Truth and Tradition*, XXXI (May 5, 1928), 126. See pages 149-90 of Mr. Smart's book.

[5]See my Appendix B, for the articles. Mr. Stoll replied to Mr. Knowlton in his recent book, *Shakespeare Studies* (1927), p. 490 n.

[6]It is to Mr. Kittredge that I owe my first interest in Shakespeare.

[7]I (June, 1928), 17.

is promulgated and known"—in short, the Ghost.[8]

In 1847 Charles Knight wrote, "It would be a dreary task to attempt to trace all that was published about Shakspere from the date of Johnson's first edition to the close of the eighteenth century. A few out of the heap of these forgotten emanations of the critical mind, the multitude of which proves the strong direction of national admiration, may not be unprofitably noted."[9] The "dreary task" is done—and it was not "dreary" at all. The lost battalion is found.

---

[8] *Blackwoods*, XXIV (1828), 585—"On the Character of Hamlet." This note was submitted to me by Mr. Jacob Haas of the University of Michigan.
[9] *A History of Opinion on the Writings of Shakspere*, p. 264.

APPENDIX A[1]

PRIMARY TEXTS OF SHAKESPEARE CRITICISM IN THE
EIGHTEENTH CENTURY

THIS bibliography of English critical Shakespeareana in the eighteenth century does not include editions, adaptations, alterations, operas, poems in general, French or German texts, articles in periodicals, etc. It is arranged chronologically, in five-year periods, from the Restoration to the early nineteenth century; but completeness has been sought for only within the years 1700-99.

An asterisk[*] signifies that the work is a rare text in the University of Michigan Library, generally the large McMillan Shakespeare Collection.

The sources of the texts here listed include a great many catalogues, among which the following are perhaps the most significant:

*The lists of "Detached Pieces of Criticism" in Johnson and Steevens' second (1778), third (1785), and fourth (1793) editions.
*Catalogue of Mr. Capell's Shakespeariana, 1779.
*Catalogue of the Boydell Shakespeare Gallery, 1791.
*Catalogue of Richard Farmer's Library, 1798.
*Catalogue of George Steevens' Library, 1800.
*Catalogue of Isaac Reed's Library, 1807.
*Catalogue of David Garrick's Library, 1823.
*Catalogue of H. Jadis' Library, 1826.
*John Wilson, *Shakspereana*, 1827.
W. T. Lowndes, "Shakespeare and His Commentators," in *Bibliographer's Manual*, 1831.
*J. O. Halliwell, *Shakespeariana*, 1841.

---

[1] A preliminary draft of this appeared in *Studies in Philology*, Extra Series I (May, 1929), 58-76. The present version represents considerable revision.

*F. Thimm, *Shakespeariana from 1564 to 1864*, 1865, 1871.
Notes and Queries, March 19, 1864, "Statistics of Shakesperian Literature."
*H. G. Bohn, *A Bibliographical Account of the Works of Shakespeare*, 1864.
*H. T. Hall, *Shaksperean Statistics*, 1874.
British Museum Cat.; Bodleian Cat.; Maggs Shakespeareana 1923 (No. 434), and 1927 (No. 493); *Camb. Hist. of English Lit.*, ix, x, xi; the Furness *Variorum Shakespeare;* Birmingham Library Cat.; University of Chicago Library Cat.; Newberry Lib. Cat.; and many others.

The spelling of the poet's name varies considerably in the eighteenth century, often even within the same text. The general spelling seems to be "Shakspeare"; hence this is the form I have used when unable to verify precisely.

The Restoration

*W. Winstanley, *England's Worthies*, *1660, *1684.
Sir R. Baker, *Theatrum Redivivum*, 1662.
Pepys' *Diary*, 1659-69.
Evelyn's *Diary*, 1641-1706.
J. Dryden, *Essay of Dramatic Poesie*, 1668, 1684, 1693.
E. Phillips, *Theatrum Poetarum*, 1675.
*R. Roderick, *Remarks on Shakespear*, 1675 (Printed in T. Edwards, *Canons of Criticism*, 6th ed., *1758).
*T. Rymer, *The Tragedies of the Last Age Considered*, *1678. *1692.
J. Dryden, *Preface to "Troilus and Cressida,"* 1679.
*N. Lee, *Preface to "Lucius Junius Brutus,"* 1681, *1713.
*W. Winstanley, *The Lives of the Most Famous English Poets*, 1687.
G. Langbaine, *Momus Triumphans*, 1688.
*G. Langbaine, *An Account of the English Dramatic Poets*, 1691.
*[C. Gildon], *The Post-boy Rob'd of His Mail*, 1692[1]

---

[1] For this reference I am indebted to Professor G. W. Sherburn, of the University of Chicago.

*J. Dennis, *The Impartial Critic*, *1693, 1697.
*J. Dennis, *Miscellanies*, 1693.
*T. Rymer, *A Short View of Tragedy*, 1693.
C. Gildon, *Some Reflections on Mr. Rymer's "Short View,"* 1694.
J. Dennis, *Letters upon Several Occasions*, 1696.
*W. Wotton, *Reflections on Ancient and Modern Learning*, *1694, 1697.
*Jeremy Collier, *A Short View of the Immorality and Profaneness of the Stage*, 1698.
*C. Gildon, A revision of Langbaine's *Lives*, 1699.

1700-1704

J. Dennis, *The Advancement of Modern Poetry*, 1701.
*[C. Gildon?], *A Comparison between the Two Stages*, 1702, *1722.
G. Farquhar, *Discourse on Comedy*, 1702.
J. Collier, *Dissuasive from the Playhouse*, 1703.
J. Drake, *Historia Anglo-Scotia*, 1703.
*J. Dennis, *The Grounds of Criticism in Poetry*, 1704.

1705-1709

*A. Bedford, *The Evil and Dangers of Stage Plays*, 1706.
Hypolitus, Earl of Douglas, *Secret History of Mackbeth*, 1708.
J. Downes, *Roscius Anglicanus*, 1708 (Continued by T. Davies, *1789).
*N. Rowe, *Some Account of the Life* . . . . . *Shakespear*, 1709.

1710-1714

*C. Gildon, *An Essay on the Art, Rise, and Progress of the Stage*, 1710 (in 1710 Edition of *Poems*).
*C. Gildon, *Remarks on the Plays of Shakespear*, 1710 (in 1710 Edition of *Poems*).
*C. Gildon, *The Life of Mr. T. Betterton*, 1710.
Lord Shaftesbury, *Characteristics*, 1711, 1714.
J. Dennis, *An Essay on the Genius and Writings of Shakespear*, 1712, *1721.

Cato Examined, 1713.
T. Parnell, *An Essay on the Different Stiles of Poetry*, 1713.

1715-1719

J. Dennis, *A True Character of Mr. Pope*, 1717.
*C. Gildon, *The Complete Art of Poetry*, 1718.
A. Bedford, *A Serious Remonstrance in Behalf of the Christian Religion*, 1719.
*Giles Jacob, *The Poetical Register*, 1719-20, *1723.

1720-1724

Golden Medley, 1720 (See *N & Q*, Oct. 10, 1874, p. 285).
Cuthbert Constable, *An Essay Towards a New English Dictionary*, c. 1720 (Excerpts quoted in Maggs Cat. No. 434, pp. 250-2).
British Curiosities in Art and Nature . . . ancient and modern, 1721.
Conduct of the Stage Considered, 1721.
*J. Dennis, *Original Letters: Familiar, Moral, and Critical*, 1721.
*L. Welsted, *Dissertation concerning the English Language*, 1724.

1725-1729

*A. Pope, *Preface* to Edition, 1725.
*L. Theobald, *Shakespeare Restored*, 1726.
W. Law, *The Absolute Unlawfulness of Stage Entertainment*, 1726.
J. Dennis, *The Stage Defended*, 1726.
J. Roberts, *An Answer to Mr. Pope's "Preface,"* 1729.

1730-1734

E. Young, *Two Epistles to Mr. Pope*, 1730.
J. Henley, *Academical Lectures*, 1731.
T. Cooke, *Considerations on the Stage*, 1731. (In *The Triumphs of Love and Honour*.)

*J. Jortin, *Miscellaneous Observations upon Authors* (ii, 242-50), 1731-32.
*C. Cibber, *Faithful Memoirs of* . . . . *Mrs. Anne Oldfield*, 1731.
A. Pope, *A Miscellany of Taste*, 1732.
*E. Coles, *English Dictionary*, 1732, *1742.
D. Mallet, *Of Verbal Criticism* [on Theobald], 1733.
*L. Theobald, *Preface* to Edition, 1733.
Some Account of the Present State of the British Islands, with a Notice of Shakspeare, 1734.
The Life of Mr. John Dennis, 1734.

1735-1739

The Dramatic Historiographer, 1735.
[Sir Thomas Hanmer?], *Some Remarks on the Tragedy of "Hamlet,"* 1736, *1864.
A. Pope, *First Epistle of the Second Book of Horace Imitated*, 1737.
*T. Hayward, *The British Muse*, 1738.
J. Dennis, *The Usefulness of the Stage* (2nd ed., with definite reference to Shakespeare), 1738.

1740-1744

*C. Cibber, *An Apology for the Life of Colley Cibber*, *1740, *1750, *1756.
J. Warton, *The Enthusiast* (ll. 167 ff.), 1740.
*[H. Fielding?], *An Apology for the Life of Mr. T. C.* [Theophilus Cibber], 1740.
*F. Peck, *Explanatory and Critical Notes on divers Passages of Shakspeare's Plays*, 1740.
*L. Riccoboni, *An Historical and Critical Account of the Theaters in Europe*, *1741, 1754.
T. Cooke, *Epistle to the Countess of Shaftesbury*, 1742.
W. Collins, *Epistle to Hanmer*, 1743 (see note under 1750-1754, on poems).

*Corbyn Morris, *An Essay towards fixing the true Standards of Wit and Humour, Raillery* . . . . . *Sir John Falstaff,* 1744.
*Sir T. Hanmer, *Preface* to Edition, 1744.

1745-1749

*T. A. Arne, *The Songs in the Comedies,* 1745 (?).
Garrick's Letter to Frank Hayman, 1745.
Letter to C. Cibber on transformation of *King John,* 1745.
*S. Say, *Poems and Essays,* 1745.
*S. Johnson, *Miscellaneous Observations on "Macbeth,"* 1745.
*J. Upton, *Critical Observations on Shakespeare,* *1746, *1748.
[Z. Grey], *A Word or two of Advice to W. Warburton,* 1746.
**Companion to the Theater,* 1747.
S. Foote, *The Roman and English Comedy Consider'd and Compar'd,* 1747.
*W. Warburton, *Preface* to Edition, 1747.
*W. Guthrie, *Essay on English Tragedy,* with remarks on the Abbé Le Blanc's *"Observations on the English Stage,"* *1747, 1749.
*J. Spence, *Polymetis,* *1747, 1765.
*T. Whincop, *Scanderbeg, A Tragedy* [with a life of Shakespeare], 1747.
*T. Edwards, *A Supplement to Mr. Warburton's Edition—being the Canons of Criticism*—1747, *1748, *1750, 1753, 1757, *1758 (6th), *1765 (7th).
*P. Whalley, *Enquiry into the Learning of Shakespeare,* 1748.
Dr. Z. Grey, *Remarks upon a Late Edition* [Warburton's], 1748, 1751, 1752.
T. Smollett, *Roderick Random* (chap. 62), 1748.
*J. Upton, *Remarks on Three Plays of Ben Jonson,* 1749.
*J. Holt, *An Attempte to Rescue that Auncient English Poet,* *1749, *1750.
M. Akenside, *The Remonstrance of Shakespeare,* 1749.
H. Fielding, *Tom Jones* (Bk. V, chap. I; Bk. VIII, chap. I), 1749.
[Moore?], *Ode to Garrick,* 1749.
*W. R. Chetwood, *A General History of the Stage,* 1749.

1750-1754

*Z. Grey, *A Free and Familiar Letter to . . . Rev. Mr. Wm. Warburton*, 1750.
J. Holt, *Proposals for Publishing an Edition of Shakespeare*, 1750.
The Diverting History and droll Adventures of Sir John Falstaff, 1750.
T. Smollett, *Peregrine Pickle* (chaps. 61, 94), 1751.
British Theater, 1752 (Cumberland—ed. by G. Daniel).
A Poetical Epistle from Shakespeare in Elysium to Garrick, 1752.[1]
*Z. Grey, *Critical, Historical and Explanatory Notes on Shakspeare*, 1752, *1754, 1755.
*W. Dodd, *The Beauties of Shakespeare*, *1752, 1757, *1780 (3rd), 1782, etc.
Miscellaneous Observations on the Tragedy of "Hamlet," 1752.
*Mrs. Charlotte Lennox, *Shakespear Illustrated*, *1753-4 (with a dedication by S. Johnson).
Letter to Miss Nossiter . . . on her playing Juliet, 1753.
*T. Cibber, *The Lives of the Poets of Great Britain and Ireland*, 1753.
History of Sophia Shakespear, 1753.
**The Present State of the Stage*, 1753.
C. Macklin, *British Inquisition*, 1754-55.
T. Warton, *Observations on the "Faery Queen,"* 1754.

1755-1759

*J. G. Cooper, *The Tomb of Shakespear, a Vision*, 1755, *1755.
A Novel, the Source of the "Merchant of Venice," 1755.
S. Johnson, *Dictionary*, 1755.
*R. Pickering, *Reflections upon Theatrical Expression in Tragedy*, 1755.
*J. G. Cooper, *Letters Concerning Taste*, 1755, 1755, 1757, *1771.
Memoirs of the Shakespeare Head in Covent Garden, 1755.
*S. Johnson, *Proposals for Printing . . . . Shakspear*, 1756.

---

[1] I have included merely a few poems, generally of this type.

Theatrical Records, 1756.
*T. Cibber, *Dissertations on Theatrical Subjects*, 1756-1759.
H. Howard, *Visionary Interview at the Shrine of Shakspear*, 1756.
J. Warton, *Essay on the Genius and Writings of Pope*, 1756, 1782.
A Letter of Abuse to D. Garrick, 1757.
E. Burke, *A Philosophical Enquiry . . . . . Sublime and the Beautiful*, 1757, 1759.
D. Hume, *Four Dissertations*, 1757.
W. Shirley, *Brief Remarks on the Original and Present State of Drama*, 1758.
Dr. J. Armstrong, *Sketches or Essays on Various Subjects*, 1758.
[J. Grove], *King Henry VIII*, with historical notes, 1758.
E. Young, *Conjectures on Original Composition*, 1759.
*S. Derrick, *A General View of the Stage*, 1759.
E. Capell, *Notes and Readings*, 1759.
T. Wilkes, *General View of the Stage*, 1759.
*A. Gerard, *Essay on Taste*, 1759, 1764, *1780 (3rd ed.).

1760-1764

T. Francklin, *A Dissertation on Ancient Tragedy*, 1760.[1]
*Robert Lloyd, *Shakespear: an Epistle to Mr. Garrick*, 1760.
*E. Capell, *Prolusions: select pieces of ancient poetry*, 1760.
*S. Foote, *A Letter to David Garrick*, 1760.
*W. Kenrick, *Falstaff's Wedding*, *1760, *1766.
B. Victor, *The History of the Theaters of London and Dublin*, 1760, (1761).
F. M. A. Voltaire, *Critical Essays on Dramatic Poetry*, Glasgow, 1761.
T. Smollett (and others), *Translation of the Works of Voltaire*, 1761.
G. Colman, *Critical Reflections on the Old English Dramatic Writers*, 1761. [In *Prose on Several Occasions*, *1787]
A Few Words in Defense of Capell, 1761.

---

[1] For this reference I am indebted to Professor G. W. Sherburn, of the University of Chicago.

Falstaff's Jests, 1761.
Henry Home, Lord Kames, *Elements of Criticism*, 1762, 1763, 1769 (4th), 1785 (6th), 1788.
*D. Webb, *Remarks on the Beauty of Poetry*, 1762.
The British Plutarch (v, 1-28, Life of Shakespeare), 1762.
[O. Goldsmith?], *The Art of Poetry on a New Plan*, 1762.[2]
J. Moor, *On the End of Tragedy according to Aristotle*, 1763.
[P. Nichols], *The Castrated Letter of Sir Tho. Hanmer*, 1763.
J. Brown, *A Dissertation on the Rise, Union, and Power . . . . of Poetry and Music*, 1763.
Companion to the Playhouse, 1764.
R. Hurd, *A Letter to T. Leland*, 1764.
J. Bowle, *Miscellaneous Pieces of antient English Poesie*, 1764.

1765-1769

*B. Heath, *Revisal of Shakespear's Text*, 1765.
*W. Kenrick, *Review of Johnson's "Shakespeare,"* 1765.
Prefaces to Shakespeare's Plays, 1765.
*S. Johnson, *Preface*, 1765.
Lord Lyttelton, *Dialogues of the Dead*, 1765.
H. Walpole, *Preface* to 2nd ed. of *The Castle of Otranto*, 1765.
*T. Tyrwhitt, *Observations and Conjectures upon some Passages of Shakespeare*, 1766.
James Barclay, *An Examination of Mr. Kenrick's Review . . . Dr. Johnson's Edition*, 1766.
[W. Kenrick], *A Defense of Mr. Kenrick's Review*, 1766.
E. Capell, *Reflections on Originality in Authors*, 1766.
C. Jemmat, *Verses on Barry as Othello*, 1766.
[D. Garrick], *The Interview, or Jack Falstaff's Ghost*, 1766.
G. Steevens, *Proposals for . . . . Edition of Shakespeare*, 1766.
*W. Kenrick, *Falstaff's Wedding* (second version), 1766.
O. Goldsmith, *Vicar of Wakefield*, (chap. XVIII), 1766.
[Q?], *The Life of Mr. James Quin*, 1766.

---

[2]For this reference I am indebted to Professor R. S. Crane, of the University of Chicago.

*R. Farmer, *Essay on the Learning of Shakespeare*, *1767; 2nd ed., 1767, *3rd ed., 1789.
W. Duff, *Essay on Original Genius*, 1767.
J. Brownsmith, *The Dramatic Time Piece*, 1767.
*R. Warner, *A Letter to David Garrick*, 1768,
*[K——], "Secret History of Macbeth," in *A Key to the Drama*, 1768.
*E. Capell, *Introduction* to Edition, 1768.
*H. Flitcroft, *Theatrical Entertainments*, 1768.
H. Walpole, *Historic Doubts on the life and reign of Richard III*, 1768.
Mrs. Elizabeth Montagu, *Essay on the Genius and Writings of Shakespear*, *1769, *1770, *1772, *1777, *1778, 1785, *1810.
*G. S. Carey, *Shakespeare's Jubilee, A Masque*, 1769.
*D. Garrick, *Ode* on Shakespeare, 1769 (with *Testimonies to the Genius . . . of Shakespeare*).
*[T. Arne], *Shakespeare's Garland*, 1769.
*Dr. Arne, Music for *An Ode upon dedicating a building to Shakespeare*, 1769.
D. Webb, *Observations on the Correspondence between Poetry and Music*, 1769.
*H. Jones, *Ode to Shakespear, in Honour of the Jubilee*, 1769.
Garrick's Vagary, 1769.
F. Gentleman, *The Stratford Jubilee*, 1769.

1770-1774

*F. Gentleman, *Dramatic Censor*, 1770.
Lamentable and True Tragedie of Mr. Arden . . . Shakspeare, 1770.
Shakespeare—Containing the Traits of his Characters (n. d.), 1770(?).
*George Colman, *Man and Wife; or the Shakespeare Jubilee*, 1770.
Shakespeare's Jests, 1770.
The Spouter's Companion, or Theatrical Remembrancer, 1770.

*J. Armstrong, *Imitations of Shakespeare and Spenser*, 1770 [in his *Miscellanies*, I, 143-66.]
"*Romeo and Juliet*," comedy originally in Spanish by Lope de Vega, built upon the same Story on which that Poet [Shakespear] has founded his tragedy, 1770.
*J. Collins, *A Letter to George Hardinge*, 1771, *1777.
*P. Hiffernan, *Dramatic Genius*, 1772.
C. Jennens, *The Tragedy of "King Lear" Vindicated from The Critical Reviewers*, 1772.
"Sir N. Nipclose," *The Theaters* [a poem], 1772.
Theatrical Review, 1772.
**Theatrical Biography*, 1772.
F. Gentleman, "*Julius Caesar*" as acted at Covent Garden, 1773.
*K. Prescot, *Letters* . . . . *with additional Classic Amusements*, 1773.
*[W. Kenrick], *Introduction to the School of Shakespeare*, 1773.
*T. Hawkins, *Origin of English Drama*, 1773.
J. Hughes, *Correspondence*, 1773.
J. Hall, *Illustrations of Shakspeare*, 1773.
**Prefaces* to Johnson and Steevens' edition, 1773.
*D. Garrick, *Dramatic Works*, 1774, *1798.
"K. P." [K. Prescot], *Shakespeare, An Essay* [on the Learning of Shakespeare], 1774.
*W. Richardson, *A Philosophical Analysis and Illustration of Some of Shakespeare's Remarkable Characters*, *1774. Reprinted 1774 (*1775, "second edition"), *1780, *1784, (*1786, "fourth edition"), *1797, *1798, *1812.
T. Warton, *History of English Poetry*, 1774, 1778.
*E. Taylor, *Cursory Remarks on Tragedy, on Shakespear*, etc., 1774.
*[F. Gentleman], *Introduction to Shakespeare's Plays* (in Bell's ed.), 1774.
*E. Capell, *Notes and Various Readings*, 1774.

1775-1779

*E. Capell, *Notes and Various Readings*, 3 vols., 1775, *1779-80.[1]

*Mrs. Griffith, *The Morality of Shakespeare's Drama*, *1775, *1777.

*W. Cooke, *Elements of Dramatic Criticism*, 1775.

Shakespeare's History of the Times, 1775.

J. H. Mortimer, *Shakspeare's Characters: 12 illustrations*, 1775.

*W. Pearce, *Haunts of Shakespeare* [a poem], 1776, *1778.

*Dr. Lawrence, *An Ode on the Spirits of Shakespear*, 1776, (Music by T. Linley). Ms.

J. Beattie, *Essays*, 1776.

English Theater, 12 vols., 1776.

*F. Pilon, *An Essay on the Character of Hamlet . . . by Henderson*, 1777.

Letter from Mr. Desenfans to Mrs. Montagu, 1777.

*M. Morgann, *An Essay on the Dramatic Character of Sir John Falstaff*, *1777, *1820, *1825.

J. Priestley, *A Course of Lectures on Oratory and Criticism*, 1777.

*T. Davies, *A Genuine Narrative of . . . . Mr. John Henderson*, 1777.

**Beauties of English Drama*, 4 vols., 1777.

Epistle from Shakspear to his Countrymen, 1777.

**Modern Characters from Shakspeare*, 2 different vols., 1778.

A. Kippis, *Biographia Britannica*, 1778.

C. Taylor, *The Beauties of Shakespeare*, 1778, 1783, 1792.

*G. Colman, *Preface to Works of Beaumont and Fletcher*, 1778.

The Theatrical Bouquet, 1778.

**Prefaces* to Johnson & Steevens' second edition, 1778.

Playhouse Pocket Companion, 1779.

Theatrical Monopoly, 1779.

Sir J. Harington, *Nugae Antiquae*, 1779.

Epistle from Little Captain Brazen [on Iago], n. d.

---

[1] "From the Press of Henry Hughs in Lincoln's Inn Fields; Feb. 21st, 1780"—at the end of vol. II in the McMillan Collection.

*J. Nichols, *Six Old Plays on which Shakespeare founded his Measure for Measure . . . and King Lear*, 1779.
*R. Griffith, *A Collection of more than 800 Prologues and Epilogues*, 1779.
*M. Sherlock, *Lettres d'un Voyageur Anglais*, 1779 (trans. *1802).

1780-1784

*W. Hodson, *Observations on Tragedy* (bound with *Zoraida*), 1780.
*E. Malone, *Supplement to the Edition of Shakspeare's Plays published in 1778*, 1780.
*M. Sherlock, *Nouvelles Lettres d'un Voyageur Anglais*, *1780, (trans. *1802).
*T. Davies, *Memoirs of the Life of Garrick*, *1780, 1784.
J. Jordan, *Original Collections on Shakespeare and Stratford*, [1780] 1864.
History of "Titus Andronicus" translated from the Italian, 1780.
Lectures on Belles Lettres and Logic, 1780.
E. Capell, *The School of Shakspeare*, 1780.
Letters from Thomas Crompton to Lord Chedworth, 1780-95.
H. Walpole, *Postscript* to *The Mysterious Mother* (1768), 1781.
[J. Ritson], *The Stockton Jubilee*, 1781.
*W. Jackson, *Thirty Letters on Various Subjects*, 1782, 1784, *1795.
*J. Nichols, *Literary Anecdotes of the Eighteenth Century*, 1782, *1812.
B. Walwyn, *An Essay on Comedy*, 1782.
*D. E. Baker, *Biographia Dramatica, or A Companion to the Playhouse*, *1782, *1812.
*S. Felton, *Imperfect Hints Toward a New Edition of Shakespeare . . . 1782*, 1787.
*J. Ritson, *Remarks Critical and Illustrative*, *1783.
E. Malone, *Second Appendix to Supplement*, 1783.
*T. Davies, *Dramatic Miscellanies*, *1783-4 (2nd ed. *1785).
J. Beattie, *Dissertations, Moral and Critical*, 1783.

H. Blair, *Lectures on Rhetoric*, 1783.
**Beauties of Shakespeare*, Dublin, 1783.
*"Thersitus Literarius"—*A Familiar Address*, 1784.
*W. Richardson, *Essays on Shakespeare's Dramatic Characters of Richard III, King Lear, and Timon of Athens*, *1784, *1785, 1786, *1797, *1798, *1812.
The Immortality of Shakespeare [a poem], 1784.

1785-1789

*J. M. Mason, *Comments on the Last Edition of Shakespeare's Plays*, 1785.
*T. Whately, *Remarks on some of the Characters of Shakspeare*, 1785, *1808, *1839.
**The Etymologist, a Comedy* [on S.'s Commentators], 1785.
*J. Pinkerton, *Letters of Literature by Robert Heron*, 1785.
*Prefaces to Johnson and Steevens' third edition, 1785.
*M. Sherlock, *A Fragment on Shakspeare*, *1786 (French version, *1780), *1802.
*J. P. Kemble, *Macbeth Reconsidered*, 1786.
J. Towers, *An Essay on Johnson*, 1786.
John Ireland, *Shakesperiana*, 1786.
An Essay on the Pre-Eminence of Comic Genius, 1786.
*A. Becket, *A Concordance to Shakespeare*, 1787.
Catalogue of the Pictures in the Shakespeare Gallery, 1787.
*G. Colman, *Prose on Several Occasions* (3 vols.), 1787.
*J. Ritson, *Quip Modest*, 1788.
Theatrical Register, 1788.
Transactions of the Royal Irish Acad., vol. ii [R. Stack on Falstaff], 1788.
*D. Simpson, *A Discourse on Stage Entertainments*, 1788.
*J. Egerton, *Theatrical Remembrancer*, 1788.
Encyclopedia of Wit, 1788.
*R. Hitchcock, *An Historical View of the Irish Stage*, 1788-94.
T. Davies, *Some Account of . . . . Massinger*, 1789.
*T. Davies, *Appendix to Downe's "Roscius Anglicanus,"* 1789.
**A Short Criticism on the Performance of Hamlet by Mr. Kemble*, 1789.

PRIMARY TEXTS

R. Potter, *The Art of Criticism*, 1789.
*Mr. Philip Neve, *Cursory Remarks on Some of the Ancient English Poets* (Private pr.), *1789.
* *The Bee, or A Companion to the Shakespeare Gallery*, 1789.
*W. Richardson, *Essays on Shakespeare's Dramatic Character of Sir John Falstaff and on his Imitation of Female Characters*, *1789, *1797, *1798, *1812.
History of Sir John Falstaff, 1789.

1790-1794

Transactions of the Royal Society of Edenburgh, vol. ii [T. Robertson on Hamlet], 1790.
A. Alison, *Essays on the Nature & Principles of Taste*, 1790.
*S. Ayscough, *Index to the remarkable passages and words.... Shakspeare*, 1790.
*T. Wilkinson, *Memoirs of His Own Life*, 1790.
*E. Malone, *Preface* to Edition, 1790.
George Mason, *Collection of English Words used by Shakespeare*, 1790.
J. Jordan, *Families of Shakespeare and Hart* [1790], 1865.
T. Monro, *Essays*, No. XVII, 1790.
G. Nicol, *Letter on Boydell's Edition*, 1791.
*E. Jerningham, *The Shakspeare Gallery, a poem*, 1791.
J. Boswell, *Life of Johnson*, 1791.
John Armstrong, *Sonnets from Shakespeare*, 1791.
J. Hurdis, *Cursory Remarks upon the Arrangement of the Plays of Shakespear*, 1792.
*J. Ritson, *Cursory Criticisms on the Edition of Shakspeare pub. by Edmond Malone*, 1792.
*E. Malone, *A Letter to the Rev. Richard Farmer*, *1792, *1792.
C. Taylor, *Shakspeare Gallery*, 1792.
A. Eccles, *Illustrations and Variorum Comments*, 1792, 1805.
*J. A. Croft, *Select Collection of the Beauties of Shakspeare*, 1792.
*E. Malone, *Prospectus of an intended Edition of Shakspeare*, 1792, *1795.
An Essay on Shakspeare, from Farrago, 1792.
G. Skene, *The Genius of Shakspeare, a summer dream*, 1793.

*A. Murphy, *Essay on the Life and Genius of S. Johnson*, 1793, *1825.
Censor Dramaticus—A Complete History of the Drama, 1793.
*J. Jackson, *History of the Scottish Stage*, 1793.
*S. and E. Harding, *Shakspeare Illustrated* (2 vols.), *1793, *1811.
**Prefaces* to Johnson and Steevens' fourth edition, 1793.
*W. Whiter, *A Specimen of a Commentary on Shakspeare*, 1794.
H. J. Pye, *Sketches*, 1794.
*Mr. A. Harrison, *The Infant Vision of Shakespeare*, 1794.
[F. G. Waldron], *Shakesperian Museum*, 1794.
**Proposals for Printing the Felton Portrait of Shakspeare* by W. Richardson (print-seller), 1794.
The Wonderful Secrets of Stage Trick, 1794.
R. Alves, *Sketches of a History of Literature*, 1794.
*[T. J. Mathias], *The Pursuits of Literature*, 1794-7, *1798.

1795-1799

J. Wallace, *Shaksperian Sketches*, 1795.
Candid and Impartial Strictures on the Performances, 1795, (1796).
*G. Steevens, *Shakspeare*, 1795. [Reprinted from *European Mag.*, Dec., 1794].
Shakespeare's Jests, 1795.
W. Parr, *The Story of the Moor of Venice*, 1795.
*James Plumptre, *Observations on "Hamlet,"* 1796.
**Essays by a Society of Gentlemen at Exeter* (Three on Shakespeare by Richard Hole), 1796.
*James White, *Original Letters of Sir John Falstaff*, *1796, *1797 (2nd ed.).
*W H. Ireland, *Miscellaneous Papers and Legal Instruments . . . William Shakespeare*, 1795 (6).
*J. Boaden, *Letter to G. Steevens . . . on S. Ireland . . W. H. Ireland*, 1796.
On W. H. Ireland Papers:
*"Philalethes" (Col. F. Webb)—Jan., 1796 (pro Ireland).
*F. G. Waldron, Feb., 1796 (vs. Ireland).

*Mat. Wyatt, Feb., 1796 (pro Ireland).
*W. C. Oulton, Feb., 1796 (pro Ireland).
*E. Malone, *Inquiry into the Authenticity of certain miscellaneous papers*, 1796.
(For complete set see S. Lee, *Shakespeareana*, ii, 265 ff.)
*[G. M. Woodward], *Familiar verses from the Ghost of Willey Shakspeare to Sammy Ireland*, 1796.
*W. H. Ireland, *Authentic Account of the Shakesperean MSS.*, Dec., 1796.
Review of the Opinions of James Boaden, 1796.
*J. Penn, *Letters on the Drama*, 1796.
*W. C. Oulton, *The History of the Theaters of London, 1771-95*, 1796.
The Poetical Preceptor, 1796
*B. Crosby, *Pocket-Companion to the Playhouses*, 1796.
J. Roach, *History of the Stage*, 1796.
*W. Richardson, *Essays on Shakespeare's Dramatic Characters*, fifth edition, *1797, *1798.
*James Plumptre, *Appendix to Observations on "Hamlet,"* 1797.
**Mr. Ireland's Vindication*, Jan., 1797 [by Samuel Ireland].
*S. Ireland, *Investigation of Mr. Malone's Claim to be the character of a scholar or critic*, Aug., 1797.
*James Caulfield, *An Enquiry into the Conduct of Edmond Malone, Esq., concerning the manuscript papers of John Aubrey*, 1797.
*G. Chalmers, *An Apology for the Believers in the Shakspeare Papers*, 1797.
*J. M. Mason, *Comments on the Plays of Beaumont and Fletcher*, 1798.
Passages on *Vortigern and Rowena*, 1798.
*G. Chalmers, *Supplemental Apology*, 1799.
*E. du Bois, *The Wreath*, 1799.
*J. T. Kirkman, *Memoirs of the Life of Charles Macklin* (2 vols.), 1799.
*Robert Anderson, *Works of the British Poets*, 1795-1807.

The Early Nineteenth Century
1800-1804

*G. Hardinge, *Essence of Malone*, 1800.
W. Wordsworth, *Preface to Lyrical Ballads*, 1800.
*G. Hardinge, *Chalmeriana*, 1800.
*E. Malone, *Historical Account of the Rise and Progress of the English Stage*, 1800.
*G. Chalmers, *Appendix to Supplemental Apology*, 1800.
A Peep into the Theater Royal, Manchester, 1800.
*T. Dutton, *Dramatic Censor*, 1800.
*C. Dibdin, *A Complete History of the English Stage*, 1800.
*A. Murphy, *Life of David Garrick*, 1801.
*G. Hardinge, *Another Essence of Malone*, 1801.
Kemble and Cooke, or A Critical Review, 1801.
*F. G. Waldron, *Shakspearean Miscellany*, 1802.
*J. T. Finegan, *An Attempt to Illustrate a few Passages in Shakespeare's Works*, 1802.
School for Satire [parody on Capell and Malone], 1802.
*C. Lamb, *G. F. Cooke in "Richard III,"* 1802.
Remarks on Mr. J. Kemble's Performance of Hamlet & Richard III, 1802.
W. H. Ireland, *Rhapsodies*, 1803.
*W. Godwin, *Life of Chaucer*, 1803.
*Johnson & Steevens, fifth edition, 1803.
[W. Cooke], *Memoirs of C. Macklin*, 1804.
*M. Sherlock, *Original Letters on Several Subjects* (originally pub. in French in 1781), 1802.

1805-1809

*A. Chalmers, *Plays of William Shakspeare*, 1805.
*E. H. Seymour, *Remarks upon the Plays of Shakspeare*, 1805.
*Lord Chedworth, *Notes upon some Passages in Shakespeare's Plays*, 1805.
F. Twiss, *A Complete Verbal Index to . . . . Shakspeare*, 1805.
*W. H. Ireland, *The Confessions of Wm. H. Ireland*, 1805.

*R. B. Wheler, *History and Antiquities of Stratford*, 1805, *1806.
*W. Cooke, *Memoirs of S. Foote*, 1805.
*F. Douce, *Illustrations of Shakspeare*, 1807.
*J. M. Mason, *Comments on the Several Editions of Shakespeare's Plays*, 1807.
*H. J. Pye, *Comments on the Commentators on Shakespear*, 1807.
*C. Lamb, *Tales from Shakespear*, 1807, *1809.
P. Stockdale, *Lectures on the Truly Eminent English Poets*, 1807.
Leigh Hunt, *Critical Essays on the Performers of the London Theaters*, 1807.
*H. Bunbury, ed., *The Correspondence of Sir T. Hanmer*, 1808, *1838.
*E. Malone, *An Account of . . . . Shakspeare's "Tempest,"* 1808-9.
J. Watkins, *Characteristic Anecdotes of Men of Learning*, 1808.
*O. Gilchrist, *Examination of . . . Ben Jonson's Enmity towards Shakspeare*, 1808.
*C. Lamb, *Specimens of the English Dramatic Poets who lived about the time of Shakspeare*, *1808, *1813.
*Mrs. Elizabeth Inchbald, *British Theater*, 1808.
S. T. Coleridge, *Lectures*, 1808, 1811, 1813, 1818 (T. Ashe, ed., 1883).
*T. Gilliland, *The Dramatic Mirror*, 1808.
Studies of Shakespeare, 1809.
*J. Plumptre, *Four Discourses on . . . The Stage*, 1809.
S. T. Coleridge, *The Friend*, 1809-10.

1810-1830

SOME REPRESENTATIVE TEXTS

*J. Croft, *Annotations on the Plays of Shakespear*, 1810.
Beauties of Shakespeare, 1811.
*Andrew Becket, *Lucianus Redivivus; or Dialogues, concerning Men, Manners, and Opinions*, 1811.
*John Huckell, *Avon, a Poem*, 1811.

*J. Poole, *Hamlet Travesties*, 1811, 1816.
*C. Lofft, *Aphorisms from Shakespeare*, 1812.
C. Lamb, *Essay on the Tragedies of Shakespear*, 1812.
*W. Richardson, Sixth Edition, to which is added: "Shakespeare's Imitation of Characteristical, and Particularly National Manners, Illustrated in the Character of Fluellen," 1812.
Mrs. Elizabeth Montagu, *Letters*, 1813.
*A Luders, An Essay on *The Character of Henry V when Prince of Wales*, 1813.
*J. Britton, *Remarks on . . . . Shakspeare*, *1814, *1818.
*A. Becket, *Shakspeare's Himself Again*, 1815.
*G. Chalmers, *Another Account of . . . . "Tempest,"* 1815.
W. Wordsworth, *Essay Supplementary to the "Preface,"* 1815.
Richard III, Travesty, 1816.
*J. Britton, *Remarks on the Monumental Bust*, 1816.
*J. Nichols, *Illustrations of the Literary History of the Eighteenth Century*, 1817-58.
*J. P. Kemble, *"Macbeth" and "Richard III,"* 1817.
*N. Drake, *Shakspeare and His Times*, 1817.
S. T. Coleridge, *Biographia Literaria*, 1817.
W. Hazlitt, *Characters of Shakspeare's Plays*, 1817.
"Macbeth," a Poem, 1817.
*Z. Jackson, *A Few Concise Examples of 700 Errors in Shakspeare's Plays*, *1818.
W. Hazlitt, *Lectures on the English Poets*, 1818.
*Z. Jackson, *Shakspeare's Genius Justified*, 1819.
A Specimen of a New Edition of Shakespeare, 1819.
W. Hazlitt, *Lectures on the English Comic Writers*, 1819.
*W. Oxberry (ed.), *Hamlet*, 1820; *Macbeth*, 1821.
W. Hazlitt, *Lectures on the Dramatic Literature of the Age of Elizabeth*, 1821.
*Sir Robert Smirke, *Illustrations to Shakspeare*, 1821-29.
Boswell's Malone Edition, 1821.
*R. Nares, *A Glossary*, *1822, *1825, *1872.
S. T. Coleridge, *Table Talk*, 1822.
C. Lamb, *Essays of Elia*, 1823.

PRIMARY TEXTS 265

*J. R. Planché, Books on Costumes of Shakespeare's Plays, 1823-30.
*T. Bowdler, A Letter to the Editor of the British Critic, 1823.
*J. Boaden, An Inquiry into the Authenticity of Various Pictures and Prints, 1824.
*A. Skottowe, The Life of Shakspeare, 1824.
*C. Sprague, Prize Ode . . . at Shakspeare Jubilee, Boston, 1824.
*J. Boaden, Memoirs of the Life of John Philip Kemble, 1825.
*John Wilson, Shakspereana, 1827.
*N. Drake, Memorials of Shakspeare, 1828.
*W. Rider, Views in Stratford-upon-Avon, 1828.
*Shaksperian Anthology: comprising the Choicest passages, 1830.

COLLECTIONS OF EIGHTEENTH-CENTURY CRITICAL TEXTS

A. Chalmers, The British Essayists, London, 1823.
N. Drake, Memorials of Shakspeare, London, 1828.
D. Nichol Smith, Eighteenth Century Essays on Shakespeare, Glasgow, 1903.
C. E. Hughes, The Praise of Shakespeare: an English Anthology, London, 1904.
W. H. Durham, Critical Essays of the Eighteenth Century, New Haven, Yale Univ. Press, 1915.
D. Nichol Smith, Shakespeare Criticism, Oxford Univ. Press, 1916.
E. D. Jones, English Critical Essays of the Sixteenth, Seventeenth, and Eighteenth Centuries, Oxford Univ. Press, 1922.

GENERAL PERIODICALS ACCESSIBLE
Pre-1766

Aberdeen Magazine, 1761.
British Magazine, 1746-50.
Dublin Magazine, 1762-65.
History of the Works of the Learned, 1699-1711.
Memoirs of Literature, 1722.
New Memoirs of Literature, 1725-27.
Republic of Letters, 1728-36.

1766-1799

Analytical Review, 1788- .
Anthologia Hibernica, 1793- .
Anti-Jacobin Review, 1798- .
British Critic, 1793- .
British Magazine, 1760-67.
Critical Review, 1756- .
European Magazine, 1782- .
Gentleman's Magazine, 1731- .
Hibernian Magazine, 1771- .
Lady's Magazine, 1770- .
Literary Magazine and British Review, 1788-94.
London Magazine, 1732-85.
Macaroni and Theatrical Magazine, 1772-73.
Monthly Epitome, 1797- .
Monthly Magazine, 1796- .
Monthly Mirror, 1795- .
Monthly Review, 1749-89.
Monthly Review, or Literary Journal, 1790- .
Royal Magazine, 1759-69.
Scots Magazine, 1739- .
Universal Magazine, 1747- .
Weekly Amusement, 1765-66.
Wit's Magazine, 1784-85.

LITERARY PERIODICALS AVAILABLE

Pre-1766

The Adventurer, 1753-54 (J. Warton, Hawkesworth, Johnson, Bathurst).
Athenian Sport, 1707.
Caribbeana, 1741.
The Connoisseur, 1754-56 (Colman and Thornton).
Covent Garden Journal, 1752 (Fielding).
The Englishman, 1714 (Steele).
Gray's Inn Journal, 1756 (Murphy).

The Guardian, 1713 (Steele).
Heraclitus Ridens, 1681.
The Herald, 1758.
The Idler, 1758-60 (Johnson).
Lay Monastery, 1714.
Miscellanea Aurea, 1720.
The Rambler, 1750-52 (Johnson).
T. Reresby's Miscellany, 1721.
The Spectator, 1711-12, 1714 (Addison and Steele).
The Sports of Wit, 1675.
The Tatler, 1709-11 (Steele).
Theatrical Review, 1763.
Universal Spectator, 1756 (Henry Stonecastle).
The Visitor, 1764 ("by several hands").
The World, 1753-56 (Edward Moore).

1766-1799

The Bee (Edinburgh), 1791-93 (W. N. Anderson).
Dramatic Censor, 1770 (Francis Gentleman).
Edinburgh Fugitive Pieces, 1791.
The Enquirer, 1797 (Godwin).
Essays, Moral and Literary, 1777 (V. Knox).
Looker-On, 1792-94 (Roberts).
The Lounger, 1785-86 (Mackenzie).
The Mirror, 1779-80 (Mackenzie).
The Observer, 1785-90 (Cumberland).
Playhouse Pocket Companion, 1779.
Theatrical Remembrancer, 1788 (T. and J. Egerton).
The Trifler, 1788 ("Timothy Touchstone") (Westminster schoolboys).
Winter Evenings, 1787 (V. Knox).
For a general summary of Eighteenth Century Periodicals see R. S. Crane and F. B. Kaye, "A Census of British Newspapers and Periodicals," *Studies in Philology*, XXIV (Jan., 1927), 1-205. Also published with same title as a book by the University of North Carolina Press, 1927; Cambridge University, 1927.

APPENDIX B[1]

A SECONDARY BIBLIOGRAPHY OF SHAKESPEARE CRITICISM IN THE EIGHTEENTH CENTURY
[Arranged chronologically]

The following abbreviations have been used:

Contemp. Rev.—Contemporary Review.
Fort. Rev.—Fortnightly Review.
Jahrb.—Shakespeare Jahrbuch.
JEGP—Journal of English and Germanic Philology.
MLN—Modern Language Notes.
MLR—Modern Language Review.
MP—Modern Philology.
N Brit. Rev.—North British Review.
N & Q—Notes and Queries.
PMLA—Publications of Modern Language Association.
PQ—Philological Quarterly.
Quart. Rev.—Quarterly Review.
RES—Review of English Studies.
SP—Studies in Philology.
SRL—Saturday Review of Literature.
TLS—London Times Literary Supplement.

[N. B. For recent books both place and publishers are generally given; otherwise only the place.]

I. General Aspects of the Century's Attitude toward Shakespeare

John Genest, *Some Account of the English Stage from* . . . . *1660-1830*, Bath, 1832.

James Boaden, *Memoirs of Mrs. Inchbald*, London, 1833.

Charles Knight, *A History of Opinion on the Writings of Shakspere* (Introd. vol. in *Studies of Shakspere* and Cabinet Edition), London, 1847.

---

[1] A preliminary draft of this appeared in *Studies in Philology*, Extra Series I (May, 1929), 77-98. The present version represents considerable revision.

[Anon.], "Stage Adaptations of Shakspeare," *Cornhill,* viii (July, 1863), 48-58.
W. Donaldson, *Theatrical Portraits* [Betterton, Garrick, Kemble], London, 1870.
L. Stephen, *History of English Thought in the Eighteenth Century,* London, 1876.
H. B. Baker, *English Actors from Shakespeare to Macready,* N. Y., 1879.
W. H. Pollock, "Shakespearian Criticism," *Nineteenth Century,* xi (1882), 915-33.
G. F. Vincke, "Shakespeare auf der englischen Bühne seit Garrick," *Jahrb.,* xxii (1887), 1-23.
G. Hallam, "Contributions to a History of Shakespearian Criticism," *Shakespeariana* of the N. Y. Shakespeare Soc., ix (Jan. and April, 1892), 30-46, 79-98.
W. H. Hudson, "Early Mutilators of Shakespeare," *Poet Lore,* iv (1892), 360-71.
L. J. Wylie, *Studies in the Evolution of English Criticism,* Boston, 1894.
E. Walder, *Shaksperian Criticism Textual and Literary from Dryden to the End of the Eighteenth Century,* Bradford, 1895.
Paul Hamelius, *Die Kritik in der Englischen Literatur des 17. und 18. Jahrhunderts,* Leipzig, 1897.
G. Saintsbury, *History of Criticism in Europe,* London, 1900-4.
T. R. Lounsbury, *Shakespeare as a Dramatic Artist,* N. Y., 1901.
J. H. Millar, *The Mid-Eighteenth Century,* London, 1902.
O. Gloede, *Shakespeare in der Englischen Litteratur des 17. und 18. Jahrhunderts,* Doberan, 1902.
F. Rae, "John Gilpin: Shakespear in 1790," *N & Q,* Ser. 9, vol. 12, July 11, 1903.
D. Nichol Smith, Preface and Introduction to *Eighteenth Century Essays on Shakespeare,* Glasgow, 1903.
L. Nelson, "Were there Shakespearean Forgers before Ireland?" *New Shakespeareana* of the N. Y. Shakespeare Soc., iii (1904), 77-81.
A. C. Bradley, "Eighteenth-Century Estimates of Shakespeare," *Scottish Hist. Rev.,* i (1904), 291-95.

F. W. Kilbourne, "Stage Versions of Shakespeare before 1800," *Poet Lore*, xv (1904), No. 2, pp. 116-25; No. 4, pp. 111-22.

L. Stephen, *English Literature and Society in the Eighteenth Century*, London, 1904.

H. A. Evans, "A Shakespearian Controversy of the Eighteenth Century," *Anglia*, xxviii (1905), 457-76. On Shakespeare's Learning—to Farmer.

F. W. Kilbourne, *Alterations and Adaptations of Shakespeare*, Boston, 1906.

M. E. Egan, *The Ghost in "Hamlet" and Other Essays* [includes Imitators of Shakespeare], Chicago, 1906.

H. B. Irving, "The English Stage in the Eighteenth Century," *Fort. Rev.*, lxxxv (1906), 895-908, 1079-1092.

J. Adler, *Zur Shakespeare-Kritik des 18. Jahrh. (Die Shakespeare Kritik im Gentleman's Magazine)*, Königsberg, 1906.

J. Sherzer, "American Editions of Shakespeare, 1753-1866," *PMLA*, xxii (1907), 633-96.

J. A. Farber, *Literary Forgeries*, London, 1907.

C. F. T. Brooke, *The Shakespeare Apocrypha*, Oxford, Clarendon, 1908.

A. I. P. Wood, *The Stage History of Shakespeare's "Richard III,"* Columbia Univ., 1909.

C. F. Johnson, *Shakespeare and His Critics*, N. Y., 1909.

F. H. Ristine, *English Tragicomedy: Its Origin and History*, Columbia Univ., 1910, 1929.

R. L. Steele, "The Shakespeares in the Eighteenth Century," *N & Q*, ser. 11, vol. iv (1911), 146, 252. [Latter by E. S. Hackaday.]

L. S. Friedland, "The Dramatic Unities in England," *JEGP*, x (1911), 56-89, 280-99, 453-67.

W. Jaggard, *Shakespeare Frauds*, Stratford, 1911.

G. Saintsbury, *A History of English Criticism*, London, 1911.

G. M. Miller, *The Historical Point of View in English Criticism from 1570-1770*, Heidelberg, 1913.

H. B. Wheatley, "Post-Restoration Quartos of Shakespeare's Plays," *The Library*, iv, ser. 3 (1913), 237-69.

G. H. Nettleton, *English Drama of the Restoration and Eighteenth Century*, N. Y., 1914.
J. Routh, *The Rise of Classical English Criticism*, New Orleans, Tulane Univ., 1915.
H. B. Wheatley, "Shakespeare Editors from 1623 to the Twentieth Century," *Transactions of the Bibliog. Soc.*, xiv (1915-7), 145-73.
W. B. Squire, "Shakespearean Operas," in *A Book of Homage to Shakespeare* [Oxford, Milford, 1916,], p. 75.
A. W. Pollard, "The Improvers of Shakespeare," *The Library*, vii, ser. 3 (1916), 265-90.
D. Nichol Smith, Introduction to *Shakespeare Criticism*, Oxford Univ., 1916.
L. B. Campbell, "The Rise of a Theory of Stage Presentation in England during the Eighteenth Century," *PMLA*, xxxii (1917), 163-200.
H. J. Götz, *Die komischen Bestandteile von Shakespeares Tragödien in der Kritik Englands*, Giessen, 1917.
E. E. Stoll, "Hamlet," *Univ. of Minnesota Studies*, No. 7, 1919.
G. C. D. Odell, *Shakespeare from Betterton to Irving*, N. Y., Scribner's, 1920; London, Constable, 1921.
R. F. Sharp, "Travesties of Shakespeare's Plays," *The Library*, i, 4th ser. (June, 1920), 1-20.
O. S. Coad, "Stage and Players in Eighteenth-Century America," *JEGP*, xix (1920), 201-23.
L. Cazamian, *L'Evolution Psychologique et la Littérature en Angleterre, 1660-1914*, Paris, 1920.
J. W. Draper, "Aristotelian Mimesis in Eighteenth-Century England," *PMLA*, xxxvi (1921), 372-400.
G. Crosse, "Shakespearean Mares-Nests in the Eighteenth Century," *London Mercury*, iv (Oct., 1921), 623-32. On W. H. Ireland.
Hugh Quigley, *Italy and the Rise of a New School of Criticism in the Eighteenth Century*, Perth, 1921.
A. Thaler, *Shakespere to Sheridan*, Harvard, 1922.
Montague Summers, *Shakespeare Adaptations*, London, Cape, 1922.

J. G. Robertson, *Studies in the Genesis of Romantic Theory in the Eighteenth Century*, Cambridge Univ., 1923.

A. W. Pollard, "Some Notes on the History of Copyright in England, 1662-1774," *The Library*, iii, 4th ser. (1923), 97-114.

A. Nicoll, *A History of Restoration Drama 1660-1700*, Cambridge Univ., 1923.

A. Nicoll, "The Editors of Shakespeare from the 1st Folio to Malone," in *Studies in the First Folio, 1623-1923*, London, 1924.

A. Bond, *Famous Actors from Burbage to Irving*, London, 1924.

H. D. de Maar, *A History of Modern English Romanticism*, London, Milford, 1924.

A. Nicoll, *A History of Early Eighteenth-Century Drama, 1700-50*, Cambridge Univ., 1925. Second Edition, 1929.

A. Nicoll, *British Drama*, New York, 1925.

A. H. Tolman, "Earnest and Jest in Shakespearean Scholarship, 1709-47," in *Falstaff and Other Shakespearean Topics*, New York, 1925. See also his succeeding chapter.

C. R. Baskervill, "Playlists and After Pieces of the Mid-Eighteenth Century," *MP*, xxiii (1925-6), 445-464.

E. B. Watson, *Sheridan to Robertson*, Harvard, 1926.

E. E. Stoll, *Shakespeare Studies*, N. Y., Macmillan, 1927.

W. P. Harbeson, *Elizabethan Influence on Tragedy of the Late Eighteenth and Early Nineteenth Century*, Univ. of Pa., 1927.

T. M. Raysor, "The Downfall of the Unities in the Eighteenth Century," *MLN*, xlii (Jan., 1927), 1-9.

T. M. Raysor, "The Study of Shakespeare's Characters in the Eighteenth Century," *MLN*, xlii (Dec., 1927), 495-500.

A. Nicoll, *A History of Late Eighteenth-Century Drama, 1750-1800*, Cambridge Univ., 1927.

S. A. Small, *Shaksperian Character Interpretation: "The Merchant of Venice,"* Göttingen, 1927.

F. D. Senior, *The Life and Times of Colley Cibber*, London, Constable, 1928.

A. Nicoll, *A History of Restoration Drama*, (2nd ed.), Cambridge Univ., 1928.

D. Nichol Smith, *Shakespeare in the Eighteenth Century*, Oxford, Clarendon, 1928.
L. Woolf, "Is Shakespeare a Great Poet?" [rev. of D. Nichol Smith], *Nat. and Ath.*, xliii (June 30, 1928), 427.
O. Elton, *A Survey of English Literature*, 1730-80, London, E. Arnold, 1928; New York, Macmillan, 1928.
J. S. Smart, *Shakespeare, Truth and Tradition*, London, Arnold, 1928.
A. Bosker, *Literary Criticism in the Age of Johnson*, Groningen, 1929.
[Anon.], "The Jubilee in Honour of Shakespeare" [1769], *TLS.*, April 18, 1929. See also April 25, May 2, 1929.
L. F. Powell, "The Stratford Jubilee," *TLS*, May 16, 1929.
R. W. Babcock, "A Preliminary Bibliography of Eighteenth Century Criticism of Shakespeare," *SP*, Extra Series, No. 1 (May, 1929), 58-98.
A. H. Thorndike, *English Comedy*, N. Y., Macmillan, 1929.
S. Vines, *The Course of English Classicism*, London, Hogarth, 1930.
M. T. Herrick, *The Poetics of Aristotle in England*, Yale Univ., 1930.
R. W. Babcock, "The Attitude Toward Shakespeare's Learning in the Late Eighteenth Century," *PQ*, ix (1930), 116-22.
R. W. Babcock, "The Attack of the Late Eighteenth Century upon Alterations of Shakespeare's Plays," *MLN*, xlv (1930), 446-51.

II. CRITICISM OF INDIVIDUAL SHAKESPEARE CRITICS OF THE EIGHTEENTH CENTURY

J. ADDISON

A. Duval, *Shakespeare et Addison*, 1786.
W. A. Henderson, F. C. Holland, E. H. Marshall, C. Russell, "Addison's Knowledge of Shakespeare," *N & Q*, Aug. 19, Sept. 9, 1893.

J. ADDISON and R. STEELE
>O. Wendt, *Steeles lit. Kritik über Shakespeare im "Tatler" und "Spectator,"* Rostock, 1901.
>Mary Child, "Mr. Spectator and Shakespeare," *The Library,* vi, ser. 2 (Oct., 1905), 360-79.
>J. H. Neumann, "Shakespearean Criticism in the *Tatler* and *Spectator,*" *PMLA,* xxxix (1924), 612-23.

JOHN BELL
>S. Morrison, *John Bell, 1745-1831,* Cambridge Univ., 1930.

J. BOYDELL
>*Shakespeareana* of the N. Y. Shakespeare Soc., iv (1887), 1-14.
>*Magazine of Art,* March, 1886; July, 1897.

E. CAPELL
>J. Nichols, "Biography of Edward Capell," *The Selector,* 1818.
>*Shakespeareana* of the N. Y. Shakespeare Soc., iii (1886), 75-80.
>W. W. Greg, "Editors at Work and Play," *RES,* ii (1926), 173-176.
>C. C. Taylor, "The Date of Edward Capell's *Notes and Readings to Shakespeare,* vol. ii," *RES,* v (1929), 317.

COLLEY CIBBER
>*The Shakespearean,* No. 4, Aug. 15, 1895, No. 9, Jan. 15, 1896.
>R. Dohse, *Colley Cibbers Bühnenbearbeitung . . . von "Richard III,"* Bonn, 1897.
>K. Kneppe, *Verhältnis von Cibbers Papal Tyranny zu Shakespeares "King John,"* Halle, 1901.
>A. C. Sprague, "A New Scene in Colley Cibber's *Richard III,*" *MLN,* xlii (1927), 29-32.
>F. D. Senior, *The Life and Times of Colley Cibber,* London, Constable, 1928.
>D. M. E. Habbema, *An Appreciation of Colley Cibber, Actor and Dramatist,* Amsterdam, 1928.

G. COLMAN, SR.
>R. Erzgraeber, *N. Tates und G. Colmans Bühnenbearbeitung des . . . "King Lear,"* Weimar, 1897.

J. Dennis
H. G. Paul, *John Dennis, His Life and Criticism*, Columbia Univ., 1911.

W. Dodd
P. Fitzgerald, *A Famous Forgery*, London, 1865.
R. W. Chapman, *Papers Written by Dr. Johnson and Dr. Dodd in 1777*, Oxford, Clarendon, 1928.

J. Downes
M. Summers, ed., John Downes' *Roscius Anglicanus*, Fortune Press, 1929.

A. Eccles
Shakespeariana of the N. Y. Shakespeare Soc., iii (1886), 510.

T. Edwards
C. Rinaker, "T. Edwards's Sonnets," [on Warburton], *MLN*, xxx (1915), 232.
A. Dobson, *Later Essays, 1917-20*, London, Milford, 1921.

R. Farmer
W. Maginn, "On the Learning of Shakespeare," in *Shakespeare Papers* (ed. S. MacKenzie, N. Y., 1856—but originally in *Fraser's Magazine*, beginning Sept., 1839).
R. W. Babcock, "The Attitude Toward Shakespeare's Learning in the Late Eighteenth Century," *PQ*, ix (1930), 116-22.

S. Foote
H. M. Belden, *The Dramatic Works of Samuel Foote*, Yale Univ., 1930.
[Anon.], "The English Aristophanes," *TLS*, May 22, 1930.

David Garrick
J. E. Schlegel, *Garrick oder die Englischen Schauspieler*, 1771.
Ida Frick, *Garrick Memoiren*, Dresden, 1849.
J. F. H., "David Garrick" [and the Shakespeare Jubilee of 1769], *Temple Bar Mag.*, xi (June, 1864), 336-55.
G. F. Vincke, "Shakespeare und Garrick," *Jahrb.*, ix (1874), 1-21.
Shakespeariana of the N. Y. Shakespeare Soc., ii (1885), 427-

38; iii (1886), 8, 97-117, 282-88, 382-83, 532; v (1888), 481-4.

G. F. Vincke, "Shakespeare auf der Englischen Bühne seit Garrick," *Jahrb.*, xxii (1887), 1-23.

[Anon.], "Garrick as a Reciter," *The Shakespearean*, No. 33, Jan. 15, 1898.

W. Goerner, *Das Verhältnis von Garricks "The Fairies" zu Shakespeares "Midsummer Night's Dream,"* Halle, 1902.

F. Haase, "David Garrick," *Deutsche Revue*, July, 1903.

R. Fischer, "David Garrick," in No. 207 of *Wiener Abendpost*, Sept. 10, 1904.

C. Gaehde, *David Garrick als Shakespeare Darsteller*, Berlin, 1904.

W. J. Lawrence, "Portraits of Garrick," *Connoisseur*, xi (April, 1905), 211-18.

Mrs. C. Parsons, *Garrick and His Circle*, London, 1906.

L. B. Campbell, "Garrick's Vagary," *Univ. of Wisconsin Studies*, 1916.

B. Münz on E. Soffé's "Garrick als Richard III," *Anglia*, xlii (1918), 330-32.

"Garrick's Lost Jubilee," *TLS*, June 25, 1927.

R. C. Alexander, *The Diary of David Garrick*, Oxford, 1928.

Notes on Sales, Garrick and Shakespeare, *N. Y. Times Bk. Rev.*, June 10, 1928 (p. 24); *TLS*, June 28, 1928 (p. 492).

["Garrick's Adaptations," *German Shakspere Soc.*, xi-xiv, No. 14]Q?

C. R. Williams, "David Garrick, Actor-Manager," *Cornhill*, No. 393 N. S. (March, 1929), 289-97.

D. M. Little, ed., *Pineapples of Finest Flavour* [Garrick Letters], Harvard Univ., 1930.

T. GRAY

"Gray and Bell on Shakespeare," *The Shakespearean*, No. 28, Aug. 15, 1897.

T. HANMER

Shakespeariana of the N. Y. Shakespeare Soc., ii (1885), 378-85.

J. HENDERSON
G. A. Sinclair, "A Successor of David Garrick," *Scottish Hist. Rev.*, i (1904), 306-13.

S. and S. W. H. IRELAND
[Anon.], "Literary Forgeries," *British Quarterly Review*, xlix (Jan., 1869), 1-30.

C. M. Ingleby, *Shakespeare: the Man and the Book*, London, 1877.

C. L. Vorbrodt, "Ireland's Forgeries," *Jahresberecht-Realschule*, Meissen, 1885.

L. Nelson, "Were There Shakespearean Forgers before Ireland?" *New Shakespeareana* of the N. Y. Shakespeare Soc., iii (1904), 77-81.

J. A. Farber, *Literary Forgeries*, London, 1907.

W. Jaggard, *Shakespeare Frauds*, Stratford, 1911.

G. Crosse, "Shakespearean Mares-Nests in the Eighteenth Century," *London Mercury*, iv (1921), 623-32.

N & Q, cxlviii (1925), 408, 447.

J. C. Young, "The Search for Shakespeare Mss. is Never Ending," *N. Y. Times Magazine*, Feb. 21, 1926.

J. L. French, *The Book of the Rogue*, N. Y., Boni and Liveright, 1926.

C. JENNENS
Shakespeariana of the N. Y. Shakespeare Soc., iii (April, 1886), 157-60.

S. JOHNSON
Shakespeariana of the N. Y. Shakespeare Soc., iii (1886), 25-30.

F. C. Hunt, "Dr. Johnson as Editor of Shakespeare," *New Shakespeareana* of the N. Y. Shakespeare Soc., ii (1903), 161-62.

W. Raleigh, *Johnson on Shakespeare*, London, 1908.

A. Morgan, "Shakespearian Criticism not largely indebted to Dr. Johnson," *New Shakespeareana* of the N. Y. Shakespeare Soc., ix (1910), 11.

Hans Meir, *Dr. S. Johnsons Stellung zu den literarischen Fragen seiner Zeit*, Zurich, 1916.

P. H. Houston, *Dr. Johnson*, Harvard, 1923.

Karl Young, "Samuel Johnson on Shakespeare—One Aspect," *Univ. of Wisconsin Studies*, 1923.

J. K. Spittal, *Contemporary Criticism of Johnson*, London, 1923.

Johnson's *Proposals* for his Edition of Shakespeare, 1756, Oxford Univ., 1923.

O. F. Christie, *Samuel Johnson, Essayist*, London, Grant Richards, 1924.

W. P. Courtney and D. Nichol Smith, *A Johnson Bibliography*, Oxford, Clarendon, 1925. [Reprint from 1915.]

J. E. Brown, *The Critical Opinions of Samuel Johnson*, Princeton Univ., 1926.

A. Cuming, "A Copy of Shakespeare's Works which formerly belonged to Dr. Johnson," *RES*, iii (1927), 208-12.

M. R. Small, "The Source of a Note in Johnson's Edition of *Macbeth*," *MLN*, xliii (1928), 34-35.

TLS, June 13, 1929, p. 480.

LORD KAMES

M. Joseph, *Die Psychologie H. Homes*, Halle, 1911.

MRS. CHARLOTTE LENNOX

T. R. Lounsbury, *Shakespeare as a Dramatic Artist*, p. 289, N. Y., Scribner's, 1901.

Karl Young, *Univ. of Wisconsin Studies*, No. 18, 1923, pp. 178 ff.

H. MACKENZIE

H. W. Thompson, ed., *Anecdotes and Egotisms of H. Mackenzie, 1745-1831*, Milford, 1927.

H. W. Thompson, *A Scottish Man of Feeling*, N. Y., Oxford University Press, 1930.

E. MALONE

Sir James Prior, *Life of Edmond Malone*, London, 1860.

Shakespeariana of the N. Y. Shakespeare Soc., iii (1886), 409-13.

J. P. Norris, "Boswell as Malone's Executor," *Shakespeariana* of the N. Y. Shakespeare Soc., iv (1887), 106-8.

[Anon.], "Edmund Malone at Stratford," *Jahrb.*, xxxi (1895), 383-84.
E. Law, *Shakespeare Forgeries*, London, 1911.
E. Law, *More About Shakespeare Forgeries* London, 1913.
W. W. Greg, "Editors at Work and Play," *RES*, ii (1926), 173-76.
S. A. Tannenbaum, *Shakespeare Forgeries in the Revels Accounts*, Columbia Univ., 1928.

J. MILLER
C. W. Nichols, "A Reverend Alterer of Shakespeare," *MLN*, xliv (1929), 30.

MRS. ELIZABETH MONTAGU
John Doran, *A Lady of the Last Century*, London, 1873.
E. J. Climenson, *Elizabeth Montagu, Queen of the Bluestockings*, New York, 1906.
R. Huchon, *Mrs. Montagu and Her Friends*, London, 1907.
R. Blunt, *Mrs. Montagu, Queen of the Blues*, London, Constable, 1923.
J. Busse, *Mrs. Montagu*, London, Gerald Howe, 1928.

M. MORGANN
W. A. Gill, ed., *Morgann's Essay on Falstaff*, London, 1912.
E. E. Stoll, "Falstaff," *MP*, xii (1914-15), 197-240.
E. C. Knowlton, "Falstaff Redux," *JEGP*, xxv (April, 1926), 193-215.
P. L. Carver, "The Influence of Maurice Morgann," *RES*, vi (1930), 320-22.
R. W. Chapman, "Maurice Morgann," *RES*, vi (1930), 455.

A. POPE
Shakespearana of the N. Y. Shakespeare Soc., ii (1885), 182-86, 337-344; iv (1887), App. xxvi-xxxvii (Reprint of *Preface*).
T. R. Lounsbury, *The Text of Shakespeare*, New York, 1906.
H. Schmidt, *Die Shakespeare-Ausgabe von Pope*, Giessen, 1912.
[Anon.], "Pope und Shakespeare," *Jahrb.*, liii (1917), 213.
R. H. Griffith, *A Pope Bibliography*, Texas Univ., 1922. [vol. i, pt. 2, 1928.]

A. Warren, *Alexander Pope as Critic and Humanist*, Princeton Univ., 1929.

J. RANN
Shakespeariana of the N. Y. Shakespeare Soc., iii (1886), 408-9.

I. REED
Shakespeariana of the N. Y. Shakespeare Soc., iii (1886), 510-14.

L. F. Powell, "George Steevens and Isaac Reed's *Biographia Dramatica*," *RES*, v (1929), 288-93. See also *RES*, vi (1930), 186-87.

W. RICHARDSON
R. W. Babcock, "William Richardson's Criticism of Shakespeare." *JEGP*, xxviii (1929), 117-36.

J. RITSON
J. Haslewood, *Joseph Ritson*, [Birmingham Pub. Lib], 1824.
H. A. Burd, "Joseph Ritson, a Critical Biography," *Univ. of Illinois Studies*, vol. ii, No. 3, 1916.
H. A. Burd, "Joseph Ritson and Some Eighteenth-Century Editors of Shakespeare," *Univ. of Wisconsin Shakespeare Studies*, 1916.
W. P. Ker, *Joseph Ritson*, Lecture, Jan. 21, 1922. [*Collected Essays*, London, Macmillan, 1925.]
B. H. Bronson, "Joseph Ritson's Unpublished Notes on Shakespeare," *TLS*, Sept. 5, 1929.

N. ROWE
Shakespeariana of the N. Y. Shakespeare Soc., ii (1885), 65-8; iv (1887), App. xiii-xxv (Reprint of *Life*).
O. Intze, *N. Rowe*, Heidelberg, 1910.
K. N. Colvile, "Shakespeare's First Critical Editor," *Nineteenth Century*, lxxxvi (1919), 266-79.
G. Saintsbury, "Nicholas Rowe," London *Bookman*, lxxvi (April, 1929), 6-8.
[Anon.], "Nicholas Rowe," *TLS*, Oct. 10, 1929.
A. Jackson, "Rowe's Edition of Shakespeare," *The Library*, x (1930), 455-73.

G. STEEVENS
Shakespeariana of the N. Y. Shakespeare Soc., iii (1886), 311-18.

L. F. Powell, "George Steevens and Isaac Reed's *Biographia Dramatica*," *RES*, v (1929), 288-93. See also *RES*, vi (1930), 186-87.

L. THEOBALD
Shakespeariana of the N. Y. Shakespeare Soc., ii (1885), 336-41.

J. C. Collins, *The Porson of Shakespearian Criticism*, London, 1895.

T. R. Lounsbury, *The Text of Shakespeare*, New York, 1906.

R. Schevell, "Theobald's Double Falsehood," *MP.*, ix (Oct., 1911), 269-85; *Jahrb.*, xlviii (1912), 256 [Anon.].

R. F. Jones, *Lewis Theobald*, Columbia Univ., 1919.

W. Mertz, *Die Shakespeare-Ausgabe von Theobald*, Giessen, 1924.

J. T. Hillhouse, ed., *The Grub Street Journal*, Durham, Duke Univ., 1927.

"Affable Hawk" [Desmond MacCarthy], *New Statesman*, xxxiii (July 6, 1929), 407.

Gordon Crosse, "Lewis Theobald," *New Statesman*, xxxiii (July 13, 1929), 433.

J. THOMSON
[G.], "Thomson and Shakespeare," *N & Q*, No. 56, p. 80, Jan. 23, 1869.

THE TONSONS
TLS, Dec. 14, 1922, and Dec. 28, 1922.

HORACE WALPOLE
"H. Walpole as a Shakespeare Skeptic," *Shakespeariana* of the N. Y. Shakespeare Soc., v (1888), 26-27.

W. WARBURTON
J. S. Watson, *Life of W. Warburton* [Birmingham Pub. Lib.], 1863.

Shakespeariana of the N. Y. Shakespeare Soc., ii (1885), 577-82.

N & Q, Feb. 25, March 18, April 8, 1893.

Otto Gans, *Die Shakespeare Ausgabe von Warburton*, Giessen, 1922.

J. WHITE

C. E. Merrill, ed., J. White, *Original Letters of Sir John Falstaff and His Friends*, N. Y., Harper's, 1924.

E. YOUNG

A. Brandl, "E. Young on Original Composition. Ein Beitrag zur Geschichte der Shakespeare-Kritik im 18. Jahrh.," *Jahrb.*, xxxix (1903), 1-42.

III. CRITICISM OF PRE-EIGHTEENTH CENTURY CRITICISM OF SHAKESPEARE

a. General

["Bibliothecary"], "A Shakespearian of the Seventeenth Century" [E. Travers], *N & Q*, June 5, 1880.

W. H. Hudson, "Early Mutilators of Shakespeare," *Poet-Lore*, iv (1892), 360-71.

W. H. Sheran, "Early Critics of Shakespeare," *Catholic World*, lxvi (1897), 74-81.

E. P. Morton, "Shakspere in the Seventeenth Century," *JEGP*, i (1897), 31-44.

J. Routh, "The Classical Rule of Law in English Criticism of the Sixteenth and Seventeenth Centuries," *JEGP*, xii (1913), 612-30.

J. Routh, "The Purpose of Art as Conceived in English Literary Criticism of the Sixteenth and Seventeenth Centuries," *Englische Studien*, xlviii (1915), 124-44.

H. T. Finck, "Shakespearean Operas," American *Nation*, March 23, 1916.

G. Thorn-Drury, *Some Seventeenth-Century Allusions to Shakespeare*, London, 1920.

B. Dobrée, *Restoration Comedy*, Oxford Univ., 1924.

A. H. Tolman, "The Early History of Shakespeare's Reputation," in *Falstaff and Other Shakespearean Topics*, New York, 1925.

H. Spencer, "Improving Shakespeare," *PMLA*, xli (1926), 727-46.
H. Spencer, *Shakespeare Improved*, Harvard Univ., 1927.
P. S. Wood, "The Opposition to Neo-Classicism in England between 1660 and 1700," *PMLA*, xliii (1928), 182-97.
E. J. Dent, *Foundations of English Opera*, Cambridge Univ., 1928.
L. Hotson, *The Commonwealth and Restoration Stage*, Harvard Univ., 1928.
B. Dobrée, *Restoration Tragedy, 1660-1720*, Oxford Univ., 1929.
H. M. Paull, *Literary Ethics: A Study in the Growth of the Literary Conscience*, N. Y., Dutton, 1929.
R. W. Babcock, "The Attack of the Late Eighteenth Century upon Alterations of Shakespeare's Plays," *MLN*, xlv (1930), 446-51.

b. Individuals

CHETTLE

G. Sarrazin, "Chettles *Kind Heart's Dream* und die vermeintliche Ehremerklärung für Shakespeare," *Jahrb.*, xli (1905), 184-86.

DAVENANT

B. Corney, "Davenant on Shakespeare," *N & Q*, July 6, 1867.
K. Elze, "Sir Wm. Davenant," *Jahrb.*, iv (1869), 121-60.
F. G. Fleay, *Davenant's "Macbeth" and Shakespeare's Witches*, 1880.
N. Delius, "Shakespeare's *Macbeth* and Davenant's *Macbeth*," *Jahrb.*, xx (1885), 69-84.
A. C. Ward, F. C. B. Terry, "Davenant on Shakespeare," *N & Q*, April 2, 1892; June 4, 1892.
J. D. E. Williams, *Sir Wm. Davenant's Relation to Shakespeare*, Strassburg, 1905.
[Anon.], "Mistress Davenant," *Jahrb.*, L (1914), 201.
H. Spencer, "Davenant's *Macbeth* and Shakespeare's," *PMLA*, xl (1925), 619-44.

DRYDEN

N. Delius, "Dryden und Shakespeare," *Jahrb.*, iv (1869), 6-40.

F. Bobertag, "Drydens Theorie des Dramas," *Englische Studien*, iv (1881), 373-404.

Max Rosbund, *Dryden als S.-Bearbeiter*, Halle, 1882.

G. S. Collins, *Dryden's Dramatic Theory*, Leipzig, 1892.

Franz Weselman, *Dryden als Kritiker*, Göttingen, 1893.

Margaret Sherwood, *Dryden's Dramatic Theory and Practice*, N. Y., 1898.

F. Hannmann, *Drydens Tragödie "All for Love"* . . . *und ihr Verhältnis zu Shakespeares "Antony and Cleopatra,"* Rostock, 1903.

H. Zenke, *Drydens "Troilus and Cressida" im Verhältnis zu Shakespeares Drama*, Rostock, 1904.

"Dryden on Shakespeare," *N & Q.*, ser. 10, vol. 1, March 19, 1904.

W. E. Bohn, "The Development of John Dryden's Literary Criticism," *PMLA*, xxii (1907), 56-139.

A. Nicoll, *Dryden as an Adapter of Shakespeare*, London, Milford, 1921. Shakespeare Assoc. Pamphlet, No. 8, 1922.

G. R. Noyes, "Crites in Dryden's *Essay of Dramatic Poesie*," *MLN*, xxxviii (1923), 333-37.

T. P. Harrison, Jr., "*Othello* as a model for Dryden in *All for Love*, Univ. of Texas Studies, No. vii, 1927.

T. S. Eliot, ed., Dryden's "*Essay of Dramatic Poesie*," London, Etchells and Macdonald, 1928.

D. T. Starnes, "More about Dryden as an Adapter of Shakespeare," Univ. of Texas Studies, No. viii, 1928.

[Anon.], "Dryden and Artificial Comedy," *TLS*, Aug, 15, 1929.

BEN JONSON

R. Cartwright, *Shakspere and Jonson*, London, 1864.

[Anon.], "Ben Jonson's Quarrel with Shakespeare," *N. Brit. Rev.*, lii (1870), 394-427.

R. Hooper, "Jonson on Shakespeare," *N & Q*, Oct. 14, 1876; March 25, 1882 [by C. M. I.].
H. Grossman, *Ben Jonson als Kritiker*, Jena, 1899.
C. A. Herpich, "Shakespeare and Ben Jonson," *N & Q*, ser. 9, vol. 9, April 12, 1902.
G. Sarrazin, "Nym and Ben Jonson," *Jahrb.*, xl (1904), 213-22.
E. Koeppel, "Ben Jonson und Shakespeare," *Jahrb.*, xlii (1906), 203-8.
C. Bastide, "Shakespeare et Ben Jonson," *Revue Critique d'histoire . . . littérature*, No. 39, Sept. 30, 1907.
M. Castelain, *Ben Jonson*, Paris, 1907.
J. J. Jusserand, *Ben Jonson's Views on Shakespeare's Art* [Stratford Shakespeare, vol. 10, 1907].
"Shakespeare et Ben Jonson," *Revue Germanique*, Jan.-Fev., Mars-Avril, 1907.
P. Butler, "The Eclipse of Ben Jonson's Comedies," *Sewanee Rev.*, xviii (1910), 32-46.
T. Davidson, "Ben Jonson's Testimony on Shakespeare," *New Shakespeareana* of the N. Y. Shakespeare Soc., x (1911), 41-48.
Mary Suddard, "Ben Jonson and Shakespeare," *Contemp. Rev.*, xcix (March, 1911), 316-28.
Rose Cords, "Ben Jonson's *Wit's Academy*," *Jahrb.*, liii (1917), 49-68.
Sir George Greenwood, *Ben Jonson and Shakespeare*, Hartford, 1921.
C. H. Herford and P. Simpson, [ed.], *Ben Jonson*, Oxford, Clarendon, 1925—.

JOHN LACY
E. Moosman, *John Lacy's "Sauny the Scot*," Halle, 1901.

PEPYS
"Pepys on Shakespeare," *N & Q*, ser. 10, vol. 1, April 9 and 30, 1904.
S. Lee, "Pepys and Shakespeare," *Fort. Rev.*, lxxxv (1906), 104-20.

[Anon.], "Pepys und Shakespeare," *Jahrb.*, xliii (1907), 326-27.

PURCELL

[Anon.], "Henry Purcell's Shakespeare Music," *Jahrb.*, lv (1919), 208.

H. Dupré, *Purcell*, Knopf, 1929.

T. RYMER

Reprint of Part of T. Rymer's Criticism of *Othello*, *New Shakespeareana* of the N. Y. Shakespeare Soc., ii (1903), 43-47.

A. Hofherr, *T. Rymer's dramatische Kritik*, Karlsruhe, 1908.

G. B. Dutton, "The French Aristotelian Formalists and Thomas Rymer," *PMLA*, xxix (1914), 152-88.

SHADWELL

W. B. Squire, "The Music of Shadwell's *Tempest*," *Musical Quarterly*, vii (Oct., 1921), 565-78.

D. M. Walmsley, "Shadwell and the Operatic *Tempest*," *RES*, ii (1926), 463-66; iii (1927), 451-53.

A. S. Borgman, *Thomas Shadwell: His Life and Comedies*, N. Y. Univ., 1928.

IV. ON THE EARLY NINETEENTH-CENTURY CRITICISM OF SHAKESPEARE

[N. B. I have ventured to put the three leading critics first.]

S. T. COLERIDGE

A. E. Brae, *Collier, Coleridge, and Shakespeare*, London, 1860. *Shakespeariana* of the N. Y. Shakespeare Soc., iii (1886), 346-52.

J. L. Haney, *The German Influence on S. T. Coleridge*, Univ. of Pa., 1902.

A. A. Helmholtz, "The Indebtedness of S. T. Coleridge to A. W. Schlegel," *Wisconsin Studies*, Old Series, vol. 3, 1907.

J. W. Mackail, *Coleridge's Literary Criticism* (selections), London, 1908.

J. Shawcross, "Coleridge's Lectures on Shakespeare," *N & Q*, ser. 10, vol. xii, July 3, 1909.

E. Pizzo, "S. T. Coleridge als Kritiker," *Anglia*, xl (1916), 201-55.

G. L. Kittredge, *Shakspere*, Harvard, 1916.

Alice D. Snyder, *Coleridge's Critical Principle of the Reconciliation of Opposites*, Ann Arbor, 1918.

A. C. Dunstan, "German Influence on Coleridge," *MLR*, xvii (1922), 272-81; xviii (1923), 183-201.

Alice D. Snyder, "A Note on Coleridge's Shakespeare Criticism," *MLN*, xxxviii (1923), 23-31.

O. Ritter, "Coeridgiana," *Englische Studien*, lviii (1924), 368-89.

T. M. Raysor, "Coleridge's MS. Lectures," *MP*, xxii (1924-25), 17-25.

W. Graham, "Henry Nelson Coleridge, Expositor of Romantic Criticism," *PQ*, iv (1925), 231-38.

H. P. Collins, "The Criticism of Coleridge," *New Criterion*, v (Jan., 1927), 45-56.

T. M. Raysor, "Some Marginalia on Shakespeare by S. T. Coleridge," *PMLA*, xlii (Sept., 1927), 762-65.

D. I. Morrill, "Coleridge's Theory of Dramatic Illusion," *MLN*, xlii (Nov., 1927), 436-44.

D. I, Morrill, "The Chronology of Coleridge's Lecture Notes," *PQ*, vii (1928), 138-50.

B. Fehr, "Das Shakespeare-Erlebnis in der Englischen Romantik," *Jahrb.*, lxv (1929), 8-22.

R. W. Babcock, "The Direct Influence of Late Eighteenth Century Shakespeare Criticism on Hazlitt and Coleridge," *MLN*, xlv (1930), 377-87.

T. M. Raysor, *Coleridge's Shakespearean Criticism*, London, Constable, 1930.

HAZLITT

S. T. Irwin, "Hazlitt and Lamb," *Quart. Rev.*, cciv (1906), 162-86.

K. Hayens, "Heine, Hazlitt and Mrs. Jameson," *MLR*, xvii (1922), 42-49.

R. W. Babcock, "The Direct Influence of Late Eighteenth

Century Shakespeare Criticism on Hazlitt and Coleridge," *MLN*, xlv (1930), 377-87.

LAMB (See also Hazlitt)

P. Fitzgerald, *The Art of the Stage as Set out in Lamb's Dramatic Essays*, London, 1885.

J. B. Matthews, ed., *C. Lamb's Dramatic Essays*, London, 1891.

J. M. Robertson, "The Paradox of Shakespeare" (on Lamb's criticism) in *A Book of Homage to Shakespeare* (ed. I. Gollancz, Oxford, Milford, 1916).

F. W. Roe, "Charles Lamb and Shakespeare," in *Univ. of Wisconsin Shakespeare Studies*, 1916.

E. M. W. Tillyard, *Lamb's Criticism*, Cambridge Univ., 1923.

BYRON

Shakespeariana of the N. Y. Shakespeare Soc., viii (1891), 226-28.

P. H. Churchman, "Byron and Shakespeare," *MLN*, xxiv (1909), 126-27.

KEATS

["S. Urban"], "Keats on Shakespeare," *Gentleman's Mag.*, cclxxx (1896), 105-8.

C. F. E. Spurgeon, *Keats's Shakespeare*, Oxford Univ., 1928.

Virginia Moore, "Keats and Shakespeare," *SRL*, v (June 8, 1929), 1105.

B. Fehr, "Das Shakespeare-Erlebnis in der englischen Romantik," *Jahrb.*, lxv (1929), 8-22.

WORDSWORTH

T. De Quincey, *Shakespeare and Wordsworth* (ed. A. H. Japp, London, 1893).

V. SHAKESPEARE AND FRANCE IN THE EIGHTEENTH CENTURY

a. General

A. Lacroix, *De l'Influence de Shakespeare*, Brussels, 1856.

F. Lotheissen, "Shakespeare in Frankreich," in *Literatur und Gesellschaft in Frankreich zur Zeit der Revolution*, Weimar, 1872.

T. W. Hunt, "Shakespearian Criticism on the Continent [French]," *Shakespeariana* of the N. Y. Shakespeare Soc., i (1884), 167-69.

J. Texte, *J. J. Rousseau et les origins du cosmopolitisme littéraire en France au XVIIIe. siècle*, Paris, 1895.

J. Engel, "Shakespeare in Frankreich," *Jahrb.*, xxxiv (1898), 66-118.

J. J. Jusserand, *Shakespeare in France*, London, 1899.

W. Butterworth, "Shakespeare's French Critics," *Manchester Quarterly*, Oct., 1900.

E. Rédard, *Shakespeare dans les pays de langue française*, Paris, 1901.

J. Rivers, "Shakespeare à la Française," *The Library*, vi, ser. 2 (1905), 78-85.

J. G. Robertson, "The Knowledge of Shakespeare on the Continent at the Beginning of the Eighteenth Century," *MLR*, i (1905), 312-21.

S. Lee, *Shakespeare and the Modern Stage*, London, 1906.

J. Fest, *"Othello" in Frankreich*, Erlangen, 1906.

[Anon.], "Der Continent und Shakespeare im 18. Jahrh.," *Jahrb.*, xliii (1907), 327-28.

F. Baldensperger, "Esquisse d'une histoire de Shakespeare en France," *Études d'Histoire littéraire*, i, 155-216, 1907-10.

G. Lanson, *Manuel bibliographique de la littérature française moderne, 1500-1900*, Paris, 1909-14.

K. Saur, *Shaksperes "Konig Lear" in Frankreich bis zum Jahre 1827*, Ansbach, 1910.

P. Van Tieghem, *L'Année Littéraire, (1754-90)*, Paris, 1917. See *MP*, xvi (1918-19), 223-24.

F. Pascal, "Shakespeare's Introduction into France," *Fort. Rev.*, cxii (1919), 369-80.

H. Thomas, *Shakespeare and Spain*, Oxford Univ., 1922.

D. F. Bond, *Fréron's "L'Année Littéraire" (1754-66) and English Literature*, Univ. of Chicago, 1923.

F. Baldensperger, *Le Mouvement des Idées dans l'Émigration française, 1789-1815*, Paris, 1924.

C. H. Herford, "A Sketch of the History of Shakespeare's Influence on the Continent," *Bulletin* of the John Rylands Library, Manchester, ix (1925), 20-62.
C. M. Haines, *Shakespeare in France*, Oxford Univ., 1925.
Margaret Gilman, "*Othello*" in *French* [from 1745], Paris, 1925.
Mme. J. de Pange, "Shakespeare en France," *Gaulois du dimanche*, Apr. 11, 1925.
O. Vocadlo, "British, French, and German Shares in Shakesperian Criticism," *Casopis pro moderni filologie*, xi, 1924-25.
A. Brandl, *Shakespeare in Frankreich*, Arch. 80, Jg. 149, Bd. 1926.
A. Dubeux, *Les Traductions françaises de Shakespeare*, Paris, 1928.

b. Individuals

DUCIS
E. Gans, *Der "Hamlet" des Ducis und des Shakspeare*, Berlin, 1834.
C. Kuhn, *Über Ducis in seiner Beziehung zu Shakspere*, Jena, 1875.
G. E. Penning, *Ducis als Nachähmer S.'s*, Bremen, 1884.
E. P. Dargan, "Shakespeare and Ducis," *MP*, x (1912-13), 137-78.
L. S. MERCIER
O. Zollinger, "Ein französischer Shakespeare-Bearbeiter des 18. Jahrhunderts," *Jahrb.*, xxxviii (1902), 98-117.
PREVOST
[Anon.], "Abbé Prévost und Shakespeare," *Jahrb.*, lv (1919), 209; lvii (1921), 125.
G. R. Havens, *The Abbé Prévost and English Literature*, Princeton Univ., 1921.
LE TOURNEUR
M. C. Cushing, *Pierre Le Tourneur*, N. Y., 1909.
VOLTAIRE
A. Schmidt, *Voltaires Verdienste um die Einführung Shakespeares in Frankreich*, Königsberg, 1864.

W. König, "Voltaire und Shakespeare," *Jahrb.*, x (1875), 259-310.

Lehmann, *Über Voltaires Reformversuch und seine Stellung zu Shakespeare*, München, 1878.

J. Strum, *"Zaïre" et "Othello,"* Crefeld, 1879.

W. Asch, *Shakespere's and Voltaire's "Julius Cæsar" Compared*, Gardeleben, 1881.

C. M. I., H. G. Hope, "Voltaire's Criticism on *Hamlet*," *N & Q*, Aug. 19, Oct. 7, 1882.

"V. contre S.," "Baretti contre Voltaire," *La Défense*, Sept. 25 et 26, 1882.

K. Adolph, *Voltaire et le théâtre de Shakespeare*, Sorau, 1883.

J. Schuhmann, "Baretti als Kritiker Voltaires," *Archiv.*, lxix (1883), 469-72.

"Voltaire et Shakespeare," *Intermédiaire*, Aug. 25, 1884.

J. C. Collins, *Bolingbroke . . . . . and Voltaire in England*, London, 1886.

Shakespeariana of the N. Y. Shakespeare Soc., ii (1885), 313-20; iv (1887), 532-33.

E. A. E. M. Déschanel, *Le Théâtre de Voltaire*, Paris, 1888.

H. Morf, *Die Cäsartragödien Voltaires und Shakespeares*, Appeln, 1888.

P. Trabaud, *Étude sur le Jules César de Shakespeare et Voltaire*, [Paris?], 1889.

A. Ballantyne, *Voltaire's Visit to England, 1726-29*, London, 1893.

E. Bertrand, *Shakespeare et Voltaire*, Grenoble, 1896.

H. Lion, *Les Tragédies et les Théories dramatiques de Voltaire*, Paris, 1896.

G. Larroumet, *V.-L'Influence de Shakespeare: "Zaïre,"* Paris, 1900.

E. Faguet, "Voltaire critique de Shakespeare," *Revue des Cours et Conférences*, Nov. 15, 1900.

T. R. Lounsbury, *Shakespeare and Voltaire*, New York, 1902.

E. J. Dubedout, "Shakespeare et Voltaire," *MP*, iii (1905-6), 305-16.

F. H. Schwartz, "Voltaire und N. Rowe," *Englische Studien*, xxxviii (1907), 134-35.
[Anon.], "Voltaire und Shakespeare," *Jahrb.*, xliii (1907) 328.
J. C. Collins, *Voltaire, Montesquieu, and Rousseau in England*, London, 1908.
J. Petkovic, *Voltaires Tragödie "La Mort de César" verglichen mit Shakespeares "Julius Cæsar,"* Wien, 1909.
H. L. Bruce, *Voltaire on the English Stage*, Univ. of California Publications, No. 8, 1918.
R. W. McKnight, "Shakespeare [and] Voltaire," *Poet-Lore*, xxxi (1920), 604-15.
C. Serrurier, "Voltaire et Shakespeare à propos du monologue d'Hamlet," *Neophilologus*, v (1919-20), 205-9.
R. S. Crane, "The Diffusion of Voltaire's Writings in England," *MP*, xx (Feb., 1923), 261-74.
R. Aldington, *Voltaire*, London, 1925.
C. B. Chase, *The Young Voltaire*, N. Y., Longmans, 1926.
E. Sonet, *Voltaire et l'Influence anglaise*, Rennes: Ouest-Eclair, 1926.
F. Baldensperger, "Voltaire anglophile avant son séjour d'Angleterre," *Revue de la littérature comparée*, ix (1929), 25.
G. R. Havens and N. L. Torrey, "Voltaire's Books: A Selected List," *MP*, xxvii (1929), 1-22.
N. L. Torrey, "Voltaire's English Notebook," *MP*, xxvi (1929), 307-25.
Mary-Margaret H. Barr, *A Century of Voltaire Study*, New York, Institute of French Studies, 1929.
R. W. Babcock, "The English Reaction Against Voltaire's Criticism of Shakespeare," *SP*, xxvii (1930), 609-25.

VI. SHAKESPEARE AND GERMANY IN THE EIGHTEENTH CENTURY

This book is not at all concerned with German criticism of Shakespeare in the eighteenth century because that criticism did not influence contemporary English critics. Inasmuch, however, as this German opinion does represent something of a parallel development with the rising idolatry in England throughout the late eighteenth century, it will perhaps be relevant to list some modern criticism of these men who helped confirm Coleridge and Hazlitt in their adoration of Shakespeare. It is obvious that Mr. L. M. Price's monumental bibliography of Anglo-German relationships (see below, 1919-20) is a fundamental work, which will brook little expansion. I shall merely venture, therefore, to present a few representative texts, the majority of which were not included by Mr. Price, in most instances simply because ten years have elapsed since the production of his book and much has been done within this decade.

a. General

E. A. Hagen, *Shakespeares Ersten Erscheinen auf dem Bühnen Deutschlands*, Königsberg, 1832.

A. Stahr, *Shakespeare in Deutschland*, Leipzig, 1843.

Shakespeare Literature in Deutschland [catalogue], Cassel, 1852.

P. H. Sillig, *Shakespeare Literature bis Mitte 1854*, Leipzig, 1854.

A. Koberstein, "Shakespeare in Deutschland," *Jahrb.*, i (1865), 1-17.

Max Ring, *Shakespeare in Deutschland*, 1867 (Sonntagsbeilage du Vossischen Zeitung).

C. C. Hense, "Deutsche Dichter in ihrem Verhältnis zu Shakespeare," *Jahrb.*, v (1870), 107-47.

R. Gericke, "Shakespeare Aufführungen in Leipzig und Dresden, 1778-1817," *Jahrb.*, xii (1877), 182-221.

Max Koch, *Über die Beziehung der englischen Literatur zur Deutschen im Achtzehnten Jahrh.*, Leipzig, 1883.

T. W. Hunt, "Shakespearian Criticism on the Continent." *Shakespeariana* of the N. Y. Shakespeare Soc., ii (1885), 55-58.

W. Kühn, *Shakespeares Tragödien auf dem deutschen theater im XVIII. Jahrh.*, Munich, 1886.

E. Walther, *Der Einfluss Shakespeares auf die Sturm und Drang periode unserer Litteratur im 18. Jahrh.*, Ostern, 1890.

"Early Knowledge of Shakespeare on the Continent in the Eighteenth Century," *New Shakespeariana* of the N. Y. Shakespeare Soc., vi (1907), 24-25.

H. Jones, *Shakespeare and Germany*, London, 1916.

B. Münz on E. Soffé's "Shakespeare auf dem deutschen Theater," *Anglia*, xlii (1918), 332-36.

M. B. Ruud, *Shakespeare in Denmark*, Univ. of Minnesota, 1920.

L. M. Price, *English-German Literary Influences*, Univ. of California, 1919-20.

J. A. Kelly, *England and Englishmen in German Literature of the Eighteenth Century*, Columbia Univ., 1921.

C. H. Herford, "A Sketch of the History of Shakespeare's Influence on the Continent, "*Bulletin* of the John Rylands Library, Manchester, ix (1925), 20-62.

F. W. Stokoe, *German Influence in the English Romantic Period: 1788-1818*, Cambridge Univ., 1926.

V. Stockley, *German Literature as Known in England, 1750-1830*, London, Routledge, 1929.

b. Individuals

GOETHE

G. R. Schottenfels, *Goethe's Shakespeare Criticism*, Univ. of Chicago, 1912.

K. Haumann, *Shakespeares Wirkung auf Goethe*, Berlin, 1916.

G. H. Eckert, *Goethes Urteile über Shakespeare*, Göttingen, 1918.

W. Diamond, "Wilhelm Meister's Interpretation of *Hamlet*," *MP*, xxiii (1925-26), 89-101.

W. Deetjen, "Goethe und Tiecks elizabethanische Studien," *Jahrb.*, lxv (1929), 175-83.

LESSING

Shakespeariana of the N. Y. Shakespeare Soc., ii (1885), 56-57.

[Review of L.'s *Hamburgische Dramaturgie*], *MLN*, xvii (1902), 318-22.

M. S. Czeke, *Lessing és Shakespeare*, Budapest, 1905.

J. G. Robertson, "Notes on Lessing's *Hamburgische Dramaturgie*," *MLR*, xv (1920), 392-405.

O. Walzel, "Der Kritiker Lessing und Shakespeare," *Jahrb.*, lxv (1929), 23-48.

LICHTENBERG

G. Betz., "Lichtenberg as a Critic of the English Stage," *JEGP*, xxiii (1924), 270-88.

SCHILLER

"Zur Aufnahme Shakespeares und Vorbereitung Schillers im deutschen Bühnendrama," *Festschrift zum 19. Neuphilologentage* (Berlin: Stolberg, 1924).

THE SCHLEGELS (See also under Coleridge).

N. Delius, *Die Schlegel-Tieckische Shakespeare-Übersetzung*, Bonn, 1846.

C. Hallam, A. W. Schlegel's "Competent Shakespearian Criticism," *Shakespeariana* of the N. Y. Shakespeare Soc., ix (1892), 85-89.

J. W. Scholl, "F. Schlegel and Goethe, 1790-1802," *PMLA*, xxi (1906), 40-192.

L. TIECK

A. Beyfuss, *Tieck und Hamlet*, Berlin, 1826.

N. Delius, *Die Schlegel-Tieckische Shakespeare-Übersetzung*, Bonn, 1846.

G. H. Danton, *Tieck's Essay on the Boydell Shakespeare*, Indianapolis, 1912.

H. Lüdecke, *L. Tieck's Shakespeare-Studien*, Frankfurt, 1917.

H. Lüdecke, "Ludwig Tieck's erste Shakespeare-Uebersetzung (1794)," *Jahrb.*, lvii (1921), 54-64.

A. Eichler, "Tieck's Shakespeare-Novellen," *Englische Studien*, lvi (1922), 254-80.

MLR, xvii (1922), 103-5; xviii (1923), 234-36.

O. Weissert, *Ludwig Tieck als Kritiker des Dramas u. Theaters*, Munich, 1928.

W. Deetjen, "Goethe und Tiecks elizabethanische Studien," *Jahrb.*, lxv (1929), 175-83.

WIELAND

M. Simpson, *Eine Vergleichung der Wielandischen Shakespeare-Übersetzung mit dem Originale*, Munich, 1898.

INDEX

Abington, Mrs., 39.
Actor, The, 9.
Adaptations, of Shakespeare's Plays. *See* Alterations.
Addison, Joseph, 5, 106, 231.
Adler, Herr J., xvii n., xxi.
Akenside, Mark, 150.
"Alciphron," presumably George Steevens, 13.
All's Well That Ends Well, 15, 186, 224.
Alterations, of Shakespeare's Plays, 9, 82-89, 217.
Analytical Review, 15, 67, 72, 75, 80, 98, 101, 102, 106, 107, 119-20, 139.
Answer to Pope's Preface, by Roberts, 20.
Anthologia Hibernica, 130, 205.
Anti-Jacobin Review, 197, 231, 234.
Antonio (in *Merchant of Venice*), 141.
"Apalachian" Mountains, 208.
Aphorisms, of Shakespeare, 213.
Apocrypha, Shakespeare, 16-17.
Apology for the Life of Colley Cibber, An, by C. Cibber, 141.
"Apology for Plagiarism, An," 193.
Apology for the Life of George Anne Bellamy, An, 146.
Appeal to Nature, 72, 75-76.
Appel à toutes les Nations de l'Europe d'un Ecrivain Anglais, by Voltaire, 91 ff., 91 n.
Ariel, 216.
Aristotle, 48-49, 53, 55, 57, 98, 215. *See* Unities.
Arne, Dr., 39.
Association of ideas, Locke's doctrine of, 178 ff.; applied to Shakespeare, 8, 176-82, 222-23.
As You Like It, 13, 117, 179, 193.
Aubrey, attacked by Farmer, 59.
Ayscough, Samuel, 14, 19, 233.

Baconian heresy, 20 n.
Banquo, 190.
Baskervill, Prof. C. R., 20-21 n.

Beattie, James, 49, 102 n., 109, 137, 178.
Beaumont, Francis, 17, 195, 199.
Beauties of English Drama, 118.
Beauties of Shakespeare, 117.
Becket, Andrew, 18-19.
"Bedlam beggar," Edgar as a, 189.
Bee, The, 29, 34, 49, 67, 69, 71, 72, 76, 77, 80, 87, 98, 101, 104, 105, 106, 107, 114, 120, 124, 125, 129, 134, 137-38, 166, 205-6, 235.
Beeston's butcher story, 59.
Bellamy, George Anne, 116.
Bell's edition of Shakespeare, 85, 102.
Belsham, Thomas, 49.
Benson, John, xix n.
Berenger, Richard, verses of quoted, 202.
Berkeley, George, xxv, 155.
Berkenhout, Dr. John, xxiii, 47, 52, 54-55, 72.
Bertram, 236.
Bibliographical Account of English Theatrical Literature, xix n.
Bibliography, Shakespearean, 20.
Bibliotheca Farmeriana, 20.
Biographia Dramatica, 17, 188, 203-4.
Biographia Literaria, xxiii.
Biography, Shakespeare, interest in, 20-27.
Blackadder, Captain, 153.
Blackwoods, 225, 243.
Blair, H., 49, 54, 66 and 66 n., 73, 102, 116, 137, 188.
Blank verse, 3, 5, 7, 79-80 (defended), 93, 100 (praised by Mrs. Montagu), 217.
Bluestockings, Mrs. Montagu leader of, 108.
Boaden, James, 25.
Bodde, D., *Shakespeare and the Ireland Forgeries*, 27 n.
Bolingbroke, 101.
Boswell, James, 24, 38, 96.
Boydell, John, 18.
Bradley, A. C., xxi, xxii, xxv, xxvi, xxviii, 242, 243.
Bristol Lectures, 236.

298 INDEX

British Critic, 33, 142, 182, 193, 234, 238, 239.
British Magazine, xxiv n., 48, 61, 67, 71, 85, 86, 102, 113, 115, 124, 235, 139, 200.
British Muse, The, 117.
Buckingham[shire], Duke of, 86.
Buffoonery, 73, 75, 146.
Bunbury, H. W., 18.
Burke, Edmund, 8, 156, 162-63, 177-78.
Burletta of Macbeth, 214.
Busts of Shakespeare, 22 n.

Calderon, 195.
Caliban, 77, 139, 216.
Capell, E., 16, 20, 29, 64, 191.
Carey, G. S., 39.
Cassio, 70, 141.
Castle of Otranto, 96.
Chalmers, George, 26, 191, 199.
Chalmers' Apology, 197, 238.
Chandos portrait of Shakespeare, 22.
Chanlieu, 101.
Characterization, Shakespeare's powers of praised, 5, 7. See Characters of Shakespeare.
Characters of Shakespeare, 135-54, 219-21. See Psychologizing of Shakespeare and also names of particular characters.
Chesterfield's Letters, 116.
Christmas Masque, Johnson's, 181.
Chronology of Shakespeare's Plays, interest in, 15, 212.
Cibber, Colley, 141, 144, 217, 231, 233.
Citizen of the World, Goldsmith's, xix.
Classical knowledge, Shakespeare's, 4, 6. See also Shakespeare's Classical Knowledge.
Closet drama, 231.
Closet scene in Hamlet, 196.
Clutton-Brock, 243.
Coleridge, Samuel Taylor, xxviii, 41, 45, 49, 130, 175, 208, 214-44 (indebtedness to late eighteenth-century critics), 233-39.
Collection and Selection of English Prologues and Epilogues . . . Garrick, by Griffith, 200.

Collection of English Words Used by Shakespeare, by George Mason, 20.
Collier's Diary, 221.
Collins, M. J. C., 242.
Coleman, George, 16, 22, 34, 40, 75, 86, 93, 109-10, 116, 136, 187, 203, 231, 59 ff. (attacked by Farmer), 60 (reaction to Farmer's work on Shakespeare's learning).
Comedy of Errors, 192, 215, 224.
Commentators, attacks on, 28-30.
Comments on the Last Edition of Shakespeare's Plays, by J. M. Mason, 13, 20.
Complete Art of Poetry, by Gildon, 118.
Concordance to Shakespeare, A, by Andrew Becket, 18-19.
Concordances, 18-19.
Congreve, William, 78.
Conventions, dramatic, 194.
Cooke, William, 49.
Cordelia, 131.
Coriolanus, 166.
Corneille, 29, 95, 99, 102.
Cornwall, Barry, 227.
Correspondent, an Original Novel, The, 138.
Costumes, in Shakespeare's Plays, 213.
Cotes, Thomas, xix n.
"The Country Girl," by "Mr. G.," quoted, 201.
Craig, 152 (article by in Lounger), 236, 243.
Crewe, Mrs., 36-37.
Critical Review, xxiv n., 20, 23, 47-48, 55, 60-61, 75, 103, 124, 154, 163-64, 172, 182, 203, 230, 231, 234, 237, 238, 239.
Criticism, historical, 72, 183-97; psychological, 155-82.
Criticism of Shakespeare in 18th cen., four stages of, xx.
Croft, J. A., 118.
Cumberland, in his Observer, 146-47.
Cursory Criticisms, 13.
Cymbeline, 103, 117.

Danes, the, in Hamlet, 95.
D'Argenson, Marquis, 101.
Darnley, Lord, 153.
Davies, Tom, 14, 17, 52-53, 63, 73, 77, 80, 87, 98, 99, 101, 109, 114,

INDEX

116, 118, 124, 129, 133, 137, 138, 139, 140, 144, 146, 151, 185, 188, 196, 204, 240.
Decorum, 3, 6, 70-80, 94 ff., 99, 216.
Dekker, Thomas, 194, 198.
Dennis, J., 5, 20.
"Dervise, the," 135, 136.
Des Cartes [Descartes], René, 178.
Desdemona, 141.
Dibdin's *History*, xix.
Dictionnaire Philosophique, Voltaire's, 96.
Die Kritik in der Englischen Literatur des 17. und 18. Jahrhunderts, by Paul Hamelius, xix.
Dissertations, Beattie's, 137.
Dissertations on the Prophecies of the Old Testament, David Levi's, 142.
Dodd, Rev. William, 58, 117, 118, 231, 241.
Double Falsehood. Theobald's, 16, 24.
Dowden, Edward, 243.
Dramatic Censor, 143.
Dramatic Miscellanies, by Tom Davies, 137, 146.
Dramatic Unities of Shakespeare, by N. J. Halpin, 242.
Drury Lane, 39.
Dryden, John, xxiv, 4, 5, 34, 58, 78, 116, 118, 217.
Dudley, Sir. H. B., 36.

Edgar (in *Lear*), 77, 189.
Edinburgh Review, 213, 214.
Editions of Shakespeare, interest in, 11-14, 15 n., 212.
Elements of Criticism, by Kames, xxiii, 156.
Elizabeth, Queen, and *Merry Wives of Windsor*, *185*; and the *Sonnets*, 26; *Hamlet* as tribute to, 153.
Elizabethan Age, 93, 189, 194.
Elizabethan drama, 105.
Elizabethan stage properties, 196.
Elliston, R. W., 214.
"Elysium of the Poets," by Ogilvie, quoted, 200.
Enquiry into the Origin of our Ideas of the Sublime and Beautiful, by Burke, 156, 162-63.
Epistle from Shakspeare to His Countrymen, 23.
Epistle to Voltaire, by Arthur Murphy, 96.

Essay (1712), by Dennis, 20.
Essay on Criticism, by Pope, 123.
Essay on Shylock, by Richard Hole, 189.
Essay on the Character of Hamlet, by F. Pilon, 119 n.
Essay on the Dramatic Character of Sir John Falstaff, by Maurice Morgann, 154, 229, 230.
Essay on the Learning of Shakespeare, by Richard Farmer, xxvi, 16 n., 58 ff., 240-41.
Essay on the Writings and Genius of Shakespeare, by Mrs. Montagu, 108 ff. and 108 n.
Essay on Tragedy, by Hume, 161, 162.
Essays, second and third series, by Richardson, 137.
Etymologist, The, title-page of, 28.
European Magazine, 21, 47, 50, 54, 76, 100, 114, 121, 144, 188.
Exeter Society *Essays*, 9, 15, 21, 33, 105, 138, 186, 193, 238.

Fairies of Shakespeare, 76.
Falstaff, 5, 103, 129, 133, 143, 145-48, 164, 170-72, 178, 195, 204, 208, 221, 229, 233, 235, 239, 240, 242, 243.
Falstaff's Letters, by White, 237.
Falstaff's Wedding, by Kenrick, 31-33.
Farmer, Richard, xxvi, 16, 18, 20, 58 ff. (on the learning of Shakespeare), 80, 184-85, 191, 193, 194, 215, 226, 231, 233, 234, 239, 240-41.
Felton, S., 18.
Felton portrait of Shakespeare, 22.
Female Mentor, 139.
Ferney, an Epistle to Mr. de Voltaire, 106.
"fishmonger passage" in *Hamlet*, 181.
Fletcher, John, 17, 67, 195.
"Flower-in-a-vase" idea of Hamlet, 152, 243.
Fool, in *Lear*, 77, 86.
Fools of Shakespeare, 140, 188.
Foote, S., 95.
Foreign translations of Shakespeare, 15 n.
Forgeries, of the Irelands, 23 ff.

INDEX

Fragment on Shakspeare, by Martin Sherlock, 137, 241.
Francisco (in *Hamlet*), 222.
French drama attacked, 101-2.
French school, of criticism, xix.
Friend, The, 234.
Fuller, Thomas, on Shakespeare's learning, 57, 58.

Garrick, David, 9 n., 20, 32, 39, 86, 87 ff., 108, 121, 124, 140, 200, 201, 202, 213, 217, 230, 231.
Garrick's Jubilee, 202.
Gascoigne, George, 191.
Genest, John, 84.
Gentleman, Francis, 40, 46-47, 70, 73, 80, 85, 89, 99-100, 113, 116, 118, 128, 131, 132, 133, 134, 136, 138, 140, 143, 144, 148, 154, 167, 173, 187, 196, 202, 231, 235, 240, 243.
Gentleman's Magazine, xxiv n., 10, 17, 31, 38-39, 40, 54, 58, 63, 66, 67, 79, 103, 108, 119, 121, 131, 139, 192, 196, 203, 206.
Gervinus, xviii.
Ghost, in *Hamlet,* 77-78, 216, 236, 244.
Ghost, in *Macbeth,* 77.
Ghosts, in *Richard III,* 77.
Ghosts, Shakespeare's, 198; Elizabethan attitude toward, 189 and n., 190.
Gildon, C., xxiv, 4, 20, 58, 118.
Glossaries, 19-20, 213.
Glossary, Hanmer's, 19.
"God of the writers idolatry," 122 n.
"God of their idolatry, the," 202, 203. *See also* Idolatry.
Goethe's *Wilhelm Meister* idea of Hamlet as a flower-in-a-vase, 152.
Goldsmith, Oliver, xxiv, 230-31.
Gravediggers, in *Hamlet,* 86.
Graveyard scene, in *Hamlet,* 73.
Greek chorus, uniqueness of, 53, 54, 63, 66.
Griffith, Mrs. Elizabeth, 16, 51, 52, 56, 67, 75, 80, 85, 98, 105, 113, 116, 123, 124-25 (eulogy on Shakespeare's natural genius), 133, 134, 136, 140, 164-65, 185, 188, 194, 203, 240.
Griffith, R., 200.

Guildenstern, 91 ff.

Haines, C. M., xxii, xxiii, xxv, 47 n.
Hall, J., 18.
Hallam, George, xvii, xviii.
Halliwell-Phillipps, J. O., xxviii.
Halpin, N. J., 242.
Hamelius, Paul, xix, xx, xxv-xxvii *passim.*
Hamlet, 30, 33 (operas based on), 73, 75, 77, 85-87 (Garrick's adaptation of), 88, 91 ff. (Voltaire's mistranslation of), 99, 116, 117, 128, 131, 153, 175, 181, 192, 224.
Hamlet, character of, 6, 7, 8, 13, 148-53, 160, 163, 172-75, 190, 196, 198, 221, 233, 236, 241. *See also* Romantic heresy of Hamlet.
Hamlet—Mary-Queen-of-Scots theory, 24.
Hanmer, Sir Thomas, xxi, 5, 6, 7, 8, 19, 231.
Harding, S. and E., 18.
Harrington, Dr., of Bath, 121.
Harris, James, 109, 151, 175, 236, 243.
Hawkins, T., 68, 196.
Hayward, T., 117.
Hazlitt, William, xxviii, 41, 175, 212-14 *passim.*
Heath, B., 59.
Henderson's acting of Hamlet, 150, 153 n., 174.
Henry IV, Part 1, 71, 74, 117, 192.
Henry IV, Part 2, 117, 133.
Henry IV, character of, 186.
Henry V, 117, 186, 192.
Henry VI, 16, 117, 192.
Henry VIII, 13, 16, 17.
Heron's Letters, 231.
Hibernian Magazine, 66, 67, 100, 101, 185, 192, 231.
Hill, Aaron, 87, 95.
Historical Account of the English Stage, by Malone, 21, 197.
Historical criticism, 72, 183-97.
Hodson, William, 18.
Hole, Richard ["T.O."], 9, 33, 105, 120, 134, 138, 141, 145, 186 n., 189, 190, 198, 241.
Holinshed, 191, 193.

INDEX

Homer, 69, 125, 135.
Horatio, 92, 128.
Howe, P. P., 222.
Hull, Thomas, 143 n.
Hume, David, xxv, 8, 155, 161, 233.
Humour, and tragicomedy, 76.
Hurdis, J., 15, 20, 241.

Iago, 140-41, 145, 172, 220, 233, 238.
Idolatry, 8, 11, 23-24, 41.
"Idolatry ad astra," 200-8, 225.
Idolatry, theatrical, 202.
Ignorance, of Shakespeare in early 18th century, 8.
Illustrations (pictures) of Shakespeare's text, 18.
Imitation of models, 6, 33-35, 214.
Imogen, 139, 163, 232.
Imperfect Hints toward a New Edition of Shakespeare, by S. Felton, 18.
Impression and understanding, Morgann's distinction between, 165, 170-78.
Index to Shakespeare. See Twiss, F.
"Index to the remarkable passages and words . . . Shakespeare," by S. Ayscough, 19.
Inquiry into the Authenticity of Certain Miscellaneous Papers, etc., by E. Malone (*in re* Ireland forgeries), 26.
"Interview at the Shrine of Shakspeare," 23.
"Interview, or Jack Falstaff's Ghost, The," 200.
Irelands, the, 20, 23 ff., 231, 237; Ireland forgeries, 23-27, 27 n., 238.
Iron Chest, The, 35.

Jackson, William, 29-30 (on commentators), 62 (praises Farmer), 114, 136-37, 143, 146, 234, 237, 241.
Jane Shore, 35.
Janssen's portrait of Shakespeare, 22.
Jerningham, E., 18.
Jews, Elizabethan attitude toward, 189 and n. See Shylock.

Johnson, C. F., xxi.
Johnson, Samuel, xviii, xix, xxiii, 6, 22, 29, 30, 46 n., 49 ff. (on the unities), 55, 56, 62 (to Dr. Farmer), 65, 67, 68, 76, 78, 80, 96, 97, 108 (on Mrs. Montagu), 119, 121, 130, 131, 133, 134, 146, 172, 183, 198, 230-31, 233, 234, 239, 241, 244.
Johnson and Steevens' edition (1773), 8, 61, 62; second edition (1778), 15, 20, 21, 22, 83, 200; edition of 1785, 9, 20; fourth edition (1793), 13, 20, 83.
Johnsonian analysis of dramatic verisimilitude, 214.
Jonson, Ben, xxiv, 21, 45, 58 (denies Shakespeare's learning), 73, 118, 181, 224.
Jubilee of 1769. See Garrick's Jubilee.
Jubilee, year of the great, 200-1.
Jubilees, 38-41, 214.
Juliet, 222.
Julius Caesar, 13, 71, 73, 103 (Voltaire's translation of), 115, 117, 181.
Julius Caesar, Buckinghamshire's, 86, 87.
Justice Shallow, 148.

Kames, Lord, xxi, xxiii, xxiv, 8, 49, 155, 156, 162, 176 n., 238.
Keate, George, 106.
Kemble, J. P., 47, 134, 144-45, 168-69, 175, 231, 232, 241.
Kenrick, William, 31, 37-38 (first public lecturer on Shakespeare), 89, 124, 131, 133, 134, 136, 145, 241.
Key to the Drama, A, 191.
King John, 117, 192.
King Lear, 9, 13, 77, 86, 117, 143, 191, 224; Cibber's, 87; Coleman's, 85, 87; Tate's, 85, 87. See also Lear, character of.
Kittredge, G. L., 243.
Knight, Charles, xvii-xviii, 240, 244.
Knowledge of the Classics. See Shakespeare's classical knowledge.
Knowlton, E. C., 243.
Kyd, Thomas, 194.

INDEX

Lady's Magazine, 70, 72, 231.
Laertes, 91.
La Fare, 101.
La Fontaine, 205.
Lamb, Charles, xxviii, 41, 212-44 passim.
La Mort de César, 101.
Language of Shakespeare. See Shakespeare's language.
La Place, 103.
Lear, character of, 77, 130, 142-43 (Lear's madness), 164, 220.
Lear. See *King Lear*.
Learning of Shakespeare. See Shakespeare's knowledge of the classics.
Le Blanc, Abbé, 105-6.
Lectures on Oratory and Criticism, by J. Priestley, 155-56.
Lectures on Shakespeare, 37-38, 214.
Lee, Harriet, 35.
Lee, Sir Sidney, xvii and xviii n.
Letter to David Garrick, by Richard Warner, 61.
Letter to the French Academy, by Voltaire, 107.
Letter to George Steevens, A, by James Boaden, 25.
Letter to the Rev. Richard Farmer, 13, 62, 194.
Letters of Falstaff, by James White. See *Original Letters of Sir John Falstaff*.
Letters on the English Nation, by Abbé Le Blanc, 105-6.
Le Tourneur, P., 103.
Levi, David, 141.
Life and Death of Cromwell, The, 17.
Life of David Garrick, by Arthur Murphy, 39.
Lloyd, R., xxiv.
Locke, John, xxv, 155, 164, 178, 179 ff.
Locrine, 17.
Lofft, C., *Aphorisms from Shakespeare*, 213.
London Magazine, xxiv n., 19, 33, 61, 81, 99, 100, 101, 103, 107, 116, 151, 163, 175, 231.
London Prodigal, The, 17.
Looker-On, 34, 185.
Lounger, 67, 147, 154, 185, 192, 197, 231, 235.

Lounsbury, T. R., 90 n., 97 n.
Love's Labour's Lost, 16.
Lowe, R. W., xix n.

Macaroni and Theatrical Magazine, 48, 50, 52, 85.
Macbeth, 13, 67, 73, 77, 78, 88, 185, 192, 231; Betterton's alterations of, 8; Davenant's, 87; Garrick's 9 n., 87.
Macbeth, character of, 44-45, 128, 134, 144, 158, 160, 167-76, 190, 220-21, 232, 241.
Macbeth, Lady, 166, 232, 234.
Macbeth Reconsidered, by Kemble, 47, 168-69.
Macduff, 193.
Macduff, Lady, 70.
Machiavel [*sic*], 141, 205.
Mackenzie, H., xxiv, 147, 236, 243.
Mackenzie, Roy, 243.
McMillan Collection, University of Michigan, 31.
Maginn, W., 65 n.
Mallet, David, 28.
Malone, E., xviii, 9, 13, 14, 15, 16-17, 18, 20, 21, 24, 25, 33, 62, 83, 144-45, 179, 184-85, 192, 194, 197, 212, 226, 231, 241.
Malone's edition (1790), 200.
Man and Wife; or the Shakespeare Jubilee, by G. Coleman, 40, 73, 110, 187.
Marlborough, Duke of, 36-37.
Marlowe, Christopher, 191.
Mason, George, 20.
Mason, J. M., 13, 17, 63, 116, 119, 120, 152, 184, 188, 195, 198, 241.
Mathias, T., 29, 182.
Measure for Measure, 87, 117, 192, 193.
Merchant of Venice, xxiv n., 13, 116, 117, 189.
Mercutio, 115.
Merope, tr. by Aaron Hill, 95.
Merry Wives of Windsor, 185.
Middleton, Thomas, 192, 217, 224, 231.
Midsummer Night's Dream, 117.
Miles Gloriosus, 195.
Milton, John, 106.
Miranda, 166.
Mirror, 154, 192, 231, 234.

INDEX 303

Modern characters from Shakespeare, 35-37, 214.
Modernity of late eighteenth-century historical criticism, 198.
Molière, 74.
Montagu, Mrs. Elizabeth, xxi, xxii, 29, 49, 52 (attacks pedants), 56, 61 (on Shakespeare's learning), 67, 68, 76, 77, 78 (on Shakespeare's puns), 79 (on blank verse), 80, 97-98, 99, 100, 102, 103, 105, 106, 109 (importance as a critic), 113, 115, 118, 119, 120, 121, 122, 123-24, 128, 131, 135, 136, 138, 144, 145, 146, 154, 158, 187, 192, 196, 200, 239, 240.
Monthly Magazine, 80, 229, 230, 231, 234, 237, 238.
Monthly Mirror, 23, 30, 33, 34, 63, 64-65, 77, 88, 125, 170, 175, 189, 190, 193, 198, 231.
Monthly Review, xxiv n., 15, 17, 46 ff., 49, 50, 52, 54, 55, 58, 61, 66, 76, 78, 79, 85, 86, 95, 99, 102, 106, 107, 109, 113-14, 118, 119, 120, 131, 134, 143, 144, 147, 148, 152-53, 154, 155, 163, 164, 165, 172, 175, 182, 187, 188, 192, 196, 200, 201, 202, 204, 231, 238.
Monuments of Shakespeare, 22 n.
Morality of Shakespeare's Drama, by Mrs. Griffith, 16 n., 133.
Morality of Shakespeare's Plays, 130-34, 219, 235.
Morgann, Maurice, xix, xxiv, xxv, 16, 17, 52, 53, 56, 63, 64, 70, 71, 77, 78-79, 80, 96-97, 98, 113, 116, 119, 121, 123, 128-29, 133, 136, 144, 146, 147, 148, 154, 165, 170-72, 175, 178, 192, 194-95, 198, 203, 207-8 (eulogy of Shakespeare), 226, 229-30, 233, 235, 239, 240, 242, 243.
Mortimer, J. H., 18.
Much Ado About Nothing, 165.
Murphy, Arthur, 38-39, 88, 96.
Mysterious Marriage, The, by Harriet Lee, 35.
Mysterious Mother, The, by Horace Walpole, 48, 102, 142-43.

Nares, R., *A Glossary*, 213.
Nature and magic compared, 77.
New Statesman (British), 242-43.

Nichols, J., 192, 193, 198.
Nicoll, Prof. A., 82, 243.
North's translation of Amyot's Plutarch, 59.

Observations on Hamlet, by Plumptre, 237.
Observations on Tragedy, by Wm. Hodson, 48.
Observer, 10, 55, 67, 146.
Of Imagination, by Beattie, 178.
Of Verbal Criticism, by D. Mallet, 28.
"Ohio, banks of the," 208.
On the Tragedies of Shakespeare, by Lamb, 230.
Operas, based on Shakespeare's plays, 33 ff., 214.
Ophelia, 91.
Original Letters of Sir John Falstaff, 186. See also White's hoax.
Origins of English drama, 196.
Orphan of China, The, by Arthur Murphy, 96.
Othello, 13, 117, 134; parodies of, 30.
Othello, character of, 133, 141.
Otway, Thomas, 9, 86.
Oulton, W. C., 25.

Pageants, 196, 197.
Palace of Pleasure, Painter's, 191.
Parodies, of Shakespeare, 30-31, 213-14.
Passions, Shakespeare's depiction of, 158-59, 222.
Peele, George, 16 n.
Pericles, 16, 17.
"Philalethes" (Col. F. Webb), 25.
Phillips, Edward, 57.
Philosophical criticism of Shakespeare, xix.
Phraseology of Shakespeare, 194.
Pictures. See Illustrations.
Picturesque Beauties of Shakespeare, by C. Taylor, 18.
Pilon, F., 74 n., 119 n., 150, 153, 174, 241.
Pistol, 148.
Planché, J. R., 213.
Plays of the Last Age Considered, by Rymer, xix.
Plays, Shakespeare's, Sources of, 191-93, 224.
Plumptre, James, 24, 153, 237, 241.

Plutarch, 59, 191.
Poetic justice, 133.
Poetical Epistle from Shakspeare in Elysium to Garrick, A, 23.
Pollock, W. H., xviii.
Polonius, 91 ff., 140, 181, 220, 232.
Poole, J., 214.
Pope, Alexander, xx, xxiv, 4, 5, 14, 51, 53, 57, 58, 65, 106, 123, 219 231, 233.
Porson, Richard, 25.
Porter scene, in *Macbeth*, 73, 216, 236.
Portraits, of Shakespeare, 18, 42.
"Praeternatural Beings," 76.
Preface to the Works of Beaumont and Fletcher, by Colman, 136, 203.
Priestley, J., 155-56.
Prince Hal, 148.
Prince of Wales, in *Henry IV*, 74.
Prompters' books, 89.
Proposals for Engraving the Felton Portrait of Shakespeare, by W. Richardson, 22.
Prose on Several Occasions, by Colman, 16 n.
Psychologizing of Shakespeare, 7-8, 155-82, 222-23.
Public Lectures on Shakespeare, 37 ff.
Public Ledger, 38, 145.
Puns, of Shakespeare, 3, 78-79, 217.
Puritan, The, 17.

Quarterly Review, 216.
Quickly, Mistress, 139, 148.
Quip Modest, by Ritson, 13.

Racine, 95, 102, 115.
Randall, R., 13-14.
Raysor, T. M., xxii, xxiii, 5 n., 212 n., 229, 230, 234, 239.
Remarks on Shylock's Reply to the Senate of Venice, by G. Coleman, 116.
Remarks on the Plays of Shakespear, by Gildon, 20.
Remarks Critical and Illustrative, by J. Ritson, 12.
Retort Courteous, by Kenrick, 241.
Rhyme, attacked, 79-80.
Ribaldry, 75.
Richard II, 117.

Richard III, 13, 77, 85 (Cibber's adaptation of), 115, 117, 219.
Richard III, character of, 128, 144-45, 147, 160, 167-76, 220-21, 232, 235, 241.
Richardson, William, xxi, xxii, xxiv, 22, 48 (on the unities), 63, 73, 75, 77, 109, 124, 129, 132, 133, 134, 137, 139, 140, 143, 144, 147-48, 149, 150, 151-52, 154, 156, 159-64, 172-75, 176-77, 188, 196, 198, 202-3, 204, 227, 229, 231, 232, 233, 234, 235, 236, 238, 239, 240, 243.
Ritson, Joseph, 12-13, 22, 25, 122 n., 123, 150-51, 184, 188, 195, 198, 231, 241.
Roberts, J., 20.
Robertson, J. M., 243.
Robertson, Thomas, 152, 236, 243.
Romantic drama, 215.
Romantic Heresy of Hamlet, 152-53, 190, 221-22, 236, 243.
Romantic school of criticism, xix.
Romantics, the, 45, 153, 172.
Romeo, 222.
Romeo and Juliet, 9, 30 (parodies of), 33 (operas based on), 85, 88 (Garrick's), 86 (Otway's), 115, 117, 224.
Rosaline (in *Romeo and Juliet*), 222.
Rosencrantz, 91.
Rowe, Nicholas, 5, 24, 34-35, 57 (on Shakespeare's learning), 65, 231.
Rowe's Life of Shakespeare, 21.
Ruling passion, theory of, 160 ff., 222.
Rümelin, 183, 198.
Rymer, Thomas, xix, xxiv, 5, 20, 231.

St. James Chronicle, 13.
Santayana, George, 243.
Saxo Grammaticus, 192.
Schlegel, 239.
Sciola, plains of, 208.
Scots Magazine, 200, 231.
Scottish Historical Review, xxi.
Select Collection of the Beauties of Shakespeare, by Croft, 118.
Sequels, to Shakespeare's plays, 31-33, 214.

INDEX 305

"Shadows of Shakespeare, The," by "C. Melmoth," 203.
Shakespeare, above the ancients, 66-67; absolved from imitation of models, 68-69, 216; affected by his age and audience, 186-91, 223-24; and British history, 185-86, 223; as actor, 21 n.; as conscious artist and man of judgment, 3, 128-30, 218-19, 220; as moral philosopher, 130-34, 219; as original genius, 123-26; as poet, 113-18, 218; as poet of nature, 119-23, 218; compared with his contemporaries, 194-95, 224; general position of in British drama, 195-97, 225.
Shakespeare apocrypha. *See* Apocrypha.
Shakespeare and His Critics, by C. F. Johnson, xxi.
Shakespeare and the Ireland Forgeries, by D. Bodde, 27 n.
Shakespeare canon, 16-17.
Shakespeariana, by Gildon, 118.
Shakespeare Illustrated, by S. and E. Harding, 18.
Shakespeare in France, by C. M. Haines, xxii.
Shakespeare in Paradise, messages from, 23.
Shakspeare-père-Davenant theory, 21.
Shakespeare Restored, by Theobald, 20.
Shakespeare's biography. *See* Biography.
Shakspeare's Characters, by J. H. Mortimer, 18.
Shakespeare's classical knowledge, Farmer's denial of, 58-65; late eighteenth-century view of, 65; early nineteenth-century view of, 215, 242.
"Shakespear's Ghost," 23.
Shakespeare's Jests, 20 n.
Shakespeare's Jubilee, by G. S. Carey, 39-40.
Shakespeare's language, 78, 184-85, 223.
Shakespeare's violation of decorum. *See* Decorum.
Shakespeare's-Walk Charity School, 23.
Shakespeare's women. *See* Women of Shakespeare.

Shakespeare's name, spelling of, 22-23.
Sherlock, Martin, 69, 74, 80, 93, 100, 114, 122 (eulogy on Shakespeare), 123, 125, 133, 137, 140-41, 188, 204-5, 241.
Shirley, Henry, 9.
"Short Encomium on the Inimitable Shakespeare, A," quoted 200.
Short View of Tragedy, by T. Rymer, 20.
Shylock, 141-42, 190, 198, 223-24, 238.
Sidney, Sir Philip, 89.
Sir John Oldcastle, 17.
Sisters, The, 9.
Six Old Play, etc., by J. Nichols, 192.
Skottowe, A., 213.
Slender, 148.
Smith, D. N., xx-xxvii *passim*, 37, 82-83, 199, 208, 226, 229, 239.
Smirke, Sir Robert, Illustrations to Shakespeare, 213.
Soest (or Zoust) portrait of Shakespeare, 22.
Soliloquy, in *Hamlet*, 116.
Some Account of the English Stage, by J. Genest, 84.
Sonnets, of Shakespeare, xix, 26.
Sophocles, 67, 99.
Sources of Shakespeare's plays. *See* Plays, sources of.
Specimen of a Commentary on Shakspeare, by Whiter, 13, 179, 241.
Spectator, the, 234.
Sprague, C., 214.
Spurious plays, 16-17, 212 and n.
Stack, Rev. Richard, 147.
Stafford, W., 16 n.
Stanley, Mrs., 89.
Steele, Richard, 8.
Steevens, George, xviii, 12-13, 16, 24, 25, 28-29, 37, 116, 148, 149, 150, 151, 191, 231, 232-33, 234, 236, 241, 243. *See also* Johnson and Steevens' editions.
Stockton Jubilee, by Ritson, 40.
Stoll, E. E., 243.
Strange Horse Race, A, by Dekker, 195.
Suckling, Sir John, 58.
Supernatural characters, attacked and defended, 76-77, 216-17.

Tacitus, 140-41.
Taming of the Shrew, 16, 192.
Tapestry pictures, 196-97.
Tate, Nahum, 9, 86, 217.
Tatler, the, 8.
Taylor, C., 18, 118.
Taylor, E., xxv, 47 (on the unities), 49, 73, 76, 103, 132, 136, 164, 166, 187, 203, 234, 241.
Tempest, The, 33 (operas based on), 77, 117, 133.
Terence, translation of, by Coleman, 59, 160.
Terrasson, 100.
Theatrical Bouquet, The, 200.
Theobald, xxi, 12-13, 16, 20, 24, 58.
Thirty Letters, by W. Jackson, 136-37.
Thrale, Mrs., 22, 119, 121.
Timon of Athens, 85 (alterations of) 180, 185.
Titus Andronicus, 16, 17.
"T. O." *See* Hole, Richard.
Tomalin Report, 212 n. ff.
Tonson, J., 13, 13 n.
Tragicomedy, 4, 6, 72-76 (attacked and defended), 99-100 (defended against Voltaire), 216.
Transactions of the Royal Irish Academy, 147.
Transactions of the Royal Society of Edinburgh, 152.
Trinder, newspaper critic, 9-10.
True Tragedy of Richard, Duke of York, by Marlowe, 191.
Twenty Plays, by Steevens, 191.
"Turtle of Literature, The," 110.
Twelfth Night, 13.
Twining, translator of Aristotle's *Poetics*, 55.
Twiss, F., *A Complete Verbal Index to Shakespeare*, 213.
Two Gentlemen of Verona, 16, 224.
Two Noble Kinsmen, 16, 17.

Unities, 4, 48 and n.; and other arts, 50-51; Aristotle's support of denied, 55; of less importance than nature, 51-53; questioned by Hanmer, 5; rejected by Johnson, 48-49; rejected by Coleridge, 214-15; rejected historically, 53-55, 214; Shakespeare's violation of, 45-48, 97; defended against Voltaire, 97-98.
Universal Magazine, 14, 23, 47, 48, 54, 64, 66, 72, 75, 86, 98, 101, 102, 106, 114, 117, 119, 120, 124, 125, 129, 134, 136, 137, 141, 143, 145, 166, 169, 186, 188, 189, 193, 201, 202, 205, 206.
Upton, J., 6, 7, 8, 58.

Vanburgh, 190.
Verisimilitude, dramatic, 214.
"Verses from the Ghost of Willey Shakespeare to Sammy Ireland," 23.
Versification, Shakespeare's, 113, 114.
Virgil, 101, 205.
Virgin Queen, The, sequel to *Tempest*, 33.
Vittoria Corombona, by Webster, 195.
Voltaire, xviii, 20, 29, 81; mistranslations of Shakespeare by, 91-93; attacked Shakespeare, 93-95; reaction of British critics toward, 95-97; British reply to traditional objections made by, 97-100; attacked as a writer, 100-2; attacked for mistranslations, 103-5; attacked for ignorance of Elizabethan drama, 105; attacked as a man, 105-8; Mrs. Montagu and, 108-9; Coleridge's opinion of, 218.
Vortigern and Rowena, 25.

Walder, E., xviii, xix, xxv, 155, 175.
Waldron, F. G., 3, 25, 213.
Walpole, Horace, 48 (on the unities), 62 (praises Farmer), 94, 96, 101-2, 105, 142, 203.
Walpole's *Winter's Tale* idea, 24, 33, 153.
Warburton, xxi, 14, 58, 120, 233, 239.
"Warm" and "moist," 180, 185.
Warner, R., 16, 19, 61, 64, 84.
Warner, W., 191.
Warton, Joseph, xix, xxi, xxii, xxiv.
"Warwickshire, A Song," by "Mr. G.," quoted, 202.
Watkins, John, 213.

Webb, Daniel, 6, 7, 8, 128.
Webster, 195, 198.
"Weed" and "suit," 181, 185.
West, Mrs., 121, 206.
Whalley, 58, 233.
Whately, T., xxi, xxiv, 52 (on unities), 128, 129, 144, 158-59, 160, 167-68, 175, 187, 192, 232.
Wheatley, H. B., 82.
White, James, 186, 193, 231.
White's hoax of the *Original Letters of Sir John Falstaff*, 148, 237.
Whiter, W., 13, 21, 103, 115, 179, 180 ff., 184, 193, 195, 196-97, 197-98, 241.
Wilson, J., 213.
Winstanley, Lilian, 153 n.
Winter's Tale, The, 13, 15, 117.
Witch, The, Middleton's, 192, 217, 231.

Witches, in *Macbeth*, 76, 216-17.
Witches, of Middleton, 224.
Wit's Magazine, 231-32.
Women, Shakespeare's, 138-39, 232, 235.
Woodward, as Polonius, 140.
Wyatt, M., 25.
Wycherley, 190.

Yorkshire Tragedy, *A*, 16, 17.
Young, E., 6, 61.
Young, Prof. Karl, xxviii, 8 n., 183, 198, 242.

Zoust (or Soest) portrait of Shakespeare, 22.
Zur Shakespeare-Kritik des 18. Jahrh., by Adler, xxi.

www.ingramcontent.com/pod-product-compliance
Lightning Source LLC
Chambersburg PA
CBHW021353290426
44108CB00010B/227